Annual Session of Scientific Papers IMT ORADEA 2017

MATEC Web of Conferences Volume 126 (2017)

Sanmartin, Romania
27 - 29 May 2017

Editors:

Gavril Grebenisan

ISBN: 978-1-5108-4969-3

Printed from e-media with permission by:

Curran Associates, Inc.
57 Morehouse Lane
Red Hook, NY 12571

Some format issues inherent in the e-media version may also appear in this print version.

Printed by Curran Associates, Inc. (2017)

For additional information, please contact EDP Sciences – Web of Conferences at the address below.

EDP Sciences – Web of Conferences
17, Avenue du Hoggar
Parc d'Activité de Courtabœuf
BP 112
F-91944 Les Ulis Cedex A
France

Phone: +33 (0) 1 69 18 75 75
Fax: +33 (0) 1 69 28 84 91

contact-edps@webofconferences.org

Additional copies of this publication are available from:

Curran Associates, Inc.
57 Morehouse Lane
Red Hook, NY 12571 USA
Phone: 845-758-0400
Fax: 845-758-2633
Email: curran@proceedings.com
Web: www.proceedings.com

TABLE OF CONTENTS

edp sciences

MATEC Web of Conferences

Statement of Peer review

In submitting conference proceedings to MATEC Web of Conferences, I certify to the Publisher that I adhere to the **Policy on Publishing Integrity** of the journal in order to safeguard good scientific practice in publishing.

1. All articles have been subjected to peer review administered by the proceedings editors.
2. Reviews have been conducted by expert referees, who have been requested to provide unbiased and constructive comments aimed, whenever possible, at improving the work.
3. Proceedings editors have taken all reasonable steps to ensure the quality of the materials they publish and their decision to accept or reject a paper for publication has been based only on the merits of the work and the relevance to the journal.

Title, date and place of the conference

ANNUAL SESSION OF SCIENTIFIC PAPERS IMT ORADEA 2017, May 27-29th, Felix SPA

Proceedings editor(s):

Gavril Grebenisan

Date and editor's signature

August 10, 2017

MATEC Web of Conferences **126**, 01001 (2017) DOI: 10.1051/matecconf/201712601001
Annual Session of Scientific Papers IMT ORADEA 2017

Algorithm for the calculation of vibration inherent frequencies bending from two-shafts transmission

Jan-Cristian Grigore[1*], *Ion* Bulac[2]

[1]University of Piteşti, jan_grigore@yahoo.com, Romania
[2]University of Piteşti, ionbulac57@yahoo.com, Romania

Abstract. The operation of the speed shaft transmissions at or near the natural frequency of the pulses at the resonance phenomenon leads to bending, when the amplitude of the oscillations increases sharply, causing deterioration or complete destruction thereof. To avoid system resonance operation is necessary to know the most accurate values its pulsations and taking appropriate constructive measures to avoid overlapping with disturbing frequency harmonics (operating speeds).This paper presents an algorithm for calculating the pulsation and vibration modes in bending, and based on numerical simulations performed on a real two-shafts transmission and will draw conclusions drawn diagrams.

1 Introduction

The frequency of variation of the outer disturbing forces are commonly known and are in most cases due to the operating condition. To establish whether resonance is likely to be determined as accurately self-oscillation frequencies of the system. Disruptive forces but do not have a single frequency spectrum from), Fl. Dudita [1], Fl. Dudita, D. Diaconescu, Cr. Bohn, M. Neagoe, and R. Saulescu [2], the multi-speed transmission, *n*, *2n*, *3n* (*n* being speed transmission). If we take into account that the angular gear also has several frequencies of oscillation own and operating speeds range between certain limits it will be clear that when working with multiple operating modes can not avoid certain harmonic disturbing forces coincide their oscillation frequencies of transmission. In this case, the task is calculation to determine the oscillation amplitudes and values of stresses occurring in the components of the transmission at resonance.

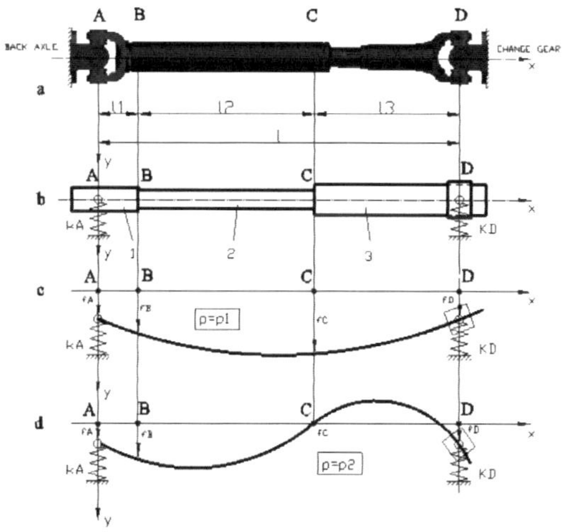

Fig. 1. The construction and mechanical equivalent model

2 Constructive model and equivalent mechanical model

The constructive solution for mobile two-shafts transmission (see Fig. 1.a.), is associated equivalent mechanical model (see Fig. 1.b.), the sections A and D elastic supports are located elastic constants k_A, k_D.

The following, using the notation f_i, θ_i, M_i, F_i respectively arrow, rotation, bending moment and shear force in a current section, R. Voinea, D. Voiculescu and FL. Simion [3], A. Ripianu and I. Craciun [4], N. Pandrea, S. Parlac and D. Popa [5].

1) Δ_i ; Δ_A ; Δ_B ; Δ_C ; Δ_D *state vectors defined by the equality:*

* Corresponding author: jan_grigore@yahoo.com

DOI: 10.1051/matecconf/201712601001

$$\begin{aligned}\Delta_i &= (f_i,\theta_i,M_i,F_i)^T\\ \Delta_A &= (f_A,\theta_A,M_A,F_A)^T\\ \Delta_B &= (f_B,\theta_B,M_B,F_B)^T\\ \Delta_C &= (f_C,\theta_C,M_C,F_C)^T\\ \Delta_D &= (f_D,\theta_D,M_D,F_D)^T.\end{aligned} \qquad (1)$$

2) $l_i, \rho_i, A_i, E_i, I_{yi}$, *respectively, the length, density, area, transverse modulus of elasticity and geometrical moment of inertia mainly for the section corresponding to the index* $i = 1,2,3$

3) *Parameter* α_i *defined by the relationship:*

$$\alpha_i = \sqrt[4]{p^2 \frac{\rho_i A_i}{E_i Iyi}}. \qquad (2)$$

where p is the vibration inherent pulse.

4) *Parameter* z_i *defined by the relationship:*

$$z_i = \alpha_i \cdot l_i. \qquad (3)$$

5) chz, shz *- sin and cos hyperbolic functions:*

$$ch(z_i) = \frac{e^{z_i} + e^{-z_i}}{2}; sh(z_i) = \frac{e^{z_i} - e^{-z_i}}{2}. \qquad (4)$$

6) $f_j(z_i)$, *j=1,2,3,4, Krâlov functions defined by relations:*

$$\begin{aligned}f_1(z_i) &= \frac{ch(z_i)+\cos(z_i)}{2}\\ f_2(z_i) &= \frac{sh(z_i)+\sin(z_i)}{2}\\ f_3(z_i) &= \frac{ch(z_i)-\cos(z_i)}{2}\\ f_4(z_i) &= \frac{sh(z_i)-\sin(z_i)}{2}.\end{aligned} \qquad (5)$$

7) $F(z)$ *– Krâlov matrixes defined by relations:*

$$F(z) = \begin{pmatrix} f_1(z) & f_2(z) & f_3(z) & f_4(z)\\ f_4(z) & f_1(z) & f_2(z) & f_3(z)\\ f_3(z) & f_4(z) & f_1(z) & f_2(z)\\ f_2(z) & f_3(z) & f_4(z) & f_1(z)\end{pmatrix}. \qquad (6)$$

8) α , α^{-1} *– for diagonal matrixes:*

$$\alpha = \begin{pmatrix} 1 & 0 & 0 & 0\\ 0 & \frac{1}{\alpha} & 0 & 0\\ 0 & 0 & -\frac{1}{\alpha^2 EI_w} & 0\\ 0 & 0 & 0 & -\frac{1}{\alpha^3 EI_w}\end{pmatrix} \qquad (7)$$

$$\alpha^{-1} = \begin{pmatrix} 1 & 0 & 0 & 0\\ 0 & \alpha & 0 & 0\\ 0 & 0 & -\alpha^2 EI_w & 0\\ 0 & 0 & 0 & -\alpha^3 EI_w\end{pmatrix}.$$

9) $R_i, i-1,2,3$, *field matrixes of sections, I. Bulac [6] :*

$$R_i = \alpha_i^{-1} \cdot F(\alpha_i x_i) \cdot \alpha_i. \qquad (8)$$

10) R *, field matrix for all two-shafts transmission limited points A, D:*

$$R = R_3 \cdot R_2 \cdot R_1. \qquad (9)$$

From boundary conditions resulting from moments A and D:

$$M_A = M_D = 0. \qquad (10)$$

and shear forces calculated with relations:

$$F_A = k_A f_A ; F_D = -k_D f_D. \qquad (11)$$

Therefore, taking into account relations (1) şi (11), state vectors of the sections A and D are:

$$\begin{aligned}\Delta_A &= \left(\frac{F_A}{k_A}, \theta_A, 0, F_A\right)^T\\ \Delta_D &= (f_D, \theta_D, 0, -k_D f_D)^T.\end{aligned} \qquad (12)$$

Using notations:

$$T_A = \begin{pmatrix} 0 & \frac{1}{k_A}\\ 1 & 0\\ 0 & 0\\ 0 & 1\end{pmatrix}$$

$$R^* = \begin{pmatrix} R_{11} & R_{12}\\ R_{21} & R_{22}\\ R_{31} & R_{32}\\ R_{41} & R_{42}\end{pmatrix} = R_3 \cdot R_2 \cdot R_1 \cdot T_A. \qquad (13)$$

state vectors of the points A şi D can be written as:

$$\Delta_A = T_A \cdot \begin{pmatrix}\theta_A\\ F_A\end{pmatrix} ; \ \Delta_D = R_3 \cdot R_2 \cdot R_1 \cdot \Delta_A. \qquad (14)$$

and the second equality in equation (14) becomes:

$$\begin{pmatrix} f_D\\ \theta_D\\ 0\\ -k_D f_D\end{pmatrix} = R^* \cdot \begin{pmatrix}\theta_A\\ F_A\end{pmatrix}. \qquad (15)$$

and hence the homogeneous system of equations is obtained in $\theta_A, F_A, \theta_D, f_D$:

* Corresponding author: jan_grigore@yahoo.com

$$\begin{cases} f_D = R_{11}\theta_A + R_{12}F_A \\ \theta_D = R_{21}\theta_D + R_{22}F_A \\ 0 = R_{31}\theta_A + R_{32}F_A \\ -k_D f_D = R_{41}\theta_A + R_{42}F_A \end{cases} . \quad (16)$$

For the system (16) to be non-trivial solution, D. Stanescu [7], must be as determinant system is zero:

$$\Psi(p) = 0. \quad (17)$$

where:

$$\Psi(p) = \begin{vmatrix} R_{11} & R_{12} & 1 \\ R_{21} & R_{22} & 1 \\ R_{31} & R_{32} & 0 \\ R_{41} & R_{42} & -k_D \end{vmatrix}. \quad (18)$$

By solving the characteristic equation (17) set their pulses p_1, p_2,…. To represent vibration inherent modes, assign arrow f_A equal to the numerical value when the system unit (16) results:

$$F_A = k_A ; \theta_A = -\frac{R_{32}}{R_{31}} k_A$$

$$f_D = k_A (R_{12} - R_{11}\frac{R_{32}}{R_{31}}) \quad (19)$$

$$\theta_D = k_A (R_{22} - R_{21}\frac{R_{32}}{R_{31}}).$$

Arrows f_B and f_C from sections B and C are the first elements of the matrixes Δ_B , Δ_C, data relationships:

$$\Delta_B = R_1 \cdot T_A \cdot \begin{pmatrix} \theta_A \\ F_A \end{pmatrix} ; \; \Delta_C = R_2 \cdot R_1 \cdot T_A \cdot \begin{pmatrix} \theta_A \\ F_A \end{pmatrix}. \quad (20)$$

3 The calculation algorithm

For the numerical calculation one uses the following algorithm:

1) *The following parameters are considered as known:*
   $k_A, k_D, A_i, \rho_i, E_i, I_i, l_i \quad i=1,2,3;$
2) *A value is chosen for the pulsation* p *and a variation step* Δp *;*
3) *Calculate parameters* $\alpha_i, i = 1,2,3$ *with relation (2) and matrixes* α, α^{-1} *with relations (7);*
4) *The parameters* z_i *and hyperbolic functions* $chz_i, shz_i, i = 1,2,3$ *using relations (4) and (5);*
5) *Calculate Krâlov functions* $f_j(z_i), j = 1,2,3,4; i = 1,2,3$ *, and Krâlov matrixes* $F(z)$*, with relations (5) and (6);*
6) *Matrixes calculus* $R_i; T_A; R^*$*,* $i=1,2,3$ *with relations (8) and (13);*
7) *Functions calculus* $\Psi(p)$ *with relation (17);*
8) *p is replaced with* $p + \Delta p$ *and the calculations are made again , up when the characteristic equation (17) is satisfied, obtaining inherent pulsations, so being obtained the own pulsations* $p_1, p_2, \ldots;$
9) *Is considered* $f_A = 1$ *and calculate* $F_A; \theta_A; f_D$ *with relations (19);*
10) *Is calculated state vectors* $\Delta_B; \Delta_C$ *with relations (20) and extracted arrow* $f_B; f_C$*;*
11) *Plot graphs vibration modes for the first two inherent pulses.*

4 Numerical application

It is considered that two-shafts transmission equips an SUV automobile constructive design of which is shown in Fig. 1., for the known:

$k_A = k_D = 85 \cdot 10^6 (N/m); l_2 = 0{,}1(m); l_2 = 1{,}0(m);$

$l_3 = 0{,}4(m); A_1 = 19{,}6 \cdot 10^{-4}(m^2); A_2 = 3{,}6 \cdot 10^{-4}(m^2);$

$A_3 = 7{,}1 \cdot 10^{-4}(m^2); \rho_1 = \rho_2 = \rho_3 = 7800(kg/m^3).$

In a first approximation be considered shaft of the transmission, consisting of three equal segments of a constant solid section resiliently supported at the ends.

Based on the presented algorithm and a computer program developed in Excel or obtained first and second pulsation own values p_1=283,2368(s^{-1}) and p_2=1117,1629(s^{-1}).

Corresponding to this pulse graphs were drawn at the bending vibration inherent modes shown in Fig. 2. and Fig. 3.

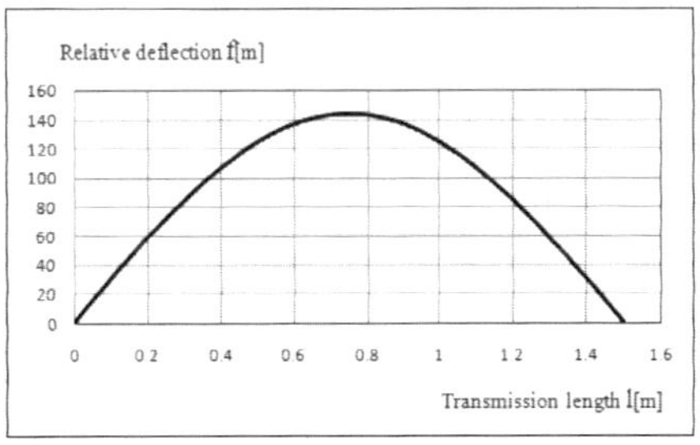

Fig. 2. Vibration mode corresponding to the first inherent pulse for shafts transmission equated with full bar of constant section

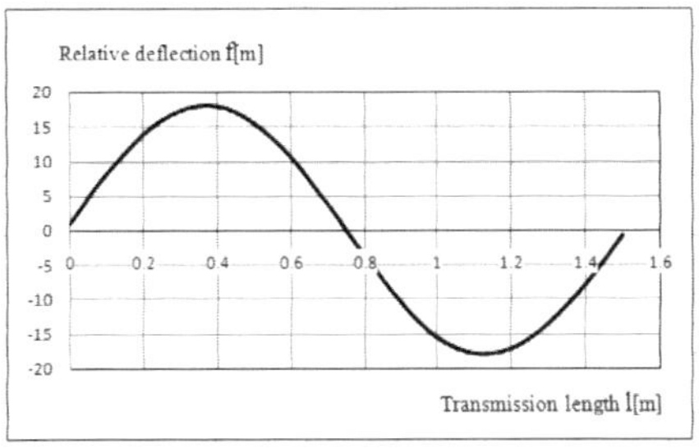

Fig. 3. Vibration mode corresponding to the second inherent pulse for shafts transmission equated with full bar of constant section

* Corresponding author: jan_grigore@yahoo.com

If real two-shafts transmission which is pipe ends with forks bond were obtained first and second inherent pulsation values p_1=325,2445(s^{-1}), p_2=1228,6995(s^{-1}) and vibration inherent modes shown in Fig. 4. and Fig. 5.

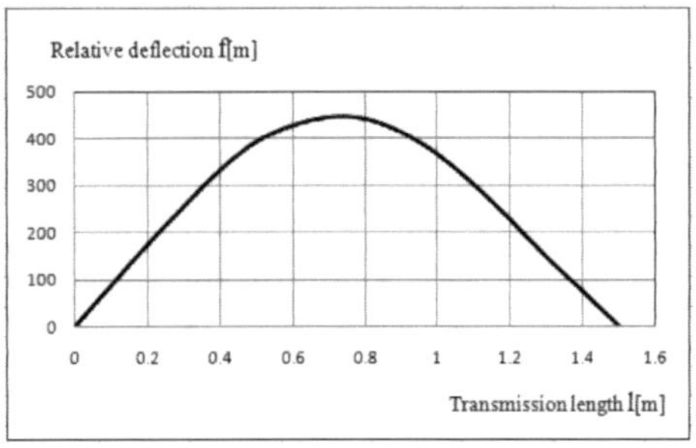

Fig. 4. Vibration mode corresponding to the first inherent pulse for real two-shafts transmission

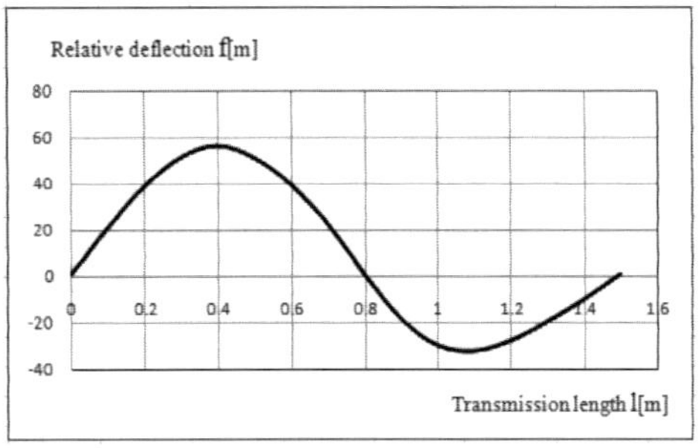

Fig. 5. Vibration mode corresponding to the second inherent pulse for real two-shafts transmission

Taking into account the results and the diagrams of variation of the relative amplitudes along the cardan joint shown in Fig. 2., Fig. 3., Fig. 4. and Fig. 5., there is the following:

1) *Two-shaft transmission values for the inherent pulsation its fitting with the shaft are higher than in the case of full drive shaft two-shaft transmission.*
2) *The positions of the maximum amplitudes occur, for two different cases considered very least, being about the middle of the shaft transmission.*
3) *For the second inherent pulse give its own shaft section for full maximum amplitudes are equal and opposite and occur at the same distance from the ends at 0,38(m) respectively 11,3(m) to point A (link shaft with rear axle of the car).*
4) *The actual two-shafts transmission of the maximum amplitudes moves to point D (connection with universal joints reducer gearbox or gearbox), at distances 0,45(m) respectively 1,2(m) to the same reference point A, being of different sizes.*

5 Conclusions

The algorithm presented in this paper and the computer program developed allows numerical study of the influence of geometrical and mechanical parameters of the two-shaft transmission constructive on inherent pulsation and vibration modes in bending.

Numerical simulations can provide important information on of the behavior of the transmission at different operating conditions and taking appropriate constructive measures to avoid negative effects of the phenomenon of resonance.

References

[1] Fl. Dudita, *Cardan shafting*, Technical Publishing House, Bucharest, 1966.

[2] Fl. Dudita, D. Diaconescu, Cr. Bohn, M. Neagoe, R. Saulescu, *Cardan shafting*, Transilvania Expres Publishing House, Brasov, 2003.

[3] R. Voinea, D. Voiculescu, FL. Simion, *Introduction in the solid mechanics with applications in engineering*, R.S.R. Academy, 1989.

[4] A. Ripianu, I. Craciun, *Axles, righteous shafts and crankshafts*, Technical Publishing House, Bucharest, 1977.

[5] N. Pandrea, S. Parlac, D. Popa, *Models for studying automotive vibrations*, Tiparg Publishing House, Pitești, 2001.

[6] I. Bulac, *Vibrations of the bicardanic transmissions with elastic supports*, 5th Symposium „Durability and Reliability of Mechanical Systems", SYMECH 2012, Târgu-Jiu, Romania, 18-19 May, 2012.

[7] D. Stanescu, *Numerical methods*, Didactic and Pedagogical Publishing House, Bucharest, 2007.

* Corresponding author: jan_grigore@yahoo.com

MATEC Web of Conferences 126, 01002 (2017) DOI: 10.1051/matecconf/201712601002
Annual Session of Scientific Papers IMT ORADEA 2017

Quadcopter thrust optimization with ducted-propeller

Endrowednes Kuantama[1*], *Radu* Tarca[2]

[1]Engineering Doctoral School University of Oradea-Romania, endrowednes@gmail.com
[2]Mechatronics Department University of Oradea-Romania, rtarca@uoradea.ro

Abstract—In relation to quadcopter body frame model, propeller can be categorized into propeller with ducted and without ducted. This study present differences between those two using CFD (Computational Fluid Dynamics) method. Both categories utilize two blade-propeller with diameter of 406 (mm). Propeller rotation generates acceleration per time unit on the volume of air. Based on the behavior of generated air velocity, ducted propeller can be modeled into three versions. The generated thrust and performance on each model were calculated to determine the best model. The use of ducted propeller increases the total weight of quadcopter and also total thrust. The influence of this modeling were analyzed in detail with variation of angular velocity propeller from 1000 (rpm) to 9000 (rpm). Besides the distance between propeller tip and ducted barrier, the size of ducted is also an important part in thrust optimization and total weight minimization of quadcopter.

1 Introduction

Quadcopter aerodynamic movement is based on thrust generated by four propellers. Movement control can be established by varying the angular velocity of each propeller independently to achieve desired attitude and altitude H. Guang, G. Hoffmann, S. Waslander, and C.J.Tomlin [1]. The magnitude of thrust depends on propeller size, magnitude of pitch, and angle of attack. At this point, analyses were done to improve quadcopter performance R. Czyba and G. Szafranski [2], V. Hrishikeshavan and I. Chopra [3]. This study focused on the design perspective of quadcopter frame by using ducted and non-ducted propeller. By using ducted-propeller, disturbance effect may be decreased and thrust can be increased and optimized, although the total weight of quadcopter will be increased J. Pereira, D. Bawek, S. Westfall, and I. Chopra [4], V. Hrishikeshavan, J. Sirohi, M. Tishchenko, and I. Chopra [5]. The most important part of ducted-propeller is how to create model and minimizing added weight of barrier for propeller while optimizing propeller performance. The distance slot between duct and propeller's tip is important part to minimize the drag effect and eliminate the friction point of barrier.

The analysis was done to observe quadcopter performance in terms of aerodynamic movement and disturbance occurred on quadcopter based on thrust generated by rotational speed. By using CFD (Computational Fluid Dynamics), both air pressure and air velocity generated by propeller rotation can be analyzed and calculated. Air motion of propeller in relation to the distance between propellers on symmetrical frame of quadcopter was analyzed with variation on rotational speed from 1000-9000 (rpm). Commercial propeller with diameter of 406 (mm) was chosen as model and analyzed in this system.

2 Quadcopter propeller model and algorithm

A two-blade propeller was designed using CAD (Computer-aided Design) and the model was analyzed using CFD method to observe air trajectory generated by propeller rotation. The magnitude of lift force from propeller depends on angular velocity and angle of attack, which in this design is 3°. The acceleration of air generated from propeller rotation can produce thrust. According to airfoil theory, it is known that pressure over the top of propeller is lower than the pressure below the propeller Y. Yang, L. L. M. Veldhuis, and G. Eitelberg [6]. Fig. 1. shows the propulsion of propeller and flow stream of the propeller. The distribution of air velocity along the propeller's blade tip through the vortex center shows that the air velocity on the tip is lower than the hub because the surface area propeller in hub is larger than in the tip. The downstream of the air

* Corresponding author: endrowednes@gmail.com

DOI: 10.1051/matecconf/201712601002

on surface area propeller will lead downward until the pressure eventually return to free stream conditions. In fact, not all air trajectory lead down but they are sucked back by propeller, which occurs on the tip located in x and y = ± 200 (mm). By knowing the air flow trajectory, one can do modeling, analyze the ducted propeller and compare each other.

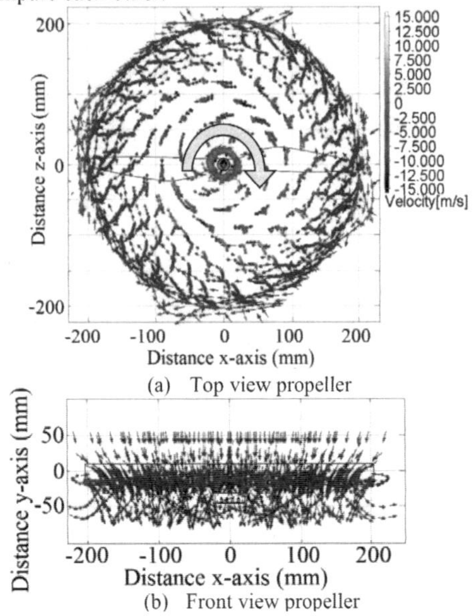

Fig. 1. Propeller air trajectory

Lift force on propeller, also known as thrust, can be calculated using momentum theory as seen on Equation (1). The generated thrust depends on propeller's air velocity which moves from upstream to downstream, and the air velocity itself depends on rotor's angular velocity and the change in momentum. There are two types of velocity generated from propeller's rotation, i.e. axial induced velocity (v_i) and free stream velocity (v_∞). Free stream velocity comes from air turbulence on wind which affect propeller H. A. Kutty and P. Rajendran [7]. Air density of $1.225(\mathrm{kg.m^{-3}})$ represented by symbol ρ and surface area propeller represented by symbol A.

$$\mathbf{T} = \rho \mathbf{A}[(2v_i + v_\infty) - v_\infty] \quad (1)$$

For ducted lift propeller, thrust can be calculated by adding variable duct diffusion ratio (σ) as seen on Equation (2) and (3). Non-ducted propeller has diffusion ratio of 0.5 and ducted propeller has diffusion ratio between 0.5-1 Y. Jiang, B. Zhang, and T. Huang [8]. Air velocity on ducted propeller can be calculated based on velocity generated by propeller (v_p) and velocity in downstream propeller (v_d).

$$\mathbf{T} = \mathbf{T_p} + \mathbf{T_d} = \rho \mathbf{A} v_p v_d \quad (2)$$

$$v_p = \sigma v_d \quad (3)$$

From flow trajectory or forward velocity (V_T) generated by rotation of rotor propeller (n), vortex impact and performance of the propeller can be analyzed through parameter advance ratio (J) and coefficient thrust (T_C), as shown in Equation (4) and (5). These equations are the standard formulas for the pressure generated by propeller rotation with diameter (D) corresponding to propeller rotation area S. B. Heinzen, C. E. Hall, and A. Gopalarthnam [9], Y. Yang, D. Ragni, L Veldhuis, and G. Eitelberge [10].

$$\mathbf{J} = \frac{\mathbf{V_T}}{\mathbf{nD}} \quad (4)$$

$$\mathbf{T_c} = \frac{\mathbf{T}}{\rho \mathbf{n^2 D^4}} \quad (5)$$

These algorithms will be used to differentiate between quadcopter performance using ducted and non-ducted propeller. Through CFD, air velocity generated by propeller can be measured, thus the magnitude of generated thrust can be analyzed.

3 Ducted propeller design and analysis

Based on air trajectory as the result of non-ducted propeller rotation, one can design three types of ducted model, presented in Fig. 2. The main focus of the modeling is minimum material addition for ducted to make as little weight gain as possible, thus optimal thrust result can be achieved. The space between tip propeller and ducted is 10 (mm) in each model.

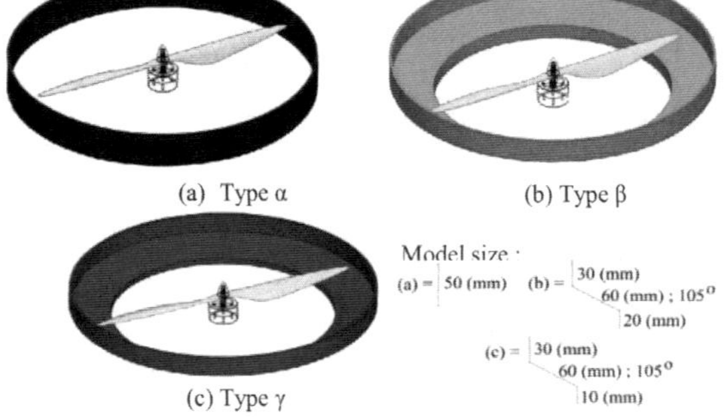

Fig. 2. Ducted propeller model

The modeling was designed based on airflow trajectory as the result of propeller rotation as seen in Fig.1. Surface area propeller around hub located on $(-140 \le x \le 140)$ and $(-140 \le z \le 140)$ generated the biggest air velocity and moving straight down to produce thrust. Meanwhile, on the propeller tip area, not all generated air velocity moving downward but they are being sucked back by propeller with circular air movement which occur on position $(-3 \le y \le 3)$. Ducted propeller type α and type β has little difference in

* Corresponding author: endrowednes@gmail.com

the bottom which was done to lessen the material load while still optimizing generated thrust. From three models of ducted propeller, the generated air velocity will be analyzed to calculate thrust value of each model. Surface area propeller in this model is 0.317 (m^2).

4 Quadcopter thrust and air trajectory analysis

CFD was used to analyze the induced velocity generated by propeller with variation between 1000 (rpm) and 9000 (rpm) with scale of 1000 (rpm). In this simulation, wind effect or outside disturbance was not taken into account thus free stream velocity was dispensed $(v_\infty = 0)$. The higher the propeller rotation, the bigger the induced velocity will be. However in this study, the generated air velocity will be compared with normal propeller, ducted and non-ducted. Ducted propeller itself was designed with three different models. Fig. 3. shows the induced velocities generated by each model.

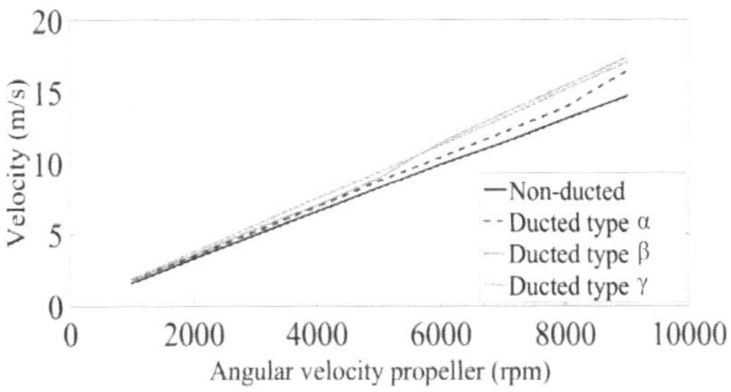

Fig. 3. Induced velocities generated by propeller

With the same propeller size and low angular velocity $(\leq 4000(\text{rpm}))$, induced velocities generated between ducted and non-ducted propeller are not differ significantly. However for angular velocity higher than 4000 (rpm), differences in induced velocities are clearly seen. Ducted propeller type β and type γ has differences in terms of surface area ducted in which type β surface area is 0.276 (m^2) and type γ surface area is 0.255 (m^2). Both ducted types produce nearly identical (not significantly differ) induced vorticities, because type γ was designed to reduce the weight of the cover material used.

In this study, the type of material used was not taken into account but from the surface area ducted it can be seen that the α type is lighter than the other ducted type of modeling. From induced velocities generated by propeller, the magnitude of thrust generated by propeller rotation can be calculated using Equation (1) and the result can be seen in Fig. 4. This equation is enough to calculate the generated thrust. Besides that, by using CFD, velocity in downstream propeller can also be analyzed where the magnitude must be smaller than the induced velocities generated by propeller.

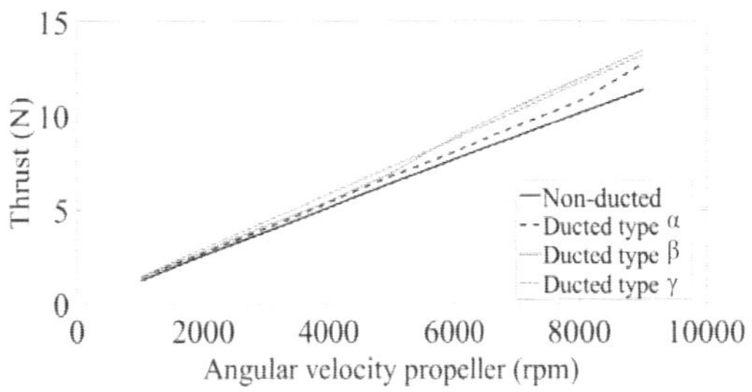

Fig. 4. Thrust propeller

Thrust optimization can be done by adding cover on propeller. However not all ducted propeller models can work to improve the thrust performance. From the test result, the ducted angle must be greater than 90° to ensure that the resulting air velocity leads downward. This modeling uses an angle of 105° to improve the propeller performance. From the thrust calculation, it can be seen that thrust optimization on ducted propeller can occur on high rotation propeller $(\geq 4000(\text{rpm}))$ with an increase in thrust value of 0.27 – 1.38 (N) for propeller type α and 0.73 – 2.1 (N) for propeller type β and γ. From previous research, angular velocity propeller 5000 (rpm) was suitable with folded size body frame with size of 560 (mm) in square size E. Kuantama, D. Craciun, and R. Tarca [11]. With the same angular velocity, ducted propeller was analyzed to examine its effect on quadcopter as a whole. With ducted propeller, the size of body frame or distance between propeller may be smaller compared with non-ducted. Body frame with width and length size 460 (mm) x 460 (mm) was designed as seen on Fig. 5. and Fig. 6.

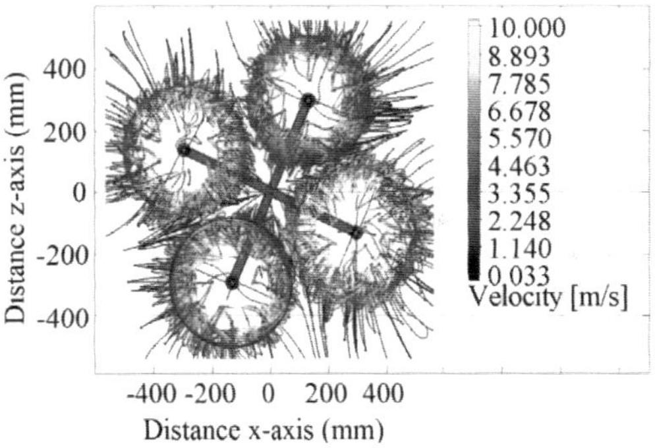

Fig. 5. Quadcopter without propeller cover (Non-ducted)

By observing the air flow trajectory generated by each propeller, it can be seen that without ducted, air velocity generated by each propeller are affecting each other $(v_\infty \neq 0)$ thus resulting in inevitable instability of quadcopter. Whereas on ducted propeller, air flow trajectory directly moves downward which means the body frame size of 460 (mm) x 460 (mm) (width x length) can be used for quadcopter with maximum angular velocity of 5000 (rpm).

* Corresponding author: endrowednes@gmail.com

 DOI: 10.1051/matecconf/201712601002

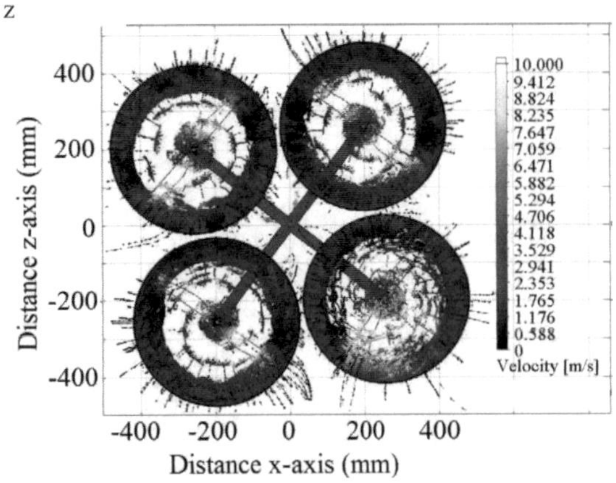

Fig. 6. Quadcopter with ducted type γ

Overall the efficiency of quadcopter propeller model can be calculated based on advance ratio propeller, thrust coefficient propeller and rotor power. The greater the advance ratio value and thrust coefficient, the greater the propeller efficiency. However, the greater the power needed to rotate the propeller, the smaller the total efficiency of propeller or vice versa O. Gur [12]. Using Equation (4) and (5), non-ducted propeller produce thrust coefficient of 0.031 with advance ratio of 0.24 and ducted propeller type γ generate thrust coefficient of 0.037 with advance ratio of 0.28. If the power generated between both models has the same value, then the ducted propeller type γ has better efficiency value. Deeper analysis can be done by calculating the correlated power rotor with the resulting thrust which is not the focus of this study.

5 Conclusion

Propeller with size of 406 (mm) can be optimized by adding cover on propeller or also known as ducted propeller. With maximum angular velocity propeller of 9000 (rpm), ducted propeller type α generate thrust of 1.38 (N) and propeller type β and γ generate thrust of 2.1 (N). This means that the addition of ducted frame material should not be more than 140 gram-force (gf) for each propeller cover type α, wheras in type γ the addition of ducted frame material should not exceed 214 (gf). Type γ is better than type β because it has lighter mass while produce the same thrust. In terms of quadcopter body frame size, ducted propeller can be designed smaller than the non-ducted propeller. Body frame size was based on maximum angular velocity of propeller rotation thus the air velocity produced between propeller will not interfere with each other. For angular velocity 5000 (rpm), a quadcopter ducted body frame with size of 460 (mm) in square size can be used.

Assuming the power required to produce propeller rotation with the same angular velocity, ducted propeller has a better efficiency than the non-ducted because the resulting airflow trajectory moves downward to generate maximum thrust with minimum disturbance.

Acknowledgment

This work has been funded under the LEADERS - Erasmus Mundus Grant (agreement number 2014-0855/001-001) by European Commission, through the Education, Audio-visual and Culture Executive Agency, in the Action Plan 2 for the years 2014-2018, and supported by PNCDI III Programme P2 - Transfer of knowledge to the economic operator (Bridge Grant PN-III-P2 2.1 BG-2016-0296) funded by UEFISCDI, Romania.

References

[1] H. Guang, G. Hoffmann, S. Waslander, and C.J.Tomlin, "Aerodynamics and Control of Autonomous Quadcopters in Aggressive Maneuvering," *International Conference on Robotics and Automation*, 2009, pp. 3277-3282.

[2] R. Czyba, and G. Szafranski, "Control Structure Impact on the Flying Performance of the Multi-Rotor VTOL Platform - Design, Analysis and Experimental Validation," *International Journal of Advanced Robotic Systems* , 2012, pp. 1-9.

[3] V. Hrishikeshavan, and I. Chopra, "Performance, Flight Testing of Shrounded Rotor Micro Air Vehicle in Edgewise Gusts," *Journal of Aircraft*, vol. 49, 2012, pp. 193-205.

[4] J. Pereira, D. Bawek, S. Westfall, and I. Chopra, "Design and Development of a Quad-Shrouded-Rotor Micro Air Vehicle," *American Helicopter Society 65th Annual Forum*, 2009.

[5] V. Hrishikeshavan, J. Sirohi, M. Tishchenko, and I. Chopra, "Design and Development of a Shrouded Rotor Micro Air Vehicle with Anti-torque Vanes," *Journal of the American Helicopter Society*, vol. 56, 2011, pp. 1-11.

[6] Y. Yang, L. L. M. Veldhuis, and G. Eitelberg, " Investigation of Propeller Induced Ground Vortices by Numerical and Experimental Methods." *AIAA Applied Aerodynamics Conference*, 2015, pp. 1-12.

[7] H. A. Kutty and P. Rajendran, "3D CFD Simulation and Experimental Validation of Small APC Slow Flyer Propeller Blade," *Aerospace Journal*, vol. 4, pp. 1-11, 2017.

[8] Y. Jiang, B. Zhang, and T. Huang, "CFD Study of an Annular-Ducted Fan Lift System for VTOL Aircraft," *Aerospace Journal*, vol. 2, 2015, pp. 555-580.

[9] S. B. Heinzen, C. E. Hall, and A. Gopalarthnam, "Development and Testing of a Passive Variable-Pitch Propeller," *Journal of Aircraft*, vol. 52, 2015, pp. 748-763.

[10] Y. Yang, D. Ragni, L Veldhuis, and G. Eitelberge, "Propeller Induced Ground Vortex," *28th International Congress of The Aeronautical Sciences*, 2012, pp. 1-11.

[11] E. Kuantama, D. Craciun, and R. Tarca, "Quadcopter Body Frame Model and Analysis," *Annals of The University of Oradea*, 2016, pp. 71-74.

[12] O. Gur, "Maximum Propeller Efficiency Estimation," *Journal of Aircraft*, vol. 51, 2015, pp. 2035-2038

* Corresponding author: endrowednes@gmail.com

The study of chain link/guide contact in relative alternative translational motion

Radu Papuc[1*], *Cătălin* Gavrilă[2], *Mihai – Tiberiu* Lateş[3]
[1] Transilvania University of Brasov, radu.papuc@unitbv.ro, Romania
[2] Transilvania University of Brasov, cgavrila@unitbv.ro, Romania
[3] Transilvania University of Brasov, latesmt@unitbv.ro, Romania

Abstract— The paper presents the study of the chain link/guide contact in relative alternative motion, by performing test and finite elements modeling. According to these, the paper presents the variation of the dynamic friction coefficient at the contact between the guide and chain links. Also, it is followed an equivalent stresses study as well as of the contact pressures variation. The conclusions are presented at the final of paper.

1 Introduction

The concepts evolution on friction nature creates conditions in order to better explain the notion of dynamic friction coefficient T. Fink [1].

It is seen that, so far, because of the friction phenomena complexity, an unanimously accepted theory that will explain the dependence of the friction coefficient on the intervening factors was not accepted D. H. Gordon, S. N. Kukureka [2]. But, there were experimentally determined, in different conditions, various numerical values of friction coefficients H. Haixia, Y. Sirong, W. Mingyu, L. Kaixin, [3].

For a more complete characterization of the dynamic friction coefficient, next there will be presented the experimental determinations for the friction coefficient between the toothed link and a guide plate by considering two testing solutions. Further, by finite elements modeling, the local contact pressures are determined.

2 Description of testing designed models

In order to determine the dynamic friction coefficient between the tensioning guide and toothed chain, used in an automobile transmission, there were designed and physically built two test models.

In Fig. 1 – 5, there are presented the used models for determining the friction coefficient, in laboratory conditions. All models were designed through CATIA V5 software and were machined in the workshops of Transilvania University of Brasov, Romania.

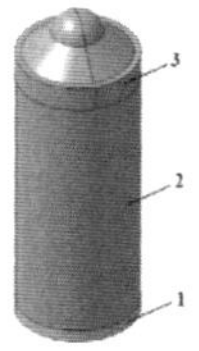

Fig. 1. Gripping - fixing device - cylinder type: 1 – guide; 2 – gripping device; 3 – applying force element.

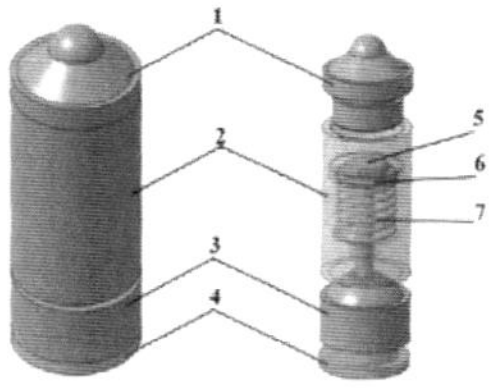

Fig. 2. Gripping - fixing device - spherical joint cylinder type: 1 – applying force element; 2 – fixing device; 3 –mobile gripping device; 4 – guide; 5 – stopping screw; 6 – washer; 7 – spring.

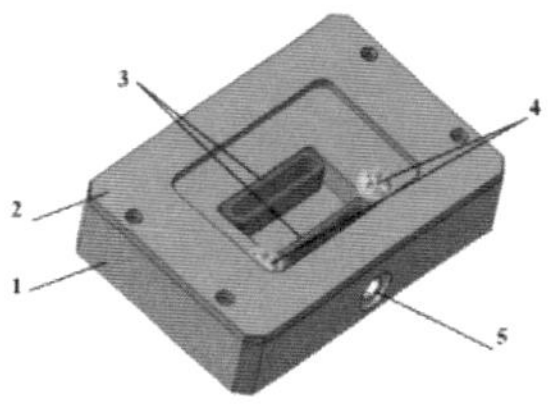

Fig. 3. Gripping - fixing device- the oil bath type: 1 – oil bath tub; 2 – bath lid; 3 – positioning and fixing screws; 4 –elastic piece; 5 –fixing screw with interior hexagonal head.

* Corresponding author: radu.papuc@unitbv.ro

 DOI: 10.1051/matecconf/201712601003

In designing and manufacturing these devices was taken into consideration the identifying of some solutions as close as possible to the real case when the chain is in contact with the tensioning guide.

For a detailed image of the two cases presented previously, in Fig. 4 and Fig. 5 are shown, in testing position, the previous devices.

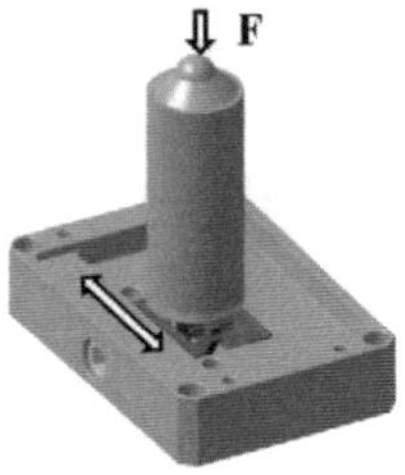

Fig. 4. The gripping - fixing devices - cylinder type

Fig. 5. The gripping - fixing devices - spherical joint cylinder type

In order to maintain the lubrication between the toothed links and the guide, it was designed a system made from two elastic elements that fixates the links into the oil bath shown in Fig. 3.

To measure the friction coefficient was used a measuring device named UMT tribometer, shown in Fig. 6, which is connected to a computer and allows to measure and to show the friction coefficient.

Fig. 5. The UMT tribometer

Fig. 6. The reciprocating module: 1 - command engine; 2 - fixing basis; 3 - friction force reading sensor; 4 – data cables.

In order to determine the friction coefficient, the reciprocating module is attached to the tribometer. This module performs an alternative rectilinear motion while the sensor 3 is measuring the friction force.

The figures from bellow present the oil bath and the devices used to determine the relative friction coefficient, in lubricated environment, for the contact between the circular guide segments (PAx and PA66) and the toothed chain links.

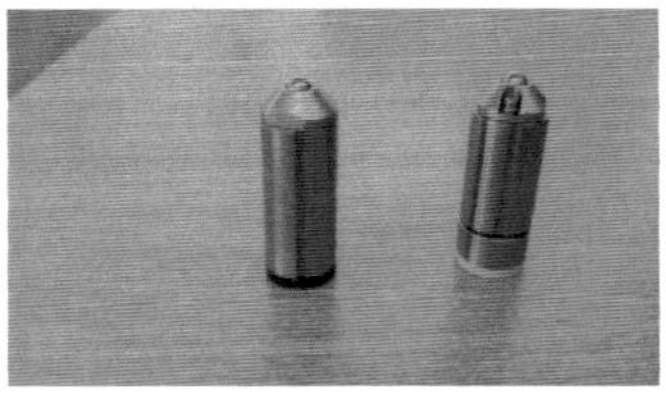

Fig. 7. The manufactured gripping - fixing devices - cylinder type and spherical joint cylinder type

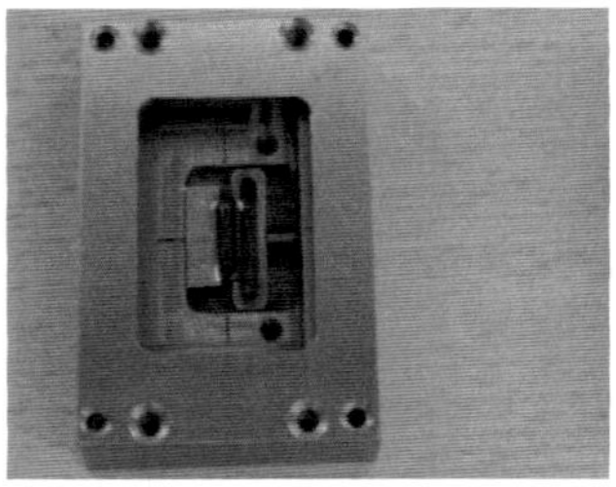

Fig. 8. The manufactured gripping - fixing device - oil bath type.

To determine the friction coefficient in lubricated environment between the toothed links and guide segment (PAx), the following initial conditions were imposed: the normal force Fn = 9 (N), which it corresponds a medium pressure pmed = 0,775 (MPa); the module stroke LV = 4,8 (mm); the working frequency f = 1 (Hz); the test period t = 2 (h); the lubricant: 15 W – 40 mineral oil.

It must be highlighted that the results regarding the obtained values for friction coefficients are presented, with some exceptions, as relative values or percentage, representing the parameters dependence for which absolute values are used; this fact was imposed by privacy clauses.

* Corresponding author: radu.papuc@unitbv.ro

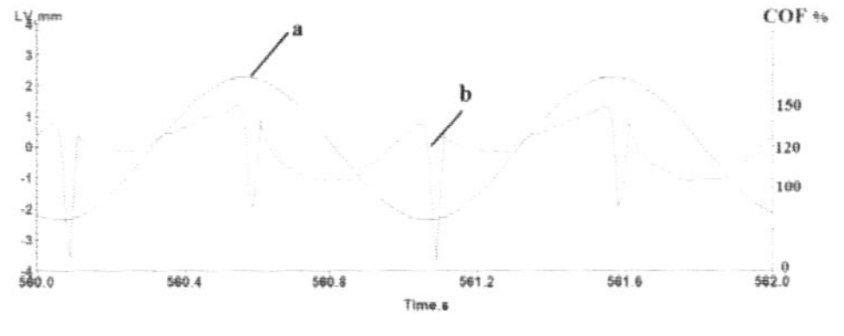

Fig. 9. The relative dynamic friction coefficient variation and the stroke for the contact between the guide segment and toothed links when using the spherical joint cylinder.

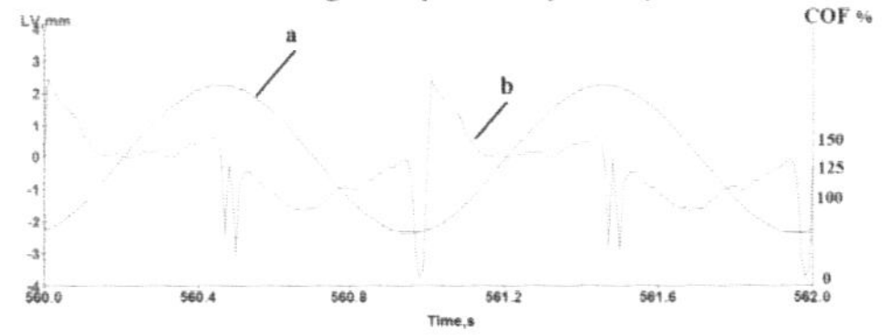

Fig. 10. The relative dynamic friction coefficient variation and the stroke for the contact between the guide segment and toothed links when using the simple cylinder.

There were performed two experimental tests, for the relative dynamic friction coefficient variations (the friction coefficient values were reported to their lowest value) between the guide and toothed links which are shown in Fig. 9 and Fig. 10. In the graphs, a is the stroke (alternative rectilinear motion) LV, and b is the relative dynamic friction coefficient COF.

By analysing in comparison the test results for the cases presented in Fig. 9 and Fig. 10 it can be concluded that on the reciprocating module the relative dynamic friction coefficient can not be rigorous determined, no matter if the the guide segment having circular form is pressed on the toothed links, by having a cylindrical holder with or without a spherical joint. This conclusion is motivated on the fact that the speed corresponding to the small linear displacement made by the module is much too small and has a constant value for a short amount of time in order to obtain a conclusive representation of the relative dynamic friction coefficient values, which later will be compared with the data found in the speciality literature.

3 The study of equivalent tensions and contact pressures

For the numerical determination was chosen the model from figure 5 due to its complexity.

This analysis assumes the deformation state and the contact distribution between the components, guide - links.

For the numerical evaluation of the studied models was used the finite element software ANSYS Workbench version .

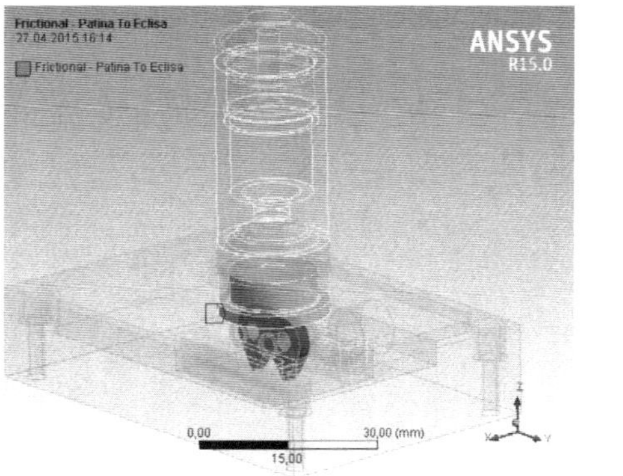

Fig. 11. Defining the contacts

In Fig. 11 is presented the defining contacts between guide and toothed links.The models were meshed with second order solids deformable finite elements with intermediary node, and for the components defined as rigide, the software used in meshing the rigide type elements J. Fish, T. A. Belychko [4].

Fig. 12. Finite elements model.

The materials used in this analysis were applied to both models as follows:

1) for the guide it was used the PAx polyamide with the following properties M. Akiyama, T. Yamaguchi [5]:

a) Young module E = 2700 (MPa)
b) Tensile Yield Strength σ = 34 (MPa)
c) Poisson coefficient ν = 0.38

2) for other components it was used steel with the following properties A. Todi-Eftimie, R. Velicu, C. Brands, F. Schlerege, M. T. Lateş [6]:

a) Young module E = 190000 (MPa)
b) Tensile Yield Strength σ = 240 (MPa)
c) Poisson coefficient ν = 0.3

The model was loaded with a static force F = 9 (N), resulted from the lubricating conditions and for the contact between the toothed links and guide it was used a friction coefficient of 0.2, determined, as well, from experimental tests.

The force is transmited from the applying point through the nonlinear contact to the guide and after to the toothed links fixed in the oil bath.

This is shown in Fig. 13.

* Corresponding author: radu.papuc@unitbv.ro

 DOI: 10.1051/matecconf/201712601003

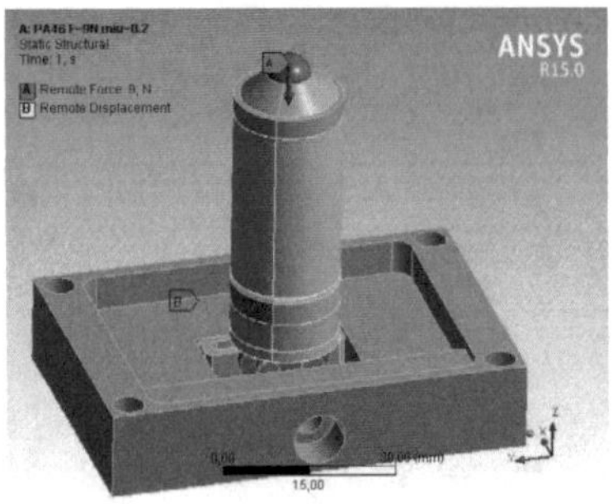

Fig. 13. Force application and freedom degrees constraints

After applying the 9 (N) force, it was obtained an uniform displacements distribution and a value of the maximum displacement which is quite small, 0.000829 (mm).

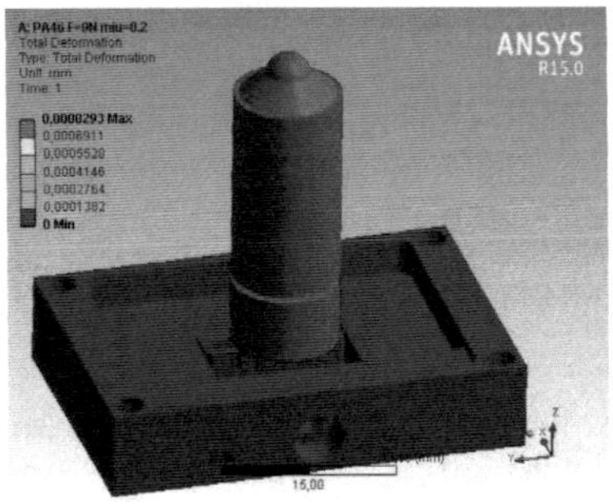

Fig. 14. Displacements distribution

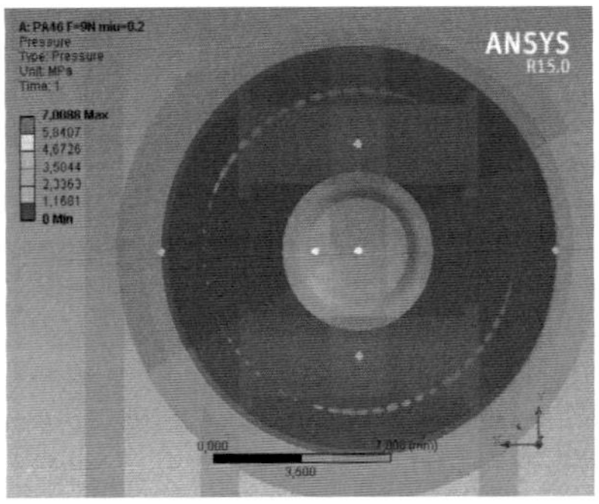

Fig. 15. The contact pressure between the mobile body and the main body.

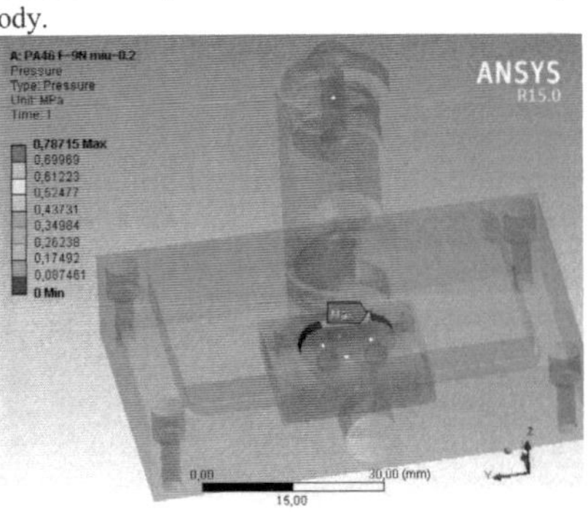

Fig. 16. The contact pressure between guide and toothed links.

This is shown in Fig. 14, where the color chart shows the precision of the model.

As it can be observed in Fig. 15, the two bodies contact pressure distribution is made on the tangent surface; the maximum value of the contact pressure in this zone is 7 (MPa).

The maximum value of the contact pressure between guide and toothed links is 0.787 (MPa) and is presented in figure 16.

4 Conclusions

The test results presented previously can be conclusive only for the start/stop situations.

This aspect is highlighted by the static friction coefficients values obtained in those situations.

By comparing these values with the speciality literature it can be concluded that in those situations it was obtained a limit friction J. Van Ruiten, R. Proost, M. Meuwissen [7].

Due to the problems identified in the reciprocating module tests, in the next stage is reccomended to perform tests on the rotary module, in order to find out the dynamic friction coefficient.

The purpose of experimental determinations for the guide - toothed links contact is to obtain a mixed friction towards fluid throughout the testing cycle and to find out the static friction coefficients which correspond to the start-stop situatuons.

Through the finite element modelling it was shown in detail the variation of the equivalent tensions and of contact pressures for the studied contact case.

References

[1] T. Fink, "Friction Reduction Potentials in Chain Drives," MTZ Worldwide Edition: Vol.72, 2011, p. 46-51.

[2] D. H. Gordon, S. N. Kukureka, „The wear and friction of polyamide 46 and polyamide 46/aramid-fibre composites in sliding–rolling contact," In: Wear, 2009, p. 669-678.

[3] H. Haixia, Y. Sirong, W. Mingyu, L. Kaixin, "Tribological behavior of polyamide 66-based binary and ternary composites," In: Polymer engineering and science, 2009, p. 2454 – 2458.

[4] J. Fish, T. A. Belychko, "First Course in Finite Elements," John Wiley & Sons Publishing House, Chichester, England, 2007.

[5] M. Akiyama, T. Yamaguchi, „Friction and wear of polyamide 66 composites filled with RB ceramics particles under dry condition," In Tribology Online No. 5 vol. 2, 2010, p. 87 – 91.

[6] A. Todi-Eftimie, R. Velicu, C. Brands, F. Schlerege, M. T. Lateş, „Friction in Bearings of Parallel Axes Transmissions," Applied Mechanics and Materials – Advanced Concepts in Mechanical Engineering I, vol. 658, 2014, ISSN 1660-9336, p. 371-376.

[7] J. Van Ruiten, R. Proost, M. Meuwissen, „How the choise of the polyamide type in timing chains tensioning systems affects the CO2 emission and fuel economy of internal combustion engines," In Presentation at VDI Veetiltrieb un Zylinderkopf 2012, November 28th, 2012.

* Corresponding author: radu.papuc@unitbv.ro

MATEC Web of Conferences **126**, 01004 (2017) DOI: 10.1051/matecconf/201712601004
Annual Session of Scientific Papers IMT ORADEA 2017

On the axioms of the forces in the mechanics of rigid bodies

Géza Lámer[1*]

[1]University of Debrecen, glamer@eng.unideb.hu, Hungary

Abstract—Newton summarised knowledge related to forces in three axioms. The first and second ones define the mechanical state and motion of the examined body when there is no force or when force is exerted on the body. The third defines the law of action and reaction. Newton did not define it as separate axiom but assumed that forces are completely independent from each other. The statics applies four axioms. The first applies to the balance of two forces while the second one applies of three forces. The third axiom defines the relationships inside an equilibrium force system. The fourth one is the axiom of action and reaction. The two axiom systems are independent from each other. Further the independent axioms are applied in case of constraint forces: frictionless reaction force orthogonal on the forced surface, friction force acts in the direction of the motion, the deformation can be elastic, plastic and viscous.

1 Introduction

Newton defined his system of axioms in „Principia" to describe the motion of objects, I. Newton [1]. Newton describes the mechanical state of the body in the axiom system if no forces are acting upon it, and also defines how the magnitude and direction of force related with quantitative measures typical of the motion of the body when forces are acting upon it, and finally summarises how the magnitude and direction of forces relate when one body acts on a second body. Newton did not refer to the relation of two or more simultaneously occurring forces and how the joint effects of these could be determined. At the same time he provided clear instructions regarding these two questions: forces are independent from each other when they occur and their effects add up according to the parallelogram rule. Newton, as his work was concentrated on the motion of (point like) bodies, did not deal with the issue of balance.

Newton's axioms did not explicitly define that forces are vector quantities; this statement is discussed in *Corollary* 1. and 2.

The axioms of statics are commonly defined for the equilibrium state of rigid bodies. These axioms define the conditions of equilibrium for two or three forces, as well as the method of conversion of one equilibrium force system into another equilibrium force system. This latter also applies to equilibrium force systems acting upon bodies in non-equilibrium states. Finally, the (Newtonian) axiom of action-reaction is also classified as an axiom of statics, although the axiom system of statics does not deal with the occurrence of forces.

The axioms of statics do not explicitly define forces as vector quantities; this statement ensues from the axiom regarding the equilibrium of three forces.

Generally, neither of the axiom systems deals with the occurrence of forces, although both include the axiom, which clearly defines the number of forces and their relationship to each other which can be interpreted as the model of effects arising between the two bodies. The two axiom systems apply to two different mechanical systems: the first one is intended to describe the motion of (point like) bodies while the second one is intended to describe the equilibrium of rigid bodies.

The fact that any triplet forms a vector is not unambiguous. There is reference that the axioms records the attributes (commutativity, associativity) of vector addition when interpreting the vector spaces and attributes of simultaneous operations with vectors and real numbers, P.R: Halmos [2]. The fact that force is a vector quantity and the joint effect of more forces is equivalent to the effect of the vectorial sum of more forces does not ensue from the fact that force is used to describe the interaction of two bodies. The study examines the two axiom systems, then an axiom system is compiled which includes the attributes of forces arising in mechanics, the operations regarding the mechanical state of bodies, i.e. the „method of use" of force.

2 The Newtonian axioms

Newton's axioms apply to motion of bodies, more

* Corresponding author: glamer@eng.unideb.hu

specifically to the motion changes of bodies, I. Newton [1].

Before presenting the axioms, a definition of force, of body, and of mechanical state is required for which the axioms apply to.

Newton defines force as the effect acting upon the body. "*Definition* 4. Impressed force is the action exerted on a body to change its state either of resting or of moving uniformly straight forward.", I. Newton [1], p. 405.

Newton uses the term matter instead of body. "*Definition* 1.: Quantity of matter is a measure of matter that arises from its density and volume." (Presently referred to as the product, I. Newton [1], p. 403.

Newton defines the „initial" mechanical state as rest or uniform motion. See i.e. *Definition* 4.

The Newtonian axioms are the following.

THE FIRST NEWTONIAN AXIOM (*Law* 1.): "Every body perseveres in its state of being at rest or of moving uniformly straight forward, except insofar as it is compelled to change its state by forces impressed", I. Newton [1], p. 416.

This axiom applies to the state when no forces are acting upon the body; in other words no other body is acting upon it.

THE SECOND NEWTONIAN AXIOM (*Law* 2.): "A changes in motion is proportional to the motive force impressed and takes place along the straight line in which that force impressed.", I. Newton [1], p. 416.

This axiom, for a force impressed on a body, is currently defined as follows: the acceleration (**a**) of an object arises in the same direction as the force (**F**) causing it while its magnitude is proportional to the magnitude of the force and inversely proportional to the mass (m) of that object.

This axiom describes the relationship between the data determining force (magnitude, direction and sign) and data describing the motion change of the body (magnitude, direction and sign). This also means that this axiom defines the data describing the force at the same time: magnitude, direction and sign. However, this axiom does not describe how force arises. This is because gravitational forces act upon objects in a Newtonian mechanical system and the value and direction of these forces is determined by the relative position, mass and universal laws of gravity. On the one hand, the second axiom describes that if force acts upon an object then it changes the motion of the object, on the other hand it also describes how the change of the motion can be calculated. The second axiom connects only the force and its consequence and it does not deal with the simultaneous effect of more forces. This has to be examined separately.

THE THIRD NEWTONIAN AXIOM (*Low* 3.): "To any action there is always an opposite and equal reactions; in other words, the actions of two bodies upon each other are always equal and opposite in direction.", I. Newton [1], p. 417.

This axiom defines that if an effect arises while two bodies act upon each other, then these are essentially two „effects", or two forces. At the same time it also defines how the data describing two forces – magnitude, direction and sign – relate to each other. It does not provide explicit information of the line of action, but it covertly assumes identical line of action in the subsequent explanation.

This axiom characterises how the force arises. Implicitly, it „follows" the first axiom. The second axiom characterises the numeric value of force and its effect, i.e. effect of one of the two occurring forces on the examined object. Therefore, the third axiom „precedes" the second axiom.

THE FOURTH NEWTONIAN AXIOM. In fact it defines not as an axiom but rather as Corollary 1. and 2.

Corollary 1. "A body acted on by [two] forces acting jointly describes the diagonal of a parallelogram in the same time in which it would describe the sides if the forces were acting separately.", I. Newton [1], p. 417.

In order to prove *Corollary* 1. Newton does not apply the previous axioms, but a logical reasoning that the forces are independent from each other; therefore, it is irrelevant which on which side of the parallelogram the body moves along first and second towards the endpoint of the diagonal. This reasoning uses the independence of forces, the attributes of which were not individually postulated by Newton. We also refer to the fact that the parallelogram rule is regarded as an axiom in linear vector spaces (see e.g. P. R. Halmos [2].

So *Corollary* 1. which is generally regarded as THE FOURTH NEWTONIAN AXIOM (see e.g. Á. Budó [3]), includes two independent statements. On the one hand, it states that the effect of forces acting upon a body are independent, on the other hand, they sum up as vectors. Since the Newtonian axioms apply to (point like) bodies, forces act upon them in one point; there are no conceptual obstacles for the vectors of forces to sum up.

Similarly to the summation of forces, Newton states in an individual *Corollary* 2. that a force can be separated to two oblique forces.

Corollary 2. "And hence the composition of a direct force AD out of any oblique forces AB and BD is evident, and conversely the resolution of any direct force AD into any oblique forces AB and BD. And this kind of composition and resolution is indeed abundantly confirmed from mechanics.", I. Newton [1], p. 418.

In order to prove this, Newton used the condition torque of forces on one point and the balance of parallel forces placed on two opposite ends of the balance beam of the scale.

The following statements can be made in connection with Newtonian axioms:

The axioms do not include information regarding the occurrence of force, i.e. the axioms do not determine the generation of force.

The second axiom, more specifically its definition in the form of $F = ma$, enables the measurement of mass and weight force (see e.g. Á. Budó [3]).

The axioms apply to the motion of bodies that can be

* Corresponding author: glamer@eng.unideb.hu

described with shifting. Instead of (point like) bodies, they can also be regarded as extensive objects (for instance rigid or deformable solid bodies), but occurring forces only act in the centre of gravity and the bodies cannot rotate around their centre of gravity.

The axioms do not deal with the movement of extensive, e.g. rigid or deformable solid, bodies. These have to be examined separately.

The axioms do not refer to equilibrium and the effect of the equilibrium force systems on motion.

The axioms do not apply to the rotation, deformation and fracture of bodies.

The axioms do not include the occurrence of constraint forces, and neither the fact that in case of a constraint created by a surface, the constraint force is orthogonal to the surface.

Newton's axioms primarily apply to the motion of bodies, i.e. the followings are excluded: deformation of bodies, fracture of bodies, equilibrium of bodies.

3 Axioms of statics

The axioms of statics apply to the equilibrium of rigid bodies (see e.g. K. Szily [4] and T. Cholnoky [5]).

Before presenting the axioms, force, body and the mechanical state to which they apply must be defined.

Force: effect occurs while two bodies act upon each other. Force is characterised by four data: point of application, line of action, magnitude and sign.

Characterisation of the body: A body is an identifiable collection of matter which moves together, the distance between any two points of the body are constant and the collection of particles remains. Generally, the rigid body is regarded as a three dimensional, finite volume region in the Euclidean space which does not change its size upon forces.

Characterisation of equilibrium: a body is motionless in equilibrium.

The axioms of statics are the following.

THE FIRST AXIOM OF STATICS: Two forces of identical magnitude and line of action, with opposite sign are in equilibrium.

This axiom captures, by providing two forces in equilibrium, that equilibrium force systems exist.

This axiom defines the equilibrium of two forces irrespective of point of application: the point of application of forces is simply not included among the conditions of equilibrium. Consequently, two forces do not have to act upon in the same point; the condition of equilibrium only depends on concordance of line of action (beyond the identical magnitude and opposite sign).

THE SECOND AXIOM OF STATICS: Three forces are only in equilibrium if the lines of action of three forces intersect in one point, and the vector of three forces constitute a closed, continuous vector polygon (triangle).

The axiom implicitly applies the fact that the force vectors are present as independent entities, as well as the fact that they can be summed as vectors. These are conditions for identifying the sum of three force vectors with the force equal that of the simultaneous effect of three forces.

The closed, continuous vector polygon indicates that the three forces must be in one plane.

THE THIRD AXIOM OF STATICS: If we connect an equilibrium force system to another equilibrium force system or an equilibrium subsystem is taken away from an equilibrium system, the obtained force system remains in equilibrium.

This axiom states how another equilibrium force system can be obtained from another equilibrium force system. Only a strictly equilibrium force system can be used to create an equilibrium force system: either two equilibrium force systems are „added", or a partial equilibrium force system constituting a part of the equilibrium force system is „subtracted". Equilibrium force system cannot be created from non-equilibrium force system. This is defined as equilibrium and non-equilibrium force systems are independent from each other.

THE FOURTH AXIOM OF STATICS: If forces arise in pairs when two rigid bodies act upon each other, the pair of forces have the same line of action, the same magnitude and opposite sign.

This axiom defines only that forces arise in pairs. It does not include information on either the number of force pairs or the point of application occurring with force pairs and neither does it refer to whether the two rigid bodies are motionless or are in motion in the moment of occurrence of force. It does not specify whether motionless bodies begin to move when force pairs arise or do the arising forces change motion in case of moving bodies or not.

The two forces, in THE FOURTH AXIOM OF STATICS, between two rigid bodies occurring as a consequence of an effect, are in equilibrium according to THE FIRST AXIOM OF STATICS.

The following statements can be made regarding the axioms of statics:

The axioms do not include information on the occurrence of forces, i.e. the axioms do not determine the occurrence of forces.

The axioms are formally applied to the equilibrium of rigid bodies. In fact, the first three axioms of statics include conditions suitable for determining equilibrium irrespective of the fact whether forces act upon rigid or deformable bodies or the forces are simply given in space. The fourth axiom of statics includes reference to rigid bodies, as long as the aforementioned axiom makes constraints regarding the force pairs occurring during the interaction of two rigid bodies.

The axioms do not refer to motion and the effect of motion on the equilibrium force system.

The axioms do not deal with the effect of forces occurring between bodies on the state of equilibrium and motion.

The axioms do not apply to the motion (shifting), rotation, deformation and fracture of bodies.

* Corresponding author: glamer@eng.unideb.hu

The axioms do not include the development of constraint forces or the fact that the constraint force is orthogonal to the surface in case of constraint created by a surface.

The axioms of statics are primarily applied to rigid bodies at rest, i.e. exclude: deformation of bodies, fracture of bodies, the motion of bodies.

We examine such tasks within statics, where the system of motionless, rigid bodies in equilibrium rearrange due to the effect of a given force system and reach a motionless state of equilibrium, but the path to this is imagined as the rearrangement of rigid body systems occurs without motion until equilibrium is reached. Bodies do not gain either velocity or acceleration during the rearrangement. Equilibrium is reached infinitely slowly.

4 Criteria of establishing the axiom system

The behaviour of bodies under forces is determined based on knowledge through experience, and from them abstracted fundamental theorems that is axioms.

We follow the following principles when setting up axiom system:

The axioms must record

1) how the force occurs,
2) what data describe (characterise) the force,
3) how the occurring force(s) can be described,
4) what the effect of two forces on each other like,
5) what mathematical object force is,
6) what state exists if there is force and if there is no force,
7) how the forces characterising a mechanical system (equilibrium force system) can be determined in case of an „elementary", or a „typical" system,
8) how can be created or derived from one specific (let understand: equilibrium) force system an another specific (that is equilibrium) system, different from beginning one.

The axioms are classified into four large groups.

The first group summarises the knowledge regarding the occurrence of forces. The second group includes interpretations of forces as mathematical objects. The third group records the effect of forces on bodies. The fourth group describes the relationship between forces and their effects.

5 A complete axiom system related to forces

The axioms are classified into four main groups: occurrence of force, force as mathematical object, effect of force on bodies, relationship between force and its effects.

B. Axioms related to the occurrence of force

The first axiom records how force occurs.

THE FIRST AXIOM (The axiom of interpretation of force): Force is the mechanical model of two interacting bodies. An effect occurring between two bodies is modelled as two forces: *one* body acts upon another body and vice versa, the *other* body acts upon *one* body. So when two bodies act upon each other, in case of *one* kind of effect, a pair of forces occur. In case of various effects, forces occur in pairs when two bodies act upon each other; as many pairs as many effects occur between the two bodies.

With two given bodies, A and B, and an existing effect between them (e.g. they are in contact in a point, or gravitational pull exists between them). The effect of body B on body A is denoted by $\mathcal{F}_{AB}$, the effect of body A on body B is denoted as $\mathcal{F}_{BA}$. Since *THE FIRST AXIOM* only records that there is an effect, so it is denoted by a „neutral" notation, by letter $\mathcal{F}$. If there are more effects between body A and B (e.g. there are contact in several points, or gravitational *and* electrical attraction, and repulsion also exists between them), then the forces occurring in pair differ from each other in accordance with more effects; $\mathcal{F}^1{}_{AB}$ and $\mathcal{F}^1{}_{BA}$, as well as $\mathcal{F}^2{}_{AB}$ and $\mathcal{F}^2{}_{BA}$ the forces occurring in contact point 1 and 2, and $\mathcal{F}^G{}_{AB}$ and $\mathcal{F}^G{}_{BA}$, as well as $\mathcal{F}^E{}_{AB}$ and $\mathcal{F}^E{}_{BA}$ the forces occurring as an effect of gravitational or electrical attraction (repulsion).

The second axiom records the data characterising the force:

THE SECOND AXIOM (The axiom of data of force): Force is characterised by the point of application, line of action, scale and direction.

We characterise the occurring forces in the third axiom.

THE THIRD AXIOM (The axiom of action and reaction): The two forces occurring between two bodies as a result of effects between two bodies are characterised as follows: the line of action of two forces is in coincidence, the magnitude of two forces is the same, and their singe is opposite. We say that there is an „action" and a „reaction" occurring for each effect between two bodies.

THE THIRD AXIOM does not have „provision" on the point of application of forces. The point of application is interpreted at different points in various modelling. For example in the case of gravitational bodies, gravitating force is connected to the centre of gravity of the gravitating body. Forces arising during the gravitational effect are far from each other in celestial body revolving around a central celestial body. Contact forces are in the same contact points in the case of contacting bodies.

It must be recorded how a force arising in the absence and presence of another force or another forces.

The fourth axiom records the method of effects of two or more forces, more specifically the independence of two or more forces from each other.

THE FOURTH AXIOM (The axiom of independence of forces): The individual forces act upon independently.

Let given three bodies, A, B and C. The effect of body B on body A when there is no body C, denoting by

* Corresponding author: glamer@eng.unideb.hu

$\mathcal{F}_{AB}(\varnothing)$, and $\mathcal{F}_{AB}(C)$, if there is the body C present, then, when body A and B act upon each other. The independence of forces means that $\mathcal{F}_{AB}(\varnothing)$ is identical with $\mathcal{F}_{AB}(C)$, i.e. the effect of body A and B on each other is not influenced by body C. Naturally, the axiom also applies to cases when more C_i ($i = 1,2,\ldots,n$) bodies are also present beyond body A and B. On this case, the $\mathcal{F}_{AB}(\varnothing)$ force arising without the C_i ($i = 1,2,\ldots,n$) bodies is identical with the $\mathcal{F}_{AB}(C_i)$ ($i = 1,2,\ldots,n$) force arising in the presence of any C_i ($i = 1,2,\ldots,n$) body, with the $\mathcal{F}_{AB}(C_i,C_j)$ ($i, j = 1,2,\ldots,n$, $i \neq j$) force arising along with any two, C_i and C_j ($i, j = 1,2,\ldots,n$, $i \neq j$) bodies and with the $\mathcal{F}_{AB}(C_i,C_j,\ldots,C_l)$ ($i \neq j$, $i \neq l$, ..., $j \neq l$, $i, j, \ldots, l = 1,2,\ldots,n$) forces arising along with any combination of bodies C_i, C_j, ..., C_l) ($i \neq j$, $i \neq l$, ..., $j \neq l$, $i, j, \ldots, l = 1,2,\ldots,n$).

C. Force as a mathematical object.

The fifth axiom records what mathematical object is force.

THE FIFTH AXIOM (The axiom of choosing the mathematical object): Force is a vector quantity.

As this axiom records that effect is modelled as a vector, effect – the force – is hereinafter denoted by a bold letter.

With the occurrence of two or more effects, i.e. two or force occurrence the fact must be recorded that if two or more forces are simultaneously interpreted, how those jointly act upon the body. This is recorded in the sixth axiom.

THE SIXTH AXIOM (The axiom of joint effect of forces): Forces with *identical point of application* acting upon independently sum up as vectors.

THE SIXTH AXIOM states that two forces with *identical point of application* sum up as vectors: their joint effects – their geometrical attributes – can be determined by vector addition. The point of application of the „summed" force is the common point of application of forces, line of action and magnitude is determined based on the rules of vector addition.

THE SIXTH AXIOM does not apply to the determination of joint effects by forces with different point of application. This requires individual examination.

D. The effect of force on bodies: motion and immobility

The following possibilities have to be separated in this section

1) No force acts upon the body
2) One force acts upon the body and no constraint exists
3) More forces act upon the body, no constraint exists and the body is in a state of inertia: the force system is in equilibrium (definition)
4) The existence of equilibrium force system
5) If there is a given equilibrium force system, how another equilibrium force system can be created from it
6) A force acts upon the body and one constraint exists

The seventh axiom records the fact that a body is in a motionless state without force.

Immobility or motion can only be interpreted compared to one or more precisely to three other bodies. Bodies providing the point of comparison can be motionless or can be in motion. Therefore new providing bodies of comparison have to be chosen. Then it must be decided whether the new (secondly chosen) providing bodies of comparison to determine the immobility of (firstly chosen) bodies are motionless or are in motion (compared to the older group of bodies). The selection of bodies for comparison to determine immobility or motion can be continued infinitely. This can only be eliminated if *absolutely motionless* bodies are chosen. This latter does not exist, as everything in the Universe is in motion. What remains is the system of bodies that can be regarded as *practically motionless*. This will simply be referred to as a motionless environment. This is what Newton refers to as system of inertia, as a system of absolute rest. As there is no information on motion (yet), immobility is regarded as a priority status. The equivalence of immobility and motion with uniform velocity can be interpreted later.

THE SEVENTH AXIOM (The axiom of immobility): A body without any forces acting upon it are at rest (compared to the environment being at rest).

This axiom refers to the state when no forces are acting upon the body; in other words no other bodies are acting upon it. A separate axiom states if a force acts upon the body. At the same time, not only one force can act upon the body, but also a support opposing the motion of its points.

DEFINITION: A body opposing the motion of some points of another body is called a *constraint* (*support*).

The effect of forces acting upon a body has to be examined separately for instances of lack of constraint and presence of constraint.

THE EIGHTH AXIOM (The axiom of motion): A body, upon which force is acted, and is not under the effect of constraint (compared to the motionless environment) does not remain motionless, it gains motion.

This axiom only records the fact that bodies without constraint start to move. The "how" of motion – depending on the type of body – can be recorded by some individual axioms.

In the presence of constraint(s), forces arising from the constraint(s) also act upon the body. This fact is recorded by the eighth axiom.

THE NINTH AXIOM (The axiom of arising support force). In body which is acted upon by a force and is under the effect of constraint, a force arises, which is opposite the direction of the constrained motion.

DEFINITION: If a motionless body is not under the effect of a constraint and is under more forces act upon it, remains motionless then the force system acting upon it are referred to as *equilibrium force system*.

Using the term of equilibrium force system the mechanical state of body under forces and constraints can be defined.

CONSEQUENCE 1: A body, which is under the effect of more forces and constraint(s) and the forces as well the

* Corresponding author: glamer@eng.unideb.hu

constraint(s) jointly
1) form an equilibrium force system, then the body is motionless,
2) do not form an equilibrium force system, then the body begins to move.

We provide the required and sufficient condition of equilibrium for two forces in the ninth axiom.

THE TENTH AXIOM (The axiom of equilibrium for two forces; the axiom of existence of equilibrium force systems): Two forces with identical line of action, identical magnitude and opposite sign are in equilibrium.

THE TENTH AXIOM records that an equilibrium force system exists by providing two forces in equilibrium.

THE TENTH AXIOM determines the equilibrium of two forces irrespective of point of application: the points of application simply are not present among the conditions of equilibrium. Consequently, two forces do not have to act upon in the same point, the condition of equilibrium only depends on the concordance of the lines action (beyond the identical magnitude and opposite sing).

A consequence of *THE TENTH AXIOM*, is that the two forces arising during action-reaction between two bodies are in equilibrium. The two bodies however, do not have to be in equilibrium; see e.g. the gravitational force among moving planets and the Sun. The fact that the two forces arising during action-reaction are in equilibrium can also be defined as the $\mathbf{F}_{AB}$ and $\mathbf{F}_{BA}$ forces arising during the interaction of A and B bodies are opposite each of other.

The eleventh axiom records the method creating an equilibrium force system from another equilibrium force system.

THE ELEVENTH AXIOM (The principle (axiom) of superposition of equilibrium force systems). If an equilibrium force system is connected to an equilibrium force system or an equilibrium subsystem is taken away from an equilibrium force system, then the obtained force system is still equilibrium.

THE ELEVENTH AXIOM states, how two equilibrium force systems, $\{\mathbf{A}_i\} \doteq \{\mathbf{0}\}$ and $\{\mathbf{B}_j\} \doteq \{\mathbf{0}\}$, can be used to create an equilibrium force system: the two independent equilibrium force systems are joined, i.e. the two joined force systems are regarded as one force system. The obtained force system is also in equilibrium: $\{\{\mathbf{A}_i\},\{\mathbf{B}_j\}\} \doteq \{\mathbf{0}\}$. Furthermore, *THE ELEVENTH AXIOM* states that if there is an equilibrium force system, $\{\mathbf{C}_i\} \doteq \{\mathbf{0}\}$, which can be separate into two subsystems in a way that one is in equilibrium, $\{\mathbf{C}_i\} \doteq \{\{\mathbf{A}_i\},\{\mathbf{B}_j\}\}$ and $\{\mathbf{B}_j\} \doteq \{\mathbf{0}\}$, then leaving the equilibrium subsystem out of the original equilibrium force system, the remaining subsystem is still in equilibrium: $\{\mathbf{A}_i\} \doteq \{\mathbf{0}\}$.

The eleventh axiom records that the state of equilibrium and motion are independent mechanical states.

THE TWELFTH AXIOM (The axiom of independence of equilibrium and motion): If an equilibrium force system acts upon a body in motion, then the motion of the body is not influenced by an equilibrium force system and vice versa.

Note. THE TWELFTH AXIOM records the independence of motion and equilibrium. At the same time, it does not separate what mechanical phenomenon occurs in equilibrium: contact, deformation, rearrangement, friction etc. This will be defined by the laws related to determining force. At least must be recorded that force arising in equilibrium must be arisen infinitely slowly and dos not acts velocity and acceleration. This is formulated in the twelfth axiom.

THE THIRTEENTH AXIOM (The axiom of effect of equilibrium force): The forces arising in equilibrium must be arisen infinitely slowly, and dos not act velocity and acceleration.

E. The relationship existing between force and its effect

The following axioms describe the relationship among various forces and their effects:

THE FOURTEENTH AXIOM (The axiom of gravitational forces). Force arising between two gravitating bodies: $\mathbf{F} = -\gamma \frac{m_1 m_2}{r^2}\frac{\mathbf{r}}{r}$, where m_1 and m_2 are the mass of the two bodies, $\mathbf{r}$ is the position vector connecting two points of the centre of gravity, γ is the universal gravitational constant.

THE FIFTEENTH AXIOM (The axiom of weight force): The weight force acting upon bodies with weight is: $\mathbf{G} = m\mathbf{g}$, where m is the mass of the body, and $\mathbf{g}$ is the gravitational acceleration on the surface of the Earth.

THE SIXTEENTH AXIOM (The axiom of constraint force): A force arises at a contact point in a body under constraint is orthogonal to the surface of constraint. Its magnitude can be determined from the conditions of equilibrium.

THE SEVENTEENTH AXIOM (The axiom of friction force): A force arises at a connection point in a body under constraint with friction is tangent to the surface of constraint. Its magnitude depends on the normal force arising between body and surface, as well as the friction constant characterising friction surfaces.

References

[1] I. Newton: *The Principia. Mathematical Principles of Natural Philosophy*, University of California Press, Berkeley – Los Angeles – London, 1999. A new translation by B. Cohen and A. Whitman assisted by J. Budenz
[2] P. R. Halmos: *Finite-dimensional vector spaces*, Springer-Verlag, 1974.
[3] Á. Budó: *Mechanika*. (Mechanics in Hungarian) 5. kiadás. Tankönyvkiadó, Budapest, 1972.
[4] K. Szily: *Mechanika* (Mechanics in Hungarian). Első kötet. Statika. Németh József technikai Könyvkiadó Vállalata, Budapest, 1921.
[5] T. Cholnoky: *Mechanika*. (Mechanics in Hungarian) I. kötet. Statika. Harmadik, átdolgozott kiadás. Tankönyvkiadó, Budapest, 1969.

* Corresponding author: glamer@eng.unideb.hu

Multiobjective optimization of planar truss girder

Imre Timár[1] and *Pál* Horváth[2*]

[1]University of Pannonia, Veszprém, Egyetem u.10, Hungary; timari@almos.vein.hu
[2] University of Pannonia, Veszprém, Egyetem u.10, Hungary; horvathp@almos.vein.hu

Abstract The continuous increasing trends in the case of the raw material-, energy-, production-, and operation costs have been made necessary, the development of the numerical methods made it possible to spread widely the optimal design methods in the technical practice.The method of optimal design with multiobjective functions is useful when the designer has to rank the different construction variations. We apply this method to optimal design of truss girder when the aim functions are the mass of girder and the deflection of the structure. We change the cross-section of beam of girder as unknown parameter. The restrictions are concerning the design resistance of tensile bars and the stability of compressed bars.

1 Introduction

Thecontinuous increasing trends in case of the raw material-, energy-, production-, and operation costs have been made necessary the development of the numerical methods have been made possible the wide spread of the optimal design methods in the technical practice. Using these methods we can ensure to fullfil not only the different requrements, but we also are able to reduce the cost level of the product. The reduction of the structural mass or volume was the target at the early stage of the optimal design studies. Later the overal cost of the product to be reducedwas the goal.

When specifying the technical optimization problems, product and process optimization is defined. The product optimization can be further specified: topology optimization, form optimization, dimension optimization and material optimization, T. Kulcsár, I. Timár [1].

2 Multiobjective optimization

The *multiobjective optimization* is widely used for solving optimization tasks of engineering problems. The method was developed by Vilfredo Pareto (1848 – 1923). The Pareto optimum is a solution point, where no other main function can be improved without the degradation of another main function. We cannot find too many papers about the theory of the multi-objective optimization by the 60-es, but a lot of papers came out in this topic after that, including also the decision making applications, K. Jármai, M. Iványi [2].

Multiobjective optimum design of structures is very significant for enhancing the quality of structural design. Multiobjective optimization is a vector optimization, each element of which represents the objective functions being optimized. The mathematical expressions are as

$$\begin{aligned} &min\ F(\underline{x}) = \{f_1(\underline{x}),...,f_n(\underline{x})\}, \\ &0 \le g_j(\underline{x}), \rightarrow j = 1,2,...,m \\ &0 = h_j(\underline{x}), \rightarrow j = m+1,...,p, \end{aligned} \qquad (1)$$

where $\underline{x} = [x_1,\ x_2,...x_n]^T$ is a column vector of design variables; $f_i(\underline{x})$ is the i-th objective function; $g_j(\underline{x})$ are inequality constraints and $h_j(\underline{x})$ are equality constraints. Several effective methods for multiobjective optimization are introduced as follows: weighting method, hierarchical optimization method and goal programming, S. Hernadez, M. El-Sayed [3]. We have applied the weighting method to the optimal design. The summation of each individual objective function multiplied by its weighting factor is considered as a new scalar objective function

$$\begin{aligned} &F(\underline{x}) = \sum_{i=1}^{3} w_i f_i(\underline{x}), \\ &\sum_{i=1}^{3} w_i = 1 \ and \ w_i \ge 0. \end{aligned} \qquad (2)$$

We should substitute a single objective optimization for the multiobjective optimization

$$min\ F(\underline{x}). \qquad (3)$$

The weighting factors represent the relative importance of the objective functions from the decision maker's view point. Because there is no practical analytical method to define the weighting factors now they are selected by experience. The weighting method

* Corresponding author: horvathp@almos.uni-pannon.hu

has been applied extensively in engineering design because of its simplicity.

3 Optimization of planar truss girder

In the most of the optimization problems of truss girder we have two cases in the optimization tasks:

- the topology of the structure is fixed, so the cross sections of the beams are unknown quantities,
- the overall topology of the structure is variable, so we have to find also the optimal overall geometry, M. P. Bendsoe [4].

At the majority of optimization task of truss girder can be related, that in the bulk of the cases the mass of the construction, his material cost or his volume are considered an objective function, what with the expenses concerning the nodal forming heavy to formulate and onto this literature data do not stand for a provision relevantly.The restriction conditions onto the stresses, the deflections, the eigenfrequencies, and they concerned the stability.The single pole cross-sections, which may record discreet or constant values, appear as unknown.The employment of beams of truss girder is tension or compression. So the tension forces have to be smaller in each beam than given by EUROCODE 3 (EC3). In the compressed beams of truss girder is the bending danger, so the force in a beam have to be smaller than the prescribed of norm (EC3). The design value of the tension force N_{Ed} at each cross-section should satisfy

$$\frac{N_{ed}}{N_{t,Rd}} \leq 1. \tag{4}$$

For sections with holes the design tension resistance $N_{t,Rd}$ should be taken as the smaller of:

a) the design plastic resistance of the gross cross-section

$$N_{pl,Rd} = \frac{Af_y}{\gamma_{M0}}, \tag{5}$$

where A is the cross sectional area of member; f_y is the yield strength; γ_{M0} partial factor for resistance of cross-section whatever the class is,

b) the design ultimate resistance of the net cross section at holes for fasteners

$$N_{u,Rd} = \frac{0,9A_{net}f_u}{\gamma_{M2}}, \tag{6}$$

where A_{net} is the net area of a cross-section, f_u is the ultimate strength, γ_{M2} is the partial factor for resistance of cross-section in tension to fracture.

The design value of the compression force N_{Ed} at each cross-section should satisfy

$$\frac{N_{Ed}}{N_{b,Rd}} \leq 1, \tag{7}$$

where $N_{b,Rd}$ is the design resistance. The design resistance of the cross-section for uniform compression $N_{b,Rd}$ should be determined as follows

$$N_{pl,Rd} = \frac{Af_y}{\gamma_{M0}}, \tag{8}$$

for class 1, 2 and 3 cross-sections,

$$N_{b,Rd} = \frac{\chi A_{eff} f_y}{\gamma_{M1}}, \tag{9}$$

for class 4 cross-section, where χ is the reduction factor for the relevant buckling mode; A is the cross sectional area of beam; A_{eff} is the effective cross-section area of the compressed member (EC3/1.5); γ_{M1} is the partial factor for resistance of members to instability. For axial compression in members the value of χ for the appropriate non-dimensional slenderness $\bar{\lambda}$ should be determined from the relevant buckling curve according to

$$\chi = \frac{1}{\Phi + \sqrt{\Phi^2 - \bar{\lambda}^2}}, \quad but \quad \chi \leq 1, \text{ where}$$

$$\Phi = \frac{1 + \alpha(\bar{\lambda} - 0.2) + \bar{\lambda}^2}{2}, \tag{9}$$

where α is an imperfection factor (EC3). The non-dimensional slenderness is given by

$$\bar{\lambda} = \sqrt{\frac{\beta\, Af_y}{N_{cr}}} = \frac{\lambda}{\lambda_1}, \tag{10}$$

for class 1, 2, and 3 cross sections,

$$\bar{\lambda} = \sqrt{\frac{\beta_A Af_y}{N_{cr}}} = \frac{\lambda}{\lambda_1}, \tag{11}$$

for class 4 cross-sections, where β is A_{eff}/A, N_{cr} is the elastic critical force for the relevant buckling mode based on the gross cross sectional properties, $\lambda = l_{cr}/i$ is the slenderness ratio, l_{cr} is the buckling length in the buckling plane considered, i is the radius of gyration about the relevant axis, determined using the properties of the gross cross-section and

$$\lambda_1 = \pi\sqrt{\frac{E}{f_y}} = 93,9\sqrt{\frac{235}{f_y}} = 93.9\varepsilon. \tag{12}$$

In the additional we show the optimization of truss girder ones on the Fig. 1., F_1 and F_2 forces loaded. We regard it as given ones the geometrical form of the structure wich consist square crosssectional beams and this cross-sections are unknown, I. Timár [5]. We solve the problem with the multiobjective optimization. The objective functions are the mass of construction and the displacements of joints "C" and "D".

3.1 Compose of the objective functions

The mass of the planar truss (Fig. 1.) is given by

$$m = f_1(x) = \sum_{i=1}^{11} A_i l_i \rho \tag{13}$$

where A_i is each beam cross-section, l_i is the length of beams and ρ is the density of the material.

The deflections of joints C and D can be calculated by Betti's law

* Corresponding author: horvathp@almos.uni-pannon.hu

$$w_c = f_2(x) = \sum_{i=1}^{11} l_i \frac{N_i n_{Ci}}{A_i E} \qquad (14)$$

$$w_D = f_2(x) = \sum_{i=1}^{11} l_i \frac{N_i n_{Di}}{A_i E} \qquad (15)$$

where N_i are the internal forces in the i-th member due to

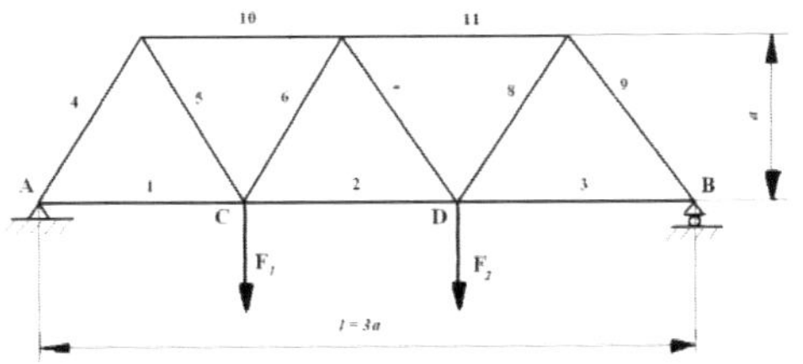

Fig. 1. The structure of truss girder

the applied load (F_1 and F_2), n_{Ci} and n_{Di} are the internal forces in the i-th member due to the load [$Q_C=1$(kN) and $Q_D=1$(kN)], E is the modulus of elasticity. Because of we have 3 main functions, the problem can be solved with the so called multiobjective optimization method. One of these methods is the so called as weighted method. The value of the weighting factors it is necessary to elect it with the respect of how important one we should award the single objective functions to in terms of the problem.

3.2 Compose of the design constrains

To the displacement of joints "C" and "D" we prescribe that should be smaller than the admissible displacements

$$w_{C_{max}} \leq w_{adm} = C_w l, \qquad (16)$$

$$w_{D_{max}} \leq w_{adm} = C_w l, \qquad (17)$$

where C_w is the allowable deflection ratio. l is the length of planar truss.

4 Numerical example

Consider the planar truss shown in Fig. 1 under the action of concentrated forces F_1 and F_2. Data: a = 1,5 (m); C_w= 1/300; E = 210 (GPa); f_y= 235 (MPa); f_u= 360(MPa); F_1 = 105 (kN); F_2 = 63 (kN); l = 4,5 (m); Q_C= 1; β_A = 1; γ_{M1} = 1,1; ρ = 7850 (kg/m^3); σ_m = 200 (MPa); value of χ calculate the software by Eurocode 3.

We solved the task with the multiobjective optimization method. Fig. 2.shows the minimal value of the optimal beams cross-sections depends on the objective functions. On the left side column the mass of truss girder was the objective function in the majority of cases (w_1=0,995, w_2=0,005, w_3=0,000) and the deflection of points "C" and "D" was practically negligible (w_2= 0.005, w_3=0,000). We got the right side higher columns that the aim was the minima of deflection of point "C" (w_1=0,005, w_2=0,995, w_3=0,000). This aim could be achieved with a more stiffness and heavier structure.

The Fig. 3.shows the mass of truss depends on the load (n*(F_1+F_2). On the left side column the mass of truss girder was the objective function in the majority of cases (w_1=0,995, w_2=0,005, w_3=0,000) and the deflection of

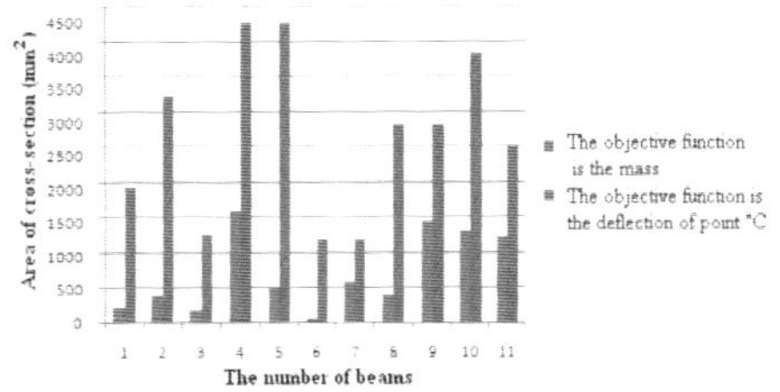

Fig. 2.Cross-section area of bars depends on the objective functions

points "C" and "D" was practically negligible (w_2= 0.005, w_3=0,000). We got the right side higher columns that the aim was the minima of deflection of point "C" (w_1=0,005, w_2=0,995, w_3=0,000), this case we got higher mass (right side columns).

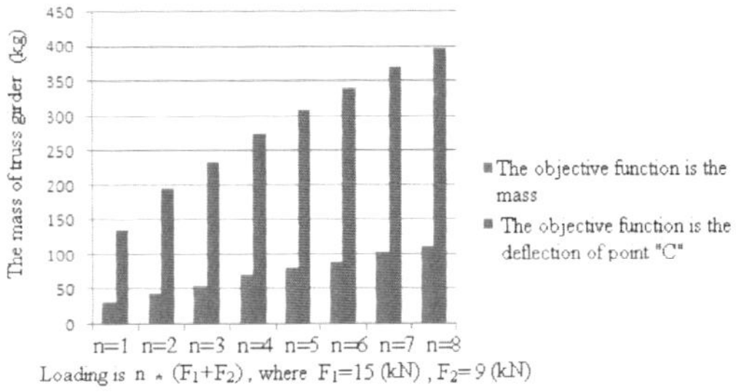

Fig. 3. Mass of truss depends on the load

The Fig. 4.shows the deflection of point "C" depends on the load (n*(F_1+F_2)).On the left side column the mass of truss girder was the objective function in the majority of cases (w_1=0,995, w_2=0,005, w_3=0,000) and the deflection of points "C" and "D" was practically negligible (w_2= 0.005, w_3=0,000). In this case the deflections are higher.

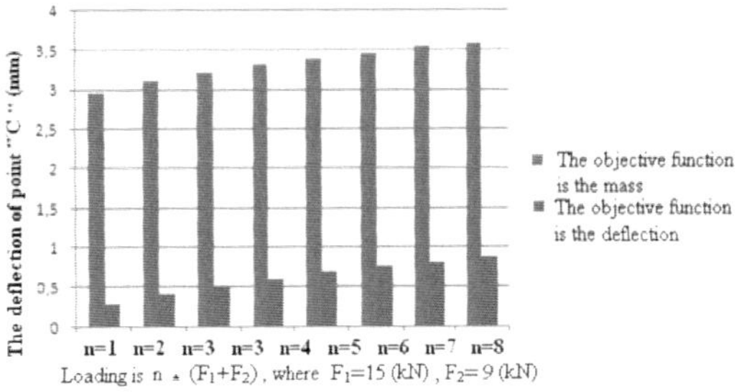

Fig. 4. Deflection of point "C" depends on the load

We got the right side higher columns that the aim was the minima of deflection of point "C" (w_1=0,005, w_2=0,995, w_3=0,000), and the deflections are smaller.

* Corresponding author: horvathp@almos.uni-pannon.hu

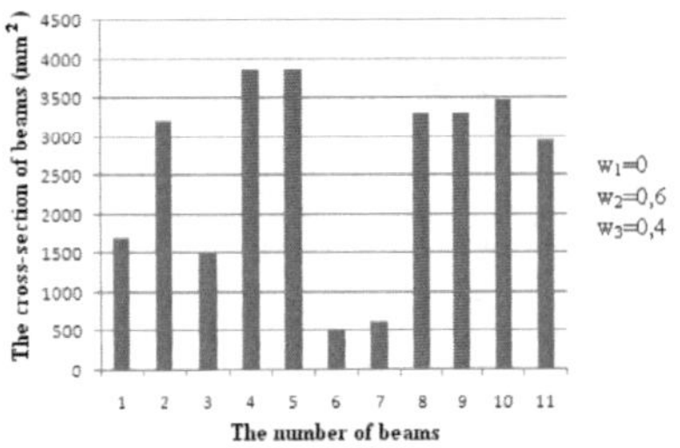

Fig. 5. The calculated cross-sections of beams

The Fig. 5. shows the the beam of planar truss girder cross-sections in this case F_1=105 (kN) and F_2=63 (kN) load. The weighting factors w_1=0,000,w_2=0,6, w_3=0,4, that mean we desire the deflection of junctions "C" and "D"at least to reduce.

Table 1. The cross-sections of beams depends on the loading

Loading	Cross-sections of beams (mm^2) (Number of beams)					
	1	2	3	4	5	6
F_1=15 (kN), F_2=9 (kN).	530	970	450	1160	1160	140
F_1=30 (kN), F_2=18 (kN).	720	1320	620	1650	1650	220
F_1=45 (kN), F_2=27 (kN).	880	1640	770	2020	2020	280
F_1=60 (kN), F_2=36 (kN).	1020	1910	890	2310	2310	320
F_1=75 (kN), F_2=45 (kN).	1140	2140	1000	2600	2600	360
F_1=90 (kN), F_2=54 (kN).	1260	2380	1100	2860	2860	400
F_1=105 (kN), F_2=63 (kN).	1360	2570	1200	3090	3090	420
F_1=120 (kN), F_2=72 (kN).	1440	2740	1280	3300	3300	440
F_1=135 (kN), F_2=81 (kN).	1530	2890	1360	3480	3480	460
F_1=150 (kN), F_2=90 (kN).	1620	3000	1440	3580	3580	480

Table 2. The cross-sections of beams depends on the loading

Loading	Cross-sections of beams (mm^2) (Number of beams)				
	7	8	9	10	11
F_1=15 (kN), F_2=9 (kN).	160	1020	1020	1100	880
F_1=30 (kN), F_2=18 (kN).	260	1380	1380	1460	1280
F_1=45 (kN), F_2=27 (kN).	330	1710	1710	1820	1560
F_1=60 (kN), F_2=36 (kN).	380	2010	2010	2100	1800
F_1=75 (kN), F_2=45 (kN).	420	2240	2240	2370	2000
F_1=90 (kN), F_2=54 (kN).	460	2440	2440	2592	2192
F_1=105 (kN), F_2=63 (kN).	480	2660	2660	2790	2370
F_1=120 (kN), F_2=72 (kN).	500	2840	2840	2970	2510
F_1=135 (kN), F_2=81 (kN).	520	2980	2980	3160	2650
F_1=150 (kN), F_2=90 (kN).	540	3120	3120	3340	2780

* Corresponding author: horvathp@almos.uni-pannon.hu

5 Conclusion

Mathematical optimization methods are generally applicable in the case of technical and economic problems. The optimization problem in general case is to build up a suitable model: to set up the multiobjective function(s) and to formulate the restrictions as mathematical functions.The truss girder optimizing received results show it, that the objective functions (mass and deflections) we receive different results differing at the time of his weighting factors. The bending of the construction with bigger mass will be smaller, but his expense will be bigger according to the meaning. The one with smaller mass (expense) we receive bigger bending on the other hand in case of a construction. The multiobjective optimising so it is possible to apply it successfully at the time of the solution of decision tasks.

"The project is co-financed by Széchenyi 2020". We acknowledge the financial support of Széchenyi 2020undertheEFOP-3.6.1-16-2016-00015.

References

1. T. Kulcsár, I. Timár: Mathematical optimization in design – Overview and application. Acta Technica Corviniensis – Bulletin of Engineering, Tome V.,Fascicule **2**, 21-26 (2012).
2. K. Jármai, M. Iványi: *Analysis and design of optimal metal structures*. (Műegyetemi Kiadó, Bp., 2001). (in Hungarian)
3. S. Hernadez, M. El-Sayed (ed.): Structural optimization. Computer Aided Optimum Design of Structures IV. Computation Mechanics Publications, Southampton, (1995).
4. M. P. Bendsoe: *Optimization of strucrural topology, shape, and material.*(Springer- Verlag, Berlin, 1995).
5. I. Timár: Optimierung von ebenen Fachwerke mit mehreren Zielfunktionen. Forschung im Ingenieurwesen, **68,** 121-125 (2003).

MATEC Web of Conferences **126**, 01006 (2017) DOI: 10.1051/matecconf/201712601006
Annual Session of Scientific Papers IMT ORADEA 2017

Cyber physical systems in mechatronic research centre

Timotei István Erdei[1], Zsolt Molnár[2], Nwachukwu C. Obinna[3], Géza Husi[4]
[1]University of Debrecen, timoteierdei@gmail.com, Hungary
[2]University of Debrecen, zsolt.molnar94@gmail.com, Hungary
[3]University of Debrecen, nwachukwucobinna@gmail.com, Hungary
[4]University of Debrecen, husigeza@eng.unideb.hu, Hungary

Abstract. In the Building Mechatronic Research Centre we started to develop our cyber-physical system. The Department provided us all necessary equipment to realize the first cyber-physical system. The main core of the project was to create an augmented reality based navigation system in our robot laboratory. In that aspect we also built an internet of things ready automated guided vehicle prototype. It must be said that the internet of things has induced a new paradigm shift in the socio-economic world. Nowadays, augmented reality and virtual reality are industrial processes development tools. In recent years, these technologies demonstrated significant improvements in real-time industrial technology.

1 Introduction

As result the efficiency of maintenance tasks may depreciate. In order to increase the efficiency in this area, augmented reality and virtual reality technology may be used.

The maintenance includes a range of complex industrial tasks and categorized into administrative, technical and management processes.

Augmented reality technology contains digital data and other technical details and is able to provide information about industrial machinery-equipment, without disassembling the equipment.

It is possible to read various data within the equipment, during its operation and in real-time. This facilitates analysis of "black box" systems.

With augmented reality technology we can measure and display the measurement data on a head-up display.

Augmented Reality enables, abnormalities to be detected quickly without special installation skills and propose several repair strategies.

2 Open computer vision based image processing

The department's robotic laboratory includes a KUKA KR5 medium payload industrial welding robot, KUKA KR3, FANUC spider and Sony scara SRX-611 and we wanted to create a unique system.

Our main goal was realizing a cyber-physical system for an industrial robot laboratory and find alternative ways of internet of things.

The head of our department G. Husi [1] had written a detailed documentation about industry 4.0. The document include the new technologies even augmented reality, virtual reality and other new industrial processes, that guided us to create our cyber-physical system.

The data and parameters have been encoded into quick response codes and other unique markers.

In the first test we use these codes as position markers and an instruction set to control a prototype automated guided vehicle robot.

The automated guided vehicle used an internet protocol based camera as vision sensors.

The Building Mechatronic Research Centre features several functional internet protocol cameras, which were interfaced to our cyber-physical system.

Behind the internet protocol cameras we used a relatively strong desktop computer. The computer has an Intel Corei7 central processing unit, 16 gigabyte random access memory, 2 terabyte hard disk drive & 2 x Nvidia GeForce GTX 650 Titan. On the other hand we chose the open computer vision which is vision library software with numerous algorithms for image processing, M. Marengoni [2].

* Corresponding author: timoteierdei@gmail.com

DOI: 10.1051/matecconf/201712601006

In order to implement the augmented reality algorithm, a special plugin/library known as augmented reality marker targeted was required.

Augmented reality gives an informative view of the world, and the main parts include a camera, J. Rubinstein [3], quick response codes with hidden information and image processing software to decode it.

With a quick response code we can detect position in real-time.

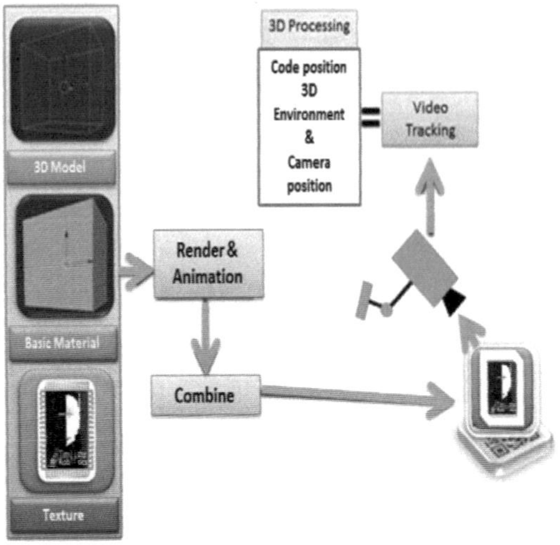

Fig. 1. Augmented reality and open computer vision

As Fig. 1. represents this type of image processing is a complex task. The proposed augmented reality system requires understanding the motion of a point in a 3 dimension coordinate system as can be seen on Fig. 2.

The field of view of a camera is a world that is seen, and detected with sensors, A. L. Kaczmarek [4].

The detection process involves the measurement of an object's velocity.

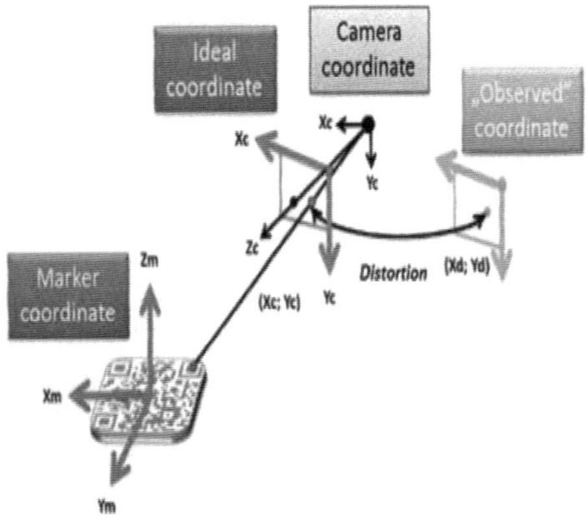

Fig. 2. Camera view and position detection of object

This is a complex method because first you need to design the 3 dimension model in a 3 dimension computer aided design software, and after it you need to decrease the polygon number of the 3 dimension model.

High polygon number values are computationally expensive. First we design all 3 dimension models in a

3 dimension computer aided design software, and after it with we decreased the numbers of the polygons to make our program run smoother, R. Inkulu [5].

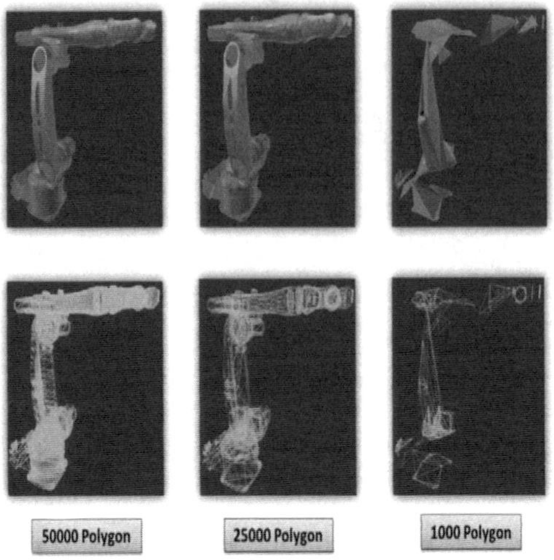

Fig. 3. Polygon reduction

We can confirm that polygon reduction on the Fig. 3. can be effective. The next step of our research was designing the automated guided vehicle prototype.

The automated guided vehicle system would include trajectory planning and tracking, as well as collision avoidance. The most important point of the robot is there are no sensors on the robot itself, it uses only the internet protocol cameras of the robotics laboratory for trajectory tracking.

Firstly we designed the automated guided vehicle concept in a 3 dimension computer aided design modeling software and made a part lists with the necessary equipment, G. Balaji [6].

Fig. 4. Augmented reality and open computer vision

* Corresponding author: timoteierdei@gmail.com

DOI: 10.1051/matecconf/201712601006

Automated guided vehicle prototype robot on Fig. 4. has an Arduino Nano, M. Banzi [7], two LM2596 direct current step down converter and a wireless fidelity to serial module.

3 Augmented reality navigation system

In the first part of our project we found a suitable place to test the system which was the robotics laboratory in the Building Mechatronic Research Centre. We designed the quick response codes/markers and printed it out in different sizes, and placed them in the right order to make the path for the robot.

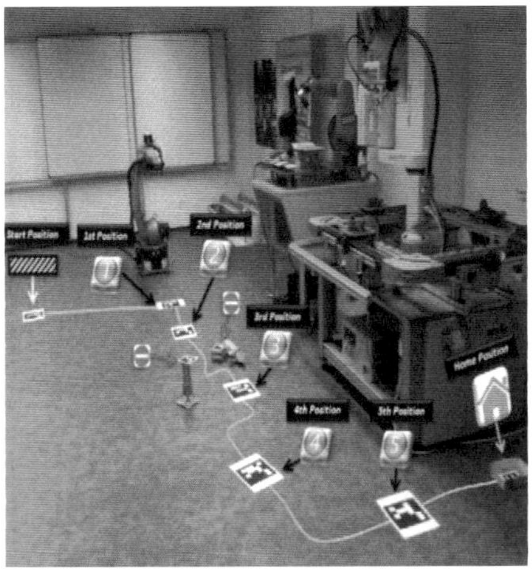

Fig. 5. Robot laboratory as isolated space

The task of the automated guided vehicle prototype robot is to leave the "Start" position go to the 1st position and wait until the KUKA KR5 goes to the position of the automated guided vehicle and put on it the steel cube. After it reach the 2nd, 3rd 4rd, 5rd positon and the Home position with the cargo. We printed a code for identifying the automated guided vehicle's orientation.

The route used for testing is represented by Fig. 5. above. The internet protocol cameras of robot laboratory see the codes and streams data to the notebook via wireless fidelity. On the desktop computer, open computer vision and augmented reality marker targeted software was required recognizes the position of the code and decodes it, sends the information to the automated guided vehicle prototype robot which plans and tracks the trajectory.

In the first test we launched/programmed the KUKA KR5 industrial robot manipulator with our electronic printed circuit board, name TiMo board, to control the robot's gripper.

Furthermore we established a new wireless fidelity network, name TP-Link router to make the wireless fidelity signal stronger in the Robot Laboratory it was very important because we sent all signals trough wireless fidelity and we wanted to avoid the lag of the stream of the mobile phone.

For the first time we noticed lag in the Desktop computer, fortunately we could set the dedicated Nvidia graphic card to calculate instead of the Corei7 central processing unit which was slower in this instance. The Fig. 6. shows the communication topology used in the robot laboratory.

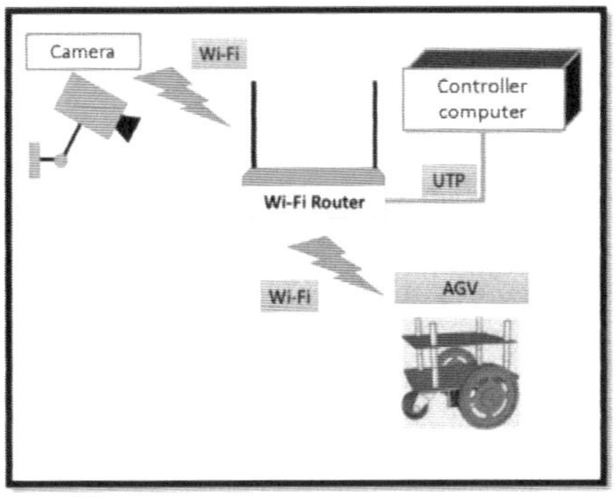

Fig. 6. Network communication system

When we began the first test, the automated guided vehicle prototype robot was in the "Start" position.

Fig. 7. Start position

After it the automated guided vehicle started from the "Start" position as we can see in Fig. 7., is heading towards to the 1st position and waited there until KUKA KR5 moved to the automated guided vehicle position and opened the gripper to put the steel cube on the automated guided vehicle.

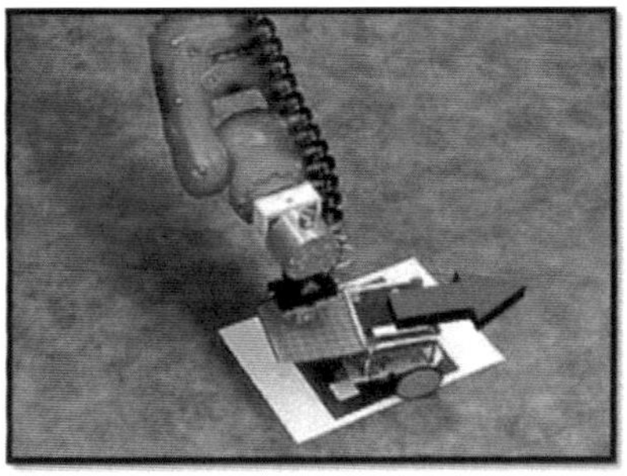

Fig. 8. 1st position

* Corresponding author: timoteierdei@gmail.com

In the Fig. 8. we can see the robot reaching the 1st position. The next step was to reach the 3rd positon marker and avoid the collision with the other objects.

To realize this we made codes with other 3D models and we set the Augmented Reality marker targeted a distance away from the other objects, and the automated guided vehicle could avoid them during the motion. When the automated guided vehicle reached the HOME positon it stopped.

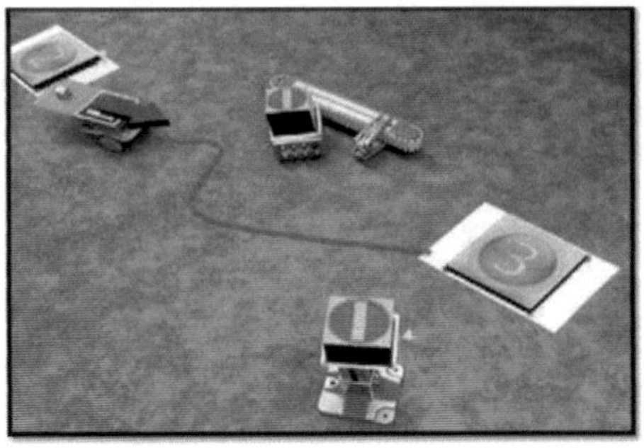

Fig. 9. Automated guided vehicle prototype first test

On Fig. 9. represents that the system can be flexible as navigation system. Because we can add any type of quick response code markers and hide commands various type.

Furthermore the robot did not have any sensors. The only sensors in the building was internet protocol based camera system.

4 Augmented reality research and development

In our next project we used quick response code as Augmented Reality marker in order to visualize the position of axis of KUKA KR5 or set position in the workspace of the robot dynamically.

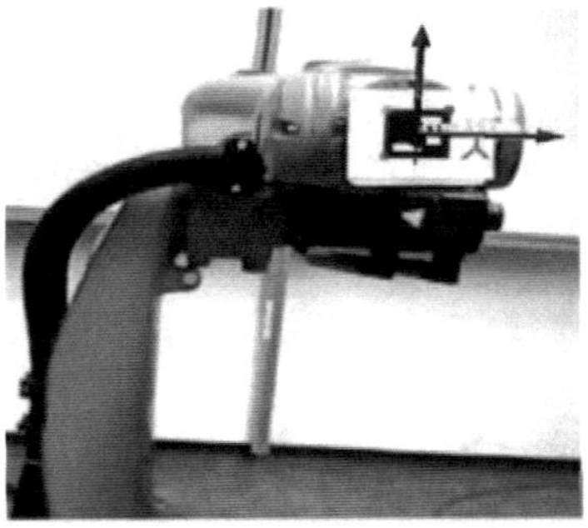

Fig. 10. Augmented reality code to set position visualization

The Augmented Reality technology is also able to test standalone systems and items. We can visualize the tool coordinate system of the robotic arm as we can see in the Fig. 10. above.We developed a gripper to KUKA KR5, we reduced the polygon number of it and mounted "virtually" on to the robot arm.

Furthermore the codes can be established interactive connection between each other.

In one of our tests we used another marker which consist of a column 3 dimension model.

Fig. 11. Virtual augmented reality items and collide

When we moved the real KUKA KR3 with the virtual mounted gripper and it could push away the virtual column in Fig. 11. above.

5 Conclusion

During test phase the Augmented Reality based navigation system was stable. We could hide information behind the quick response codes/markers. These information can be commands to any kind of robots in the future. Moreover with this technique we can replace the 3 dimension printer, because we do not need to print out the 3 dimension model itself, we should only hide the 3 dimension model behind quick response codes/markers.

In the future we will create real Automated Guided Vehicle to our Augmented Reality based navigation system.

The project was supported by University of Debrecen, Electrical Engineering and Mechatronics Department.

References

[1] G. Husi, "*Industry 4.0 technology in University of Debrecen*", https://www.researchgate.net/publication/301607839_Industry_4 0_Hungarian, accessed on May 2017.

[2] M. Marengoni, "*High Level Computer Vision Using OpenCV, Graphics*", (Unpublished work style)," unpublished.

[3] J. Rubinstein, "*Signal Delay in RC Tree Networks*", IEEE Transactions on Computer-Aided Design of Integrated Circuits and Systems, Volume: 2, Issue: 3, July 1983, pages. 202 – 211.

[4] A. L. Kaczmarek, "*Stereo vision with Equal Baseline Multiple Camera Set (EBMCS) for obtaining depth maps of plants*", CEA Volume 135 Issue C, April 2017 pages. 23-37.

[5] R. Inkulu, "*Incremental Algorithms to Update Visibility Polygons*", Algorithms and Discrete Applied Mathematics, LNCS, Volume: 10156 pages. 205-218.

[6] G. Balaji, "*Automated Guided Vehicle Navigated using Fuzzy Cognitive Maps and Intelligent Space*" Ijraset Volume 5 Issue III, March 2017 pages 41-44

[7] M. Banzi, "*Arduino Nano system*", https://www.arduino.cc/en/uploads/Main/ArduinoNanoManual23 .pdf, accessed on April 2017.

* Corresponding author: timoteierdei@gmail.com

MATEC Web of Conferences **126**, 01007 (2017) DOI: 10.1051/matecconf/201712601007
Annual Session of Scientific Papers IMT ORADEA 2017

Defects detection on the welded reinforcing steel with self-shielded wires by vibration tests

Ion Crâştiu[1*], *Eva* Nyaguly[2], *Sorin* Deac[3], *Mircea* Vodă[4], *Dorin* Simoiu[5], *Liviu* Bereteu[6]

[1]Politehnica University Timisoara, ion_crastiu@upt.ro, Romania
[2]Politehnica University Timisoara, pintiutza@gmail.com, Romania
[3]Politehnica University Timisoara, sorin.deac@upt.ro, Romania
[4]Politehnica University Timisoara, mircea.voda@upt.ro, Romania
[5]Politehnica University Timisoara, dorin.simoiu@upt.ro, Romania
[6]Politehnica University Timisoara, liviu.bereteu@upt.ro , Romania

Abstract. The aim of this paper is the development and validation of a vibroacustic technique to welding defects detection, especially for welded reinforcing structures. In welded structures subjected to dynamic cyclic loads may appear and propagate fatigue cracks due to local structural damage. These cracks may initiate due to the technological parameters used in welding process, or due to environmental operating conditions. By the means of Finite Element Method (FEM), the natural frequencies and shape modes of more welded steel specimens are determined. The analysis is carried out in undamaged condition as well as damaged one, after artificially induced damages. The experimental measurement of the vibroacustic response is carried out by using a condenser microphone, which is suitable for high-fidelity acoustic measurements in the frequency range of 20 – 20.000 Hz. The vibration responses of the welded specimens, in free-free conditions, are carried out using algorithms based on Fast Fourier Transform (FFT), and Prony's series. The results are compared to modal parameters estimated using FE Analysis.

1 Introduction

Reinforced concrete is a composite material in which the tensile strength and the ductility are balanced by the inclusion of the concrete reinforcements to give the tensile strength and/or ductility higher than that of concrete. The reinforcement is usually, though not necessarily, made of steel bars, called reinforcements, and is embedded passive in concrete. Reinforcement schemes are generally designed to withstand concrete in certain regions where tensile stresses may cause cracks unacceptable and/or structural failure. Modern reinforced concrete as a reinforcing material can contain a variety of steel, polymer or composite materials. The metal can alternate with composite materials. Reinforced concrete may also be subjected to the permanent compression, so as to improve the structural behavior under work load. The most common methods for achieving this state of pre and post-application are the straining.

Weldable reinforcing steel and stainless reinforcing steel, in accordance with the relevant standards or technical specification may be used. For refurbishment and extensions of buildings, the weldability of the existing reinforcing steel shall be verified. Other types of steels, weldable structural or stainless steels, may be welded to reinforcing steel, SR EN 481-1/2012 [1], and M. Burcă and St. Negoiţescu [2].

In this paper we determine the changes of resonance frequencies of welded reinforcing steel bars PC 52 with surface defect using a nondestructive technique based on experimental determination of resonance frequencies, L. Bereteu, M. Burca, R. Moisa, D. Simoiu, Gh. Draganescu, St. Pavel, and C. Nes [3], L. Bereteu, M. Voda, T. Medgyesi, Gh. Draganescu and D. Simoiu [4].

The results are used to introduce three quality indicators of the welding, about the name of analysis method.

2 Materials and methods

2.1 Samples obtaining

Reinforcing steel PC 52 is a low alloy steel with a periodic profile. The chemical composition of the steel

* Corresponding author: ion_crastiu@upt.ro

grade is as follows: maximum 0.22% C; maximum 0.55% Si; than 1.6% Mn; maximum 0.045% S; maximum 0.045% P and 0.06% Ti or Nb maximum. Preparation of the ends of bars and choice of joints form were made according to norm SREN 438/1-2012 [5] for concrete steel bars with a diameter greater than 16 mm. The norm is applicable for welding weldable steel bars and concrete that can transmit loads. The legislation specified requirements for materials, design and construction, welded joints, and quality requirements. Welding processes are given which can realize concrete reinforcement welded steel.

To obtain the samples was chosen arc welding process together with or without the root, and in the process of arc welding fittings was chosen tubular wire welding with self protection. Butt welding fittings concrete can be done without root support if the diameter of the steel bar is more than 16 mm, respectively with root support if bar diameter is greater than 12mm.

2.2 Resonant vibration tests

In the following, the samples consist of welded reinforcing steel, shall be considered circularly bars, having a constant section, and no subject to external tensions. To study the free vibration of these bars can consider different boundary conditions. The best known cases in the literature are: free – free conditions.

2.3 Free-free vibration of welded reinforcing steel bars

Vibratory motion of the bar is governed by a differential equation with partial derivate Euler-Bernoulli as in Meirovitch [6]:

$$EI\frac{\partial^4 v}{\partial x^4} + \rho A\frac{\partial^2 v}{\partial t^2} = 0, \tag{1}$$

where : E is Young's modulus, I is the geometric moment of inertia of the cross-sectional area, A is the area of this section, and ρ is material density. With v(x, t) was noted the transverse deflection of the bar at a distance x from the end. To determine the transverse vibrations of the specimen must be known boundary conditions. In the physical model developed was assumed a free-free bar.

In table 1 are calculated the characteristic equation and the first five solutions on the free-free boundary conditions for the flexural vibration.

Table 1. The characteristic equation and the five solutions

Characteristic equation	X_1^2	X_2^2	X_3^2	X_4^2	X_5^2
1-chxcosx=0	22.4	61.7	120.9	199.8	298.5

In this table was noted:

$$X_r = \lambda_r L, \tag{2}$$

where λ is:

$$\lambda_r = \sqrt[4]{\frac{\rho A p_r^2}{EI}}, \tag{3}$$

and r =1,2.....5, represent the number of the natural mode.

From (3) there are obtained the natural frequencies:

$$f_r = \frac{X_r^2}{2\pi L^2}\sqrt{\frac{EI}{\rho A}}. \tag{4}$$

where, X_r are the routs of the characteristic equation Euler – Bernoulli, table I. If the cross area and geometric moment of inertia are modified by surface defect, the natural frequencies becomes

$$f_r' = f_r - \frac{1}{2f_r}\frac{\{X\}_r^T[\Delta K]\{X\}_r}{\{X\}_r^T[M]\{X\}_r}, \tag{5}$$

where [ΔK] is stiffness structural modification matrix and [M] is mass matrix, L. Bereteu [7].

2.4 Finite Element Analysis

To validate the shape of vibration modes of the sample and correlation with resonance frequencies experimentally obtained is necessary to make a modal analysis. The modal parameters are obtained by Finite Element Analysis using ANSYS.The shape and size of the sample are given in Fig.2.

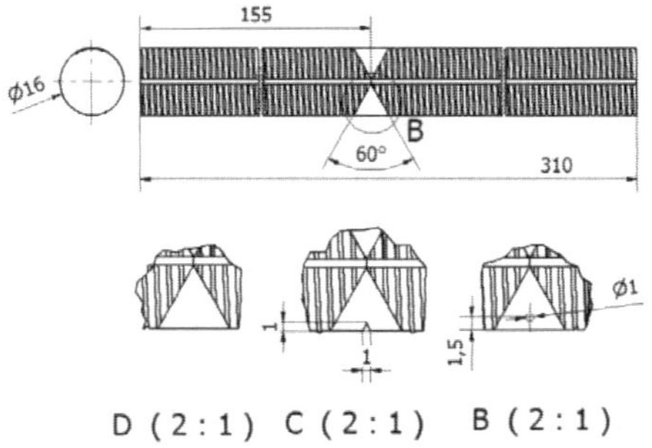

Fig. 1. The shape and size of the experimental sample

3 Experimental setup

The experimental stand for non-contact measurement of free vibrations of the sample is shown in Fig. 2. and it is composed by: the sample *1,* which is the mechanical structure to be analyzed; impulsive mini hammer *2;* brackets to support the sample *3;* elastic threads for support of the structure in boundary conditions with the free ends *4;* the acoustic sensor one condenser microphone *5,* and the computer that has embedded and acquisitions plate *6.*

* Corresponding author: ion_crastiu@upt.ro

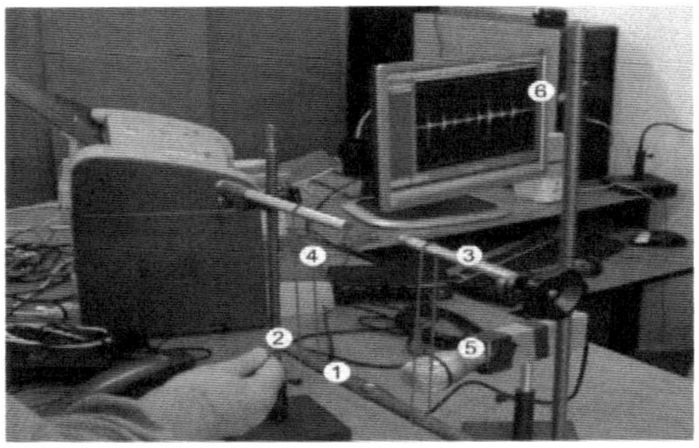

Fig. 2. Experimental stand for vibroacustic measurements

4 Numerical results

The sizes mechanical characteristics of the PC 52 steel bar analyzed by ANSYS software are: L=310 mm, $\phi = 16$ mm, $\rho = 7850 kg/m^3$ and E_1=200GPa. The frequencies and the shape modes of the sample without any defect are given in table 2, and the frequencies and the shape modes of the sample with surface defect are given in the table 3.

5 Experimental results

To determine the resonance frequencies of reinforcing bars without any surface defect and with induced surface defect, Fast Fourier Analysis are required for two signals. Signal acquired for reinforcing bar without surface defect is shown in Fig. 3.

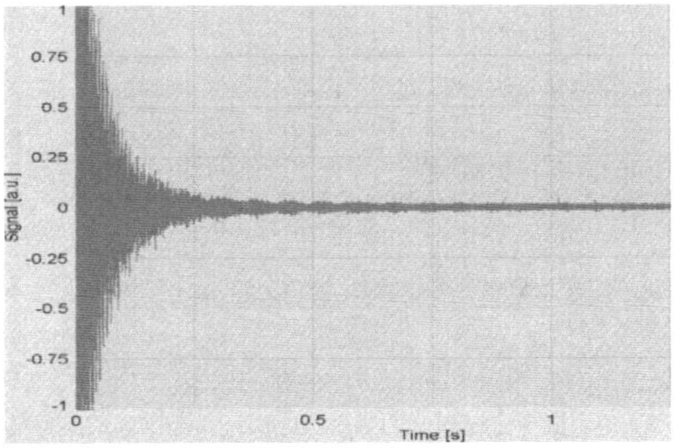

Fig. 3. Experimental acquired signal

A similar signal is obtained for a bar with surface defect induced. The two signals are processed using Fast Fourier Transform method, S.W.Park [8] and Prony's series method, D.J. Trudnowski [9]. The Fourier Frequency Spectrum in 0 Hz to 4000 Hz for without defect bar in the Fig. 4 is presented. A similar spectrum, but with changes in natural frequencies, it was obtained for surface defect induced bar.

To characterize weld quality depending on the method used to determine the resonant frequencies three indicators are introduced. The first indicator shows the relative deviation of the resonance frequencies of the bar

Table 2. The first six frequencies and the mode shape of the bar without dfect

Mode	Frequency [Hz]	
1.bending	718	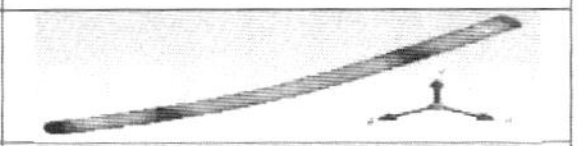
2.bending	754	
3.bending	1946.7	
4.bending	2000.8	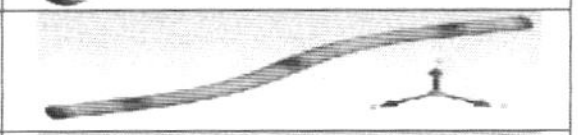
5.bending	3755.4	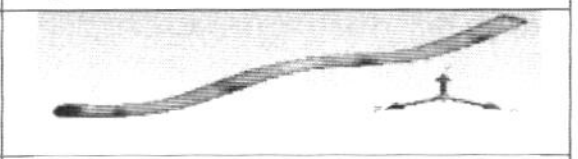
6.torsion	3917.2	

Table 3. The first six frequencies and the mode shape of the bar with surface dfect

Mode	Frequency [Hz]	
1.bending	717.1	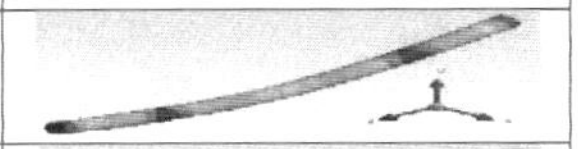
2.bending	752.4	
3.bending	1943.5	
4.bending	2019.2	
5.bending	3750.4	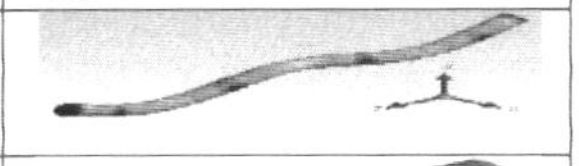
6.torsion	3911.7	

without defect compared with resonant frequencies of the bar with surface defect. The frequencies were obtained based on Modal Analysis Method using the Finite Element Method. Finite Element Method Indicator (FEMI) is defined as

$$FEMI\% = \frac{f_{rFEM} - f'_{rFEM}}{f_{rFEM}} \cdot 100, \qquad (6)$$

where f_{rFEM} is the r-th mode frequency of the bar without defect and f'_{rFEM} is the r-th mode frequency of the damaged bar. Similarly the other two indicators are introduced: Fast Fourier Method Indicator (FFMI) as,

$$FFTMI\% = \frac{f_{rFFTM} - f'_{rFFTM}}{f_{rFFTM}} \cdot 100, \qquad (7)$$

and Prony Method Indicator (PMI) as

$$PMI\% = \frac{f_{rPM} - f'_{rPM}}{f_{rPM}} \cdot 100, \qquad (8)$$

* Corresponding author: ion_crastiu@upt.ro

DOI: 10.1051/matecconf/201712601007

where the frequencies marked with an apostrophe (') are denoted bar modes frequencies with surface defects, and without (') the frequencies of the undamaged bar.

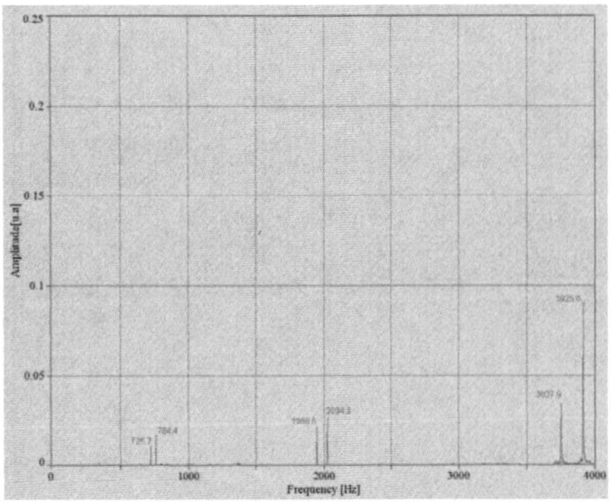

Fig.4. Fourier Frequency Spectrum for undamaged bar

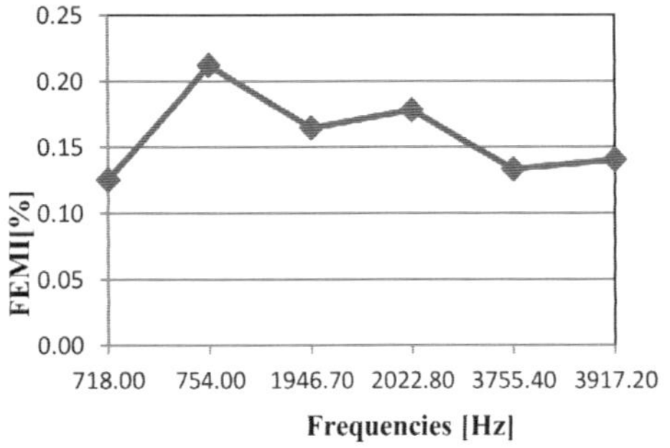

Fig. 5. FEM indicator by frequency

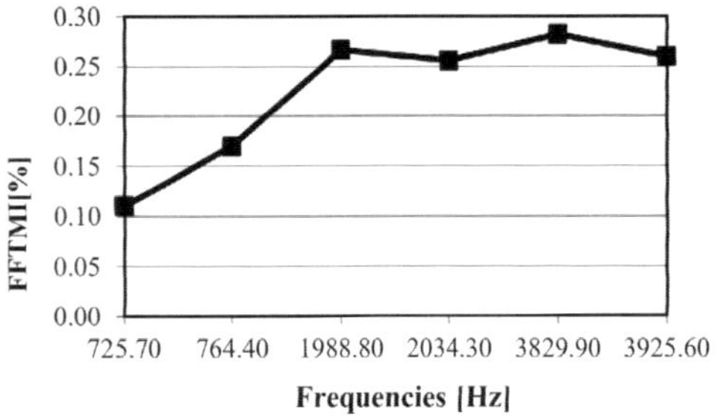

Fig.6. FFT indicator by frequency

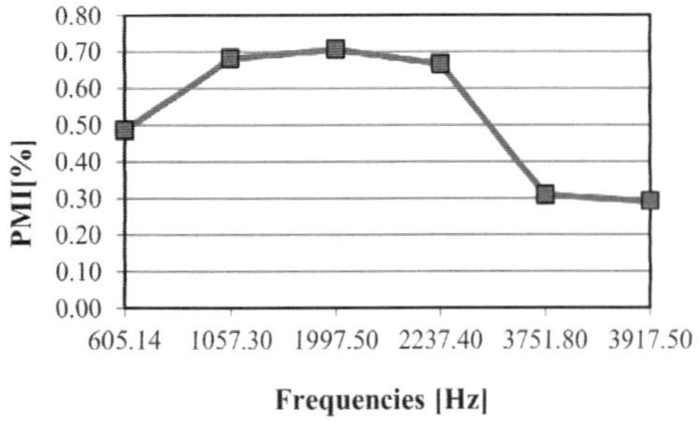

Fig. 7. PM indicator by frequency

FEM indicator depending on the frequencies of the first six modes of bar vibration is shown in Fig.5. Change in other two indicators, according to the resonance frequencies are given in Figs.6 and 7.

6 Conclusions

The results obtained in this work show that the signals and data analysis method for free vibration of the samples can be considered between nondestructive methods that can be used to determine the quality of the welding. The changing of resonance frequencies through structural modifications as a consequence of welding defects obtained in experiments come to validate the numerical results obtained on modal analysis by FEM, and the results obtained by applying the formulas (5). There is a good convergence of results obtained by the two methods of experimental analysis of signals: Prony's Series Method and Fast Fourier Transform Method, compared with numerical method (FEM). It finds that the three indicators give a weak sensitivity for a surface defect, especially for first resonant frequency of vibration. However, the sensitivity is double or even triple for higher frequencies mode of vibration. The best stability is given for high resonance frequencies of the modes by FFT Indicator.

References

[1] SR EN 481-1/2012, Welding - Welding of Reinforcing Steel.

[2] M. Burcă, St. Negoiţescu, MIG/MAG Welding (in romanian), Editura SUDURA, Timişoara, 2004

[3] L. Bereteu, M. Burca, R. Moisa, D. Simoiu, Gh. Draganescu, St. Pavel, C. Nes, "Determination of some mechanical properties of welded reinforcing steel with self-scielded wires by vibration tests", *Advanced Material Research,* Vol 1029, pp 206-211, 2014.

[4] L. Bereteu, M. Voda, T. Medgyesi, Gh. Draganescu, D. Simoiu, "Defect detection on the welded thin steel plates using vibroacustic method", *Advanced Material Research,* Vol 1029, pp 212-217, 2014.

[5] SR 438-1/2012, Steel Products for Concrete Reinforcement. Part 1. Hot rolled Structural Steel, Grades and Technical Quality Requirements.

[6] L. Meirovitch, Fundamentals of Vibrations, Waveland Press, Inc. 2010

[7] L. Bereteu, The vibrations of mechanical structures (in romanian), Editura Mirton, Timisoara, 2000

[8] S.W.Park, "Analytical Modeling of Viscoelastic Dampers for Structural and Vibration Control", *Int. J. Solids Struct.* 38, pp 8065-8092, 2001.

[9] D.J. Trudnowski, Characteristics of Identifying Linear Dynamic Models Response Data Using Prony Analysis, Battelle, 1992.

* Corresponding author: ion_crastiu@upt.ro

Impulse tests to determine the mechanical properties of aluminum alloys used to manufacture auto rims

Eva Nyaguly[1*], *Sorin* Deac[2], *Ion* Crâştiu[3], *Dorin* Simoiu[4], *Teodor* Heput[5] and *Liviu* Bereteu[6]

[1]Politehnica University Timisoara, pintiutza@gmail.com, Romania
[2]Politehnica University Timisoara, sorin.deac@upt.ro, Romania
[3]Politehnica University Timisoara, ion.crastiu@upt.ro, Romania
[4]Politehnica University Timisoara, dorin.simoiu@upt.ro, Romania
[5]Politehnica University Timisoara, teodor.heput@upt.ro, Romania
[6]Politehnica University Timisoara, liviu.bereteu@upt.ro, Romania

Abstract—The purpose of this paper is to analyze the improvement of quality rims made of different aluminum alloys for road vehicles. The modulus of elasticity, shear modulus and Poisson's ratio are mechanical parameters that characterize, together with mass and geometrical dimensions, dynamic behavior of auto rims. To reduce the weight of the rims, the steel is replaced with the aluminum and magnesium alloys or composite materials. The natural frequencies and the shape of the natural modes are determined for different aluminum samples, using the Finite Element Method and Modal Analysis in the ANSYS software. The vibroacoustic signal is recorded through a condenser microphone that has a high fidelity in the audible range of 20-20,000 Hz. The vibration responses of the aluminium specimens, in free-free conditions, are carried out using algorithms based on Fast Fourier Transform (FFT), and Prony's series.

1 Introduction

After iron, aluminum is now the second most widely used metal in the world. Aluminum and its alloys have become widely used metals in recent decades, mainly due to their properties, among which the most important are: densities and thus low weight, high strength, high resistance to corrosion, easy mechanical processing etc. It is noteworthy that aluminum has a very good weldability and not least, the best property is its high rate of recycling.

The popularity of aluminum and its alloys derive from its use in various areas such as: first of all in machine construction, automotive, food industry, chemical industry, civil construction, shipbuilding and aerospace industry, railway transport industry, areas where the use of aluminum is substantial.

In the commercial process, this material is called unalloyed aluminum. It is very easy to be processed, it has very good anticorrosive properties, it can be anodized and painted, and it can be varnished. It also has excellent bending properties and excellent weldability properties. It is used to various surfaces in advertising production, or it is used frequent in common surfaces plating.

In the use of unalloyed aluminum, the main issue that it is considered is that in the corrosion process, the surface does not become matt. This material can be very well anodized in the natural state or in the painted state. Anodized sheets not only looks much better in terms of aesthetics, but also presents much better features anticorrosive and erosion properties than the natural aluminum. These can be maintain and clean up much easier.

Aluminium and its alloys have increased machinability characteristics: can be excellent processed by lathering and these have a good weldability with the MIG/WIG procedures. For these reasons, these materials are widespread in industrial applications, including shipbuilding, as shown T. Anderson in paper [1]. The arc welding method - MIG is the most common method of joining aluminum alloys used in shipbuilding, and the research results on the mechanical properties of aluminium alloys and its MIG welded joints were carried out using a static tensile test by K. Dudzik [2]. .

To achieve the new fuel efficiency standards requires the use of vehicle weight reduction. Achieving this goal involves the use of new materials and alloys. Aluminium alloy 6082, according to SR 1706: 2000 is such alloy and is used in manufacturing car rims by hot plastic deformation [3]. Performance rims are closely related to the mechanical properties of the material, and any

* Corresponding author: pintiutza@gmail.com

chemical composition changing, in order to improve the structure of aluminum-alloys must be found in increasing the mechanical properties values, were presented by R.Pradeep, B.S. Praveen Kumar and B. Prashanth in [4], and by N.Bularda and T. Heput in [5] and [6].

In all these works, to determine the elastic properties of aluminum and its alloys were used classical methods based on shear and tensile test respectively.

In recent years a strong development took nondestructive methods based on the resonance tests to determine the elastic properties of metals and their alloys. In the paper [7], M. Alfano and L. Pagnotta reviews the latest patents in the field of non-destructive tests for the determination of mechanical characteristics of materials. The use of the vibroacoustic signals for determining the elasticity modulus of the hydroxiapatite or welded joints is presented in [8] by L. Bereteu, M. Vodă, Gh. Draganescu and in [9] by O. Suciu, L. Bereteu, Gh. Draganescu.

The purpose of this paper is to show that by analyzing a vibration signal obtained after applying a mechanical impulse on the sample can be determined all three elastic properties of the material: the longitudinal modulus (Young's), the shear modulus and the Poisson coefficient. This is possible by validating the results given by the spectrum analysis with the results of modal analysis based on Finite Element Method. For signal acquisition uses an acoustic sensor one condenser microphone and for signal processing it is used an adequate software [10].

2 Theoretical background

2.1 Resonant vibration tests

In the following, the samples consist of welded aluminum, shall be considered rectangular beam, having a constant section, and no subject to external forces. To study the free vibration of these beams can consider different boundary conditions. The best known case in the literature is free–free conditions. The elastic properties of the material can be determined by measuring the frequencies of the free vibrating bar excited by mechanical impulse. Vibratory motion of the beam is governed by a partial differential equation with partial derivate Euler-Bernoulli, as it is given by Meirovics [11].

$$EI\frac{\partial^4 Y(x,t)}{\partial x^4}+\rho A\frac{\partial^2 Y(x,t)}{\partial t^2}=0, \tag{1}$$

where Y(x,t), E, I, A, ρ are the displacement of neutral axis of the beam at x distance to the left end, the longitudinal elastic modulus, geometric moment of inertia of the cross - section of the beam, the area of this section and material density. The characteristic equation for free-free boundary conditions is:

$$1\text{-ch}X\cos X=0 \tag{2}$$

where

$$X=\sqrt[4]{\frac{4\pi^2 f^2 L^4 \rho A}{EI}}, \tag{3}$$

f is one of the bending resonance frequencies and L is the length of the beam.

The first two roots of the characteristic Eq.°2 are $X_1=4{,}730$, $X_2=7{,}853$, and for natural modes r>2, it is easy to show that

$$X_r=\frac{(2r+1)\pi}{2} \tag{4}$$

From Eq.°3 and Eq.°4 it can obtained the relation between free vibration frequency f_r of the sample and its Young's modulus

$$E=\frac{4\pi^2 f_r^2 L^4 \rho A}{X_r^4 I} \tag{5}$$

This relationship is valid only for the bending modes of the sample.

By a similar procedure could be obtained the relation between the shear modulus and the corresponding resonance frequencies of the torsion modes:

$$G=\frac{4\rho f_r^2 L^4 K_f}{r^2}, \tag{6}$$

where r is the torsion mode number and K_f is a coefficient that takes into account the geometrical shape of cross-section and it is equal to 1 only for circular section. For a rectangular section has the expression:

$$K_f=\frac{\frac{b}{h}+\frac{h}{b}}{4\left(\frac{h}{b}\right)-2.52\left(\frac{h}{b}\right)^2+0.21\left(\frac{h}{b}\right)^6}, \tag{7}$$

where b is the sample breadth, and the h is sample thickness.

To determine Poisson's ratio noted by υ it is used the well-known relationship between the three mechanical parameters that characterize the behavior of a metal to simple tensile and torsion tests:

$$\upsilon=\frac{E}{2G}-1. \tag{8}$$

2.2Finite Element Analysis

To validate the sample shape modes of vibration and correlation with experimental resonance frequencies is necessary to make a modal analysis. For an n-degree of freedom system, by Finite Element Method meshing (Fig. 1) the free motion equation of sample can be expressed as follows:

$$[M]\{\ddot{q}\}+[C]\{\dot{q}\}+[K]\{q\}=\{0\} \tag{9}$$

where {q} is the vector of the displacement, and [M], [C] and [K] are mass, damping and stiffness matrices, respectively. In this approach the mechanical system is modeled as Rayleigh damping which is associated with symmetric matrix [C] proportionally with [M] and [K] matrices.

* Corresponding author: pintiutza@gmail.com

DOI: 10.1051/matecconf/201712601008

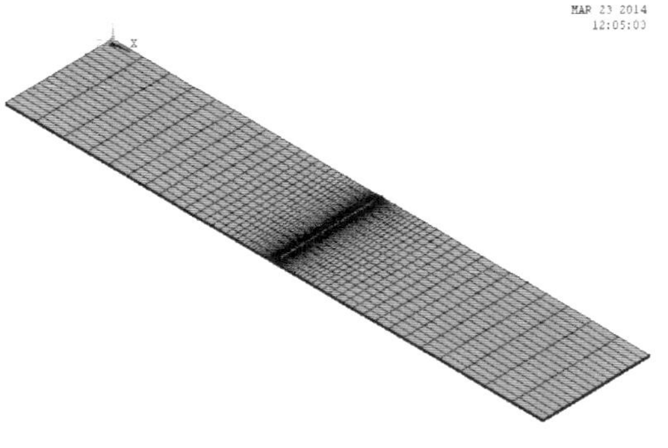

Fig. 1. Experimental stand for vibroacustic measurements

The resonance frequencies and modal shapes are obtained by Finite Element Analysis, using ANSYS [12].

3 Experimental setup

The experimental stand for non-contact measurement of free vibrations of the samples is shown in the Fig. 2. below, and it is composed by: the sample *1*, which is the mechanical structure to be analyzed; impulsive mini hammer *2*; brackets to support the sample *3*; elastic threads for support of the structure in boundary conditions with the free ends *4*; the acoustic sensor one condenser microphone *5*, and the computer that has embedded and acquisitions plate *6*.

Fig. 2. Experimental stand for vibroacustic measurements

4 Numerical results

The sizes of laminate aluminum sample analyzed by ANSYS software are: L=206 mm, b=39.5mm, h=1.5mm. The frequencies and the shape modes are given in Table I. This analysis is necessary to determine the order of the form of natural modes, that is, to determine which modes correspond to bending vibrations, respectively which modes correspond to torsional vibrations.

Table 1. The shape modes and their frequencies for laminate aluminum sample

Modes and frequencies [Hz]	Shape mode
First bending mode 184.97 Hz	
Second bending mode 512.80 Hz	
First torsion mode 578.18 Hz	
Third bending mode 1017.7 Hz	
Second torsion mode 1176.9 Hz	

5 Experimental results

Equation (5) is used to determine the experimental values of the longitudinal elasticity module, E, with the frequencies corresponding to the first three bending modes of vibration, which are obtained from Fast Fourier Transform of the vibroacoutical signal obtained from experimental measurements. From Fig. 3, correlating with the results in Table 1 can determine the frequencies corresponding to the bending modes, respectively the torsion modes.

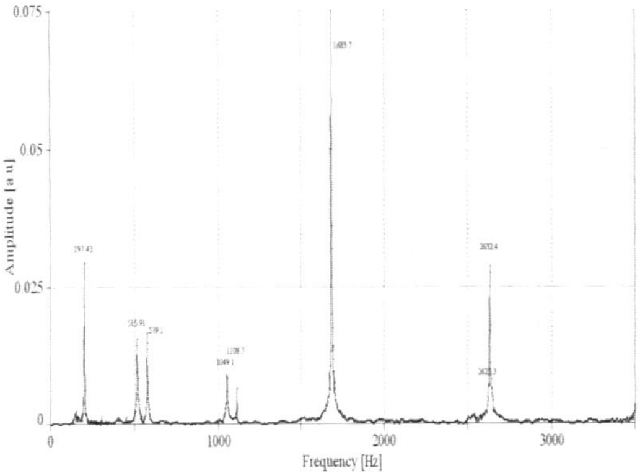

Fig. 3. Fourier Frequency Spectrum

The same formula is used to determine the experimental values of Young's modulus with frequencies determined by analyze the acquired signal with Prony's Series Method, D.J. Trudnowski [13].
Equation (6) is used to determine the experimental values of the shear modulus G, corresponding to the first two torsion modes of vibration, which are obtained also from Fast Fourier Transform, Fig. 3.

* Corresponding author: pintiutza@gmail.com

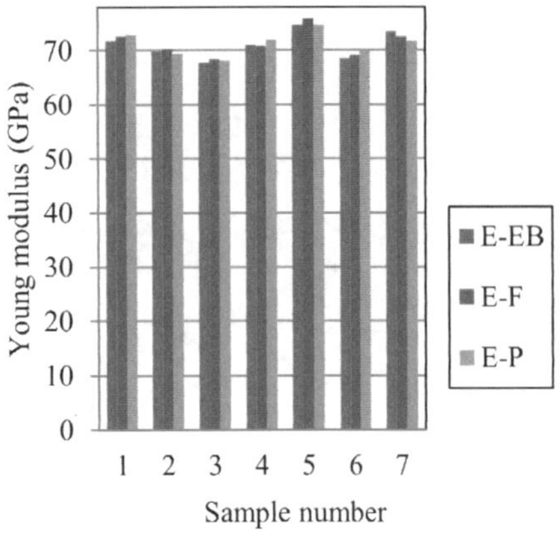

Fig. 4. Young's modulus (E) by different methods

The values of the modulus of elasticity obtained by three methods: Euler Bernoulli equation (E-EB), Fast Fourier Transform (E-F) and the series Prony method (E-P), for seven samples are represented in Fig. 4.

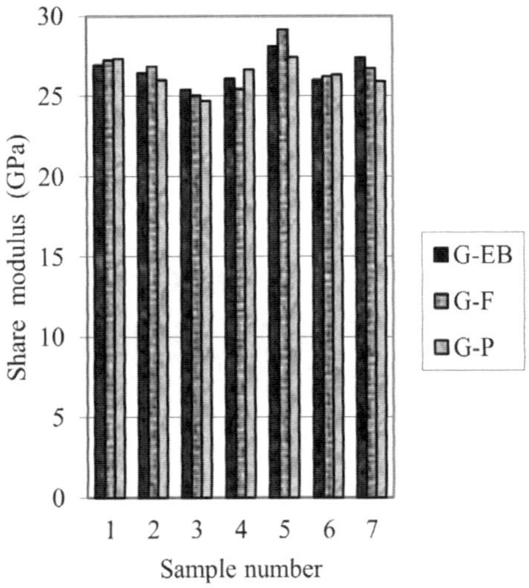

Fig. 5. Share modulus (G) by different methods

The same three methods are used to determine the shear modulus of elasticity. Their values for seven samples of molten batches are shown in Fig. 5.

6 Conclusion

Method of measurement of Young's modulus, shear modulus and Poisson coefficient by modal analysis of vibrations excited by impulse is extremely simple to use.

The results for the elastic moduli are better than those obtained using standard tensile or shear tests.

This method does not require specific form for samples and does not introduce errors due to the fastening system.

Modulus variation depending on various alloying elements of aluminum, will be of particular interest and will constitute an upcoming issue.

References

[1] T. Anderson, "New developments within the Aluminum Shipbuilding Industry", *Svetsaren*, 58(1), pp. 3-5, 2003.

[2] K. Dudzik, "Mechanical Properties of 5083, 5059 and 7020 Aluminum Alloys and their Joints Welded by MIG", *Journal of KONES Powertrain and Transport,* 18(3), pp 1-5, 2011.

[3] SR EN 1706:2000, Aluminum and aluminum alloys. Molded pieces. Chemical composition and mechanical characteristics (Aluminiul şi aliaje de aluminiu. Piese turnate. Compoziţie chimică şi caracteristici mecanice, in romanian)

[4] R.Pradeep, B.S. Praveen Kumar, B. Prashanth, "Evaluation of mechanical properties of aluminum alloy 7075, reinforced with silicon carbide and red mud composite", *International Journal of Engineering Research and General Science, Vol. 2, Issue* 6, pp. 1081-88, 2014.

[5] N. Bularda, T. Heput, „Mathematical modeling concerning the influence of chemical composition on the 6082 aluminum alloy on the phisical and mechanical characteristics", 12-th *International Conference of Numerical Analysis and Applied Mathematics*, 22-28 September 2014, Rhodos, Greece, Vol. 1648 2014.

[6] N.Bularda, T. Heput, Reconditioning by welding of rims manufactured from nonferrous alloys, *TIMA* 1029, pp 61-66, 2014.

[7] M. Alfano, L. Pagnotta, "Recent Developments and Selected Patents on Vibration Based Methods for the Elastic Characterization of Isotropic Materials", *Recent Pat on Mec. Eng.* 2, pp 130-143, 2009.

[8] L. Bereteu, M. Vodă, Gh. Draganescu, "Measurement of Young's Modulus and Shear Modulus of some Structures Welded Using Flux Cored by Vibration Tests", *Solid State Phenomena*, Vol 216 pp 151-156, 2014.

[9] O. Suciu, L. Bereteu, Gh. Draganescu, Determination of Mechanical Properties of Hydroxyde Apatite Doped with Magnesium, *AIP Conference Proceedings* Vol 1564 pp. 132-137, 2013.

[10] Simulation driven product development | ANSYS, http://www.ansys.com.,accessed on Mars 2017

[11] AutoSignal, Cutting edge signal analysis software http://www.sigmaplot.co.uk/products/autosignal/autosignal.php., accessed on Mars 2017

[12] L. Meirovitch, *Fundamentals of Vibrations*, Waveland Press, Inc. 2010

[13] D.J. Trudnowski, *Characteristics of Identifying Linear Dynamic Models Response Data Using Prony Analysis*, Battelle, 1992

* Corresponding author: pintiutza@gmail.com

 DOI: 10.1051/matecconf/201712602001

3d modeling and fem analysis for solar panel mounting system on a house roof

Cornel Cătălin Gavrilă[1*], *Radu* Velicu[2], *Mihai -Tiberiu* Lateş[3]

[1] Transilvania University of Brasov , cgavrila@unitbv.ro, Romania
[2] Transilvania University of Brasov , rvelicu@unitbv.ro, Romania
[3] Transilvania University of Brasov , latesmt@unitbv.ro, Romania

Abstract— Mechanical structures 3D modeling in the aim of real-time simulation of the product dynamic behavior, using computer performing software, is a necessity. In the paper, there are presented some aspects regarding the 3D modeling and FEM analysis for a mounting system used to fix solar panels or collectors on house roof. First, there are presented some general aspects of the mounting systems used to fix solar panels on the house roof. Then there are presented the aspects of virtual modeling of these parts, using CATIA software. Then, there are presented some aspects of the Finite Element Analysis and the results of this. In the final part of the paper, there are presented the conclusion.

1 Introduction

THE paper presents some aspects regarding the virtual modeling and FEM analysis for a mounting system used to fix solar panels (or collectors) on house roof. Generally, for the solar panels or collectors, the producers are also providing the adequate fixing kit, Innoterm Katalog [1]. Mainly, the solutions refer more to the solar panels used than the roof surface used for it. However, an increased number of solar panels are placed to be used on classic house roofs, previously manufactured by ceramic tiles. For these old roofs types, the kits provided are not matching very well. This mismatching lead usually to the new tiles is breaking and rainfall water drip inside the construction.

The ceramic tiles produced and used in Romania are standardized according to SR EN 1304 + A1: 2001 [2] (the former Romanian STAS 515 – Ceramic Tiles and Ridges). According to the standard, the tiles can be in a big format, with drains and shafts, or in smaller standard format, type "sawtooth" or "scales". The scales tiles type main dimensional characteristics are presented in Fig. 1. It can be observed that the tiles can be produced with one nose, as in Fig. 1, a, or with two nose, as in Fig. 1, b.

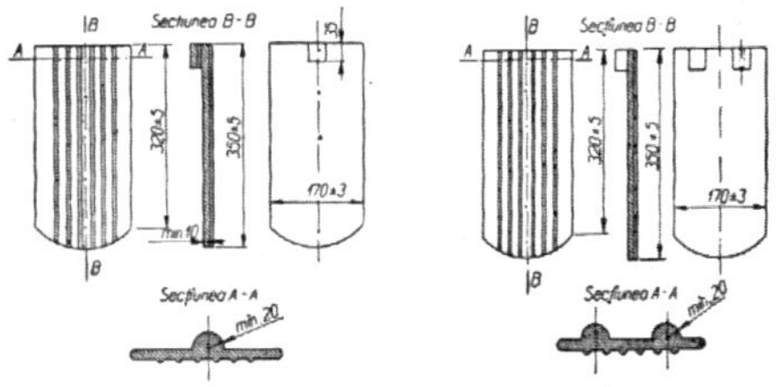

Fig. 1. The scale tiles.

Usually, the tiles are arranged in the network (Fig. 2) or line, on the roof structure made of thin wide woods placed on wood timbers. For scale tiles, in a network arranged, the wide woods distance is 160 mm Tondach Catalogue [3].

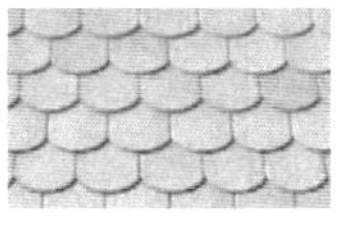

Fig. 2. The scale tiles in a network arrangement.

One particular aspect for tile roofs can be observed in section (Fig. 3). Because of rows tiles superposition, the declination of tile, given by the angle α_t, differs by the general roof declination, provided by the angle α_r. If the manufacturing of the roof is well done, all tiles should have the same declination.

* Corresponding author: cgavrila@unitbv.ro

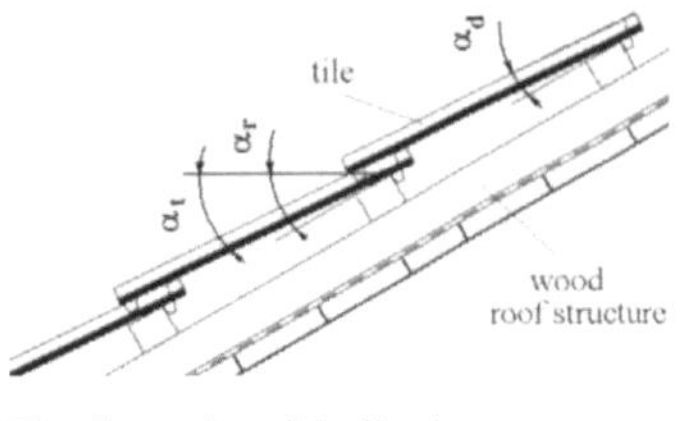

Fig. 3. The tiles and roof declination.

The difference between the declinations of roof and tile is given by relation

$$\alpha_d = \alpha_r - \alpha_t .(1)$$

The angle α_d= 2…7 degrees, and may vary depending on the tile dimensions, shape or misalignments and also by wood roof structure Tondach Catalogue [3]. Because of these, the contact surface between each tile and wood wide is reduced, at the limit, to a contact line under the tile nose. Usually, to prevent the rainfall water drip inside the construction, the fixing solutions to place different installations on the roof, consist of metal clips inserted between the tiles and fixed on roof wood structure. An example of solar panel fixing solution, offered by the producer, is presented in Fig. 4, a, and b Innoterm Katalog [1].

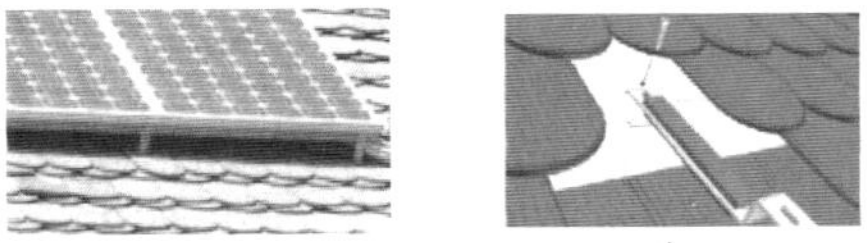

a. b.

Fig. 4. An example of solar panel fixing solution.

As it was presented, any object inserted between tiles should change the declination of the tiles placed above. If the metallic clip width, the above tiles declination changes and, as a consequence, the fit with other tiles and roof elements is worst and lead to premature tiles breaking in subjected area.

2 The 3D modeling

The virtual model is developed, using CATIA software, for the metallic clip and the ceramic tile as the main parts involved in solar panel fixing operation on the roof C. Alexandru [4] and I. G. Ghionea[5]. The wood roof structure, which serves to support the entire assembly, is considered as rigid.

For the metallic clip, the first step is to sketch the main section. To fit the clip in the roof structure, the main dimension is corresponding to this, especially the difference between the declinations, α_d = 2 degrees, for scale tiles. Also, the clip width is 25 mm. Then, using Part Design module, the virtual model is completed, as is presented in Fig. 5.

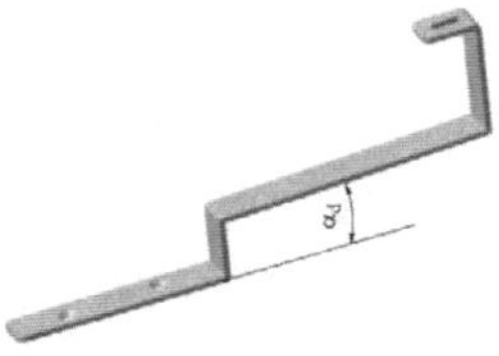

Fig. 5. The metallic clip virtual model

For scale tile, the first step is to sketch the main section. Because there is two type of tiles, with one nose and with two noses, the virtual model are made for both types. Then, using Part Design module, the virtual models are completed, as is presented in Fig. 6, a, for one nose tile, respectively, in Fig. 6, b, for two nose tile.

a. b.

Fig. 6. The scale tiles virtual models

3 The Finite Element Analysis

For analysis, the previous models for the metallic clip and also for the tiles will be used. The material properties, as Young modulus, Poisson coefficient, Tensile Yield Strength, Ultimate Strength should be defined.

For the metallic clip, the material is steel R. Velicu [6]. For the analysis, the loading force for metallic clip depends on solar panel weight, including the frame and fixing kit and also the wet snow weight. The considered snow layer is 150 mm Technical regulation CR 1-1-3/2012 [7], and the snow mass which covers a solar panel, dimension 1650 x 990 mm, is 64 kg. Taking account that the clip number is 6, results in the loading force on one clip, F = 291N. The force is applied vertically on the clip, corresponding to a tile declined at 30 degrees by horizontal reference. For simulation, the metallic clip is considered fixed on the surface fixed on timber wood. To estimate the deformations, the metallic clip will be also considered with no tile above. The model needs to mesh into finite elements, solids and deformable, type hexahedral and tetrahedral, with integration node M. T. Lateş, R. Velicu, and R. Papuc [8]. The metallic clip model, with a defined force, is presented in Fig. 7.

* Corresponding author: cgavrila@unitbv.ro

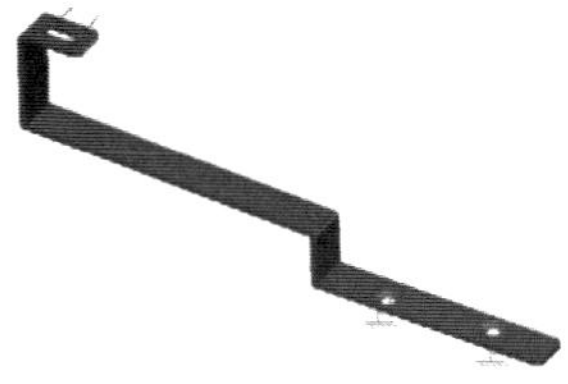

Fig. 7. The metallic clip model with defined force

For the scale tiles, the material is ceramic, with the main properties given by C. Bob, and P. Velicu [9] and I. Teoreanu, N. Ciocea, A. Bărbulescu and N. Ciontea, [10]. The ceramic materials are fragile – under the load, are subjected to break before some elastic deformations. Also, the ceramic materials present the static fatigue – for an increased time of load application, the break resistance is decreasing. For analyze, the ceramic material for tiles is considered having fine texture: homogeneous granulation, without material failures, as breaks or inclusions. For ceramic material, the limit stress is 15 MPa.

Also, the model needs to mesh with finite elements, solids and deformable, type hexahedral and tetrahedral, with integration node. The tile is declined at 30 degrees by horizontal reference, and the force is the same as the metallic clip, applied on a contact surface with this. The tile is considered fixed above the nose, on the line contact and on the bottom corners, which correspond to the placing on the tiles above. The tile model with defined force is presented in Fig. 8. For results comparing, are made the models for one and two nose tiles.

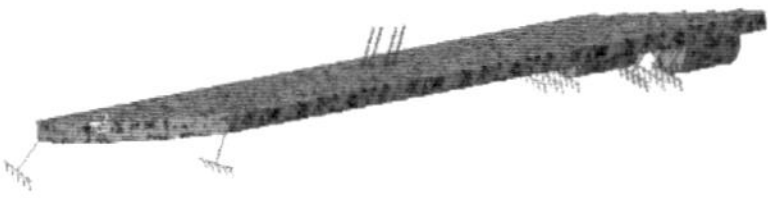

Fig. 8. The tile model with defined force

4 Simulation and Results

For simulation, the metallic clip is considered fixed on the surface placed on timber wood. Because of the roof manufacturing misalignments and clearances, the metal clip can be put in different positions, as it is presented in Fig. 9, a - c. The ideal positioning is presented in Fig. 10, a, where the clip is in contact with tile on the full subjected area.

In fig. 9, b, is presented a real positioning, where the contact without loading appear at the top of the tile and the folding corner of the clip. When loading, the contact surface increase.

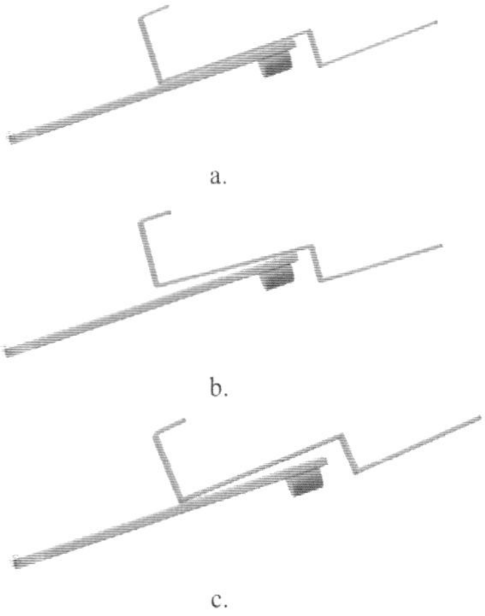

Fig. 9. Positions between the metallic clip and tile

Another real positioning is presented in fig. 9, c, where the contact surface appears between the tile surface and the above portion of the clip. In this case, when loading, the contact remains reduced to a small area.

To estimate the metallic clip deformations, there will be considered with no contact with the tile above, corresponding to the situation from Fig. 9, b.

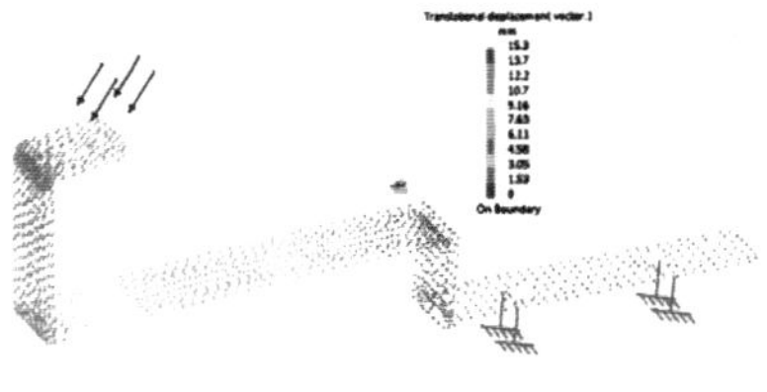

Fig. 10. Metallic clip model with deformation values

In Fig. 10 there are presented the deformations, and it can be observed that the maximum deformation value appear in the in the solar panel assembling area and exceed 15 mm. Under the load, the metallic clip deformation increase just until its bottom end is touching the tile surface, depending on the misalignment size. Then, the load is also taken by tile.

In Fig. 11 is presented the stress on the metallic clip; the maximum value is 491 MPa and appears in the middle zone, where the clip is folded.

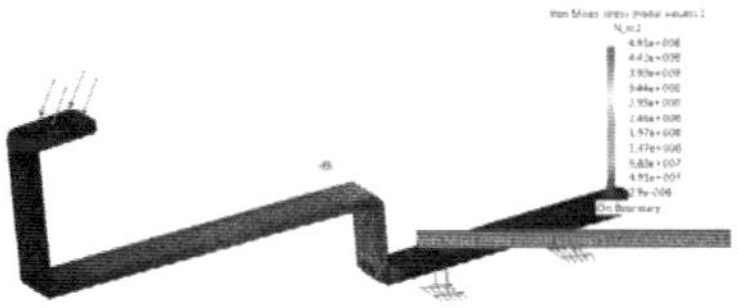

Fig. 11. Metallic clip model with stress values

* Corresponding author: cgavrila@unitbv.ro

For the tile simulation, are considered the both models, with one and also with two noses. The load on the tile is applied distributed on the contact area with the bottom end of the metallic clip. Because the contact area may vary, depending on the tile and clip folding radius and also by positioning on the roof structure, there are considered few cases of contact surfaces. Because the tiles are subjected to break before some elastic deformations, only the stress values are presented.

The first situation is when the tile contact area with clip is reduced to 25x5 mm, which corresponds to increased misalignments and increased clip deformations.

The obtained stress maximum values are 20,9 MPa for one nose tile (fig. 12, a), and, respectively 25,2 MPa for two nose tile (fig. 12, b). It can be observed that the maximum value appears, for both tile models, at contact area with clip; the value exceed the recommended stress value So, the tile break is in the contact area (tile is breaking in two parts).

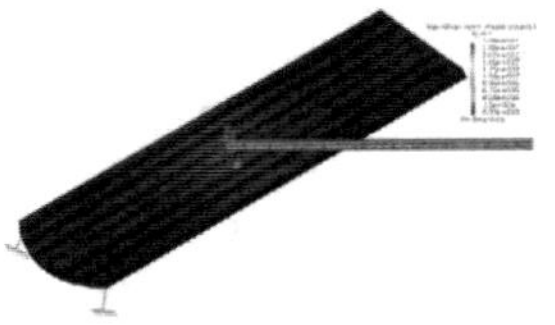

a.

b.

Fig. 12. Stress values on tile reduced contact area

The second situation is when the tile contact area with clip is increased to 25x10 mm, which correspond to reduced misalignments and reduced clip deformations.

a.

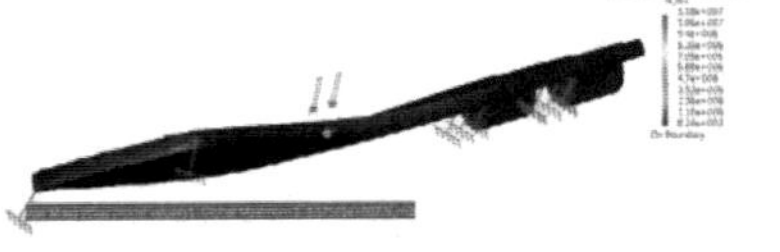

b.

Fig. 13. Stress values on tile, contact area length increased

The obtained stress maximum values are 11,2 MPa, for one nose tile (fig. 13, a), and appears under the nose, where the tile is arranged on wide wood. For the two nose tile, the maximum value is 11,8 MPa for (fig. 13, b) and appears on the tile above corners. So, at the one nose tile appears the possibility to break the tile nose properly. For two nose tile, appears the possibility to break its corners.

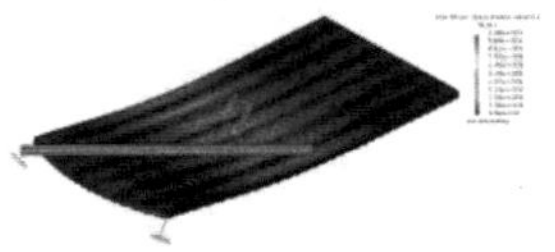

a.

b.

Fig. 14. Stress values on tile, contact area width increased

The third situation is when the tile contact area with clip is increased by increasing the metallic clip width to 40 mm. So, the contact surface increases to 40x5 mm.

The obtained stress maximum values are 10,8 MPa for one nose tile (fig. 14, a), and, respectively 10,9 MPa for two nose tile (fig. 14, b). It can be observed that the maximum value appears, for both tile models, on the tile above corners. So, for both tile models, appears the possibility to break the corners.

5 Conclusion

On solar panels roof assembly, there are situations when, because of surfaces misalignments, the contact surface between the studied parts may be different.

For the metallic clip, the deformations and stresses values are lower than the limit values recommended in the literature for steel.

For tiles with reduced contact surface with metallic clip, appear the tile break. If the contact with metallic clip is improved, the maximal stress values are lower than the limit values recommended in the literature for the ceramic material. Taking account that the ceramic materials are fragile and present the static fatigue – for an increased time of load application, the break resistance is decreasing in subjected locations.

So, to avoid the tile breaking, the main solution is to improve the contact with the metallic clip, for example by increasing the clip width or by increasing the folding clip radius.

Also, the analysis presented lead to the conclusion that is better to use a two nose scale tile above the clip.

Similar can be created and simulated a lot of 3D models for any needed tiles and roof types. In this way, with reduced costs can be reduced the roof failures.

References

[1] Innoterm Katalog, *Solar-Kollektoren*, 2009 (in German).

* Corresponding author: cgavrila@unitbv.ro

[2] Romanian Standard, SR EN 1304 + A1: 2001, *Ceramic Tiles and Ridges*, 2001.
[3] Tondach Catalogue, *Sibiu Classic Scale Tiles (Ţiglă solzi clasic Sibiu)*, 2008 (in romanian).
[4] C. Alexandru, *Mechanical Articulated Systems Simulation on Computer (Simularea pe calculator a sistemelor mecanice articulate)*, Ed. Lux Libris, Braşov, 2000 (in Romanian).
[5] I.G. Ghionea, *CATIA v5. Application in Mechanical Engineering (CATIA v5. Aplicaţii în ingineria mecanică)*, Editura Bren, Bucureşti, 2009 (in romanian).
[6] R. Velicu, *Machine Elements (Organe de Maşini)*, Ed. Universităţi Transilvania din Braşov, 2003 (in romanian).
[7] Technical regulation CR 1-1-3/2012, *Design Code: Snow Action On Construction Evaluation (Cod de proiectare. Evaluarea actiunii zapezii asupra constructiilor)*, 2012 (in romanian).
[8] M. T. Lateş, R. Velicu, R. Papuc, *Multiscale modeling of chain-guide contact by using tests and FEM*. 11th World Congress on Computational Mechanics WCCM XI, Barcelona, Spain, 20-25 July 2014, pp.1062-1069.
[9] C. Bob, P. Velica, *Construction Materials (Materiale de construcţii)*, Ed. Didactică şi Pedagogică, Bucureşti, 1978 (in romanian).
[10] I. Teoreanu, N. Ciocea, A. Bărbulescu, N. Ciontea, *Ceramic and Refractory Material Technology (Tehnologia produselor ceramice şi refractare)*, Vol. I, Ed. Tehnică, Bucureşti (in romanian).

* Corresponding author: cgavrila@unitbv.ro

Automated production based model of flexible cell using Timed Colored Petri Nets

Sanjib Kumar Saren[1,*], *Florin* Blaga[2], and *Tiberiu* Vesselenyi[1]

[1]University of Oradea, Mechatronics Department, Romania
[2]University of Oradea, Industrial Engineering Department, Romania

Abstract. The purpose of this paper is to develop a model of a flexible manufacturing cell to identify the production strategies using various types of product processing. To model the system, Petri Net Theory is implemented with the extension of Timed Color Petri Nets (TCPN). To improve the production of various types of parts in the system, tool management plays an important role during system modeling. The proposed model is based on the flexible manufacturing cell from the Faculty of Technological Engineering and Management, University of Oradea. CPNTools software is used to model the system and analyze the overall production and performance in the system.

1 Introduction

This paper deals with modeling and simulation of production of multiple parts using a single machine cell and tool management implementation for various operations of multiple parts. Multi-product and multi-stage flexible manufacturing system (FMS) modeled using Colored Petri Nets and multi-factor optimized by design of experiment is presented by T. Aized, K. Takahashi and I. Hagiwara [1]. H. Hosseini-Nasab and A. Sadri [2] described Multi-purpose plant designed using Stochastic Colored Petri Nets to determine shared resources and idle time through simulation. TCPN used to model and simulate wood flexible manufacturing system by Z. Yuerong, C. Jun and S. Liping [3]. FMS with shared resources and automatic transport system model using Colored-Timed Extended Petri nets explained by H. V. Brussel, Y. Peng, P. Valckenaers [4]. Timed place petri nets are used to model a FMS on scheduling problem defined by Z. Ye, T. Wang and P. Sun [5]. M. Copik and J. Jadlovsk'y [6] explained the analysis of production systems and the state of design analysis, calculation of the reachability and firing sequence for every reachable state from initial to required state use of Petri Nets. Colored Petri Net used to model the FMS and implement of object-oriented method for evaluation of dynamic tool allocation with performance of the model proposed by J. Chen and F.F. Chen [7]. Focus on modeling and analysis of dynamic behavior of automated manufacturing systems using Colored Time Object Oriented PNs by L.C. Wang and S.Y. Wu [8]. F. Blaga, I. Stanasel, A. Pop, V. Hule and T. Buidos [9] describe the usefulness of CPNTools software in Flexible manufacturing cell (FMC).

2 Part processing sequences

In this model time for arrivals of the parts are associated with resources from place. The part arrival time for P1= 0 (sec), P1=800 (sec), P1= 1300 (sec), P2= 500 (sec), P2= 2000 (sec), P2= 2500 (sec), P3= 3000 (sec), P3= 4200 (sec), P3= 5500 (sec), P4=7700 (sec), P4=9450 (sec), P4= 11600 (sec), and P5= 14500 (sec), P5= 18000 (sec), P5= 20500 (sec) in the system. The processing time for each part are: (P1, M1) = 336 (sec); (P2, M1) = 458 (sec); (P3, M1) = 1158 (sec); (P4, M1) = 2160 (sec) and (P5, M1) = 2460 (sec).

3 Definition of places and transitions

The modeled FMC consists of one CNC machine, two ABB robots and separate storage area for specific raw material and storage area for finish part. The model is based on the Flexible cell from University of Oradea, department of Mechatronics. During modelling each resource corresponds to places and each transition follow significant meaning. In the Table 1 and Table 2 below, each place and transition is mentioned in detail.

4 Modeling of flexible manufacturing cell

1) Color set definitions for raw material and finished part, machine and robots:

The color set for each raw material is declared in place P_A with color P1, P_B with color P2, P_C with color P3, P_D with color P4, P_E with color P5.

The color set for robot1 is described as a 1`R1. The color set for robot2 is described as a 1`R2. The color associated with machine is “machine” with color set M1.

* Corresponding author: sanjibksaren@gmail.com

The complex color for each part combines with robot1 to define that the position for part is on the robot1 gripper. The complex color set is declared below:

Table 1. Places and their notations

Places	Interpretation	Initial Token
P_A	Storage for P1	5
P_B	Storage for P2	2
P_C	Storage for P3	1
P_D	Storage for P4	1
P_E	Storage for P5	2
R1P1	Part 1 on robot1 gripper	0
R1P2	Part 2 on robot1 gripper	0
R1P3	Part 3 on robot1 gripper	0
R1P4	Part 4 on robot1 gripper	0
R1P5	Part 5 on robot1 gripper	0
R2P1	Part 1 on robot2 gripper	0
R2P2	Part 2 on robot2 gripper	0
R2P3	Part 3 on robot2 gripper	0
R2P4	Part 4 on robot2 gripper	0
R2P5	Part 5 on robot2 gripper	0
T1	Tool_1	1
T2	Tool_2	1
T3	Tool_3	1
T4	Tool_4	1
T5	Tool_5	1
T6	Tool_6	1
T7	Tool_7	1
R1	Robot_1 for loading	1
R2	Robot_2 for unloading	1
MC	Machine for processing	1
CA	T3 allotted for P1	0
CB	T3 allotted for P2	0
CC	T6, T1, T3, T4 allotted for P3	0
CD	T6,T7 allotted for P4	0
CE	T6,T5,T2 allotted for P5	0
P_A1	Final storage for P1	0
P_B1	Final storage for P2	0
P_C1	Final storage for P3	0
P_D1	Final storage for P4	0
P_E1	Final storage for P5	0

Table 2. Transitions

Transitions	Interpretation	Delay(sec)
ACT_1	Part1 is in robot1 gripper	30
ACT_2	Part2 is in robot1 gripper	30
ACT_3	Part3 is in robot1 gripper	30
ACT_4	Part4 is in robot1 gripper	30
ACT_5	Part5 is in robot1 gripper	30
ACT_6	Part1 is in robot2 gripper	30
ACT_7	Part2 is in robot2 gripper	30
ACT_8	Part3 is in robot2 gripper	30
ACT_9	Part4 is in robot2 gripper	30
ACT_10	Part5 is in robot2 gripper	30
ACT_11	Part1 is near final storage	0
ACT_12	Part2 is near final storage	0
ACT_13	Part3 is near final storage	0
ACT_14	Part4 is near final storage	0
ACT_15	Part5 is near final storage	0
PR1	Part1 is ready to processing	0
PR2	Part2 is ready to processing	0
PR3	Part3 is ready to processing	0
PR4	Part4 is ready to processing	0
PR5	Part5 is ready to processing	0

P1R1= complex color p1xr1.
P2R1= complex color p2xr1.
P3R1= complex color p3xr1.
P4R1= complex color p4xr1.
P5R1= complex color p5xr1.
The color set for tools are:
T1= with complex color Tool_1.
T2= with complex color Tool_2.
T3= with complex color Tool_3.
T4= with complex color Tool_4.
T5= with complex color Tool_5.
T6= with complex color Tool_6.
T7= with complex color Tool_7.

The complex color set for robot2 and parts are mentioned below:
P1R2= complex color p1xr2.
P2R2= complex color p2xr2.
P3R2= complex color p3xr2.
P4R2= complex color p4xr2.
P5R2= complex color p5xr2.

To process all the parts in the cell is import to create the complex color for the connection between machine, tools and parts. The complex colors are:
Color set t3xp1xm1, color set t3xp2xm1, color set t6xt1xt3xt4xp3xm1, color set t6xt7xp4xm1 and color set t6xt5xt2xp5xm1.

2) *Variables for raw material and finished part, machine and robots:*

In Timed Color Petri Nets the network connection between all places and all transitions are defined by arcs. In this Petri model arc is assigned with the variables to create connection between place and transition. The variable for part is defined by "p1, p2, p3, p4, p5" and it has values P1, P2, P3, P4, and P5.

$$\mathbf{P1 \in \{p1\}} \quad (1)$$

$$\mathbf{P2 \in \{p2\}} \quad (2)$$

$$\mathbf{P3 \in \{p3\}} \quad (3)$$

$$\mathbf{P4 \in \{p4\}} \quad (4)$$

$$\mathbf{P5 \in \{p5\}} \quad (5)$$

The variables for machine M1 is defined by respectively m1.

$$\mathbf{M1 \in \{m1\}} \quad (6)$$

The variable for robot1 and robot2 can be defined by "r1 and r2" which have the values:

$$\mathbf{R1 \in \{r1\}} \quad (7)$$

$$\mathbf{R2 \in \{r2\}} \quad (8)$$

The variables for tool_1, tool_2, tool_3, tool_4 and tool_5 are mentioned below:

$$\mathbf{T1 \in \{t1\}} \quad (9)$$

$$\mathbf{T2 \in \{t2\}} \quad (10)$$

$$\mathbf{T3 \in \{t3\}} \quad (11)$$

* Corresponding author: sanjibksaren@gmail.com

$$\mathbf{T4} \in \{\mathbf{t4}\} \tag{12}$$

$$\mathbf{T5} \in \{\mathbf{t5}\} \tag{13}$$

$$\mathbf{T6} \in \{\mathbf{t6}\} \tag{14}$$

$$\mathbf{T7} \in \{\mathbf{t7}\} \tag{15}$$

During modeling of the flexible manufacturing cell the position of places for all raw parts are designed separately due to part identity. All the five raw parts have separate storage areas. The places for raw parts are connected through arc to transitions and transition to places to define the connection between parts and robot1. The delay time for making connection between part and robot are consider 30 seconds. The color token for raw parts are P1=3, P2=3, P3=3, P4=3 and P5=3 respectively. The token for robot R1=1 meaning we have one robot for loading operation of the cell. Resource Places R1P1, R1P2, R1P3, R1P4 and R1P5 are the complex connection places for parts and robot1. Below in Fig. 1 we show the connections using timed colored petri nets.

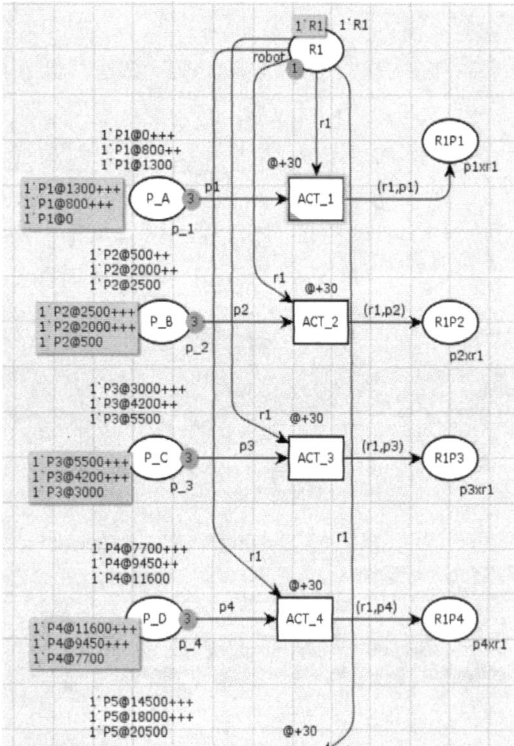

Fig. 1. The complex color connection between parts and robot1.

5 Tool assignment for part processing

* Corresponding author: sanjibksaren@gmail.com

In this flexible manufacturing cell the tool magazine have tool slots for 40 different tools. The tools are changed using the automated tool changer (ATC) mechanism. Here in this flexible model we are processing five different parts and all five parts have different kinds of machining operation. To process all those five parts seven different tools are arranged for machining operation. The Tools are T1, T2, T5, T6, T29, T30 and T39. Below in Fig.2 the tool magazine is illustrated.

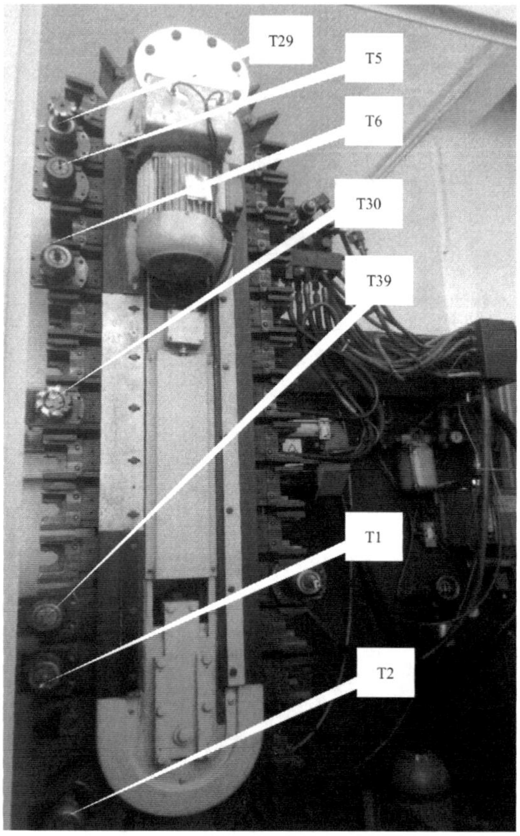

Fig. 2. Tool arrangement for different parts processing.

In the tool magazine we consider seven tools for processing five different parts. The places for all seven tools are T1 with color tool_1, T2 with color tool_2, T3 with color tool_3, T4 with color tool_4, T5 with color tool_5, T6 with color tool_6 and T7 with color tool_7. We create the connection between parts, machine and tools through transitions respectively, PR1, PR2, PR3, PR4 and PR5 for performing machining operation. In transition PR1 we define the guard function [p1=P1] because that transition is assigned for part1 only, respectively PR2 with guard function [p2=P2], PR3 with guard function [p3=P3], PR4= [p4=P4] and PR5 with guard function [p5=P5].

Complex color set CA provides the information of connection for tool3, part1 and machine, CB provides connection for tool3, part2 and machine, CC provides connection of tool6, tool1, tool3, tool4, part3 and machine, CD defines the connection of tool6, tool7, part4 and machine and CE define the connection of tool6, tool5, tool2, part5 and machine respectively. The transitions ACT_1, ACT_2, ACT_3, ACT_4 and ACT_5 means that parts are processed and ready for unloading from the machine after a delay time of 30 (sec).

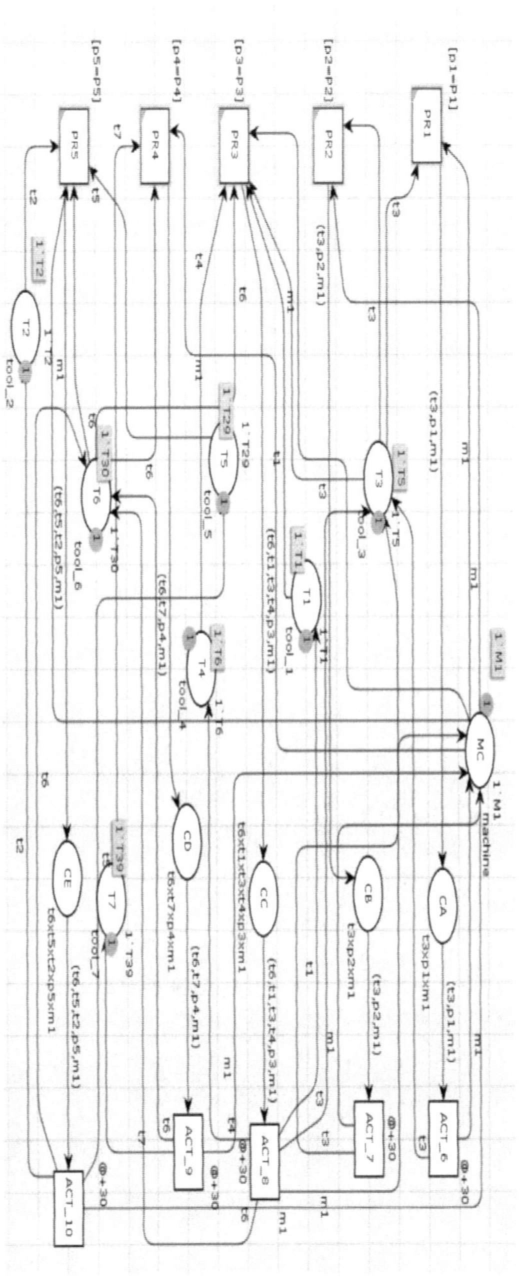

Fig. 3. Tool arrangement design for processing different parts using colored Petri Net techniques.

6 Simulation of the manufacturing cell

The simulation is implemented in the flexible manufacturing cell using Timed Colored Petri Nets. In this production based model, we are processing five different types of parts with different processing times.

In resource places P1, P2, P3, P4 and P5 we define different part arrival times. Fig. 1 shows all the part arrival time for all five parts. Place P1 contain 3 token color, it defines that in total 3 parts P1 will be processed, all other parts P2, P3, P4, P5 also contains 3 token color in their places. Here, we are basically processing 15 parts in this flexible cell.

During simulation we can observe that robot1 take the part from the storage area and load it in the machine for processing and after finish robot2 unload the part from machine and load the finished part in final storage area.

The program is implemented in all resource places to follow the sequence of operation to complete the simulation process.

From simulation we observed that, robot1 first take the part1 from the storage area with a delay time of 30 (sec) when transitions ACT_1 is firing, after that, place R1P1 defines that the part is in robot gripper. After that robot1 loads the part in the machine, robot1 returns back to its own place with token color 1. In transition PR1, the processing time for part1 is mentioned and the guard function [p1=P1] is activated.

In transition PR1, we observed part1; machine and tool_3 are activated and perform machining operation. Place CA defines that the part is complete and machine and tool_3 are now free and the color token returns to their places after firing ACT_6 transition. Now robot2 unloads the part from the machine and R2P1 place shows that part1 is now in robot2 gripper and after firing ACT_11 robot2 loads the part in the final storage place P_A1 and robot2 is free to perform the next operation. So, during simulation, P2 will arrive after 500 (sec) in the system and process the part with processing time 456 seconds. In this situation transition PR2 and guard function [p2=P2] are activated. After finishing P2, robot2 unloads the part from the machine and stores it in place P_B1. After we observed the system follow the part arrival time for part1 to complete the operation for remaining part1 and then it complete remaining part2 operation.

For part3, part4 and part5 the part arrival time is declared in such a manner that first all part3 will be completed, then part4 and part5. For part3 the guard function [p3=P3] and transition PR3 are activated with processing time 1148 (sec) for machining the part. For part4 the guard function [p4=P4] and transition PR4 are activated with processing time 2160 (sec) for machining the parts. For part5 the guard function [p5=P5] and transition PR5 are activated with processing time 2460 (sec) for machining the parts.

* Corresponding author: sanjibksaren@gmail.com

Here, we processed in total 15 parts with five different processing times using seven different tools. The allocations of tools are observed during simulation when transitions PR1, PR2, PR3, PR4 and PR5 are activated.

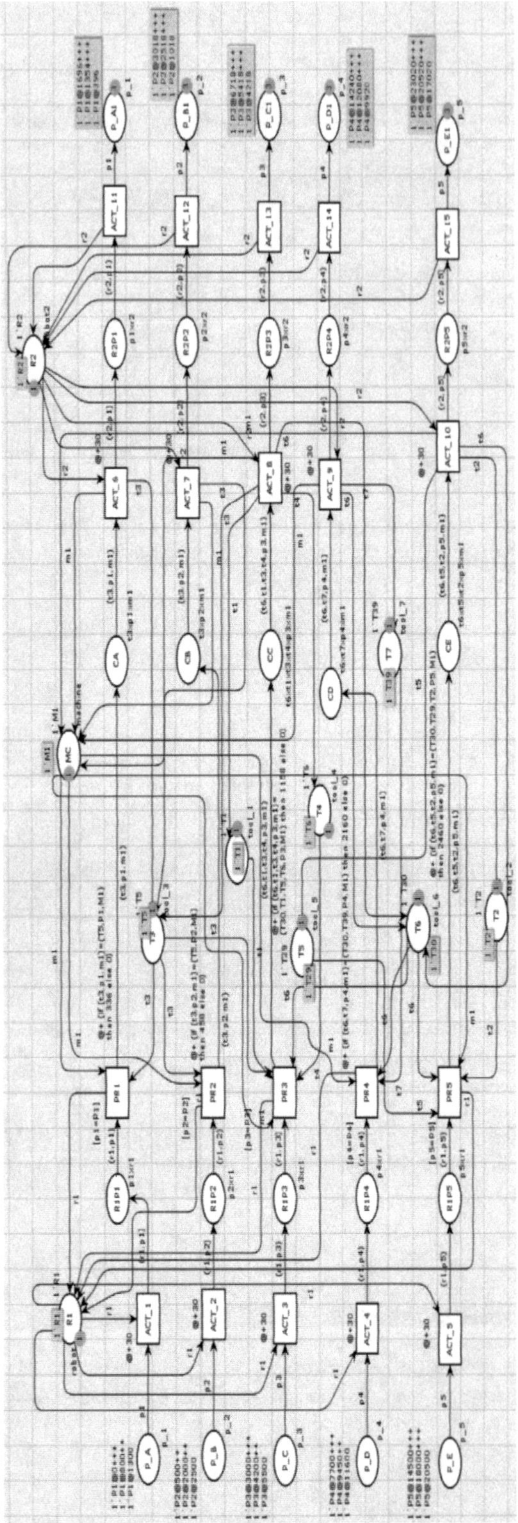

Fig. 4. Simulation results after processing all the parts using CPNTools software.

7 Simulation results

In Timed Colored Petri Nets simulation we notice that all the five types of parts with different processing times are machined and in total 15 parts are processed and the times appears in all final storage areas respectively, place P_A1, P_B1, P_C1, P_D1 and P_E1. The total time is 23020 (sec) after processing all 15 parts and total 60 steps are required to complete the simulation process in CPNTools software mention in Fig.4. The times are mentioned in Table 3 according to the arrival of processed parts.

Table 3. Total Time (sec.)

Part	Place	Time (sec)
P1	P_A1	396
P1	P_A1	1354
P1	P_A1	1696
P2	P_B1	1018
P2	P_B1	2518
P2	P_B1	3018
P3	P_C1	4218
P3	P_C1	5418
P3	P_C1	6718
P4	P_D1	9920
P4	P_D1	12080
P4	P_D1	14240
P5	P_E1	17020
P5	P_E1	20520
P5	P_E1	23020

We also observed from the simulation the involvement of the tools for each part in Colored Petri Nets. It is found that each in simulation, the tool place is free when the tool is allotted for performing the operation and after performing the operation the tool color token returns back to its place meaning that the tool is available for the next operation. For part1, tool_3 with token color T5; for part2, tool_3 with token color T5; for part3, tool_6, tool_1, tool_3, tool_4 with token color T30, T1, T5, T6; for part4, tool_6, tool_7 with token color T30, T39; for part5, tool_6, tool_5, tool_2 with token color T30, T29, T2;

In this, production based model no conflict situation were found, all the transitions are firing appropriately and parts have arrived in the system according to mentioned part arrival times in the resource places. The arcs contain the variables for parts, robots, tools and machine to create a connection for the mentioned places.

Overall the simulations for all the parts are successfully made and the system follows all the sequences to complete the simulation.

* Corresponding author: sanjibksaren@gmail.com

8 Conclusion

The Colored Petri Nets are implemented in various type of flexible manufacturing modeling. Here we attempted to model a production type flexible manufacturing cell. In this, model, the employment of different tools for different parts is a challenging work in order to complete the production model. The advantage of this production model is that all the places are represented by color tokens to construct the system. When a token is moved from place to the transition and transition to places it carries the information. The purpose of the simulation is to analyze if the production of different parts can be successfully carried out for a given production setup. Part arrival times also play very important role in planning the operation sequences and can be very useful for decision making and resource planning.

This research has been sponsored under the Erasmus Mundus partnership program agreement with number 2014-0855/001-001 coordinated by and between University of Oradea and City University of London Under Action Plan 2 for the year 2015-2018.

References

1. T. Aized, K. Takahashi and I. Hagiwara, "Modeling and Optimization of multiple product EMS using Colored Petri Net and Design of Experiment" Networking, Sensing and Control, 2007 IEEE International Conference on London, ISBN: 1-4244-1076-2, pp-334-339, (2007).
2. H. Hosseini-Nasab and A. Sadri, "Using Stochastic Colored Petri nets for Designing Multi-Purpose Plants," Engineering, Vol. 4 No. 10, pp. 655-661, (2012). doi: 10.4236/eng.2012.410083.
3. Z. Yuerong, C. Jun and S. Liping, "Modeling and Analysis of the Wood Flexible Manufacturing System Based on TCPN" Electronic Measurement & Instruments, 2009. ICEMI '09. 9th International Conference on Beijing, China, ISBN: 978-1-4244-3864-8, pp.483- 487, (2009).
4. H. V. Brussel, Y. Peng and P. Valckenaers, "Modelling Flexible Manufacturing Systems Based on Petri Nets" CIRP Annals - Manufacturing Technology Volume 42, Issue 1, pp.479–484, (1993).
5. Z. Ye, T. Wang and P. Sun, "A Petri-Net Based Approach for Flexible Manufacturing System Modeling" International Conference on Automatic Control and Artificial Intelligence (Acai 2012), pp. 252 – 254, (2012).
6. M. Copik and J. Jadlovsk'y, "Utilization of petrinets for the analysis of production systems" Procedia Engineering 48, pp.56-64, (2012).
7. J. Chen and F.F. Chen, "Performance modelling and evaluation of dynamic tool allocation in flexible manufacturing systems using Coloured Petri nets: an object-oriented approach". International Journal of Advanced Manufacturing Technology 21(2), 98–109, (2003).
8. L.C. Wang and S.Y. Wu, "Modeling with colored timed object-oriented Petri nets for automated manufacturing systems". Computers and Industrial Engineering 34(2), pp. 463–480, (1998).
9. F. Blaga, I. Stanasel, A. Pop, V. Hule and T. Buidos, "Consideration on flexible manufacturing cell modeling with timed coloured petri nets" ANNALS OF THE ORADEA UNIVERSITY, Fascicle of Management and Technological Engineering , Issue #1, May 2014, pp 299- 302, http://www.imtuoradea.ro/auo.fmte.(2014)

* Corresponding author: sanjibksaren@gmail.com

Tribological tests of steel on polyamide 66, polyamide 46 type surface contacts

Radu Papuc[1], *Cătălin* Gavrilă[2], *Mihai – Tiberiu* Lateş[3]
[1] Transilvania University of Brasov, radu.papuc@unitbv.ro, Romania
[2] Transilvania University of Brasov, cgavrila@unitbv.ro, Romania
[3] Transilvania University of Brasov, latesmt@unitbv.ro, Romania

Abstract. Improving the efficiency of mechanical transmissions is made, mostly, by finding new materials characterized through antifriction properties, specific reduced mass, wear resistance and by keeping the mechanical properties at high working temperatures (until 220 °C). The paper presents the experimental tests for the surface type contacts between a steel made pin and different types of polyamides; finally there are presented the processing of the experimental data.

1 Introduction

The need of identifying the solutions for friction reduction between the components of the mechanical transmissions in relative motion, as well as the reduced wear, has led to researched by universities, research institutes and specialized companies to create new materials with antifriction properties; in this sense, the polyamides is a class of materials that answer to these demands - especially the groups: Polyamide 66(PA66) and Polyamide 46 (PA46), T. D. Mehnmet, D. Hayrettin, Y. Rifat [1]. Through research, in the first step there were developed the polyamides PA66 being characterized by high rigidity, low dimension variations with temperature variation, abrasion resistance, low dimension variations in high load case (because of high Young module values). These polyamides are used in the case of high loads (pressure) and temperatures up to 100 (°C), M. W. Shin, S. S. Kim, H. Jang, [2]. Considering the exploitation conditions, it appeared the necessity to improve the antifriction properties, wear resistance and keeping the mechanical properties at temperatures up to 220 (°C); in this manner, it was developed, by deep research, the PA46 polyamide class which keeps its characteristics up to these high temperatures and are characterized, at these temperatures, by friction coefficients of contact with steel components lower than the polyamides PA66, J. Van Ruiten, R. Proost, M. Meuwissen [3]. Lately, by recent research, there were brought notable improvements to polyamides by adding graphite to their composition and Teflon. By adding graphite in the internal composition of polyamides PA46 there will be obtained materials with specific reduced mass, high mechanical resistance, self lubricating properties (due to graphite), shock and vibration amortization properties, corrosion resistance, technological simplicity and reduced fabrication costs. Adding Teflon is the main concern of the polyamide producing companies with direct application in automobiles industry, with good antifriction properties and wear resistance at high temperatures (up to 220 °C), specific low mass, and keeping the material properties at these temperatures, K. Randall, B. R. Antoni [4].

2 Experimental determination of the friction coefficient

For determining the friction coefficient between a steel pin and 3 types of polyamides (PA66, PA46, Teflon modified PA46) it will be used the UMT tribometer, presented in figure 1 which is equipped with the rotary module presented in figure 2.

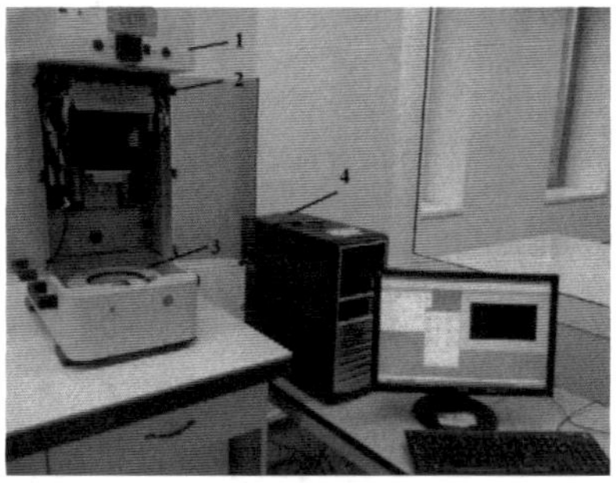

Fig.1. Tribometer UMT: 1 – command engine; 2 – positioning device; 3 – positioning and fixation rim; 4 – computer.

* Corresponding author: radu.papuc@unitbv.ro

This tribometer has the following characteristics: it allows making the mechanical and tribological determinations for different types of materials; the measured physical quantities are processed by data processing software and then there are presented as diagrams.

In Fig. 1, are identified the principal components: the command motor and the positioning devices.

The UMT tribometer is connected to the computer through data cables.

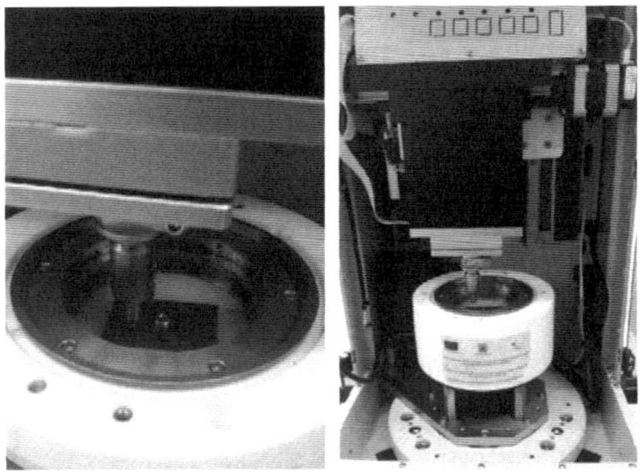

Fig. 2. The rotation module.

The PA66, PA46 and, respectively Teflon modified PA46 materials are used as plates, presented in figure 3 and mounted on a disk which is presented in figure 4.

Fig. 3. The PA66, PA46 and, respectively Teflon modified PA46 plates.

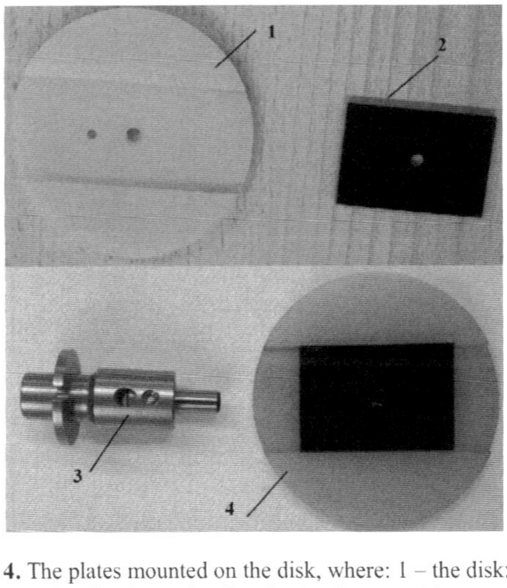

Fig. 4. The plates mounted on the disk, where: 1 – the disk; 2 – the plates; 3 – the pin; 4 – the assembly.

The disk is mounted inside the tribometer rotation module and the contact is made between the normal pressing force pin and the PA66, PA46 and, respectively Teflon modified PA46 plates presented in the figure 4.

In order to study in comparison the tribological properties of the three polyamides, in the following steps, there are performed tests in lubricated conditions, at a test environment temperature of T=120 (^{o}C), for the peripheral speeds v=1,6 (m/s) and 3,2 (m/s) in the conditions of a normal pressing force F=7 (N). The friction coefficient values are presented in the figure 5.

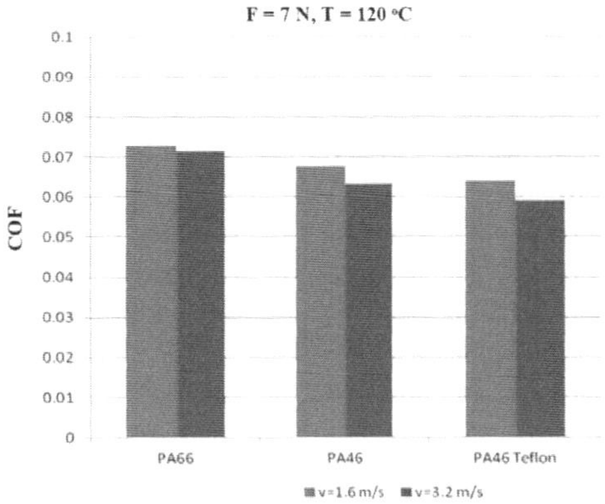

Fig. 5. The friction coefficient.

The friction coefficient value, for all polyamides, drops when the peripheral speed is increasing; the lowest values of the friction coefficient are in the case of Teflon modified PA46 polyamide.

Figure 6 presents, in percentages, the difference, by dropping down, of the friction coefficients for PA46 and Teflon modified PA46 polyamides relative to the PA66 polyamide friction coefficient, determined for the normal pressure force F=7 (N), peripheral speed **v**=3,2 (m/s) and the temperature T=120 (^{o}C).

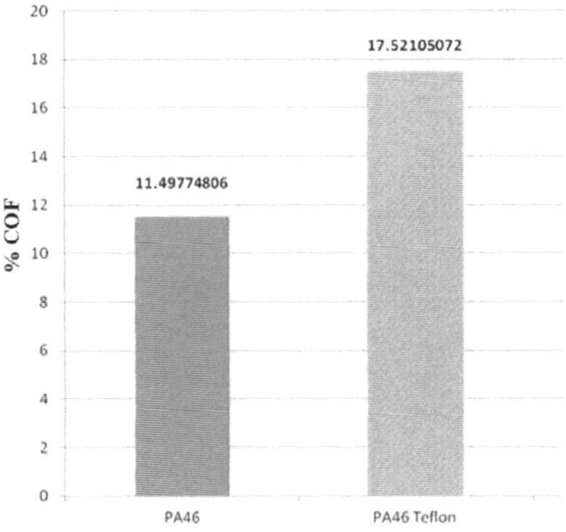

Fig. 6. The difference of friction coefficients to PA66; F=7 N, v=3,2 m/s, T=120 ^{o}C.

* Corresponding author: radu.papuc@unitbv.ro

As it can be seen, the PA46 polyamide has the friction coefficient with 11,5 (%) lower than the PA66 friction coefficient, and the Teflon modified PA46 polyamide has the friction coefficient with 17,5 (%) lower than PA66; the percentage difference to the PA46 friction coefficient is 6.8 (%).

3 Experimental processing data

Measuring the physical quantities implies multiple measurements of the same quantity in the same testing conditions. The measurement process generates a random value set for the same physical quantities which can lead to wrong conclusions regarding the physical phenomena reproduced by testing.

The random value set resulted by measurement in the same conditions can have as fault the lack of control over some variables which affect the measurement process or a reduced precision for the measurement system.

The question is, for a value set obtained through n measurements, which from these values can be kept as "good" values and which of these values must be eliminated as "bad". For example, it is considered as study the previously shown data, and as method used for data selection was chosen the modified Thompson τ technique from the document Measurement Uncertainty -American Society of Mechanical Engineers – ASME, 1998.

For the tests between the steel stud and the three polyamides (PA66, PA46 and Teflon modified PA46) there were made 5 measurements. By applying the modified Thompson τ method, the steps are presented as it follows.

For each of the 5 value sets there is calculated their average

$$\bar{x} = \frac{1}{n}\sum_{i=1}^{n} x_i \tag{1}$$

with n=5 representing the tests number performed on the same type of materials, in the same test conditions and x_i the measured value of the friction coefficient of test i from the same set.

Next, for each of the n=5 value sets it is calculated their standard deviation with the relation.

$$S = \sqrt{\frac{1}{n-1}\sum_{n-1}^{n}\left(x_i - \bar{x}\right)^2} \tag{2}$$

and, further it is arranged inside each of the n=5 value sets, the measured values in increasing order; the minimum and maximum values are likely to be eliminated from the set.

For the minimum and maximum values measured in every set, the value deviation is calculated with the relation.

$$\delta_m = \left|x_{min} - \bar{x}\right| \tag{3}$$

for the minimum value deviation and

$$\delta_M = \left|x_{min} - \bar{x}\right| \tag{4}$$

for the maximum value deviation; it is chosen

$$\delta_{Max} = \max\left(\delta_m, \delta_M\right) \tag{5}$$

Next, according to the numbers of the measurements on the same material, in the same conditions (in this case n=5) from the document Measurement Uncertainty it is chosen the value for τ parameter - for n=5, τ=1,572, R. Velicu, M. T. Lateş, G. Moldovean [5], for n=4, τ=1,393 and for n=3, τ=1,150, A. J. Wheeler, A. R. Ganji, [6].

If the condition

$$\delta_{Max} > \tau S \tag{6}$$

is accomplished, then the measured value corresponding to the maximum deviation is eliminated. The steps 1 ... 6 are retaken until the condition 6 is no longer accomplished and, in this case, the accepted measured value is considered to be equal with the mean calculated with the value 1.

After applying this algorithm, it can be concluded that, from 30 measured values, there were eliminated 4 values (13,33 % values – presented in Fig. 7); the repartition of the eliminated and kept values for each of the polyamides tested is presented in Fig. 8. So, in the case of 27 sets of values there where used for computing the average mean all 5 values from the set, in two cases there were used 4 values from the set and in this case the mean was computed by using only 3 values from the set of 5 measured values set is presented in Fig. 9.

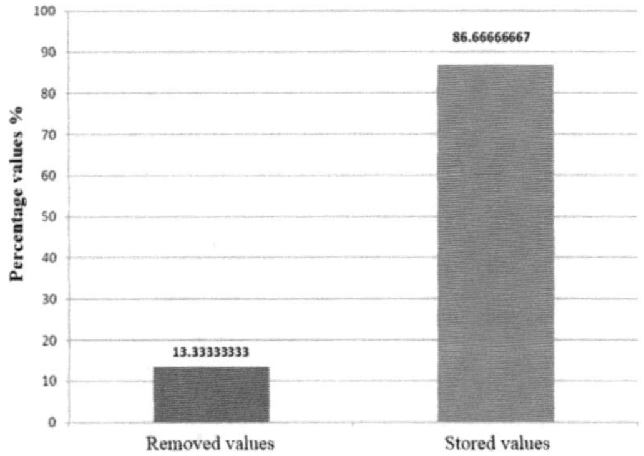

Fig. 7. The overall number used in data processing for PA66, PA46, Teflon PA46.

The friction coefficient values before and after

* Corresponding author: radu.papuc@unitbv.ro

 DOI: 10.1051/matecconf/201712602003

applying the modified Thompson τ technique, in the cases where measured values were eliminated are presented in Fig. 10.

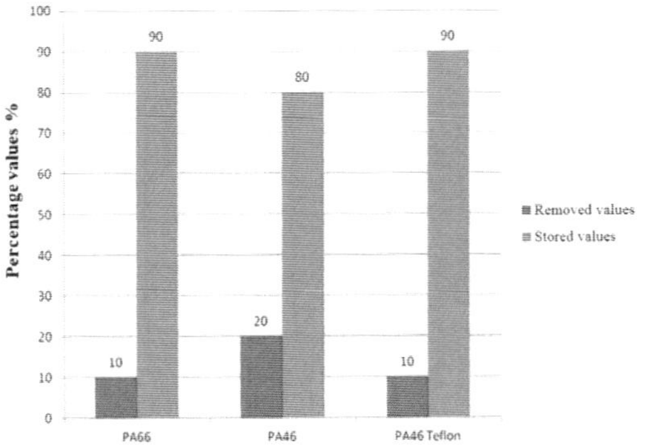

Fig. 8. Repartition of the overall number of values used on tested polyamides.

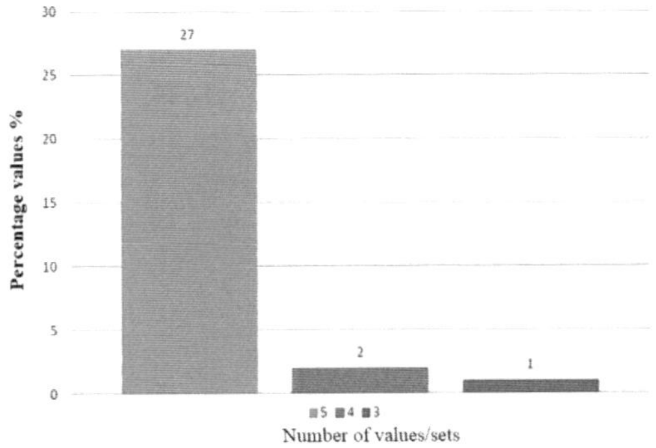

Fig. 9. The number of values/set used for calculating the average mean.

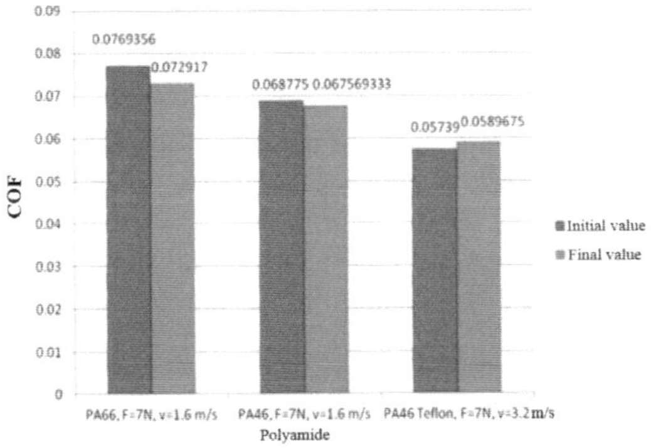

Fig. 10. The friction coefficient before and after applying the modified Thompson τ technique.

4 Conclusions

The differences between the friction coefficient values before and after applying the modified Thompson τ technique are not big; theses differences can be seen in percentage, for every material.

As it can be seen in Fig. 11, the percentage differences in the case of friction coefficients determined before and after applying the modified Thompson τ technique, are quite small (as far as 5%), but they give compliance for the final data, in accordance with the specialty literature from the researched field – document Measurement Uncertainty (American Society of Mechanical Engineers – ASME, 1998).

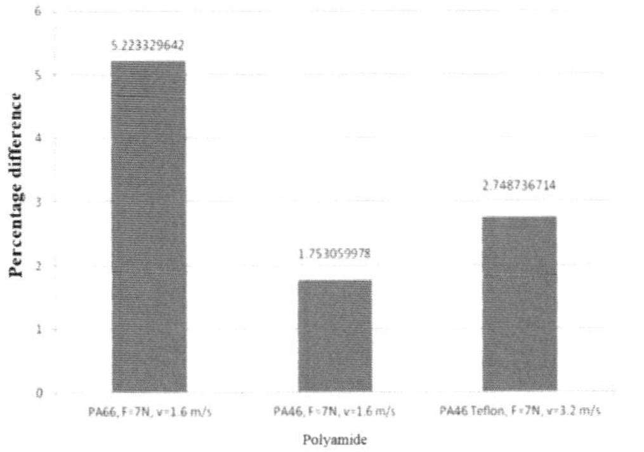

Fig. 11. The percentage difference between the friction coefficients before and after applying the modified Thompson τ technique.

References

[1] T. D. Mehnmet, D. Hayrettin, Y. Rifat, "Investigation of temperature effects on tribological properties of glass fiber and MoS2 reinforced PA6.6 and PA66 journal bearings," In: Journal of materials science and engineering, No. A 3 (11), 2013, pp. 738 – 742.
[2] M. W. Shin, S. S. Kim, H. Jang, "Friction and wear of polyamide 66 with different weight average molar mass," In: Tribology letters, No. 44 (2), p. 151 – 158, 2011.
[3] J. Van Ruiten, R. Proost, M. Meuwissen, "How the choise of the polyamide type in timing chains tensioning systems affects the CO2 emission and fuel economy of internal combustion engines," In Presentation at VDI Veetiltrieb un Zylinderkopf 2012, November 28th, 2012.
[4] K. Randall, B. R. Antoni, "Rolling bearing element diagnostics – A tutorial," Journal of Mechanical Systems and Sygnal Processing, Elsevier Publishing House, nr.25, 2011, p. 485-520.
[5] R. Velicu, M. T. Lateş, G. Moldovean, "Loading Cases and Forces on Azimuthal Solar Tracking Systems with Linear Actuators," Proceedings of SYROM 2009, Braşov, Romania, p. 723-733.
[6] A. J. Wheeler, A. R. Ganji, "Introduction to Engineering Experimentation," Third Edition. Pearson Education Publishing House, 2010.

* Corresponding author: radu.papuc@unitbv.ro

A novel design of an air-cushion vehicle and its implementation

Zsolt Molnár[1*], *Timotei István* Erdei[2], *Nwachukwu* C. Obinna[3], *Géza* Husi[4]

[1]University of Debrecen, zsolt.molnar94@gmail.com
[2]University of Debrecen, timoteierdei@gmail.com
[3]University of Debrecen, nwachukwucobinna@gmail.com
[4]University of Debrecen, husigeza@eng.unideb.hu

Abstract— Recent advancements of unmanned aerial vehicles (UAVs) has led to an increase in public acceptance and availability of manufacturing technologies for these vehicles. This paper is concerned with the development of an air-cushion vehicle (ACV) utilizing the aforementioned manufacturing technologies. Exploiting similarities between UAVs and ACVs, and compensating for their differences, a unique hovercraft is designed and fabricated. The goal of the project is designing an ACV which can be controlled as an UAV without the dangers of easily damaging it. An overview of the development procedure of the hardware, software and implementation of the design is presented within this text.

1 Introduction

Currently, there is a vast amount of commercially available UAVs (Unmanned Aerial Vehicles). However these platforms tend to be closed source, and are of relatively high cost. In addition, making modifications to these UAVs is limited. In the midst of these limitations, it is still possible to design a drone which consists of an open-source controller. The open-source controllers utilized within the framework of this paper, include an Arduino and a Linux operating system-based controller.

The University of Debrecen, Faculty of Engineering, Department of Electrical Engineering and Mechatronics, Building Mechatronic Research Centre, G. Husi [1] made provision for all the necessary equipment required by this research project.

2 Design considerations

Several types of quadrotors has been developed within the research centre. By analysing the construction of these quadrotors, and on the basis of ACV (Air-Cushion Vehicle) design requirements, a layout of the hovercraft presented in this paper is achieved.

In comparison to classical hovercraft, S.A.M. Ali [2], flight is not necessary to achieve translational inertial motion of the presently proposed hovercraft. Furthermore, the proposed hovercraft features less navigation power consumption and is easily repaired. For these reasons, the lifecycle of this hovercraft is estimated at three times the average lifecycle of a quadrotor.

The first step of design was to find low density materials, and produce a Google Sketch Up 3D model of the hovercraft's geometry.

Google Sketch Up [3] software was very useful in enabling modifications of the 3D model to be made quickly and precisely. It is interesting to note that with the hovercraft's 3D model, one may develop a Computer Numerical Control (CNC) prototype to cut out the materials.

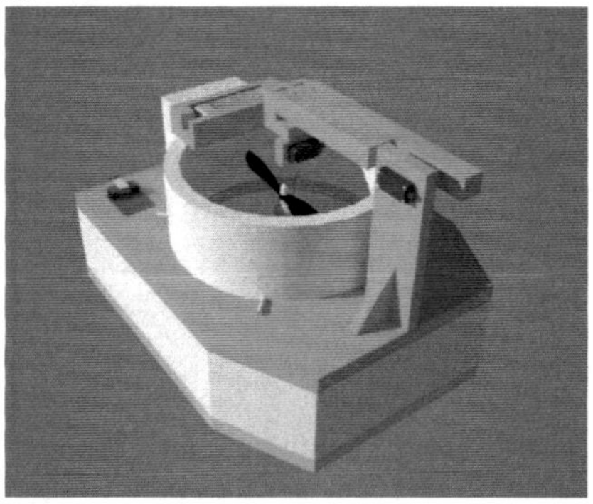

Fig. 1. 3D model of hovercraft

* Corresponding author: zsolt.molnar94@gmail.com

DOI: 10.1051/matecconf/201712602004

3 Construction materials

The hovercraft houses three brushless DC (Direct Current) motors, and two of which provide the vehicle's buoyancy. They rotate in opposite directions, so that net torque generated by the motors is equals to zero. As a result, the vehicle is able to achieve vertical thrust, without redundant inertial rotation. Horizontal thrust is induced by the third brushless DC motor, which is housed at the rear of the vehicle. In order to optimize lift control, the motors responsible for lift generation are placed at the vehicle's centre.

On board the hovercraft is a controllable robot arm which contains within its frame, 20 dices of size (14x14x14 (mm)) each. The robot arm has one degree of freedom, and is capable of carrying out pick and drop tasks, with the dices. In addition the robot arm may also serve as a counterbalance for the whole structure of the hovercraft. Using the robotic arm is most effective in situations where the aircraft demands autonomous task handling and weight modification during flight. Control perspective, this requires careful consideration by the governing party. The robot arm position is shown below the vehicle.

Fig. 2. The robot arm on the hovercraft

In terms of the physical parameters of the air-cushion vehicle has the following: a hovercraft including cube size: 480 (mm) long, 380 (mm) wide, 330 (mm) high (with robot arm state shown in fig. 2.). The mass is small relative to its dimensions. With the battery and dices, the total weight of vehicle is 1.27 (kg).

The two hoist motors and the forward force providing one are the same type, A2212 / 13T brushless DC motors. They have the following parameters [4] :

Motor weight: 52.7 (grams), the maximum operating voltage: 11.1 (V) (Lithium-Polymer battery cell 3) maximum operating current: 10 (A), the maximum achievable operating power (non-continuous operation): 150 (W), shaft diameter: 3.2 (mm), speed Kv: 1000 (RPM / V). The brushless DC motors with high efficiency (over 80%) and a high power / weight ratio. The robot arm with two MG995-type servo motor is housed.

One of the joints of the robotic arm provides the robotic arm movement, and the other will ensure the functioning of the mechanism performing the removal of the dice. The servos as data having the following main characteristics [5]:

Weight: 55 (grams), the maximum operating voltage 7.2 (V), the maximum torque of 0.98 (Nm) capable of rotating 180 (degrees), can be positioned within this range.

4 The circuit of hovercraft

The circuit was designed in KiCAD [6], the main part is the PIC18F type microcontroller. This controls the brushless motors with production of the PWM (Pulse Width Modulation) signal, controls the robot arm servo motors, measures the battery voltage level and communicates via Bluetooth module to the control computer.

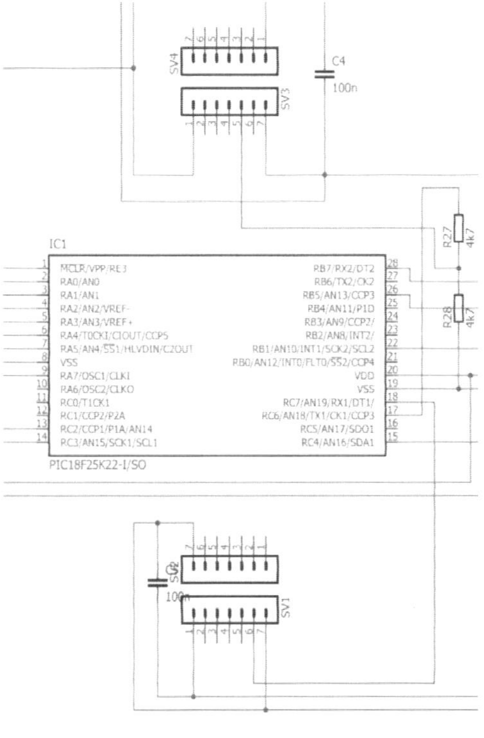

Fig. 3. Connection of the microcontroller used for Hovercraft

The Bluetooth module type was HC-05. This will allow two-way communication, so can be transmitted to the control computer the battery voltage and the position of servo motors of the robot arm. The battery type used capable of 3-cell Li-Po (Lithium-polymer) battery of 2200 (mAh) and 11.1 (V) voltage delivery. It fell Li-Po battery of choice, as the ratio of capacity / weight applied to large, making it ideal for remote-controlled vehicles.

Furthermore, large currents are able to deliver. The circuit is housed in two voltage stabilizer integrated circuits. One provides 3.3 (V) voltage supply necessary

* Corresponding author: zsolt.molnar94@gmail.com

for the Bluetooth module and the other necessary stable 5 (V) power supply for the microcontroller.

The power required for the production of servo motors, DC brushless motors with control electronics provides, because they have a built-in 5 (V) voltage stabilizer and able to lead a 1 (A) current.

5 The construction of hovercraft and material selection

During the build-out should strive to get the materials used are lighter, but they should have a high resistance against arise in the performance of their functions and management of conflicts of mistakes. Based on these considerations, the choice fell polystyrene insulation versions of different densities. Indicatively three different density polystyrene have been used.

The completed 3D model allows you to weigh the volume of polystyrene various types of air-cushion vehicle designed to scale.

Thus, knowing the density of polystyrene [7], calculate the mass of the vehicle frame even before designing.

The following table provides a summary of the different types of polystyrene density and volume of this calculated mass used.

Table 1. The mass of vehicle

	Density (g/cm^3)	Volume(cm^3)	Mass (g)
Expanded polystyrene (White)	0.015	7490	112,35
Extruded polystyrene (Blue)	0.03	3073	92.19
Expanded polystyrene (Green)	0.052	815	42.38

The summing calculated values in the table, the main body of the air mass of 246.92 (g), which is added to the electronics, motors, fasteners, adhesives, dice weight, battery used. The total weight of the assembled hovercraft is 1.27 (kg). The polystyrene has high physical resistance, low density and can be well machined.

The foam cutter uses a glowing thin electrical conductor, which may be of polystyrene cut to size even and smooth cuts. As our own design with the help of CNC machine, which also functions as a foam cutter. The 3D plans have been required to file generating CNC control, then executed the finished polystyrene parts.

Such assembly has polystyrene glue [8] and by means of hot melt [9] is performed.

6 Remote control and software

The remote control of the hovercraft Bluetooth HC-05 module has been used, which can directly communicate with Bluetooth module built into laptops or commercially available Bluetooth adapter with a USB (Universal Serial Bus) connection. In the project a Dell Inspiron Mini 1018 netbook has been carrying out the tests and was used for control because of the mobility and long battery life.

The netbook has the following specifications [10]:

1) *Processor: Intel Atom N455 1.66 (GHz)*
2) *RAM: 1 (GB) DDR3*
3) *Display: 10 ", 1366 x 768 resolution*
4) *Video card: Integrated Intel NM10 Express*
5) *Storage: 250 (GB) HDD, 5400 (RPM)*
6) *Weight: 1.33 (kg)*
7) *Battery capacity: 48 (Wh)*
8) *Built-in Bluetooth 2.1 and 802.11b / g WiFi (Wireless Fidelity)*

These specifications make it suitable to run a hovercraft made software to control and communicate with it via Bluetooth. The software has been designed so that users can directly from the computer control the vehicle or can take control over by using a glove with accelerometer.

The glove is measuring the hand tilt and sends out this data to the computer software which generates the control data for the vehicle microcontroller.

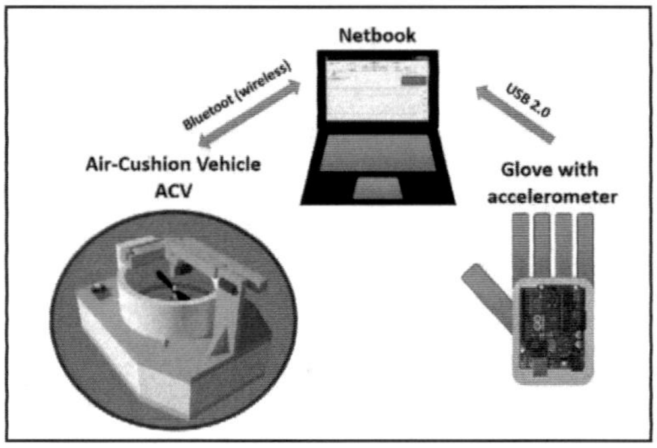

Fig.4. Remote control concept

The figure shows that the netbook communicates wirelessly via Bluetooth. The acceleration sensor glove is directly connected to the notebook via a USB cable. The acceleration sensor type used is MMA7361 sensor three-axis, micro-machined type. The sensitivity can be adjusted ± 1.5 (g) and ± 6 (g). The (g) value means that many times the acceleration of gravity will be the maximum measured acceleration value. The gravitational acceleration is 9.81 (m / s2).

For tilt measurement we consider that it points to the Earth's surface perpendicular to the sensor direction and heeling 1 (g) acceleration, which is the Earth's gravitational field distributed to varying degrees among the three axes. From these values can be determined the orientation of the glove thus the orientation of the operator hand with respect to the Earth's surface. For the control of the air-cushion vehicle was used 1.5 (g) of sensitivity range to achieve the high sensitivity of the sensor. The output of analog signals, varies from 0 (V) to 3.3 (V) range. These signals must be converted to digital values prior processing.

For the sake of completion of an analog to digital conversion has been Arduino UNO [11] used. It has the

* Corresponding author: zsolt.molnar94@gmail.com

required analog inputs and a USB connection in order to connect to the netbook.

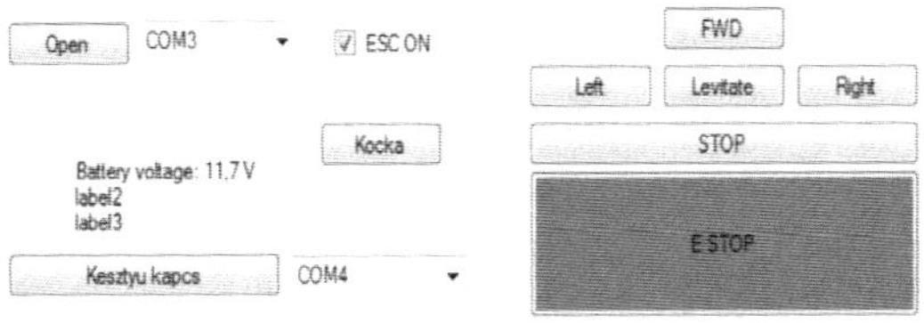

Fig.5. The GUI (Graphical User Interface) of the controller

The main task of the software running on the computer is to provide continuous communication between the computer and the hovercraft. It is important that in case of loss of communication, the hovercraft controller will detect and control the motors automatically to shut down for safety. Since the hovercraft and acceleration sensing glove, both are treated as serial port by the computer, so we have two serial communication port selection drop-down list on the GUI. These are 'COM3' and 'COM4' by default.

The interface also reads the actual battery voltage, which is important in case of Li-Po batteries since the excessive discharge leads to damage. The button and a stop button enabling control in four directions housed in the user interface, if you want to control your vehicle from your computer.

In addition, it is equipped with an 'E-STOP' (Emergency-STOP) button on the user interface which performs an immediate emergency stop, the motors shuts down and interrupts the communication.

The adjustable 'Levitate', 'Turn', 'FWD' are the values of the maximum power of the motors, which operate while floating or turning. The turning is higher value, because in such a case, only one lift motor functions due to the use of the torque to turn and it must ensure the inoperative motor performance as well. In addition, the program has three control modes. The first is the 'cushion'. In this mode, with the tilt of the glove the motors can be switched on and off in order to rotate the hovercraft. There are no transitional values, the inclination of the glove is only used by the software for thresholds that the engine is turned on or off.

This control mode is recommended when walking next to the hovercraft and cannot be guaranteed the stability of the governing hand of the person. The following is the 'Robot arm', in this case with the tilt of the glove can be varied the inclination of the robot arm. The third mode is the 'Analog Control' when it comes to managing people can keep their hands firmly and properly in this mode, the software controls the engine speed to the degree of inclination of the glove.

The control software is written for Windows 7 64-bit operating system, the software is in C # using Visual Studio [12] development environment that is free for student use.

7 Conclusion

The planned hovercraft was built and tested. Functionally, as expected, it is difficult to control, the ability to move with great speed, it requires attention, as in the case of quadrotors.

During testing, smaller collisions occurred, which causes no damage in vehicle frame due to the polystyrene impact absorbing ability.

The remote control works in terms of a stable, open space of 30 m range is also available with it.

In terms of battery life depending on terrain, indoors, where the floor is smooth to operate the hoist motors small amount of power is required, but outdoors more power is needed in order to avoid any uneven ground.

In summary it can be said that it meets the expected conditions, however, with further software development various flight situations can be implemented, such as the simulation of air turbulence for quadrotors becomes possible.

The project was supported by University of Debrecen, Department of Electrical Engineering and Mechatronics.

References

[1] G. Husi, "*Industry 4.0 technology in University of Debrecen*", https://www.researchgate.net/publication/301607839_Industry_4 0_Hungarian, accessed on May 2017
[2] S.A.M. Ali, "*Guidance, Navigation, modeling and control of a hovercraft*", https://www.researchgate.net/publication/277776432_Guidance_Navigation_modeling_and_control_of_a_hovercraft, accessed on February 2017
[3] SketchUp Pro, http://www.sketchup.com/download?sketchup=pro, accessed on January 2017
[4] A2212/13T TECHNICAL DATA, http://www.rhydolabz.com/documents/26/BLDC_A2212_13T.pdf, accessed on April 2017
[5] MG995 High Speed Metal Gear Dual Ball Bearing Servo, http://www.electronicoscaldas.com/datasheet/MG995_Tower-Pro.pdf, accessed on April 2017
[6] KiCad EDA, http://kicad-pcb.org/, accessed on January 2017
[7] Kunststoffe international, Rigid Polystyrene Foam (EPS, XPS), http://www.plasticsportal.net/wa/plasticsEU~it_IT/function/conversions:/publish/common/upload/technical_journals/plastics_trendreports/Rigid_polystyrene_foam.pdf, accessed on February 2017
[8] Polystyrene Foam Adhesive, http://www.genkem.co.za/genkem/index.php/diy-with-genkem/item/polystyrene-foam-adhesive, accessed on March 2017
[9] Hot Melt Glue Gun, https://www.amazon.com/CCbetter-Temperature-Melting-Flexible-Projects/dp/B01178RVI2, accessed on February 2017
[10] Dell Inspiron Mini 1018, http://www.dell.com/en-us/shop/productdetails/inspiron-mini1018, accessed on April 2017
[11] Arduino UNO & Genuino UNO, https://www.arduino.cc/en/main/arduinoBoardUno, accessed on April 2017
[12] Microsoft, Visual Studio IDE, https://www.visualstudio.com/, accessed on March 2017

* Corresponding author: zsolt.molnar94@gmail.com

Industrial robot trajectory optimization- a review

Mariana Ratiu[1*], *Mariana Adriana* Prichici[2]

[1]University of Oradea, e-mail: mratiu@uoradea.ro, Romania
[2]University of Oradea, e-mail: mprichici@uoradea.ro, Romania

Abstract. This paper is the result of the literature review on the trajectory optimization of the serial industrial robots, a study developed in a wider research in the field of the trajectory generation mechanisms of the serial industrial robots. After a short presentation of the importance of the industrial robots in the current context and future challenges, are presented the main optimal trajectory planning criteria approached in several specialized scientific papers, especially in the last few years.

1 Introduction: Current Context

In one of the many definitions of the industrial robots in ISO 8373:2012 [1] is said that an industrial robot is an "actuated mechanism programmable in two or more axes with a degree of autonomy, moving within its environment, to perform intended tasks". There are different types and models of industrial robots, which can be classified, as M. W. Spong, S. Hutchinson and M. Vidyasagar [2] say, according to different criteria, such as the power source or the way in which their joints are actuated, their mechanical or kinematic structure, the payload capacity, the volume of their workspace, their method of control or their intended application area.

Current and future challenges to effectively respond to the global competitiveness and the consumer behaviour, and using the advantages of the new technologies, aim, as M. Hägele, K. Nilsson, N. Pires and R. Bischoff say [3], to design the industrial robots after new principles, so they can be used in many fields and industries, to be more performance and less expensive, to interact intuitively with workers. H. Chen, B. Zhang and G. Zhang [4] note that such intelligent industrial robotics systems are attracting more and more attention of the specialists because of the growing need for adaptation to the complex and flexible industrial processes. C. Mineo, S. G. Pierce, P. I. Nicholson and I. Cooper [5] prove that automatic programming of control systems based on robots does increase flexibility by minimizing the effort and time needed for implementation.

R. Bloss [6] shows that a class of robots that successfully meet such challenges is the category of the collaborative robots, which can be used in many applications where traditional robots fail, providing rapid major improvements in productivity, safety, ease of programming, portability and costs over time. R. Bogue [7] and B. Carlisle [8] take into account the use of the collaborative robots in applications such as the manufacture and assembly of the electronic products or those from the automotive; they can be used by the small and medium-sized companies or by the companies seeking agile production methods. Z. Lu, C. Xu, Q. Pan, D. Xiao, F. Meng and J. Hao [9] analyse the use of the collaborative robots for non-destructive testing of curved surfaces. O. Madsen, S. Bogh, C. Schou, R. S. Andersen, J. S. Damgaard, M. R. Pedersen and V. Krüger [10] present the integration of two autonomous mobile robots in a real manufacturing environment.

It is expected to expand to new areas the applicability of the industrial robots, such as deburring of custom parts with complex geometry, high-speed processing, such as milling with a high degree of accuracy, as A. Klimchik, A. Ambiehl, S. Garnier, B. Furet and A. Pashkevich [11] present, or arc welding. J. Léger and J. Angeles [12] say that all these require high precision robots, robots whose components are built and assembled with precision and the trajectory planning and control algorithms are also designed to improve the accuracy execution of the tasks. T. Messay, R. Ordóñez and E. Marcil [13] note that an improvement of the accuracy of the robot can be obtained by a computationally efficient and kinematic calibration method.

According to G. Berselli, M. Gadaleta, A. Genovesi, M. Pellicciari, M. Peruzzini and R. Razzoli [14], the industrial robots could be an effective alternative to the dedicated machine tools, because of the increased

* Corresponding author: mratiu@uoradea.ro

flexibility of the possibility of location and cost, being estimated a reduction of 20-50% costs compared to the machining with the traditional CNC machines. To ensure efficiency of the entire robotic system in the production processes, the researchers seek, study and propose various machining strategies and robot settings leading to improved geometric accuracy and surface quality processed using industrial robots, M. Halbauer, C. Lehmann, J. P. Städter, F. Leali [15], the robot stability to the vibrations occurring in the machining process (chatter), S. Mousavi, V. Gagnol, B. C. Bouzgarrou, P. Ray [16].

In the context of the extensive use of the industrial robots in automated production processes, P. Tavares, J. Lima, P. Costa and A. P. Moreira [17] seek the best solutions to optimize and streamline the entire process. In this regard, G. Boschetti [18] proposes and experimentally implements a path planning technique for a robot so that it can pick-up parts "on the fly" of the circular feeder without to need to stop its rotation. To overcome the problems of the occurrence of the equipment failures, C. Müller, C. Weckenborg, M. Grunewald and T. S. Spengler [19] propose taking into consideration of the redundancy in the configuration of the automated assembly lines, by creating a buffer space between the stations, so that the downstream stations to take over the operations of the failed stations.

Nowadays, when it is imperative to develop environmentally friendly products and production processes, many studies in robotics are conducted regarding the reduction of the energy consumption, in special through the optimization of the robot's motions, as L. Wang [20] says. D. Constantinescu and E. Croft [21] demonstrate that the optimization through the smoothing trajectories provides a superior feasible optimal time and leads to the reduced energy consumption, as Paryanto, M. Brossog, M. Bornschlegl and J. Franke [22] show. To ensure a sustainable manufacturing, recently was appeared the concept "Industrial Cloud Robotics" presented by J. Liu, W. Xu, J. Zhang, Z. Zhou and D. Pham [23].

P. Tavares, J. Lima and P. Costa [24] propose a solution for the need to adapt the robots at the multiple loads and environments by creating a Robotic Operative System (ROS), a set of software libraries and tools that can be used for building robot applications by putting together more simple algorithms, in order to obtain a modular solution to a complex problem, thus increased flexibility. There are also available open-source educational platforms, with robots with different degrees of freedom, which can provide academic training to those interested without charge, as S. Manzoor, R. Ul Islam, A. Khalid, A. Samad and J. Iqbal [25] show.

Considering the role of the robots in the present and future industrial processes, a lot of recent studies are conducted to streamline and optimize the trajectories and the motions of the industrial robots.

2 Industrial robot trajectory optimization

Optimization of the movement of an object manipulated by an industrial robot, between two given positions, involve both optimization of the movement of the object manipulated respectively of the end-effector relative to the robot base, as well as the optimization of the positioning of the robot base relative to the application defined by the two positions, or vice versa, the positioning of the application relative to the robot base. D. Spensieri, J. S. Carlson, R. Bohlin, J. Kressin and J. Shi [26] demonstrate experimentally that the optimal position of the robot base into a cell assembly in automotive, depending on the tasks to be performed, leads to a reduction of up to 20% of the execution time of the tasks.

The purpose of such optimization is to minimize/maximize at least one of the following objective functions:

1) *minimizing the execution time, respectively maximizing the robot productivity, considering that the relative speeds of the actuator's elements are limited constructively;*
2) *minimizing the energy consumption or mechanical work necessary for execution, leading to a reduction of the mechanical stresses in actuators and on the robot structure and obtaining smooth trajectories, easy to follow;*
3) *minimizing the maximum power required for operating the robot;*
4) *minimizing the maximum actuation forces and moments.*

Often, to get better results, multi-criteria optimization is achieved when the objective function that minimizes/maximizes express simultaneously more of the above criteria.

The most common optimization criteria used in the literature are: minimum time trajectory planning; minimum energy trajectory planning or minimum actuation effort; minimum jerk trajectory planning, or hybrids criteria, such as, for example, minimum time and minimum energy, when is a compromise between the time necessary for trajectory and the energy of the actuators; minimum time and minimum jerk, both minimized simultaneously.

J. Kim and E. A. Croft [27], following a study in terms of the industrial applications of the available optimization methods, claime that these methods are limited to use, if not taken into account some important considerations such as the precision tracking trajectory, the importance of the minimum time criteria, the need to minimize the cycle time by online planning, the motion controllers' performance.

3 Minimum time trajectory planning

Minimum/optimal time trajectory planning is the first and most frequently method of optimization discussed in the literature, especially due to its direct connection with the reduction of the manufacturing time respectively with the productivity increase. Over time, have been used

* Corresponding author: mratiu@uoradea.ro

various techniques or different algorithms for this type of optimization but most of them neglect the actuator dynamics, which lead to discontinuation of the actuators' accelerations and torques. To overcome this disadvantage, D. Constantinescu and E. Croft [21] solve the optimization problem by using a flexible tolerance method and limits for the torque rates to obtain the desired smoothness for trajectory which provides a feasible time-optimal motion. X. Gao, Y. Mu and Y. Gao [28] use for optimization an improved teaching-learning algorithm while respecting the kinematic constraints. J. Kim, S. R. Kim, S. J. Kim and D. H. Kim [29] recommend an approach for online implementation by using the dynamic model of the robot to find the maximum kinematic constraints that are used with the conventional trajectory models. F. Abu-Dakka, I. Assad, R. Alkhdour and M. Abderahim [30], after an exhaustive analysis of the optimization methods presented in the literature, prefer the optimization by minimizing the time, using a parallel populations genetic algorithm and three different types of constraints: kinematics, dynamics and payload constraint, instead of minimizing the jerk, the latter being placed constraints within the meaning of imposing limits given in the literature.

In the context in which was found that the redundant robots have some advantages in comparison with the conventional robots, there are numerous studies on optimizing their motions. A. Reiter, K. Springer, H. Gattringer and A. Müller [31] present a method that uses, besides of the standard optimization techniques, a decomposition of the joint space and inverse kinematics analysis for obtaining a minimum-time trajectory of the joint. G. Erdős, A. Kovács and J. Váncza [32] propose the optimization method for a redundant industrial robot that execute a set of tasks in a complex work environment with multiple technological and geometric constraints, consists of selecting, from the set of configurations obtained by solving inverse kinematics, of those which avoid collisions, after which, pursuing the time minimization by ensuring the shortest trajectory, is selected the optimal combination, respecting all kinematic constraints of the robot.

Starting from the observation that only a few studies approach the working times in direct connection with the analysis of the productivity, F. Rubio, C. Llopis-Albert, F. Valero and J. L. Suñer [33] demonstrate, by using two methodologies, an optimization procedure, and a simulation technique, that the optimization procedure, with multiobjective functions, leads to lower working times and greater annual revenue in comparison with those obtained with a simulation technique.

4 Minimum energy trajectory planning

The trajectory optimization by minimizing the energy has several advantages. On the one hand, it produces smooth trajectories that are easier to follow and reduces mechanical stresses in actuators and on the robot structure. On the other hand, this method saves energy, which is important not only regarding the cost but also regarding the quantitative limitation, in the case of specific applications where the power supply is limited by technical factors such as robotic applications in outer space or underwater exploration or for certain military tasks.

This type of optimization, developed in recent times in industrial applications, due to the need to reduce the energy consumption, is found in several studies: T. Mashimo, T. Urakubo and T. Kanade [34]; D. Meike, M. Pellicciari and G. Berselli [35]; O. Wigstrom, B. Lennartson, A. Vergnano and C. Breitholtz [36]; J. Gregory, A. Olivares and E. Staffetti [37]". In these studies are used different algorithms or methods for trajectory planning, including modeling and simulation. In some of these studies it was not succeeded obtaining the continuous accelerations and torques in joints, but in other ones, this inconvenience has removed. In one such study, L. P. Luo, C. Yuan, R. J. Yan, Q. Yuan, J. Wu, K. S. Shin and C. S. Han [38], by using the Lagrange interpolation method and through imposing position and stability constraints were obtained the smoothness of the joint angular positions, velocities, accelerations, and joint torques. R. F. Fung and Y. H. Cheng [39] use genetic algorithms and high-degree polynomials to optimize, by minimizing energy, the point-to-point trajectory of a robot, introducing constraints of the angular displacement, speed, acceleration, and jerk at the start and end times. M. Jin and D. Wu [40], in a concrete study on a manipulator redundant with six degrees of freedom, to ensure the safety motions and to reduce the energy consumption, it was adopted an improved algorithm type "particle swarm optimization" (PSO) for optimizing the trajectory of the arm system.

Starting from the finding that the position-controlled servo systems, widely used and efficient, are energy intensive, G. Berselli, F. Balugani, M. Pellicciari and M. Gadaleta [41] demonstrate that the trajectory optimization by minimizing the energy leads to the best performance of these servo systems. Other approaches in this regard are found in several other recent studies: E. Oliva, G. Berselli, M. Pellicciari and A. Andrisano [42]; M. Pellicciari, G. Berselli and F. Balugani [43]; Y. Wang, K. Ueda and S. Bortoff [44]; M. Huang, Y. Hsu and R. Fung [45].

5 Minimum jerk trajectory planning

Jerk is the third derivative of the position in time and indicates how quickly the joints change its forces. Jerk's reduction ensures the trajectory continuity and leads, on the one hand, to the reduction of the joint positioning errors or more accurately tracking trajectory and, on the other hand, to the reduction of the robot vibration limits, which leads to the wear reduction and thus to the increasing the duration of the exploitation.

The trajectory planning through jerk minimization is performed in specialized researches by two approaches: by using predefined via points, called nodes, node points or control points used for interpolation and without the use of node points. H. I. Lin [46] presents a quick and unified method for joints' trajectory planning, by minimizing the jerk, using the PSO algorithm integrated

* Corresponding author: mratiu@uoradea.ro

with the K-means clustering. Using a computer simulation method has been proved that this method is easy and efficient in comparison with other methods taken into consideration.

6 Multi-criteria optimization

Z. Miljković and M. Petrović [47] present, in an optimization study regarding the planning of a flexible manufacturing process, a hybrid optimization criterion, minimum production time and minimum production cost, by using an improved particle swarm optimization algorithm, with crossover, mutation and shift operator.

By applying the combination minimum time and minimum energy, which is a compromise between the time necessary for trajectory and the energy of the actuators, D. Gleeson, S. Bjorkenstam, R. Bohlin, J. S. Carlson and B. Lennartson [48] show that can achieve a 10% reduction in energy consumption of an industrial robot standard used in a welding station.

The hybrid optimization criterion minimum time and continuous jerk is applied in a study by H. Liu, X. Lai and W. Wu [49] for obtaining efficient and smooth motions for the robot. In another studies by the same type, the criterion applied is: time-optimal and jerk-bounded for a pick and place operation, by S. Perumaal and N. Jawahar [50]; time-jerk optimal, taking into account more constraints: the joints' velocity, acceleration and jerk by A. Gasparetto and V. Zanotto [51], A. Gasparetto, A. Lanzutti, R. Vidoni and V. Zanotto [52], and the heavy payload and high speed handling, F. Liu, F. Lin [53].

To optimize the trajectory of a glass-handing robot, in a study H. Duan, R. Zhang, F. Yu, J. Gao and Y. Chen [54] present a multi-criteria approach, through weighting the execution time, acceleration, and jerk, and the results of the mathematical simulations show not only improving the working efficiency but also ensuring smoothing robot' motions.

By using for optimization the objective functions minimum transmission time and maximum load carried, H. Esfandiar and M. H. Korayem [55] have planned an optimal point to point trajectory for a flexible manipulator under large deformation, by imposing kinematic constraints (maximum velocity and acceleration), dynamic constraint (maximum torque applied to the arms) and also the constraint of final point accuracy.

To increase flexibility and manoeuvrability, are sometimes used snake robots, which have a high degree of freedom, which prevents their control, but facilitates their motions on uneven surfaces. There are several studies that seek the best algorithms for the motion control of the joints of the snake robots, as M. Jafari and A. Shahmansoorian [56] show. In one such study, P. Costa, J. Lima, A. I. Pereira, P. Costa, A. Pinto [57]" propose a multi-criteria optimization for a robot with 12 degrees of freedom, Tentacle Robot, by minimizing the Euclidean distance between the target positions and by minimizing the effort of the servomotors.

To perform a complex robotic assembly task was developed by F. Anton, S. Anton, S. Răileanu and T. Borangiu [58] an algorithm based on the dynamic equations of the robot, to obtain the optimal speed-trajectory length, taking into account the load of the robot and the stopping points on the trajectory.

In an attempt to solve the kinematic redundancy of a 6R industrial robot used for five axes milling process, W. Xiao, J. Huan [59] propose a numerical multi-criteria method to optimize the singularities, joint limits and collisions, critical constraints for the milling process.

To planning the trajectory of industrial robots with payload constraint, into a research S. S. Chiddarwar and N. R. Babu [60] impose six objective functions: weighted balance of traveling time, actuator torques, singularities avoidance, joint jerks, joint accelerations and gripping force.

7 Optimization of the robotic task sequence

In many industrial applications, the robots are used to perform a set of tasks and the tasks sequencing and how the robot moves between them greatly influence the overall performance of the application. In many such applications, the motions of the robots are still optimized manually, this being expensive and predisposing to errors. Therefore, in recent years the researchers are working to search algorithms for automatic calculation of optimal trajectories of the robot motions. This approach proved to be quite complicated, because of several factors, such as redundant kinematics, collision avoidance, ambiguous possibilities for performing the tasks, complicated objective functions, a set of possible locations for the robot base, etc., as S. Alatartsev, S. Stellmacher and F. Ortmeier [61] show. Also, it found that is difficult to compare existing approaches because they address various case studies in various industrial applications and various types of robots with different characteristics and constraints.

S. Alatartsev, starting from the finding that many kinds of tasks allow some freedom of execution, develop more studies to search a more efficient sequence of tasks. In a such study, S. Alatartsev, V. Mersheeva, M. Augustine and F. Ortmeier [62] propose a new heuristic and effective way to solve such problems by TSPN (Traveling Salesman Problem with Neighbourhoods) method, a combination of TSP (Traveling Salesman Problem) and TPP (Touring-a-sequence-of-Polygons Problem) focused only on optimizing the Euclidean distance, showing the applicability of this method.

In trying to solve an integrated problem, of tasks sequencing and path planning for a process of robotic remote laser welding, A. Kovács [63] introduces a new model, an extension of TSP method, Traveling Salesman Problem with Neighbourhoods and Duration visits (TSP-ND). He demonstrates through ample computational experiments, that the new approach effectively solves the relevant problems in this industry, and achieves a substantial improvement in cycle time.

* Corresponding author: mratiu@uoradea.ro

In tracking a path between two target points, the robot must usually pass by so-called via-points, placed in general to avoid certain obstacles in the workspace, or to impose a particular direction, preferred. In some cases these points must be strictly visited, in other cases, we are dealing with pseudo-via-points not intended to be strictly visited, but the passing is effected by their immediate vicinity. In this respect, H. Liu, X. Lai and W. Wu [64] sustain that the robot must follow exactly the path of the end effector and its laws of motion, and via-points must be strictly visited, without any deviation, to obtain an optimal trajectory. In opposition to this opinion, S. Alatartsev, A. Belov, M. Nykolaychuk and F. Ortmeier [65] demonstrate in another study on the problem of optimizing the tasks sequencing of the industrial robots, that if it is relaxed the path through small changes in position or orientation of the end-effector, the motion law can be strictly followed, and this can lead to a significant cost reduction.

By studying several existing approaches to find a path suitable to a robot in a certain environment and their advantages and disadvantages, T. Nierhoff, S. Hirche and Y. Nakamura [66] propose a new approach to deform trajectories, while keeping their similar local shape. This new approach is based on discrete Laplace-Beltrami operator, well-known in computer graphics, but still untapped in robotics problems.

8 Conclusion

In the current context, the optimizations of any kind, including those in engineering, are regarded as being of particular importance, this being demonstrated by a huge number of researches, publications and scientific events dedicated to this topic. In the context of using the industrial robots on a more widely scale, and in which the optimal trajectory planning of the industrial robots proved to be a complex and difficult task, more and more researchers and specialized companies develop different theoretical and experimental studies, with different approaches to optimizing the motions of the industrial robots.

References

[1] ISO 8373:2012(en) *Robots and robotic devices – Vocabulary*
[2] M. W. Spong, S. Hutchinson, M. Vidyasagar, *Robot modeling and control*, Wiley, 2006.
[3] M. Hägele, K. Nilsson, N. Pires, R. Bischoff, "Industrial robotics", *Springer Handbook of Robotics*, 2nd Edition, 2016, pp. 1385-1421.
[4] H. Chen, B. Zhang, G. Zhang, "Robotic assembly", *Handbook of Manufacturing Engineering and Technology*, Springer, 2015, pp. 2347-2401.
[5] C. Mineo, S. G. Pierce, P. I. Nicholson, I. Cooper, "Robotic path planning for non-destructive testing – A custom MATLAB toolbox approach", *Robotics and Computer-Integrated Manufacturing* 37, Elsevier, 2016, pp. 1-12.
[6] R. Bloss, "Collaborative robots are rapidly providing major improvements in productivity, safety, programing ease, portability and cost while addressing many new applications", *Industrial Robot: An International Journal*, 43(5), 2016, pp. 463-468.
[7] R. Bogue, "Europe continues to lead the way in the collaborative robot business", *Industrial Robot: An International Journal*, 43(1), 2016, pp. 6 – 11.
[8] B. Carlisle, "Collaborative robots: design challenges and applications", *Robotic Industries Association, International Collaborative Robots Workshop*, 2016.
[9] Z. Lu, C. Xu, Q. Pan, D. Xiao, F. Meng, J. Hao, "Kinematic constraint analysis in a twin-robot system for curved-surface nondestructive testing", *Industrial Robot: An International Journal*, 43(2), 2016, pp. 172-180.
[10] O. Madsen, S. Bogh, C. Schou, R. S. Andersen, J. S. Damgaard, M. R. Pedersen, V. Krüger, "Integration of mobile manipulators in an industrial production", *Industrial Robot: An International Journal*, 42(1), 2015, pp. 11 – 18.
[11] A. Klimchik, A. Ambiehl, S. Garnier, B. Furet, A. Pashkevich, "Comparison study of industrial robots for high-speed machining", *Mechatronics and Robotics Engineering for Advanced and Intelligent Manufacturing, Part of the series Lecture Notes in Mechanical Engineering*, 2016, pp. 135-149.
[12] J. Léger, J. Angeles, "Off-line programming of six-axis robots for optimum five-dimensional tasks", *Mechanism and Machine Theory*, 100, Springer, 2016, pp. 155–169.
[13] T. Messay, R. Ordóñez, E. Marcil, "Computationally efficient and robust kinematic calibration methodologies and their application to industrial robots", *Robotics and Computer-Integrated Manufacturing*, 37, 2016, pp. 33–48.
[14] G. Berselli, M. Gadaleta, A. Genovesi, M. Pellicciari, M. Peruzzini, R. Razzoli, "Engineering methods and tools enabling reconfigurable and adaptive robotic deburring", *Advances on Mechanics, Design Engineering and Manufacturing*, 2016, pp. 655-664.
[15] M. Halbauer, C. Lehmann, J. P. Städter, F. Leali, "Milling strategies optimized for industrial robots to machine hard materials", *IEEE*, 978-1-4799-0864-6/13, 2013.
[16] S. Mousavi, V. Gagnol, B. C. Bouzgarrou, P. Ray, "Model-based stability prediction of a machining robot", *New Advances in Mechanisms, Mechanical Transmissions and Robotics, Mechanisms and Machine Science*, vol. 46, 2016, pp. 379-387.
[17] P. Tavares, J. Lima, P. Costa, A. P. Moreira, "Multiple manipulators path planning using double A", *Industrial Robot: An International Journal*, 43(6), 2016, pp. 657-664.
[18] G. Boschetti, "A Picking Strategy for Circular Conveyor Tracking", *Journal of Intelligent and Robotic System*, 81, 2016, pp. 241–255.
[19] C. Müller, C. Weckenborg, M. Grunewald, T. S. Spengler, "Consideration of redundancies in the automated flow lines", *Logistics Management*, 2016, pp. 173-185.
[20] L. Wang, "Redefining the shop floor - make it as cool as a computer game", published on Sep 10, 2015, http://www.kth.se/en/forskning/artiklar/redefining-the-shop-floor-1.590274.
[21] D. Constantinescu, E. Croft, "Smooth and time-optimal trajectory planning for industrial manipulators along specified paths", *Journal of Robotic Systems*, 17 (5), 2000, pp. 233–249.
[22] Paryanto, M. Brossog, M. Bornschlegl, J. Franke, "Reducing the energy consumption of industrial robots in manufacturing systems", *International Journal of Advanced Manufacturing Technology*, 78, 2015, pp. 1315–1328.
[23] J. Liu, W. Xu, J. Zhang, Z. Zhou, D. Pham, "Industrial cloud robotics towards sustainable manufacturing", *Proceedings of the ASME 11th International Manufacturing Science and Engineering Conference*, vol. 2, 2016.
[24] P. Tavares, J. Lima, P. Costa, "Double A* path planning for industrial manipulators", *Advances in Intelligent Systems and Computing*, 418, 2016, pp. 119-130.
[25] S. Manzoor, R. Ul Islam, A. Khalid, A. Samad, J. Iqbal, "An open-source multi-DOF articulated robotic educational platform for autonomous object manipulation", *Robotics and Computer-Integrated Manufacturing*, 30, 2014, pp. 351–362.
[26] D. Spensieri, J. S. Carlson, R. Bohlin, J. Kressin, J. Shi, "Optimal robot placement for tasks execution", *6th CIRP Conference on Assembly Technologies and Systems (CATS)*, Procedia CIRP 44, 2016, pp. 395 – 400.
[27] J. Kim, E. A. Croft, "Trajectory planning for robots: the challenges of industrial considerations, Motion Planning for Industrial Robots", *IEEE International Conference on Robotics and Automation (ICRA)*, 2014.
[28] X. Gao, Y. Mu, Y. Gao, "Optimal trajectory planning for robotic manipulators using improved teaching-learning-based optimization algorithm", *Industrial Robot: An International Journal*, 43(3), 2016, pp. 308-316.

* Corresponding author: mratiu@uoradea.ro

[29] J. Kim, S. R. Kim, S. J. Kim, D. H. Kim, "A practical approach for minimum-time trajectory planning for industrial robots", *Industrial Robot: An International Journal*, 37(1), 2010, pp. 51–61.

[30] F. Abu-Dakka, I. Assad, R. Alkhdour, M. Abderahim, "Statistical evaluation of an evolutionary algorithm for minimum time trajectory planning problem for industrial robots", *International Journal of Advanced Manufacturing Technology*, 2016, DOI 10.1007/s00170-016-9050-1.

[31] A. Reiter, K. Springer, H. Gattringer, A. Müller, "An explicit approach for time-optimal trajectory planning for kinematically redundant serial robots", *PAMM Proceedings in Applied Mathematics and Mechanics*, 15, 2015, pp. 67–68.

[32] G. Erdős, A. Kovács, J. Váncza, "Optimized joint motion planning for redundant industrial robots", *CIRP Annals - Manufacturing Technology*, 65, 2016, pp. 451–454.

[33] F. Rubio, C. Llopis-Albert, F. Valero, J. L. Suñer, "Assembly Line Productivity Assessment by Comparing Optimization-Simulation Algorithms of Trajectory Planning for Industrial Robots", *Mathematical Problems in Engineering*, , Hindawi Publishing Corporation, 2015, Article ID 931048.

[34] T. Mashimo, T. Urakubo, T. Kanade, "Singularity-based four-bar linkage mechanism for impulsive torque with high energy efficiency", *Journal of Mechanisms and Robotics*, 7(3), 2015.

[35] D. Meike, M. Pellicciari, G. Berselli, "Energy efficient use of multirobot production lines in the automotive industry: detailed system modeling and optimization", *IEEE Transactions on Automation Science and Engineering*, 11(3), 2014, pp. 798–809.

[36] O. Wigstrom, B. Lennartson, A. Vergnano, C. Breitholtz, "High-level scheduling of energy optimal trajectories", *IEEE Transactions on Automation Science and Engineering*, 10(1), 2013,pp. 57–64.

[37] J. Gregory, A. Olivares, E. Staffetti, "Energy-optimal trajectory planning for robot manipulators with holonomic constraints", *Systems & Control Letters*, 61(2), Elsevier, 2012, pp. 279–291.

[38] L. P. Luo, C. Yuan, R. J. Yan, Q. Yuan, J. Wu, K. S. Shin, C. S. Han, "Trajectory planning for energy minimization of industry robotic manipulators using the Lagrange interpolation method", *International Journal of Precision Engineering and Manufacturing*, 16(5), 2015, pp. 911–917.

[39] R. F. Fung, Y. H. Cheng, "Trajectory planning based on minimum absolute input energy for an LCD glass-handling robot", *Applied Mathematical Modelling*, 38, 2014, pp. 2837–2847.

[40] M. Jin, D. Wu, "Collision-free and energy-saving trajectory planning for large-scale redundant manipulator using improved PSO", *Mathematical Problems in Engineering*, Hindawi Publishing Corporation, Volume 2013.

[41] G. Berselli, F. Balugani, M. Pellicciari, M. Gadaleta, "Energy-optimal motions for Servo-Systems: A comparison of spline interpolants and performance indexes using a CAD-based approach", *Robotics and Computer-Integrated Manufacturing*, 40, Elsevier, 2016, pp 55–65.

[42] E. Oliva, G. Berselli, M. Pellicciari, A. Andrisano, "An engineering method for the power flow assessment in servo-actuated automated machinery: mechatronic modeling and experimental evaluation", *Robotics and Computer-Integrated Manufacturing*, 38, Elsevier, 2016, pp. 31–41.

[43] M. Pellicciari, G. Berselli, F. Balugani, "On designing optimal trajectories for servo-actuated mechanisms: detailed virtual prototyping and experimental evaluation", *IEEE/ASME Transactions of Mechatronics*, 20(5), 2015, pp. 2039–2052.

[44] Y. Wang, K. Ueda, S. Bortoff, "A hamiltonian approach to compute an energy efficient trajectory for a servomotor system", *Automatica*, 49(12), 2013, pp. 3550–3561.

[45] M. Huang, Y. Hsu, R. Fung, "Minimum-energy point-to-point trajectory planning for a motor-toggle servomechanism", *Transactions on Mechatronics*, 17(2), 2012, pp. 337–344.

[46] H. I. Lin, "A fast and unified method to find a minimum-jerk robot joint trajectory using particle swarm optimization", *Journal of Intelligent and Robotic System*, 75, 2014, pp. 379–392.

[47] Z. Miljković, M. Petrović, "Application of modified multi-objective particle swarm optimisation algorithm for flexible process planning problem", *International Journal of Computer Integrated Manufacturing*, 30(2-3), 2017, pp. 271-291.

[48] D. Gleeson, S. Bjorkenstam, R. Bohlin, J. S. Carlson, B. Lennartson, "Towards energy optimization using trajectory smoothing and automatic code generation for robotic assembly", *6th Conference on Assembly Technologies and Syatems (CATS)*, Procedia CIRP, vol. 44, 2016, pp. 341-346.

[49] H. Liu, X. Lai, W. Wu, "Time-optimal and jerk-continuous trajectory planning for robot manipulators with kinematic constraints", *Robotics and Computer-Integrated Manufacturing*, 29(2), 2013, pp. 309–317.

[50] S. Perumaal, N. Jawahar, "Synchronized trigonometric curve trajectory for jerk-bounded time-optimal pick and place operation", *International Journal of Robotics and Automation*, 27(4), 2012, pp. 385-395.

[51] A. Gasparetto, V. Zanotto, "Optimal trajectory planning for industrial robots", *Advances in Engineering Software*, 41, 2010, pp. 548–556.

[52] A. Gasparetto, A. Lanzutti, R. Vidoni, V. Zanotto, "Experimental validation and comparative analysis of optimal time-jerk algorithms for trajectory planning", *Robotics and Computer-Integrated Manufacturing*, 28(2), 2012, pp. 164–181.

[53] F. Liu, F. Lin, "Time-jerk optimal planning of industrial robot trajectories", *International Journal of Robotics and Automation*, 31(1), 2016, pp. 1-7.

[54] H. Duan, R. Zhang, F. Yu, J. Gao, Y. Chen, "Optimal trajectory planning for glass-handing robot based on execution time, acceleration and jerk", *Journal of Robotics, Hindawi Publishing Corporation*, 2016.

[55] H. Esfandiar, M. H. Korayem, "Optimal point to point path planning of flexible manipulator under large deformation by using harmony search method", *Journal of Theoretical and Applied Mechanics*, 54(1), 2016, pp. 179-193.

[56] M. Jafari, A. Shahmansoorian, "PI/Backstepping control of snake robot optimazed by genetic algorithm", *IEEE* 978-1-4799-3010-9/14/, CCECE, Toronto, Canada, 2014.

[57] P. Costa, J. Lima, A. I. Pereira, P. Costa, A. Pinto, "An optimization approach for the inverse kinematics of a highly redundant robot", *Advances in Intelligent Systems and Computing*, 427, Springer, 2016, pp. 433-442.

[58] F. Anton, S. Anton, S. Răileanu, T. Borangiu, "Optimizing trajectory points for high speed robot assembly operations", *Advances in Robot Design and Intelligent Control*, 371, 2016, pp. 127-135.

[59] W. Xiao, J. Huan, "Redundancy and optimization of a 6R robot for five-axis milling applications: singularity, joint limits and collision", *Production Engineering*, 6(3), 2012, pp. 287-296.

[60] S. S. Chiddarwar, N. R. Babu, "Optimal trajectory planning for industrial robot along a specified path with payload constraint using trigonometric splines", *International Journal of Automation and Control*, 6(1), 2012.

[61] S. Alatartsev, S. Stellmacher, F. Ortmeier, "Robotic Task Sequencing Problem: A Survey", *Journal of Intelligent and Robotic System*, 80, 2015, pp. 279–298.

[62] S. Alatartsev, V. Mersheeva, M. Augustine, F. Ortmeier, "On Optimizing a Sequence of Robotic Tasks", *IEEE/RSJ International Conference on Intelligent Robots and Systems (IROS)*, November 3-7, 2013. Tokyo, Japan.

[63] A. Kovács, "Integrated task sequencing and path planning for robotic remote laser welding", *International Journal of Production Research*, 54(4), 2016, pp. 1210–1224.

[64] H. Liu, X. Lai, W. Wu, "Time-optimal and jerk-continuous trajectory planning for robot manipulators with kinematic constraints", *Robotics and Computer-Integrated Manufacturing*, 29(2), 2013, pp. 309–317.

[65] S. Alatartsev, A. Belov, M. Nykolaychuk, F. Ortmeier, "Robot trajectory optimization for the relaxed end-effector path", *Informatics in Control, Automation and Robotics (ICINCO)*, Vienna, Austria, 2014.

[66] T. Nierhoff, S. Hirche, Y. Nakamura, "Spatial adaption of robot trajectories based on laplacian trajectory editing", *Autonomous Robots*, 40, Springer, 2016, pp. 159–173.

* Corresponding author: mratiu@uoradea.ro

Parameterized finite element analysis of a superplastic forming process, using Ansys®

Gavril Grebenişan[1*], *Sanda* Bogdan[2]

[1]University of Oradea, e-mail: grebe@uoradea.ro
[2]University of Oradea, e-mail: sandaromocea@yahoo.com

Abstract: A theoretical and experimental analysis was carried out, after superplastic forming, of Al-Ti-V-based alloy sheets, of hemispherical parts, as the start point of research. Based on the measurements i.e. the quantitative and qualitative determinations of the manufactured parts, work reports have been prepared to contain the magnitude of variations in the thickness of the parts, in cross-section, as well as references to the surface quality and the local thinning of the walls of the part. The experimental study was followed by a parameterized finite elements analysis of the process, using Ansys®, Explicit Dynamics Module, This being for examining the next step of our study, comparing the experimental results with the theoretical analysis, based on two input parameters: and discussing the results, and very necessary, the correlation between input and output parameters, mainly the influence magnitude rate of input parameters on output parameters.

1 Introduction

The parameterized analysis has as its main objective the discovery and accentuation of the role of each input parameter on the evolution of the process, mainly on the output parameters chosen by the operator. It is known that superplastic forming is a process whose duration is superior to similar plastic deformation processes, primarily due to the extremely low strain rate. This major disadvantage in the economy of the process and the calculation of economic efficiency is countered by the broad applicability of this process in areas of particular interest: aeronautics, automobiles, medicine, and robotics.
The superplasticity is defined in the scientific literature as a more metallurgical phenomenon and is manifested in some materials, mainly alloys based on Al, Ti, V, Zn, Cu, but also on some low carbon steels. These alloys or metals, which have superplastic characteristics, exhibit a long and uniform deformation at extremely low deformation rates and relatively high temperatures (> $0.5T_{melt}$), and the grain structure is characterized by grain sizes of about 10 micrometers. The term "superplasticity" was introduced in 1945 by A.A. Bochvar and Z.A. Sviderskaia [1] when analyzing the behavior of the Zn + 22% Al eutectic alloy, having an ultrafine structure. Since 1960, the phenomenon has been researched for promising practical applications, which has determined that the main conditions for the development of superplastic behavior are elucidated and then created in metallurgical research labs. In particular, the realization of the granular microstructure, the methods of grinding the rough structure, and the reduction of grain sizes up to 10 μm, have been achieved successfully. Another parameter of superplastic deformation, namely strain rate, which was estimated to be effective, in the range (10^{-5} to 10^{-1} [s^{-1}]), at relatively high temperature (> 0.5 T_{melt}, where T_{melt} is the melting temperature of the alloy expressed in [K]) at low values of deformation pressure., made this technology to be received with caution by engineering technology science. But the advantages that superplastic deformed parts exhibit, the dimensional fidelity, the accuracy of multiple profiles, and the dimensional stability at temperature variations in the operating environment, such as those in the aerospace industry, have recommended this process as an extremely efficient and suitable one for cutting edge technology. Using alloy Zn + 22% Al alloy, W.A. Backofen, I.R. Turner, and D.H. Avery [2] conducted tests and researches on the behavior of this material in simple traction and extrusion respectively, then processing, from this material, parts with a relatively complex configuration as a geometric profile. The Zn + 22% Al superplastic alloy plate had a thickness of s = 0.76 (mm), the diameter of the die was 100 (mm), and the working air pressure in the die was 0.1 to 0.2 (MPa).
The special structure, i.e. the ultrafine structure, as the most significant constraint on the superplastic behavior

* Corresponding author: grebe@uoradea.ro

of the material, is the size of the ultra-fine granules, which must be less than 10 micrometers. From the metallurgical phenomena that characterize superplastic behavior, the balance between maintaining the ultra-fine grain structure, coagulation development, and growth (at deformation temperature) is one of the main objectives of the study of superplastic behavior in the world. Methods of refining the structure, which can be summarized in the following consecutive types: phase separation, the phase transformation or mechanical processing accompanied by recrystallization are used for the majority of superplastic materials.

It should be emphasized, however, that the realization of ultra-fine structures is not a sufficient condition to guarantee the behavior of a superplastic material but must provide methods and conditions for maintaining the fine grain size. Grain growth is highlighted in superplastic areas deformed, and non-deformed areas are less (experimental observations).

The superplastic behavior of materials is characterized by law established by W.A. Backofen, I.R. Turner, and D.H. Avery [2], known as an extended power-law model:

$$\bar{\sigma} = K \cdot \varepsilon^n \cdot \dot{\varepsilon}^m \quad (1)$$

where $\bar{\sigma}$ s is the equivalent flow stress, K is the strength coefficient, ε is the equivalent strain, n is the work-hardening index, $\dot{\bar{\varepsilon}}$ is the equivalent strain rate, and m is the strain rate sensitivity index, the mathematical expression of which is given by $m = \ln(\text{stress}) / \ln(\text{strain rate})$ the gradient of the logarithmic curve. Other authors, N. Chandra [3], proposed a more comprehensive expression of the uniaxial flow stress. This is seen to be a highly dependent of inelastic strain-rate $\dot{\bar{\varepsilon}}$ and a weak function of strain ε and grain size d:

$$\sigma = f(\varepsilon, \dot{\varepsilon}, d) \quad (2)$$

which expressed in the logarithmic form, become:

$$\ln\sigma = F(\ln\varepsilon, \ln\dot{\varepsilon}, \ln d) \quad (3)$$

That may be written in the manner expanded as Taylor series, at a given equilibrium state, with neglecting the higher order terms:

$$\sigma = K_1 \cdot \varepsilon^n \cdot \dot{\varepsilon}^m \cdot d^p \quad (4)$$

Where we denoted K_1, m, n, p, are the material's coefficients, having the mathematical forms: $n = \frac{\partial(\ln\sigma)}{\partial(\ln\varepsilon)}$; $m = \frac{\partial(\ln\sigma)}{\partial(\ln\dot{\varepsilon})}$; $p = \frac{\partial(\ln\sigma)}{\partial(\ln d)}$, with the following significant expressions: m is the strain rate sensitivity, n is the strain hardening exponent, and p is the grain growth exponent.

For the study that we are going to accomplish, we should, theoretically at least, to find some evaluations regarding the influence of some of the geometric parameters, material parameters, respectively technological parameters, on the output parameters, in a design study. These assessments, in the alternative, could lead to a project optimization analysis using either single objective or multi-objective methods, depending on project constraints. Thus, using the studies presented by P, F. Dunne and N. Petrinic [4], a cylindrical specimen with the initial dimensions L (length) and A (undeformed area) upon which a force acts, will be characterized, after deformation, by the following parameters: A + dA, L + dL, σ + dσ, $\dot{\varepsilon}$+ d$\dot{\varepsilon}$, respectively. By imposing the incompressibility condition, so the volume remains constant, by neglecting the infinitesimal small terms, it is obtained:

$$\mathbf{AL = (A + dA)(L + dL) \approx AL + LdA + AdL} \quad (5)$$

one obtain

$$\frac{dA}{dt} = -\dot{\varepsilon}A \quad (6)$$

which, become (applied for deformed zone):

$$\frac{d(A+dA)}{dt} = -(\dot{\varepsilon} + d\dot{\varepsilon})(A + dA) \quad (7)$$

so:

$$\frac{d}{dt}(dA) \approx -(Ad\dot{\varepsilon} + \dot{\varepsilon}dA) = -\dot{\varepsilon}dA\left(\frac{A}{dA}\frac{d\dot{\varepsilon}}{\dot{\varepsilon}} + 1\right) \quad (8)$$

As the force is constant, we obtain:

$$\sigma A = (\sigma + d\sigma)(A + dA), \text{ or } \frac{d\sigma}{\sigma} = -\frac{dA}{A} \quad (10)$$

Applying the constitutive equation, expressed in effective values(we neglect, for the seek of comprehensibility and mathematical simplification): $\sigma = K\dot{\varepsilon}^m$, one obtain:

$$\sigma + d\sigma = K(\dot{\varepsilon} + d\dot{\varepsilon})^m = K\dot{\varepsilon}^m\left(1 + \frac{d\dot{\varepsilon}}{\dot{\varepsilon}}\right)^m = K\dot{\varepsilon}^m\left[1 + m\frac{d\dot{\varepsilon}}{\dot{\varepsilon}} + \cdots\right] \quad (11)$$

This relationship may be written as:

$$\frac{d\sigma}{\sigma} \approx m\frac{d\dot{\varepsilon}}{\dot{\varepsilon}}, \text{ or } \frac{A}{dA}\frac{d\dot{\varepsilon}}{\dot{\varepsilon}} = -\frac{1}{m} \quad (12)$$

so that

$$\frac{d}{dt}(dA) \approx -dA\dot{\varepsilon}\left(1 - \frac{1}{m}\right) \quad (13)$$

The previous relationship shows that the magnitude of deformation $\frac{d}{dt}(dA)$, depends on value of $\left(1 - \frac{1}{m}\right)$ term. Thus, it can be concluded that the strain rate sensitivity, m, increases, and takes 1 as value, while local necking, $\frac{d}{dt}(dA)$ decreases to zero. Hence, the significance of

* Corresponding author: grebe@uoradea.ro

strain sensitivity in the superplastic forming process resides: that is, the high value for there is no local gouging, which allows for a pronounced stretching. This is the essence of superplastic deformation: the ability of materials to exhibit very broad, uniform deformations without the appearance of local rusting. This is the explanation for which we chose *Sample_Diameter*(this determine, or not(this will be revealed, after parameterized analysis results will be obtained) the magnitude of necking, as the first of the input parameters, with the objective of studying the influence of this parameter on stress deformation, strain deformation and total deformation(the output parameters).

2 Experiments and parameterized analysis

In order to setup the parameterized analysis a second input parameter was chosen: *Sample_Thickness*. We'll show, next steps, why we chosen this second geometrical parameter as an input parameter, to study the influence of output parameters, above named: stress deformation, strain deformation, and total deformation. Our demonstration is based on applying the membrane theory, G. Giuliano [5], in order to reveal the stress state in a thin sheet loaded by pressure *P*, with *s* as thickness, R_θ and R_φ are the curvature radii ($R_\theta - meridian\ radius; R_\varphi - circumpherential\ radii$), fig. 1:

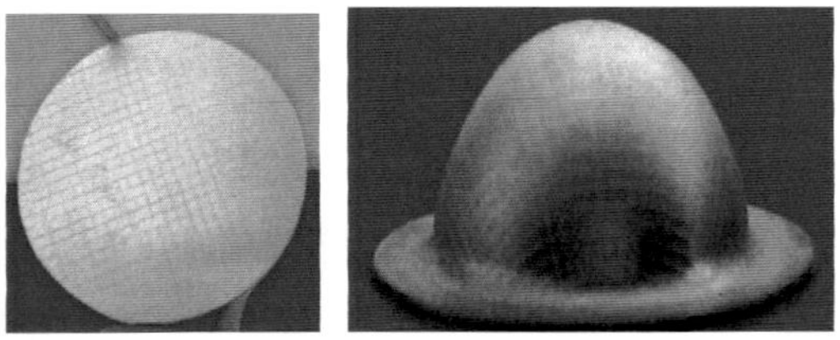

Fig. 1. The meshed sample(before the forming)-left; The meshed part, superplastic formed-right, G. Grebenişan and S. Mureşan [6]

Follow the assumptions, the state of equilibrium is described as:

$$\mathbf{2\sigma_\varphi sin\left(\frac{d\varphi}{2}\right) sR_\theta d\theta + 2\sigma_\theta sin\left(\frac{d\theta}{2}\right) sR_\varphi d\varphi = pR_\varphi d\varphi R_\theta d\theta}, \quad (14)$$

moreover, assuming the forced approximation, $\mathbf{sin}\left(\frac{d\varphi}{2}\right) \cong \frac{d\varphi}{2}$, the previous equation may be rewritten as:

$$\frac{\sigma_\varphi}{R_\varphi} + \frac{\sigma_\theta}{R_\theta} = \frac{p}{s} \quad (15)$$

Using the evidence $\mathbf{\sigma_\theta sin(\varphi) \cdot 2\pi rs = p\pi r^2}$, and $\mathbf{r = R_\varphi sin(\varphi)}$, than, the tangential stress, and the circumferential stress are estimated, respectively, with relationships:

$$\sigma_\theta = \frac{pR_\varphi}{2s} \quad (16)$$

$$\sigma_\varphi = \frac{pR_\varphi}{2s}\left(2 - \frac{R_\varphi}{R_\theta}\right) \quad (17)$$

One may apply the von Mises criterion, for calculating the equivalent stress, for plain stress condition(assuming that the $thickness\ stress\ \sigma_t = 0$):

$$\bar{\sigma} = \sqrt{\sigma_\theta^2 + \sigma_\varphi^2 - \sigma_\theta\sigma_\varphi} = \frac{pR_\varphi}{2s}\sqrt{\left(\frac{R_\varphi}{R_\theta}\right)^2 - 3\frac{R_\varphi}{R_\theta} + 3} \quad (18)$$

Considering that the elastic strain is negligible, a relationship between stresses and strains magnitude, in the plastic domain, using the Levy-Mises flow rule to obtain the expressions for tangential($\dot{\varepsilon}_\theta$), circumferential($\dot{\varepsilon}_\varphi$) and thickness($\dot{\varepsilon}_t$) strain rate are as follows:

$$\dot{\varepsilon}_\theta = \frac{\dot{\bar{\varepsilon}}}{\bar{\sigma}}\left[\sigma_\theta - \frac{1}{2}(\sigma_\varphi + \sigma_t)\right]$$

$$\dot{\varepsilon}_\varphi = \frac{\dot{\bar{\varepsilon}}}{\bar{\sigma}}\left[\sigma_\varphi - \frac{1}{2}(\sigma_\theta + \sigma_t)\right] \quad (19)$$

$$\dot{\varepsilon}_t = \frac{\dot{\bar{\varepsilon}}}{\bar{\sigma}}\left[\sigma_t - \frac{1}{2}(\sigma_\varphi + \sigma_\theta)\right]$$

Considering the incompressibility law, so the volume variation is null ($\mathbf{\varepsilon_\theta + \varepsilon_\varphi + \varepsilon_t = const,\ \dot{\varepsilon}_\theta + \dot{\varepsilon}_\varphi + \dot{\varepsilon}_t = 0}$), the equivalent strain rate, calculated based on von Mises criterion is:

$$\dot{\bar{\varepsilon}} = \frac{2}{\sqrt{3}}\sqrt{\dot{\varepsilon}_\theta^2 + \dot{\varepsilon}_\varphi^2 + \dot{\varepsilon}_\theta\dot{\varepsilon}_\varphi} \quad (20)$$

The analyzed part is a hemisphere, and, by definition, $R_\theta = R_\varphi = R$, so one may write:

$$\sigma_\theta = \sigma_\varphi = \frac{pR}{2s} \quad (21)$$

and Levy- Mises equations are:

$$\dot{\bar{\varepsilon}} = -\dot{\varepsilon}_t = 2\dot{\varepsilon}_\theta = 2\dot{\varepsilon}_\varphi \quad (22)$$

We may use an empirical relationship for estimate the stresses:

$$\sigma_\theta = \frac{pR}{2s}$$

$$\sigma_\varphi = \frac{\sigma_\theta}{2} \quad (23)$$

$$\bar{\sigma} = \sqrt{3} \cdot \sigma_\varphi = \frac{\sqrt{3}}{2}\sigma_\theta$$

and strains are:

$$\dot{\varepsilon}_\theta = 0$$

* Corresponding author: grebe@uoradea.ro

 DOI: 10.1051/matecconf/201712603001

$$\dot{\varepsilon}_{\varphi} = -\dot{\varepsilon}_{t} \tag{24}$$

$$\dot{\bar{\varepsilon}} = \frac{2}{\sqrt{3}}\dot{\varepsilon}_{\varphi} = -\frac{2}{\sqrt{3}}\dot{\varepsilon}_{t}$$

Using the considerations of F. Jovane [7], also F.U Enikeev and A.A Kruglov [8], respectively, of which the thickness is uniform on all directions, one may obtain a relationship for R and average thickness, $\bar{s}$, respectively, :

$$\mathbf{R} = \frac{a^2+h^2}{2h} \tag{25}$$

and

$$\bar{\mathbf{s}} = \mathbf{s_0}\frac{a^2}{a^2+h^2} \tag{26}$$

where h is the sphere height at the instance t, and a is the initial radius of the sample sheet (the input parameter *Sample_diameter*).

Although, for an optimal strain rate, $\dot{\bar{\varepsilon}}_{opt}$, experimentaly obtained, at which one may consider that the forming process occurs, i.e. the strain rate that the sensitive index m has the highest value, and the process temperature known, G. Giuliano [5] had obtained the expressions for the preasure, as function of the sphere relative to height, H=h/a:

$$\bar{\sigma} = \frac{pa}{4s_0}\frac{(1+H^2)^2}{H} \tag{27}$$

$$\dot{\bar{\varepsilon}} = \frac{2H}{1+H^2}\cdot\dot{\mathbf{H}} \tag{28}$$

and

$$\mathbf{p} = \frac{4s_0K\dot{\bar{\varepsilon}}^{m}_{opt}}{a}\frac{H}{(1+H^2)^2};\ \text{where } \mathbf{H} = \sqrt{\mathbf{e}^{\dot{\bar{\varepsilon}}_{opt}t} - \mathbf{1}} \tag{29}$$

3 Results and discussion

There were setup two input parameters, namely: P1-Sample_diameter and P8- Sample_Thickness, and three output parameters P5-Equivalent Stress Maximum, P6-Total Deformation Maximum and P7-Equivalent Plastic Strain Maximum, respectively, shows in fig. 2. For each of these parameters was monitored the only influence, the Parameter Correlation operation was done for this reason after the Design Points was calculated and updated, fig. 3. Updating the Design Points were realized the map of the Correlation Parameter System, fig. 4. This update offers a complete set of tools for study and analyzes the influence of input parameters, on output parameters, fig. 5. Examples of the Correlation Scatter between input parameters and output parameters(pairs composed by one input parameter and one output parameter) are shown in fig. 6 to fig. 8. The fig. 9 shows the influence magnitude of one input parameter on one output parameter: the value 1 means good influence,

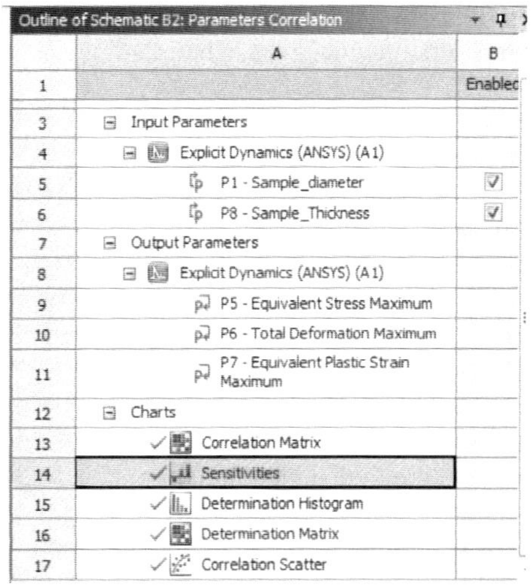
Outline of Schematic B2: Parameters Correlation

	A	B
1		Enabled
3	Input Parameters	
4	Explicit Dynamics (ANSYS) (A1)	
5	P1 - Sample_diameter	✓
6	P8 - Sample_Thickness	✓
7	Output Parameters	
8	Explicit Dynamics (ANSYS) (A1)	
9	P5 - Equivalent Stress Maximum	
10	P6 - Total Deformation Maximum	
11	P7 - Equivalent Plastic Strain Maximum	
12	Charts	
13	Correlation Matrix	
14	Sensitivities	
15	Determination Histogram	
16	Determination Matrix	
17	Correlation Scatter	

Fig. 2. The input and output parameters settings

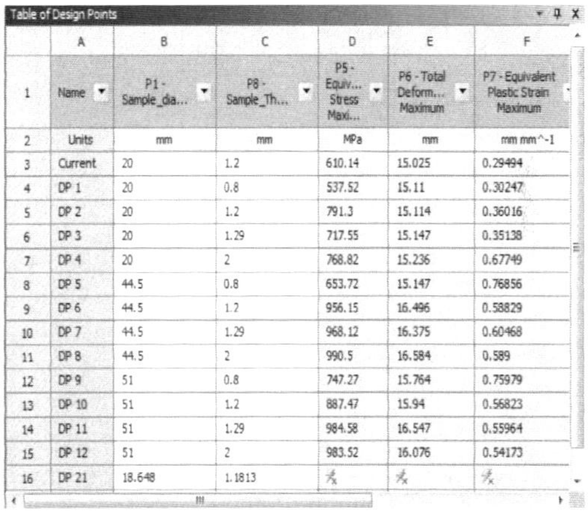
Table of Design Points

	A	B	C	D	E	F
1	Name	P1 - Sample_dia...	P8 - Sample_Th...	P5 - Equiv... Stress Maxi...	P6 - Total Deform... Maximum	P7 - Equivalent Plastic Strain Maximum
2	Units	mm	mm	MPa	mm	mm mm^-1
3	Current	20	1.2	610.14	15.025	0.29494
4	DP 1	20	0.8	537.52	15.11	0.30247
5	DP 2	20	1.2	791.3	15.114	0.36016
6	DP 3	20	1.29	717.55	15.147	0.35138
7	DP 4	20	2	768.82	15.236	0.67749
8	DP 5	44.5	0.8	653.72	15.147	0.76856
9	DP 6	44.5	1.2	956.15	16.496	0.58829
10	DP 7	44.5	1.29	968.12	16.375	0.60468
11	DP 8	44.5	2	990.5	16.584	0.589
12	DP 9	51	0.8	747.27	15.764	0.75979
13	DP 10	51	1.2	887.47	15.94	0.56823
14	DP 11	51	1.29	984.58	16.547	0.55964
15	DP 12	51	2	983.52	16.076	0.54173
16	DP 21	18.648	1.1813			

Fig.3. The Design Points updated table

Fig. 4. Analysis system settings

---
[*] Corresponding author: grebe@uoradea.ro

DOI: 10.1051/matecconf/201712603001

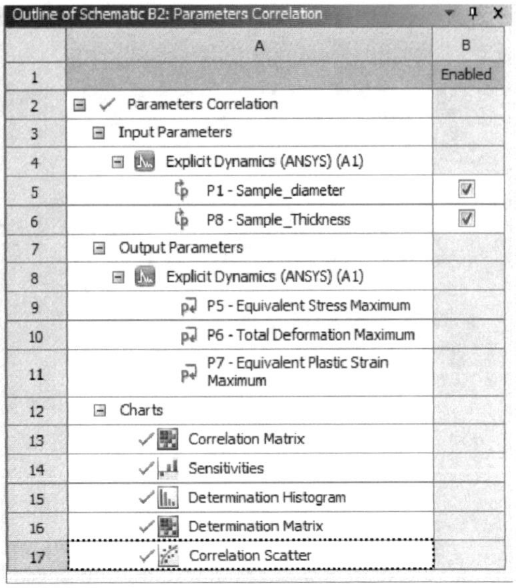

Outline of Schematic B2: Parameters Correlation

	A	B
1		Enabled
2	⊟ ✓ Parameters Correlation	
3	⊟ Input Parameters	
4	⊟ Explicit Dynamics (ANSYS) (A1)	
5	P1 - Sample_diameter	☑
6	P8 - Sample_Thickness	☑
7	⊟ Output Parameters	
8	⊟ Explicit Dynamics (ANSYS) (A1)	
9	P5 - Equivalent Stress Maximum	
10	P6 - Total Deformation Maximum	
11	P7 - Equivalent Plastic Strain Maximum	
12	⊟ Charts	
13	✓ Correlation Matrix	
14	✓ Sensitivities	
15	✓ Determination Histogram	
16	✓ Determination Matrix	
17	✓ Correlation Scatter	

Fig. 5. The Parameters Correlation updated table

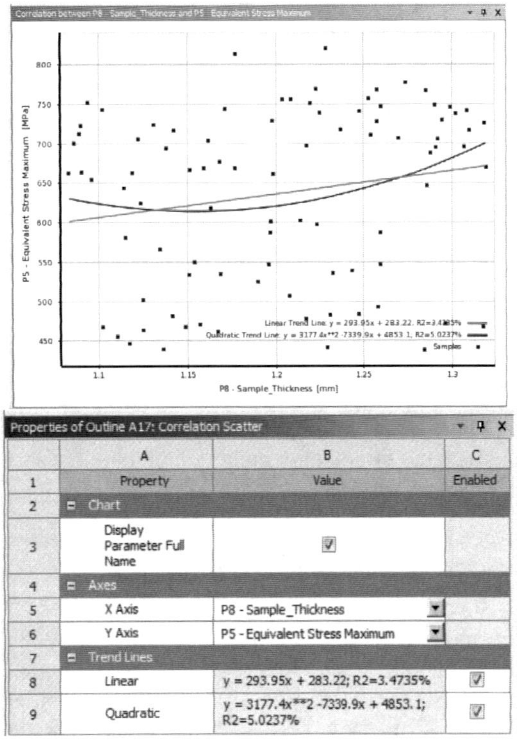

Properties of Outline A17: Correlation Scatter

	A	B	C
1	Property	Value	Enabled
2	⊟ Chart		
3	Display Parameter Full Name	☑	
4	⊟ Axes		
5	X Axis	P8 - Sample_Thickness	
6	Y Axis	P5 - Equivalent Stress Maximum	
7	⊟ Trend Lines		
8	Linear	y = 293.95x + 283.22; R2=3.4735%	☑
9	Quadratic	y = 3177.4x**2 -7339.9x + 4853.1; R2=5.0237%	☑

Fig. 6. The Correlation Scatter, between P8 and P5 parameters

otherwise, the increasing of the input parameter, produce an increasing of one output parameter. A negative value means an inverse influence: the increasing of the input parameter, produce a decreasing of the output parameter. The Sensitivities of the output parameters with respect to the input parameters represents the major influence(positive graph), or minor influence(negative graph). The fig. 11 presents the determination (the high value means the strong influence). The greatest value possible is 1.

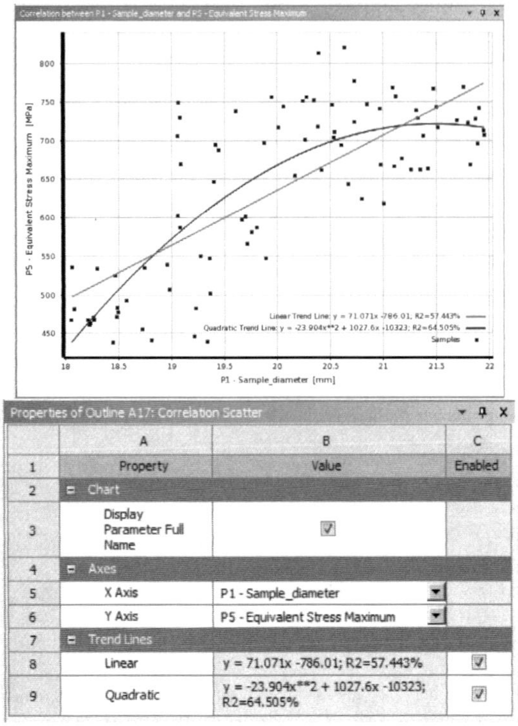

Properties of Outline A17: Correlation Scatter

	A	B	C
1	Property	Value	Enabled
2	⊟ Chart		
3	Display Parameter Full Name	☑	
4	⊟ Axes		
5	X Axis	P1 - Sample_diameter	
6	Y Axis	P5 - Equivalent Stress Maximum	
7	⊟ Trend Lines		
8	Linear	y = 71.071x -786.01; R2=57.443%	☑
9	Quadratic	y = -23.904x**2 + 1027.6x -10323; R2=64.505%	☑

Fig. 7. Correlation Scatter between P1 and P5 parameters

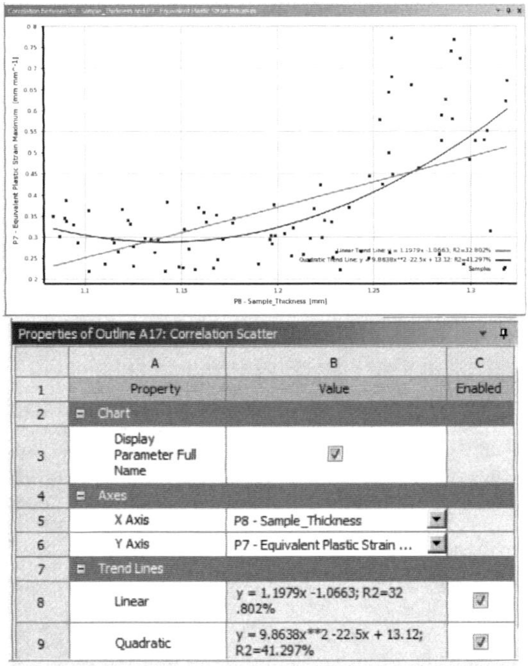

Properties of Outline A17: Correlation Scatter

	A	B	C
1	Property	Value	Enabled
2	⊟ Chart		
3	Display Parameter Full Name	☑	
4	⊟ Axes		
5	X Axis	P8 - Sample_Thickness	
6	Y Axis	P7 - Equivalent Plastic Strain ...	
7	⊟ Trend Lines		
8	Linear	y = 1.1979x -1.0663; R2=32 .802%	☑
9	Quadratic	y = 9.8638x**2 -22.5x + 13.12; R2=41.297%	☑

Fig. 8. Correlation Scatter between P8 and P7 parameters

* Corresponding author: grebe@uoradea.ro

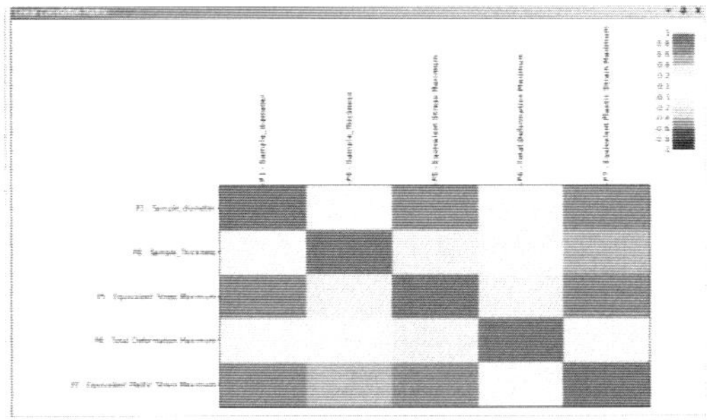

Fig. 9. The Correlation Matrix

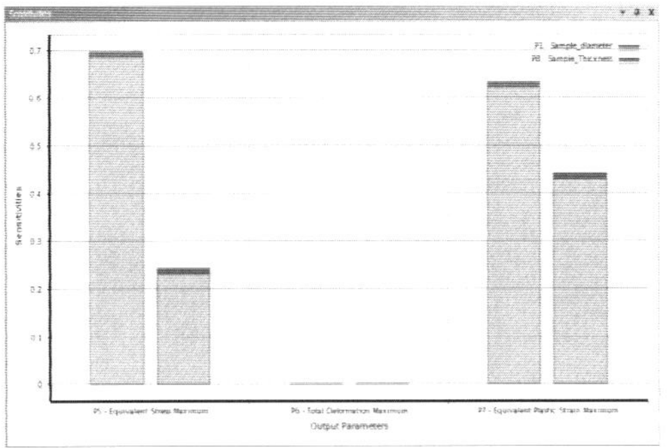

Fig. 10. The Sensitivities of output parameters on input parameters

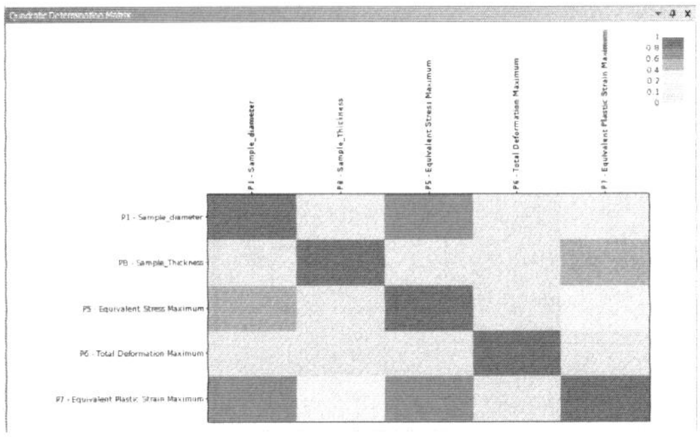

Fig. 11. Determination Matrix

The fig. 12 shows the summary of the Correlation Parameters expressed in value comprised between -1 and +1. The table highlighted in fig. 12 presents, also, the start of Design Points table.

Table of Schematic B2: Parameters Correlation

	A	B	C	D	E	F
1	Name	P1 - Sample_diam... (mm)	P8 - Sample_Thic... (mm)	P5 - Equivalent Stress Maximum (MPa)	P6 - Total Deformation Maximum (mm)	P7 - Equivalent Plastic Strain Maximum (mm mm^-1)
2	Correlation Matrix (Linear)					
3	P1 - Sample_diamet	1	-0.084372	0.6966	-0.053422	0.6332
4	P8 - Sample_Thickne	-0.084372	1	0.24299	-0.062564	0.4427
5	P5 - Equivalent Stress Maximum	0.6966	0.24299	1	-0.1093	0.72782
6	P6 - Total Deformation Maximum	-0.053422	-0.062564	-0.1093	1	-0.075077
7	P7 - Equivalent Plastic Strain Maximum	0.6332	0.4427	0.72782	-0.075077	1
8	Determination Matrix (Quadratic)					
9	P1 - Sample_diamet	1	0.0085432	0.64505	0.071996	0.11209
10	P8 - Sample_Thickne	0.030544	1	0.050237	0.018609	0.41297
11	P5 - Equivalent Stress Maximum	0.59291	0.055711	1	0.0045101	0.29454
12	P6 - Total Deformation Maximum	0.093859	0.00899	0.085034	1	0.026319
13	P7 - Equivalent Plastic Strain Maximum	0.6882	0.33202	0.66502	0.0035194	1
14	Design Points					
15	1	20.168	1.0961	654.06	15.344	0.28696
16	2	21.325	1.1979	728.44	15.285	0.37769
17	3	20.674	1.114	643.21	15.11	0.2959
18	4	21.01	1.163	618.72	15.065	0.33633
19	5	18.082	1.1414	481.59	15.319	0.21869

Fig. 12. Values of input and output parameters correlation

References

[1]. A.A. Bochvar, and Z.A. Sviderskaia, "Superplasticity in Zinc-Aluminum Alloys," Izv. Akad. Nauk SSSR, Otd. Tekh. Nauk, 9 (1945), 821-827.

[2]. W.A. Backofen, I.R. Turner, D.H. Avery - Superplasticity in an Al-Zn Alloy, Trans. ASM, 57 (1964), pp. 980-990.

[3]. N. Chandra, Constitutive behavior of superplastic materials, International Journal of Non-Linear Mechanics 37 (2002) 461}484

[4]. F. Dunne, N. Petrinic, Introduction to Computational Plasticity, Oxford University Press, 2005.

[5]. G. Giuliano, Superplastic forming of advanced metallic materials, Methods and Applications, Oxford, © Woodhead Publishing Limited, 2011.

[6]. G. Grebenişan and S. Mureşan, *Numerical Study Of Volumic Forming On Superplastic Behaviour,* Annals of The University of Oradea. Fascicle of Management and Technological Engineering, Volume XVI (VI), ISSN 1583-0691, DOI: 10.15660/AUOFMTE.2007.714, 2007.

[7]. F. Jovane, An approximate analysis of the superplastic forming of a thin circular diaphragm: theory and experiments, Int. J. Mech. Sci., Pergamon Press. 1968. Vol. 10, pp. 405-427. Printed in Great Britain.

[8]. F.U. Enikeev and A.A. Kruglov, An analysis of the superplastic forming of a thin circular diaphragm *International Journal of Mechanical Science*, 37 (5): 473 – 483

* Corresponding author: grebe@uoradea.ro

Simulating the electrical characteristics of a photovoltaic cell based on a single-diode equivalent circuit model

Syeda Adila Afghan[1*], *Husam* Almusawi[2], *Husi* Geza[3]

[1]University of Debrecen, Doctoral School of Informatics, adila@eng.unideb.hu, Pakistan
[2] University of Debrecen, asd_sw@ymail.com, Hungary
[3] University of Debrecen, husigeza@eng.unideb.hu, Hungary

Abstract. This research work presents the simulation based study of a commercial solar cell for analyzing the real-time behavior of a PV module. The mathematical modelling is based on Equivalent circuit of the solar cell and demonstrating the practical approach for using the single diode five parameters (IM5P) mechanism. This research involves purely mathematical formulation to extract the unknown parameters of PV cell by applying the Lambert W function. The I – V and P – V characteristics are emulated under different temperature and radiation levels by using the Linear Technology's LTSpice simulator.

1 Introduction

The world is facing huge energy crises and we will run out of fuel coal and gases by 2071 as it is predicted by CIA (Central Intelligence Agency) [1].This is an alarming situation which emphasizes the researchers and scientists around the globe to make alternative possible solutions. Energy harvesting is the only hope to overcome this issue, however, renewable energy sources can be utilized to tackle most of the energy hungry devices whether it is in form of a large-scale applications like solar systems power generators or a small scale domestic use like cell phone, Ipods, and wireless sensor networks, elaborated in a recent review by A. S. Adila, A. Husam, J. H. Sana G. Husi [2]. The most viable source which can equip greener ways successfully since last decade is solar energy.

The Photovoltaic market have seen rapid growth for solar power systems that entertains the possible gap of renewable energy interpretation for both macro and micro systems as reported in Ren21 [3]. A Photovoltaic system converts the sunlight directly into electricity and the main device is solar cell in the system. Solar cell arrays are formed by grouping them together. The electronic converters play a viable role for processing the electricity from the PV system as defined by M. G. Villalva, J. R. Gazoli, E. R. Filho [4]. A solar cell is made of semiconductor diode which is exposed to light and consists of various types of semiconductors using different manufacturing processes as reviewed by A. S. Sedra, K. C. Smith [5]. M.A. Eltawil, Z. Zhao discussed that the incoming solar radiations and the intrinsic properties are responsible for the electric energy generation in a solar cell [6]. The solar radiation is composed of photons of various energies, some of them are absorbed at p-n junction as shown in Fig 1., described in Union of Concerned Scientists [7]. If the photons with energies are lower than the bandgap of the solar cell, they are useless and will not generate electric current or voltage. Whereas, photons with energy higher than the bandgap will generate electricity and the energy corresponding to the bandgap will be used only. The remaining energy is dissipated as heat in the body of solar cell as mentioned by J. Bikaneria, S. P. Joshi, A. R. Joshi [8].

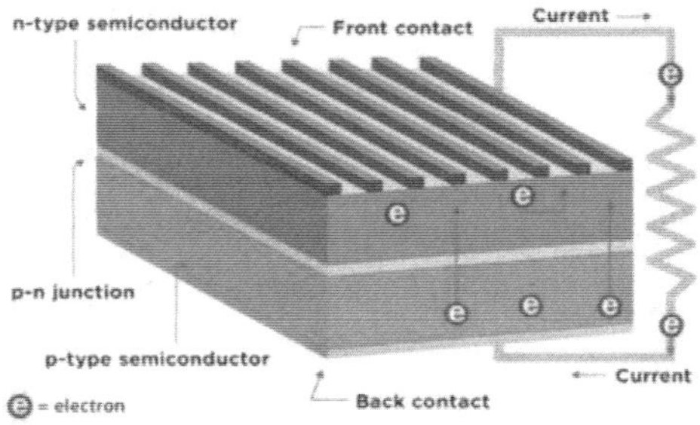

Fig 1. Schematic diagram demonstrating the operation of p-n junction of a Solar Cell

* Corresponding author: adila@eng.unideb.hu

Despite of widely adopted renewable solar solution, there's still lack of understanding the performance efficiency and power extraction, when it comes to the selection of solar panels or arrays by the end users. Many mathematical models are highlighted for demonstrating the non-linear response of a PV system as highlight by E. M. G. Rodrigues, R. Melicio, V. M. F. Mendes and J. P. S. Catalao [9]. The common technique is to model the solar equivalent circuit and amongst all possible parametric models, the single diode model is the popular one, which is also known as 1M5P (Single Mechanism, Five Parameters). It is used to predict the real-time behavior of a solar cell mentioned by Yetayew and Jyothsna [10]. For I – V and P – V characteristics, the complicated procedure is required which involves certain equations and calculations. The solar cell involves non-linear and exponential expressions that results the equations as implicit, which is complicated, iterative, and time consuming. J. Cubas, S. Pindado, C. D. Manuel [11] demonstrated in their research that the explicit technique is required which consists of analytical formulation with use of Lambert W function for making the parametric model simpler. In this paper, the single diode equivalent circuit is being modelled for a commercial solar cell for obtaining the unknown parameters from the manufacturer's datasheet. Matlab is used for the formulation of the explicit expressions whereas, the LTSpice circuit simulator is used to model and simulate the performance of solar cell by demonstrating the I – V and P – V curves at temperature and irradiations variations of solar equivalent circuit.

2 Modelling of solar cell

2.1 Ideal single diode model for photovoltaic cell

The photovoltaic technology is based on the principle of electron hole creation in each cell that consists of two different layers; p type and n type. However, The I - V curve characteristics of a solar cell are like the exponential characteristics of the ideal diode as described by Walker [12]. To understand the phenomenon of any solar cell, panel or an array, it is needed to derive the electrical parameters of PV cell in to the equivalent circuit as a necessary requirement.

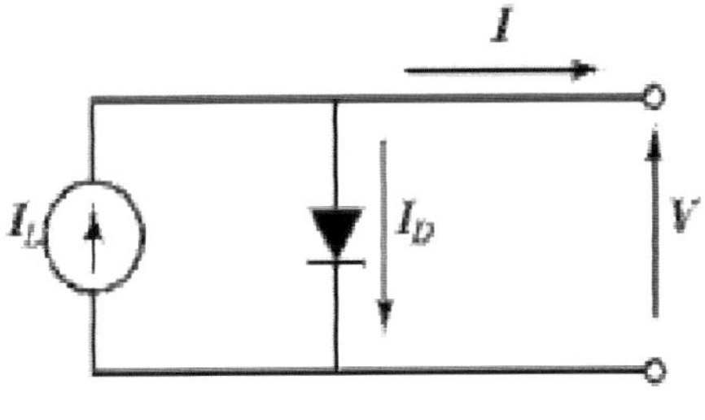

Fig. 2. Ideal Single Diode Model (1M3P)

As shown in the Fig. 2, the ideal solar cell consists of current source I_L, which is parallel to the diode I_D. The model containing 3 parameters also known as 1M3P (Single mechanism three parameters) suggested by M. Azzouzi, D. Popescu and M. Bouchahdane [13].

Therefore, the equation can be derived by using the Kirchhoff's law:

$$\mathbf{I = I_L - I_D} \quad (1)$$

Where I_D equals to,

$$\mathbf{I_D = I_O \left[\exp\left(\frac{V}{AV_T}\right) - 1\right]}$$

The output current is represented by the following non-linear I – V equation:

$$\mathbf{I = I_L - I_O \left[\exp\left(\frac{V}{AV_T}\right) - 1\right]} \quad (2)$$

However, this model does not be able to produce accurate results for modelling I – V and P – V curves of a solar cell.

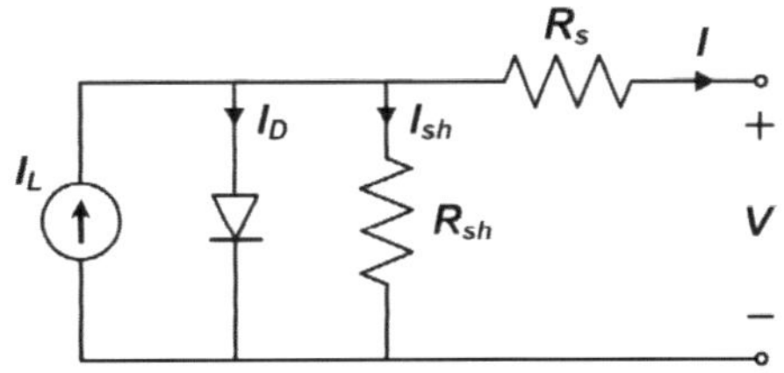

Fig. 3. Single Diode Equivalent Circuit (1M5P)

2.2 Single diode model with series and shunt resistors

To specify the most popular and practical functioning of a solar cell, M. Wolf and H. Rauschenbach [14] denoted the representation of losses by the resistors as shown in the Fig. 3, having a current source connected in parallel with a diode and two resistors, one in series and other in parallel.

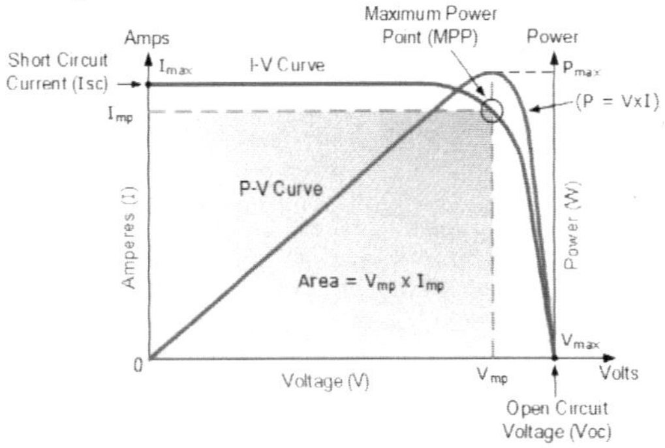

Fig. 4. I – V and P – V characteristics of a typical solar cell

Azzouzi, Popescu and Bouchahdane [13] also mentioned that this model composed of five parameters for which it known as 1M5P (Single mechanism, five parameters), as current, voltage, and power curves can be easily deduced by this model by calculating the five unknown parameters. Mostly the short circuit, open

* Corresponding author: adila@eng.unideb.hu

circuit and maximum power points are included in the datasheet of solar cells as illustrated in Fig. 4.

3 Mathmatical modeling of single diode equivalent circuit

A. Wafaa, A. M. Ashraf, A. Fouad, S. Saad [15] described that it is important to derive the characteristics equations for solar cell for calculating the five-parameters of an equivalent solar circuit. Considering the Fig. 3, the equation is given as:

$$I = I_L - I_D - I_{sh} \quad (3)$$

To fully define the relationship between the output current of photovoltaic cell and the terminal voltage for the single diode model is given by the following equation:

$$I = I_L - I_o\left[\exp\left(\frac{V+IR_s}{aV_T}\right) - 1\right] - \frac{V+IR_s}{R_{sh}} \quad (4)$$

Along with Thermal Voltage; $V_T = n\frac{KT}{q}$ [V]

Where I_L denotes the current generated by the incidence of light, I_D denotes the diode current, R_S represents the series resistance, for leakage current R_{sh} is denoted as Shunt resistor, a is the ideality factor, Vt is the thermal voltage, q as an electron charge, the Boltzman constant K; the n as number of cells in series and T as the temperature.

Solar cell is required to be characterized by the short circuit current Isc, the open circuit voltage Voc, and ideality factor a. Equation (4) can be rewritten as:

Short Circuit current: I = Isc, for V=0

$$I_{sc} = I_L - I_o\left[\exp\left(\frac{I_{sc}R_s}{aV_T}\right) - 1\right] - \frac{I_{sc}R_s}{R_{sh}} \quad (5)$$

Open circuit Voltage: I = 0 for V = Voc

$$0 = I_L - I_o\left[\exp\left(\frac{V_{oc}}{aV_T}\right) - 1\right] - \frac{V_{oc}}{R_{sh}} \quad (6)$$

Maximum power point equation: I = Imp, for V = Vmp

$$I_{mp} = I_L - I_o\left[\exp\left(\frac{V_{mp}+I_{mp}R_s}{aV_T}\right) - 1\right] - \frac{V_{mp}+I_{mp}R_s}{R_{sh}} \quad (7)$$

3.1 Required equations for calculating unknown parameters

In order to obtain the value of series resistor, it is need to calculate the implicit expression, which is unstable and time consuming at the same time, for the sake of making expression decoupled, analytical formulation is required to make it explicit. Therefore, the implicit current - voltage expression is converted as an explicit one by applying the technique to solve the voltage as a function of current and vice versa, it is intended to make use of popular strategy as suggested by J. Amit, S. Sandeep, K. Avinashi [16], Villegas [17], K. Roberts, S. R. Valluri [18] that is known as Lambert W function.

For calculating ***Rs***:

$$Rs = A\left(W_{-1}\left(B\exp(C)\right) - (D + C)\right) \quad (8)$$

Where,

$$A = \frac{aV_T}{I_{mp}}$$

$$B = -\frac{V_{mp}\left(2I_{mp} - I_{sc}\right)}{V_{mp}I_{sc} + V_{oc}\left(I_{mp} - I_{sc}\right)} \quad (9)$$

$$C = -\frac{2V_{mp} - V_{oc}}{aV_T} + \frac{\left(V_{mp}I_{sc} - V_{oc}I_{mp}\right)}{\left(V_{mp}I_{sc} + V_{oc}\left(I_{mp} - I_{sc}\right)\right)}$$

$$D = \frac{V_{mp} - V_{oc}}{aV_T}$$

For calculating ***Rsh***:

$$R_{sh} = \frac{\left(V_{mp} - I_{mp}R_s\right)\left(V_{mp} - R_s\left(I_{sc} - I_{mp}\right) - aV_T\right)}{\left(V_{mp} - I_{mp}R_s\right)\left(I_{sc} - I_{mp}\right) - aV_TI_{mp}} \quad (10)$$

For calculating I_0:

$$I_0 = \frac{(R_{sh} + R_s)I_{sc} - V_{oc}}{R_{sh}\exp\left(\frac{V_{oc}}{aV_T}\right)} \quad (11)$$

For calculating I_L:

$$I_L = \frac{R_{sh} + R_s}{R_{sh}}I_{sc} \quad (12)$$

4 Methodology

4.1 Parameter identification and calculation from manufacturer's datasheet

In order to evaluate the unknown parameters (I_L, I_O, Rs, Rsh) and to simplify the calculations for specific model, P. M. Cuce, E. Cuce [19] elaborated that the ideality factor should be considered as generic value which is suggested for monocrystalline cell type as a = 1.2 and is independent of any temperature and irradiation. The following procedure is followed for calculating the parameters from manufacturer's datasheet.

* Corresponding author: adila@eng.unideb.hu

*1) Approximating the ideality factor **a** as 1.2 for Monocrystalline Cell*
*2) Calculating the Series Resistance **Rs** with Equation (8)*
*Calculating the Shunt Resistance **Rsh** with Equation (10)*
3) Calculating the Saturation Current I_O with Equation (11)
4) Calculating the Photodiode Current I_L with Equation (12)

The electrical characteristics are given in the TABLE I, which demonstrates the perquisite data for insertion in to the expressions. The input parameters from the datasheet at (STC) Standard Test Conditions are 1000 W/m2 incident normal radiance, Cell temperature is 25 ^{0}C and Air Mass AM1.5g.

Table 1. Electrical specifications of ixolar solarmd slmd481h081

I – V Curve Characteristics	Specifications	Units
Open Circuit Voltage (Voc)	5.04	V
Short Circuit Current (Isc)	0.2	A
Voltage at maximum power point (Vmpp)	4.0	V
Current at maximum power point (Impp)	0.178	A
Maximum Peak Power (Pmpp)	0.714	W
Temperature Coefficients of Isc (alpha)	0.12	mA/(cm^2) K
Temperature Coefficient of Voc (beta)	-2.1	mV/K

The obtained parameters are demonstrated in TABLE II, where the unknown parameters have been calculated by the defined equations and pushing the ideality factor as constant and independent.

Table 2. Calculated parameters of ixolar solarmd slmd481h081

Parameters	Calculated Values
I_0	9.0837e-10
I_L	0.2009
Rs	1.7795
Rsh	398.4280
a	1.2

4.2 Simulating the solar equivalent circuit

In this paper, the commercial solar cell iXolar SolarMD SLMD481H08L [20] is being selected for analyzing I – V and P – V curves based on mathematical formulation and using the Linear Technology's LTSpice (Linear Technology Simulation Program with Integrated Circuit Emphasis) software. However, the obtained values will be modelled on the solar equivalent circuit for evolving the behavior of solar module on simulator. As defined in section IV. A, the input parameters have been calculated for modelling and simulation purpose for solar equivalent circuit as shown in Fig. 5.

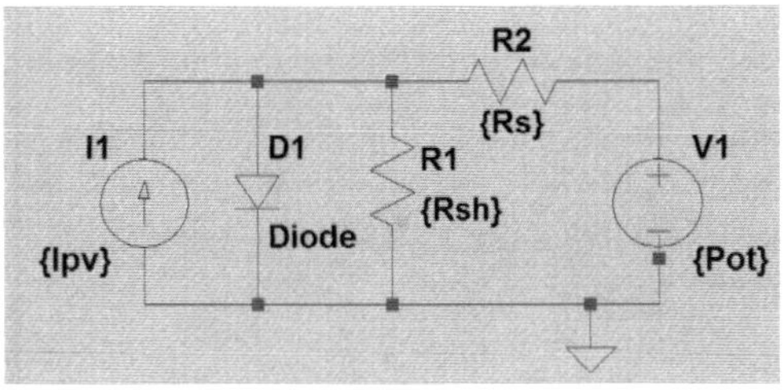

Fig. 5. Single diode Equivalent circuit for iXolar SolarMD SLMD481H08L

5 Results and discussions

5.1 I – V and P – V curve simulation

The generated I – V and P – V curve for commercial solar cell has been plotted as demonstrated in Fig. 6 and Fig. 7. The simulations are mathematically formulated based on the datasheet information. These plots are being further simulated based on two variations for solar equivalent circuit. The environment dependence has been modelled to analyze the PV cell response and the characteristics points to adequate the output performance of the cell. For this purpose, the temperature and irradiations levels are adopted to configure the system response in the real-time environment.

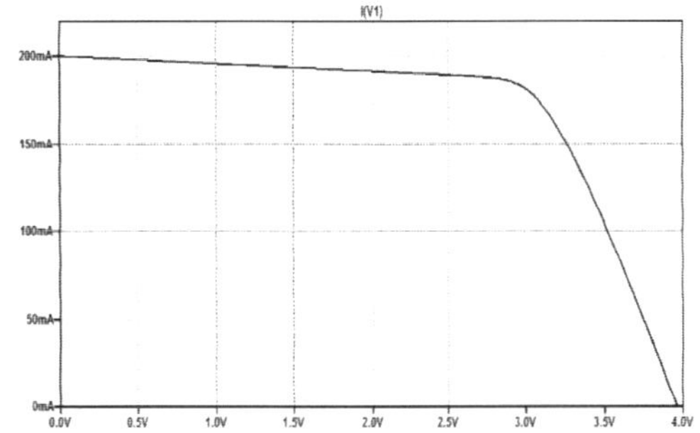

Fig. 6. I – V curve of Solar Equivalent Circuit of iXolar SolarMD SLMD481H08L

* Corresponding author: adila@eng.unideb.hu

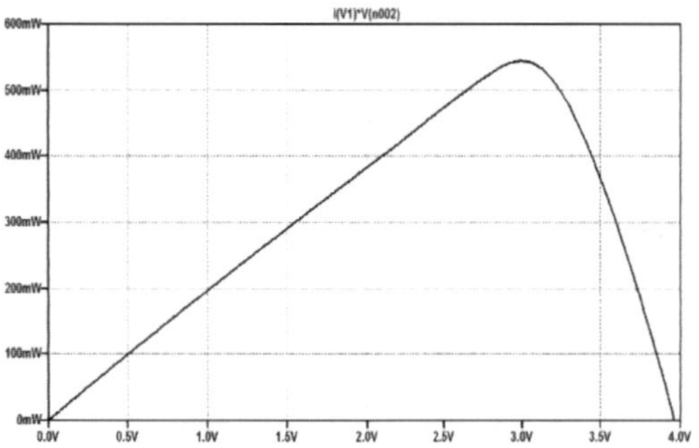

Fig. 7. P – V curve of Solar Equivalent Circuit of iXolar SolarMD SLMD481H08L

5.2 Effect of solar irradiation on i – v curve

The simulation is being performed on the same solar circuit for different levels of solar irradiation, which varies from 200 W/m^2 to 1000 W/m^2 by maintaining the temperature constant at 25 °C. It can be seen in Fig. 8, that the generated current depends on the incident light, as long as the irradiation is increasing the current also increases. As there is slight change of voltage with respect to the increment of the current.

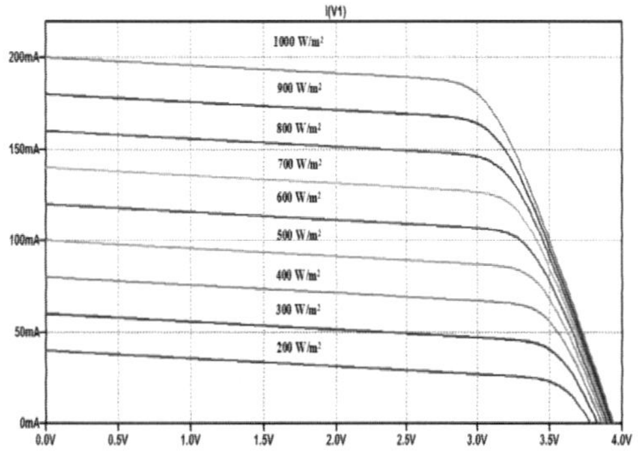

Fig. 8. Solar Irradiation levels from 200 W/m^2 to 1000 W/m^2 at 25 ^{0}C

5.3 Effect of temperature on I – V and P – V curve.

In this simulation, the temperature is being varied from 15 ^{0}C to 85 ^{0}C and keeping the irradiation level constant at 1000 W/m^2. Fig. 9 and Fig. 10, shows the I – V and P – V curve generated on different temperature ranges. As it is clearly indicated that by varying the temperature from low to high, the voltage is being affected. Increasing the temperature causing the decreased voltage and maximum power point at the same time. While the current generated by incident light remained constant.

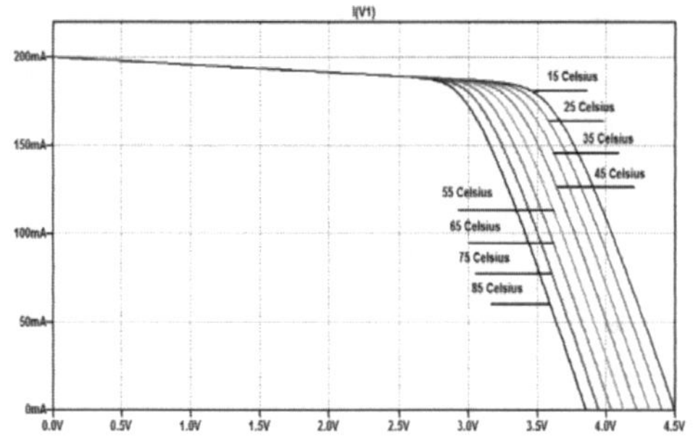

Fig. 9. I – V Characteristics for Temperature variation between 15 ^{0}C to 85 ^{0}C at 1000 W/m^2

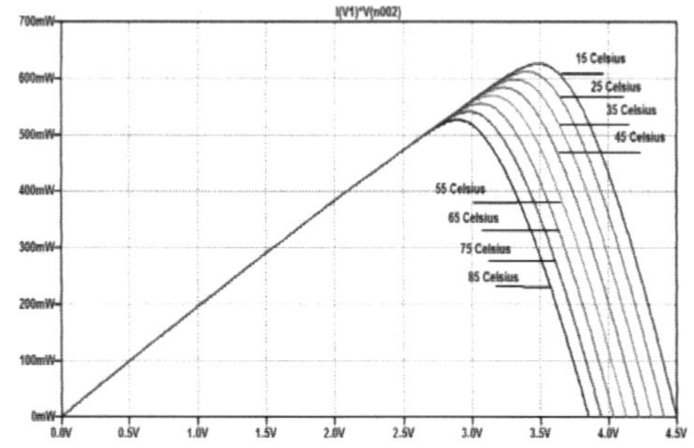

Fig. 10. P – V Characteristics for Temperature variation between 15 ^{0}C to 85 ^{0}C at 1000 W/m^2

6 Conclusion

In this research work, the commercial solar cell is being examined to predict the solar cell response on the simulator based on the I – V and P – V characteristics. For such study, the solar cell is being modelled as a single diode equivalent circuit (1M5P), the only source available is the manufacturer's datasheet that is being considered to extract the unknown parameters. Certain calculation and explicit expressions have been performed to get most of the optimal values of the module. This way the calculation is being done on the Matlab software and the obtained parameters were simulated on LTSpice simulator on the equivalent circuit. The results have been analyzed on the two cases; one on the temperature variation and keeping irradiation constant and second on the irradiation levels keeping temperature constant. The plots of I -V curves indicate that as far as temperature increases the cell current slightly increases and the voltage is being decreased. It is observed that P – V characteristics of solar cell denotes the decrease in voltage as the temperature is being decreased which proportionally affects the power output of the cell. However, the increment in the irradiation levels also increases the output power. Finally, this simulation based study provides the end users to establish the realistic mathematical modelling of solar cell, panel or an array to estimate the electrical behavior of PV systems for planning their own systems.

* Corresponding author: adila@eng.unideb.hu

References

[1] Fuels, The End of Fossil. Ecotrcity Britain's Greenest Energy, https://www.ecotricity.co.uk/our-green-energy/energy-independence/the-end-of-fossil-fuels, (Date of Access: November 2016).

[2] A. S. Adila, A. Husam, J. H. Sana G. Husi. "Estimation of minimum output power threshold for energy harvesting module: An inspection of battery and charging parameters of cell phones." *Proceedings of 4th International Mechatronic Student Micro-Conference Budapest*, 56-71, 2017.

[3] REN21. *Renewables Global Status Report 2016*. Paris: REN21 Secretrait: REN21 Publications, 2016.

[4] M. G. Vilalva, J. R. Gazoli, E. R. Filho, "Comprehensive approach to modeling and simulation of photovoltaic arrays",*IEEE Transactions on Power Electronics*, Vol. 24, No. 5, 1198-1208, May 2009.

[5] A. S. Sedra, K. C. Smith, *Microelectronic Circuits*, Oxford University Press, London, U.K. 2006.

[6] M. A. Eltawil, Z. Zhao, "Grid-connected photovoltaic power systems: Technical and potential problems- A review", *Renewable and Sustainiable Energy Reviews*, Vol. 14, No. 1, 112-129, Jan 2010.

[7] Union of Concerned Scientists- Science for a healthy planet and safer world. "How solar panels work", *http://ucsusa.org/*, (Date of Access: April 2016).

[8] J. Bikaneria, S. P. Joshi,A. R. Joshi, "Modeling and simulation of a pv cellusing one-diode model", *International Journal of Scientifc Research Publications,* Vol. 3, No. 10, 1-4, Oct 2013.

[9] E. M. G. Rodrigues, R. Melicio, V. M. F. Mendes, J. P. S. Catalao. "Simulation of a Solar Cell considering Single-Diode Equivalent Circuit Model." *Renewable Energy and Power Quality Journal* Vol. 1. No. 9, 369-373, 2011.

[10] T. T. Yetayew, T. R. Jyothsna,. "Improved single-diode modeling approach for photovoltaic modules using datasheet." *Annual IEEE India Conference (INDICON)*. Bombay, 1-6, 2013.

[11] J. Cubas, S. Pindado, C. D. Manuel. "Explicit Expressions for Solar Panel Equivalent Circuit Paramaters Based on nalytical Formulation and the Lambert W-Function ." *Energies* Vol.7, No.7 4098-4115, 2014.

[12] G. R. Walker. "Evaluating MPPT topologies using a Matlab PV model." *Journal of Electrical & Electronics Engineering* Vol. 21, No.1, 49-56, 2001.

[13] M. Azzouzi, D. Popescu, M. Bouchahdane. "Modeling of Electrical Characteristics of Photovoltaic Cell." *Journal of Clean Energy Technologies* Vol.4, No.6, 414-419, 2016.

[14] M. Wolf, H. Rauschenbach,. "Series resistance effect on solar cll measurements." *Advance Energy Conversions* 3 (1963): 455-479.

[15] A. Wafaa, A. M. Ashraf, A. Fouad, S. Saad,. "Mathematical Model for Photovoltaic Cells." *Leonardo Journal of Sciences* Vol.12, No. 23, 13-28, 2013.

[16] J. Amit, S. Sandeep, K. Avinashi,. "Solar cell array parameters using Lambert W-function." *Solar Energy Material & Solar Cells* 90, 25-31, 2006.

[17] D. Villegas, "Analysis of solar cell using the Lambert W function with Maple." *Proceedings of SPIE - Energy Harvesting and Storage: Materials, Devices, and Applications V*. Baltimore, Vol. 9115, 2014.

[18] K. Roberts, S. R. Valluri. "Solar Cells and the Lambert W Function." *Celebrating 20 years of the Lambert W function*. London, Canada, 2016.

[19] P. M. Cuce, E. Cuce,. "A novel model of photovoltaic modules for parameter estimation and thermodynamic assesment." *International Journal of Low-Carbon Technology* Vol. 7, 159-165, 2011.

[20] iXolar SolarMD SLMD481H08L,Available online http://ixapps.ixys.com/DataSheet/ixys_solar.pdf (Date of Access: January 2017).

* Corresponding author: adila@eng.unideb.hu

MATEC Web of Conferences **126**, 03003 (2017) DOI: 10.1051/matecconf/201712603003
Annual Session of Scientific Papers IMT ORADEA 2017

The multi-objective genetic algorithm optimization, of a superplastic forming process, using ansys®

Gavril Grebenişan[1,*], *Nazzal* Salem[2]

[1]University of Oradea, e-mail: grebe@uoradea.ro, Romania
[2] ZAQRA University, nsalem@zu.edu.jo, Jordan

Abstract: In the industrial practice, the product is intended to be flawless, with no technological difficulty in making the profile shapes. If this product results without defects, then any Finite Elements Method (FEM) based simulation can support that technology. A technology engineer does not propose, very often to analyze the simulation of the design technology, but rather to try to optimize a solution that he feels feasible. Experiments used as the basis for numerical optimization analysis support their research in the field of superplastic forming. Determining the influence of input parameters on the output parameters, Determining the optimal shape of the product and the optimal initial geometry, the prediction of the cracks and possibly the fractures, the prediction of the final thickness of the sheet, these are the objectives of the research and optimization for this project. The results of the numerical simulations have been compared with the measurements made on parts and sections of the parts obtained by superplastic forming. Of course, the consistency of the results, costs, benefits, and times required to perform numerical simulations are evaluated, but they are not objectives for optimizing the superplastic forming process.

1 Introduction

The engineering design system is an extremely laborious and delicate interdisciplinary process that requires co-operation between designers in various engineering fields. This means the technological design is considered to be a complex process and needs to be approached very carefully. Design engineering requires hypotheses that need to be adopted for the further development of models that can undergo analysis, verification, and experiments. The project starts, always with the analysis of several variants. For most applications, the entire design project can be subdivided into different subproblems that can then be independently addressed. Each subproblem can thus be presented as a design optimum to be mathematically solved, M. Diehl, F. Glineur, E. Jarlebring, W. Michiels [1].

For technology engineers to apply optimization methods to a project, they need to have a detailed understanding of both theory and algorithms and their specific techniques. This is due, first of all, to the fact that considerable effort is needed to apply optimization techniques to practical problems to achieve an improvement in the performance of the studied product. For this reason, perhaps, optimization has been used, in particular, to help the projection process, namely to support decision-making, not to develop concepts, or to develop a detailed project.

Generally, for technology engineers, optimization issues are reduced to minimization a function (a cost function, for example), or maximizing a function (a "profit" function), a function that is subject to constraints (mathematically, these may be some inequalities or equations), the optimization problem being called the nonlinear programming problem. Its general form is, A. D. Belegundu and T. R. Chandrupatla [2]:

Minimize:

$$\mathbf{f(x,y)} \tag{1}$$

subject to:

$$\mathbf{g_i(x,y) \leq 0 \quad i = 1, \ldots, m} \tag{2}$$

$$\mathbf{h_j(x,y) \geq 0, \quad j = 1 \ldots \ell} \tag{3}$$

* Corresponding author: grebe@uoradea.ro

where

$$\mathbf{x} \in \mathbb{R}^{n_c},\ \mathbf{y} \in \mathbb{R}^{n_i}$$

$$\mathbf{x_l} \leq \mathbf{x} \leq \mathbf{x_u}$$

$$\mathbf{y_l} \leq \mathbf{y} \leq \mathbf{y_u}$$

Not often (it can be said that this is the real challenge for an engineer regarding a genuinely delicate optimization problem), both a minimization and a maximization may be required, of course, on various criteria, clearly set, the problem is extremely complex and cost-generating. For example, a structural engineer may like to minimize the mass of the product, but would also like to increase mechanical rigidity. At this point, several goals can be discussed simultaneously. Mathematically, the problem with multiple targets (or "attributes") may be stated as, A. D. Belegundu and T. R. Chandrupatla [2]:

$$\text{minimize } \mathbf{f} = [\mathbf{f_1(x)}, \mathbf{f_2(x)}, \ldots,\ \mathbf{f_m(x)}]$$

$$\text{subject to } \boldsymbol{x} \in \boldsymbol{\Omega}$$

When, very rarely, it happens that only one optimum criterion $\mathbf{x_{opt}}$ minimizes all the objectives, the problem is solved instantly. Most of the time, however, the optimization criteria are in conflict. In this situation, the optimization problem is solved by weighting the criteria:

$$\text{minimize } \mathbf{f} = \boldsymbol{\omega}_1\mathbf{f_1(x)} + \boldsymbol{\omega}_2\mathbf{f_2(x)} + \cdots$$

$$\text{subject to } \boldsymbol{x} \in \boldsymbol{\Omega}$$

where the weights $\boldsymbol{\omega}_i$ are positives, and $\sum \boldsymbol{\omega}_i = \mathbf{1}$. Choosing the sizes of these weights is based on experimental data.

Another approach, quite common, is to designate one of the criteria as a priority, and to constrain the values for the weights of the other criteria:

$$\text{minimize } \mathbf{f_1(x)}$$

$$\text{subject to } \mathbf{f_2(x)} \leq \boldsymbol{c}_2$$

$$\ldots$$

$$\mathbf{f_m(x)} \leq \boldsymbol{c}_m$$

$$\boldsymbol{x} \in \boldsymbol{\Omega}$$

Even if the use of a set of values for weights, $\boldsymbol{\omega}_i$, or limits, $\boldsymbol{c}_i$, generates an optimum, $\mathbf{x_{opt}}$, that coresponds to all criteria, an engineer must be able to answer the question, what if the diferent selection of set of values will done, the results are different? Then comes the answer: we must take into account the sensitivities of the output parameters with respect to the input parameters, and the Parameters Correlation, the computation and optimization module, provided by ANSYS as a feature, mathematics and graphics at the same time.

2 Optimization procedure

The studied part, shown in Fig. 1, is hemispherical with flange, G. Grebenişan and S. Mureşan [3]. The blank is fixed, with friction, between the two components of the forming die, on its perimeter and the entire assembly is heated in a horizontal oven, for superplastic forming at high temperature (under the half of melting temperature of the material, i.e. approximately 460[°C], for Supral 100, commercial named, this Aluminium alloy. The gas pressure will act and deform the sample, with a very low strain rate $\dot{\varepsilon} = 2.5\text{x}10^{-3}\ [s^{-1}]$. The material is modeled with an Anand Viscoplasticity law as described by M.M. Rahman [4]. The strain distribution on the workpiece section and resultant thickness of the specimen it's possible to be very variable from one area to another, leading to a nonhomogeneous thickness distribution in the final component. This will also induce higher stress zones.The authors J.-P. Ponthot, J.-P. Kleinermann [5] proposed an approach to avoid these problems. The mentioned authors proposed to use the following procedure: to determine the initial piece geometry that would lead, at the end of forming process, to the prescribed uniform distribution of the thickness of the final workpiece transversal section. Furthermore, we chosen as input parameters the sample diameter and the thickness of the sample.

a)-hemispherical parts

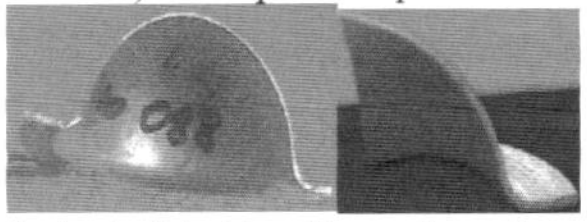

b)-hemispherical (midsection and quarter section)

Fig. 1. Studied parts

Later, in this workpaper, a Design of Experiments(DOE) is presented and is easy to found that the study involves a sampling point which not always conducive to lowering the time needed for the analysis.

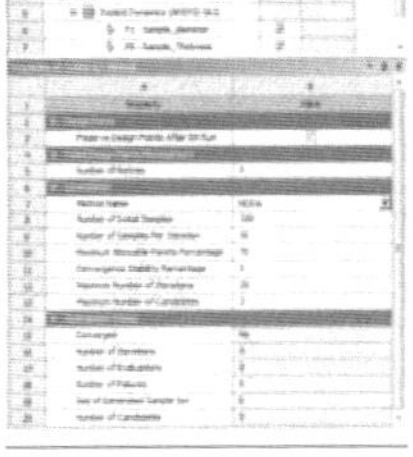

Fig. 2. The Settings of Direct Optimization

* Corresponding author: grebe@uoradea.ro

Table 1. Raw optimization data

Name	P1 - Sample_diameter (mm)	P8 - Sample_Thickness (mm)	P5 - Equivalent Stress Maximum (MPa)	P6 - Total Deformation Maximum (mm)	P7 - Equivalent Plastic Strain Maximum (mm mm^-1)
1	18.02	1.08	488.91	15.08	0.24
2	18.06	1.20	495.75	15.31	0.22
3	18.10	1.14	484.52	15.22	0.22
4	18.14	1.26	485.42	15.44	0.24
5	18.18	1.11	494.11	15.20	0.22
6	18.22	1.23	535.34	15.38	0.22
7	18.26	1.17	499.01	15.30	0.22
8	18.30	1.29	517.91	15.15	0.23
9	18.34	1.10	491.14	15.25	0.22
10	18.38	1.22	554.64	15.19	0.23
11	18.42	1.16	466.27	15.15	0.23
12	18.46	1.28	476.75	15.13	0.25
13	18.50	1.13	533.48	15.34	0.24
14	18.54	1.25	505.48	15.24	0.24
15	18.58	1.19	520.15	15.14	0.24
16	18.62	1.31	433.10	15.16	0.25
17	18.66	1.09	513.64	15.35	0.25
18	18.70	1.21	484.48	15.06	0.24
19	18.74	1.15	466.67	15.09	0.25
20	18.78	1.27	492.00	15.10	0.73
21	18.82	1.12	470.99	15.13	0.27
22	18.86	1.24	522.50	15.04	0.26
23	18.90	1.18	538.05	15.19	0.25
24	18.94	1.30	723.67	15.09	0.73
25	18.98	1.10	468.50	15.10	0.27
26	19.02	1.22	612.17	15.11	0.26
27	19.06	1.16	441.66	15.08	0.26
28	19.10	1.28	667.51	15.04	0.73
29	19.14	1.13	604.14	15.25	0.27
30	19.18	1.25	462.46	15.14	0.27
31	19.22	1.19	560.77	15.24	0.27
32	19.26	1.31	654.86	15.33	0.65
...	...	...	...	...	...
371	20.95	1.31	748.18	15.24	0.43
372	21.98	1.32	702.80	15.21	0.70
373	21.44	1.26	775.84	15.16	0.57
374	21.77	1.29	707.99	15.20	0.68

For example, applying a CCD in a fractional factorial scheme, a dozen times more sampling points are required for some input parameters, that is, as many evaluations as Finite Element Analysis, which means a significant computational time is consuming, G. Gantar, T. Pepelnjak, K Kuzman [6].

The MOGA method (Multi-Objective Genetic Algorithm), fig. 2, is a variant of the popular Non-dominated Sorted Genetic Algorithm-II (NSGA-II) based on controlled elitism concepts. It supports multiple objectives and constraints and aims at finding the global optimum, Ansys manual [7].

The method's Configuration is: will generate 100 samples initially, 50 samples per iteration and find 3 candidates in a maximum of 20 iterations, fig. 3.

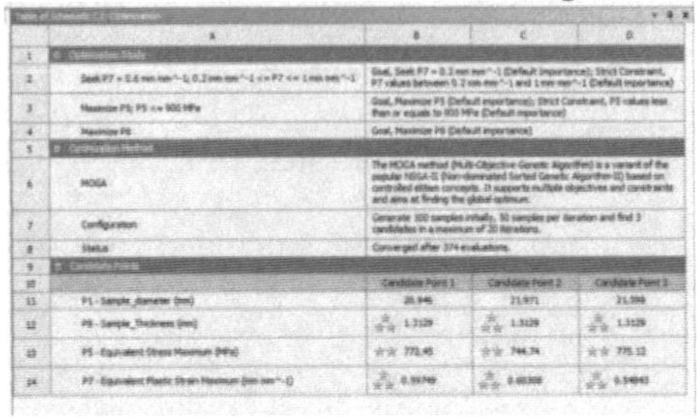

Fig. 3. Table of Schematic C2: Optimization(Optimization Study; Optimization Method; Candidate Points)

Our application was realized after 4 hours of computing time; the results are concentrated on four modules: Candidate Points, Tradeoff, Samples, and Sensitivities. The method converged after 374 Design Points evaluated(Table 1).

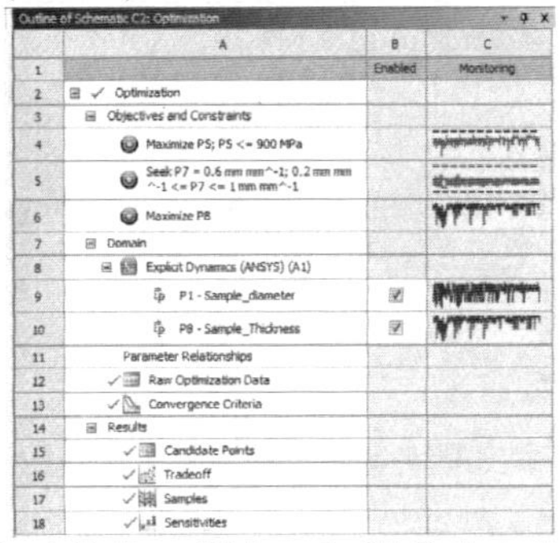

Fig. 4. Outline of Schematic C2: Optimization

3 Results of the Multi-Objective Genetic Algorithm (MOGA)

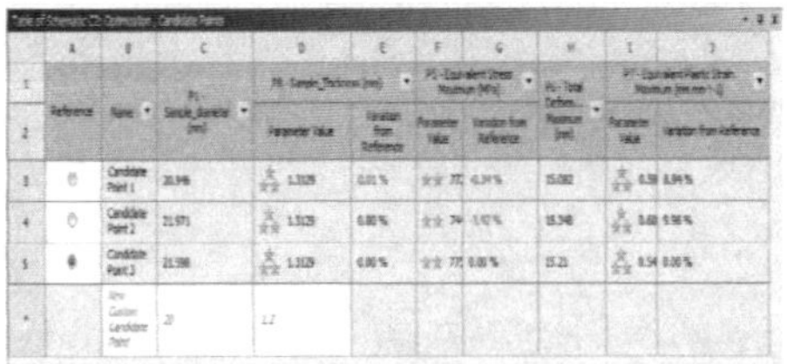

Fig. 5. Table of Schematic C2: Optimization, Candidate Points

* Corresponding author: grebe@uoradea.ro

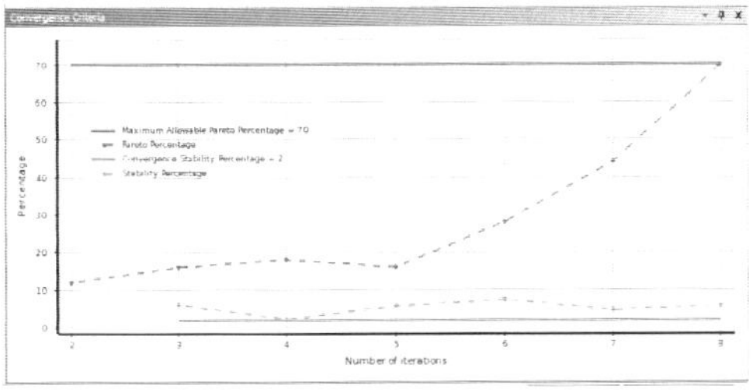

Fig. 6. Convergence Criteria

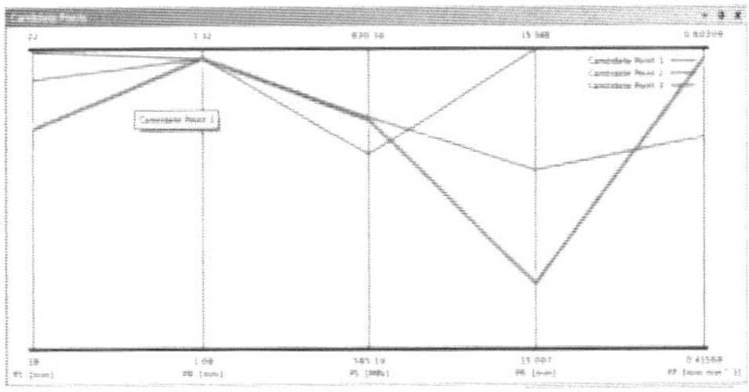

Fig. 11. Candidate Points

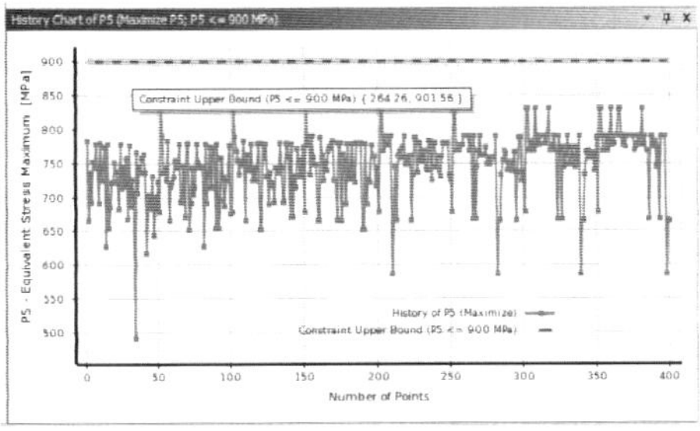

Fig. 7. History Chart of parameter P5 (Maximize P5- Equivalent Stress Maximum)

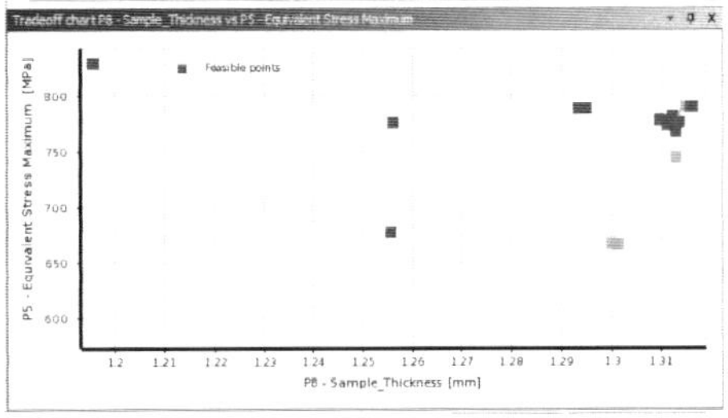

a)-Sample_Thickness vs. Equivalent Stress Maximum

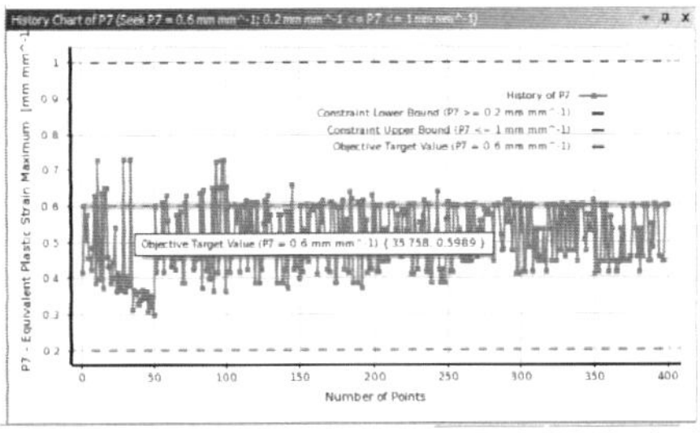

Fig. 8. History Chart of parameter P7 (Seek P7- Equivalent Plastic Strain Maximum)

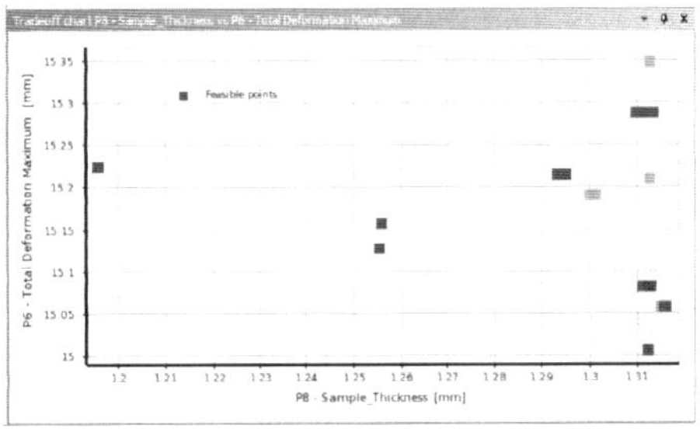

b)- Sample_Thickness vs. Total Deformation Maximum

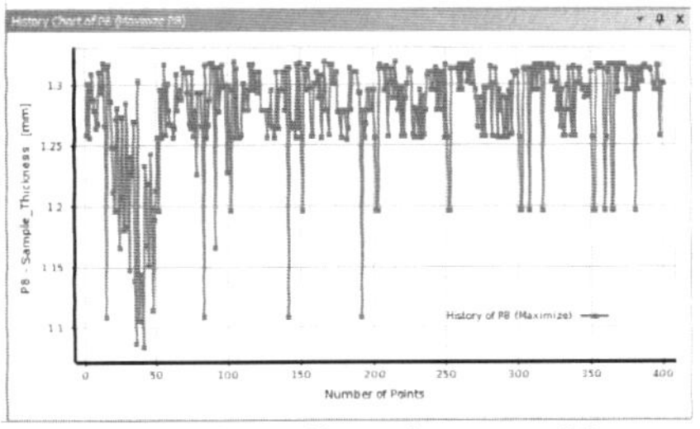

Fig. 9. History Chart of parameter P8 (Maximize P8- Sample_Thickness)

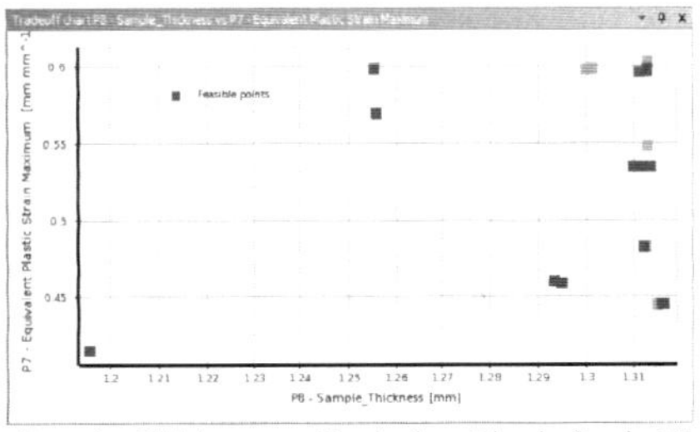

c)- Sample_Thickness vs Equivalent Plastic Strain Max.

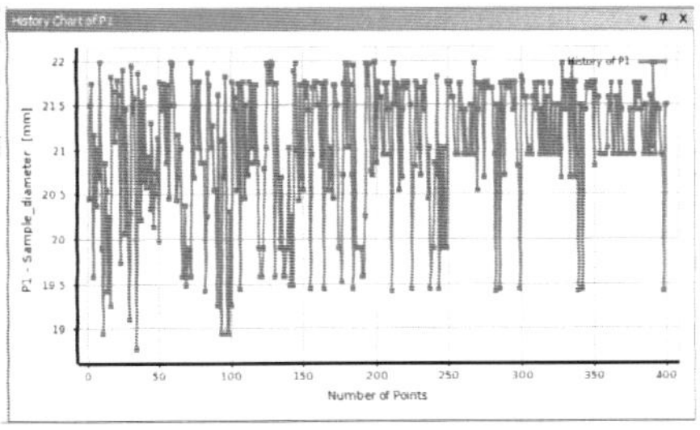

Fig. 10. History Chart of parameter P1 (Sample_diameter)

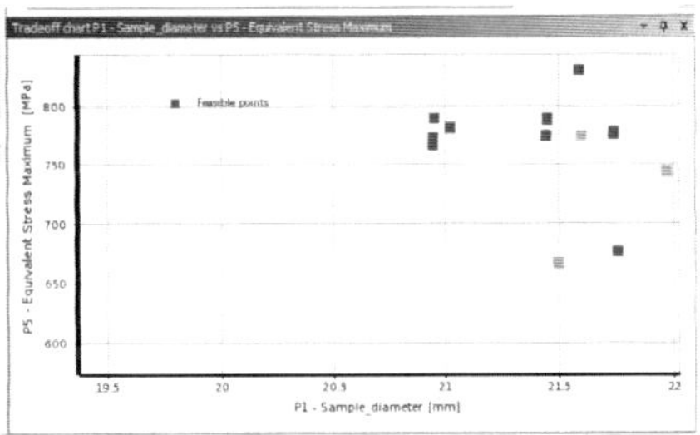

d)- Sample_diameter vs Equivalent Stress Maximum

* Corresponding author: grebe@uoradea.ro

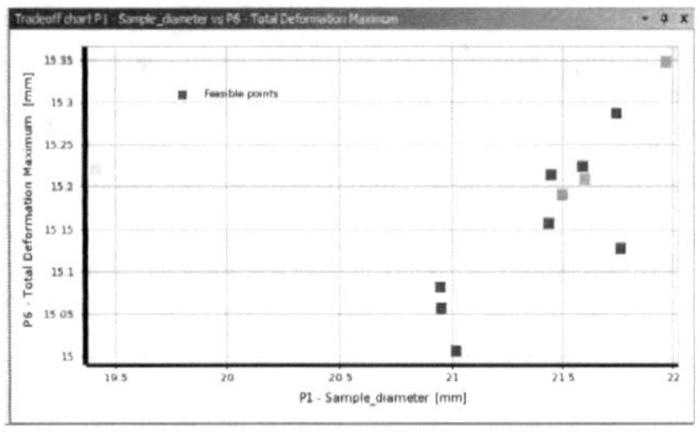

e)- Sample_diameter vs Total Deformation Maximum

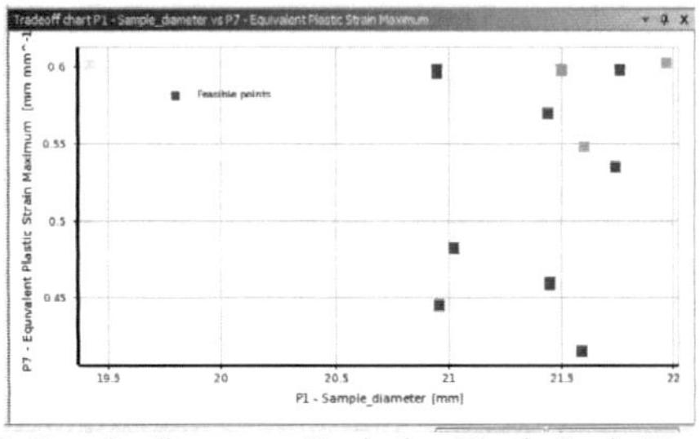

f)- Sample_diameter vs Equivalent Plastic Strain Max.

Fig. 12. Tradeoff-feasible points-2D

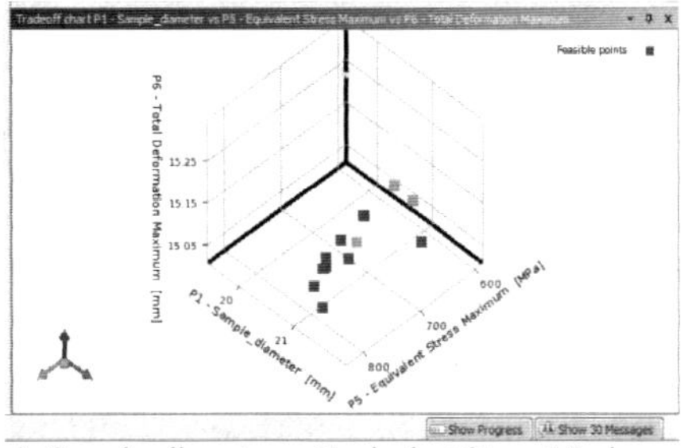

a)- Sample_diameter vs Equivalent Stress Maximum vs Total Deformation Maximum

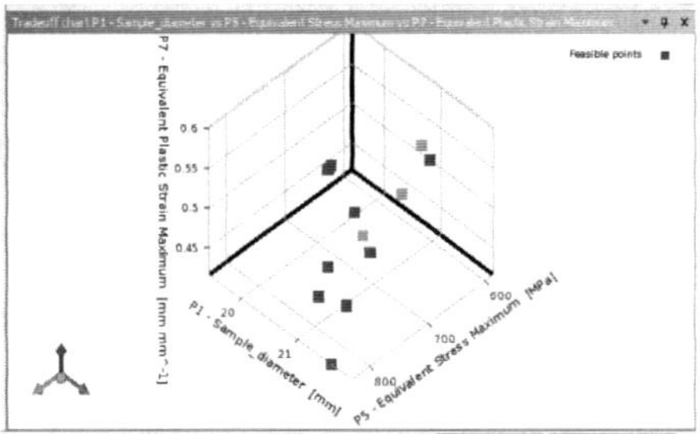

b)- Sample_diameter vs Equivalent Stress Maximum vs Equivalent Plastic Strain Maximum

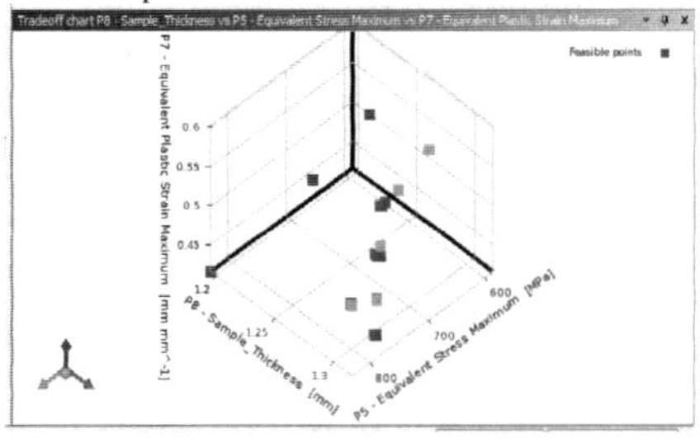

c) -Sample_Thicknrss vs Equivalent Stress Maximum vs Equivalent Plastic Strain Maximum

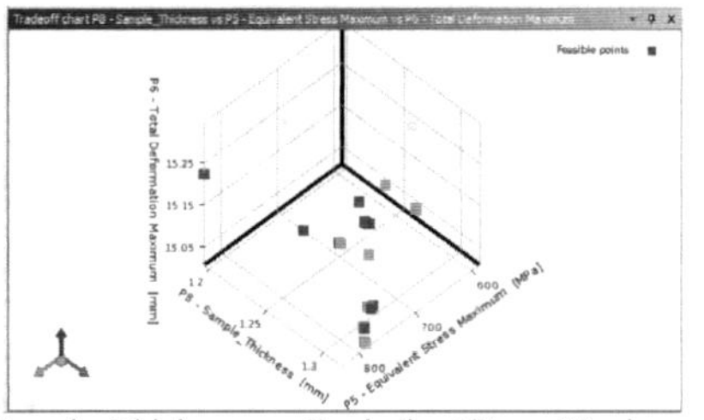

d) - Sample_Thicknrss vs. Equivalent Stress Maximum vs. Total Deformation Maximum

Fig. 13. Tradeoff-feasible points-3D

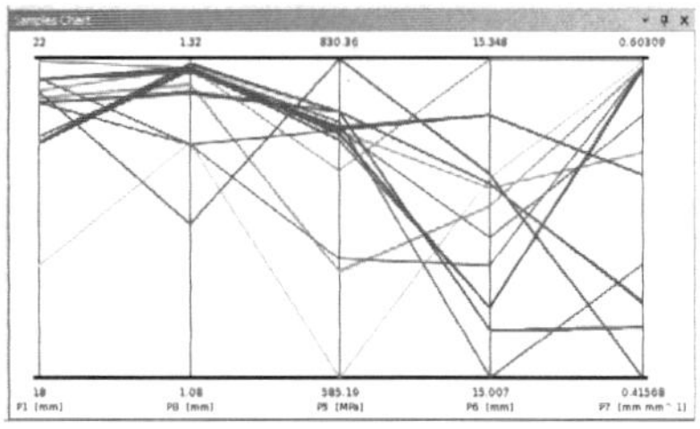

Fig. 14. Samples Chart

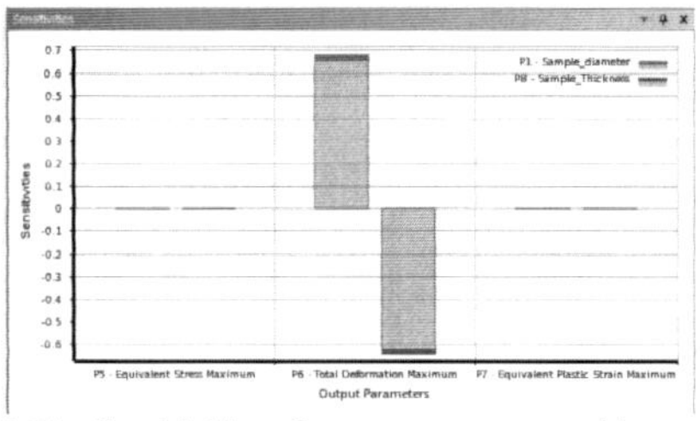

Fig. 15. The Sensitivities of output parameters with respect on input parameters

Response Surface created based on MOGA Optimization are:

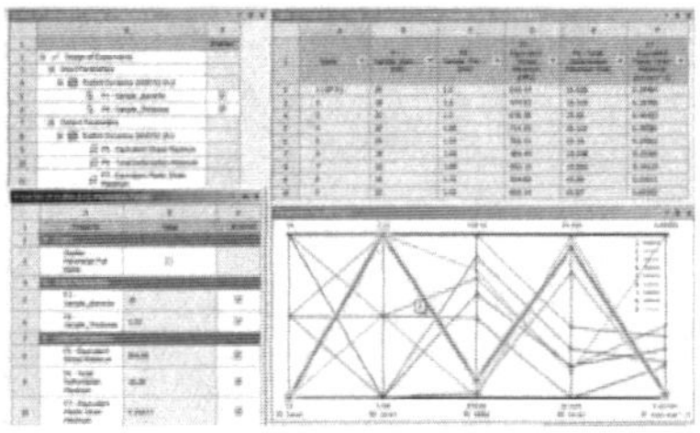

Fig. 16. Design of Experiments(Central Compozite Design) and Parameters Parallel Chart

Fig. 17. Table of Outline A14: Goodness Of Fit

* Corresponding author: grebe@uoradea.ro

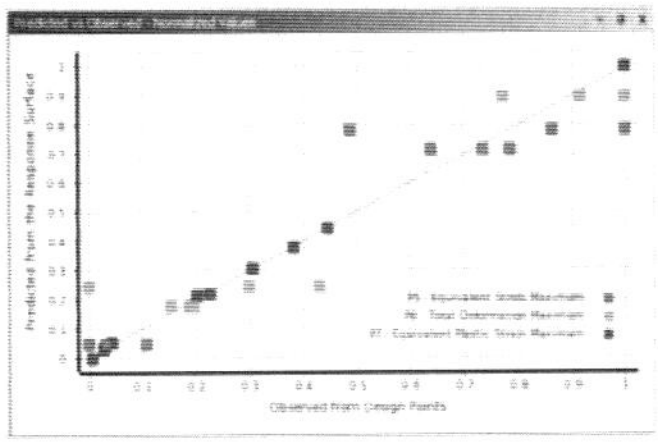

Fig. 18. Goodness of fit for Predicted Point vs. Observed Point

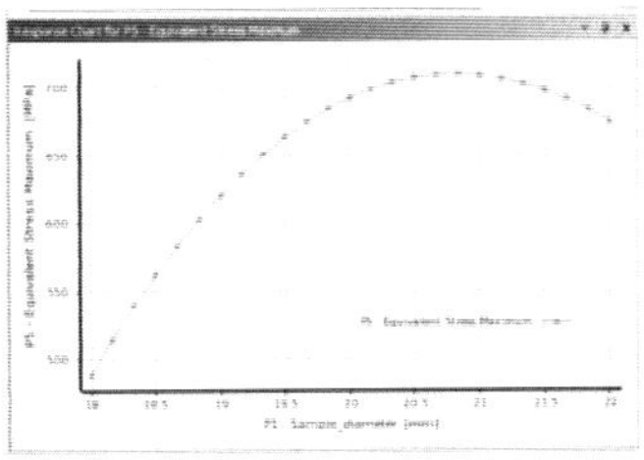

a) Sample_diameter vs Equivalent Stress Maximum

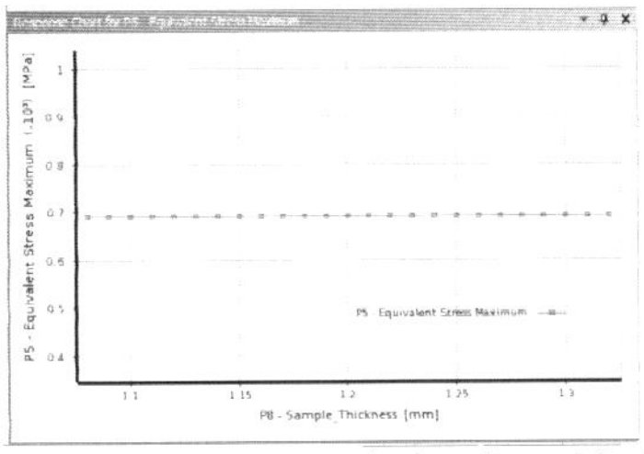

b)- Sample_Thickness vs. Equivalent Stress Maximum

Fig. 19. Response Surface(2D)

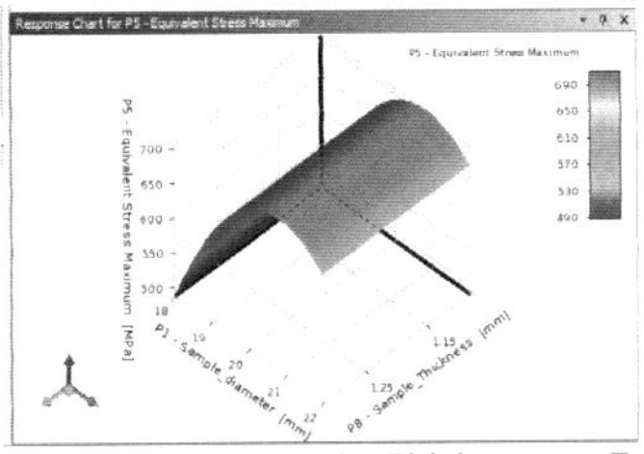

a)-Sample_diameter vs. Sample_Thickness vs. Equivalent Stress Maximum

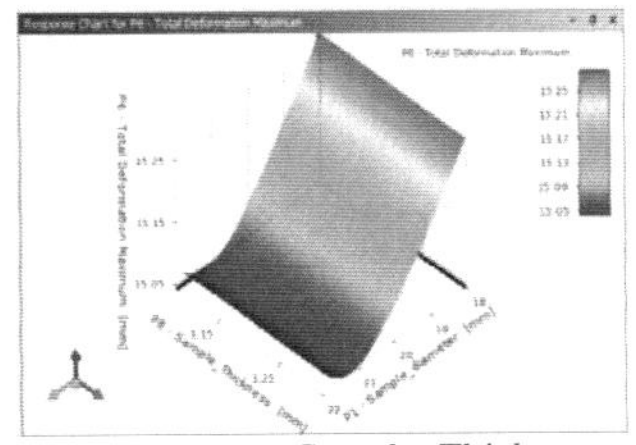

b)- Sample_diameter vs. Sample_Thickness vs. Total Deformation Maximum

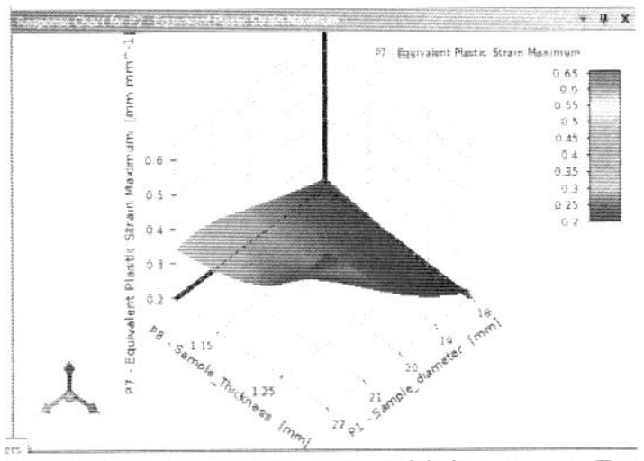

c)- Sample_diameter vs. Sample_Thickness vs. Equivalent Plastic Strain Maximum

Fig. 20. Response Surface(3D)-Equivalent Stress Maximum

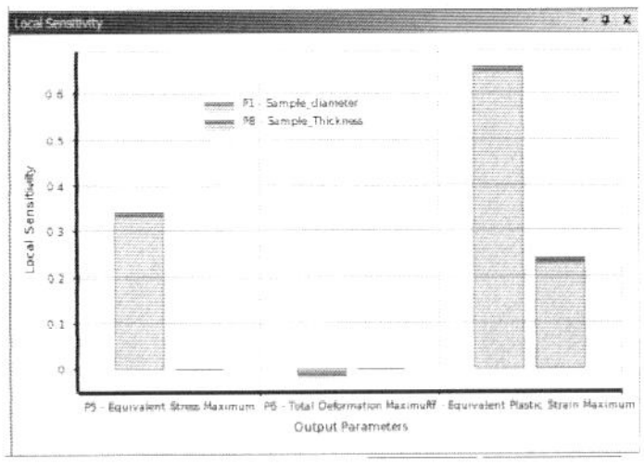

Fig. 21. Local Sensitivity of output parameters with respect on input parameters

References

[1] M. Diehl, F. Glineur, E. Jarlebring, W. Michiels, Recent Advances in Optimization and itsApplications in Engineering, Springer, 2010.

[2] A. D. Belegundu and T. R. Chandrupatla, Optimization Concepts and Applications in Engineering, Prentice Hall 1999.

[3] G. Grebenişan and S. Mureşan, *Numerical Study Of Volumic Forming On Superplastic Behaviour,* Annals of The University of Oradea. Fascicle of Management and Technological Engineering, Volume XVI (VI), ISSN 1583-0691, DOI: 10.15660/AUOFMTE.2007.714, 2007.

[4] M.M. Rahman, "Optimization of Process Parameters on Ti-6Al-4V Using Central Composite Design Method", Advanced Materials Research, Vols. 189-193, pp. 1393-1400, 2011

[5] J.-P. Ponthot, J.-P. Kleinermann, A cascade optimization methodology for automatic parameter identification and shape/process optimization in metal forming simulation, Elsevier Science B.V., Comput. Methods Appl. Mech. Engrg. 195 (2006) 5472–5508.

[6] G. Gantar, T. Pepelnjak, K Kuzman, Optimization of sheet metal forming processes by the use of numerical simulations, Elsevier Science B.V., Journal of Materials Processing Technology 130–131 (2002) 54–59.

[7] Ansys manual, (ANSYS Help Viewer).

* Corresponding author: grebe@uoradea.ro

MATEC Web of Conferences **126**, 03004 (2017) DOI: 10.1051/matecconf/201712603004
Annual Session of Scientific Papers IMT ORADEA 2017

Dynamic behavior of the horizontal milling and drilling machine spindle assembly with Dynrot software

Nicoleta Luminița Căruțașu[1*], *Nicoleta Elisabeta* Pascu[2], *George* Căruțașu[3]

[1] University Politehnica of Bucharest, nicoletacarutasu@yahoo.com, Romania
[2] University Politehnica of Bucharest, nicoletaelisabeta_pascu@yahoo.ro, Romania
[3]Romanian-American University, carutasu.george@profesor.rau.ro, Romania

Abstract. This article presents research conducted to study the dynamic behavior of the assembly of a horizontal milling CNC machine spindle at the speed of 10 000 rpm and 50 000 rpm. This step aims to determine the critical rotation speeds of the complex system "spindle – bearings", by drawing Campbell diagrams. The rotor is a subset of these machines, consisting of a shaft, in which the one or more discs, and which executes a rotating motion around the axis propyl. The curve Campbell contours in the diagram represents the variation of natural pulsations of spindle system, depending on the speed bearing spindle.

1 Introduction

About high speed processing machines cutting, quality of a product is based on the fulfillment of all customer requirements, presented by A. Dugas, J.-J. Lee, and J.-Y. Hascoët in [1]. For this reason, it is necessary to use all the knowledge about quality assurance since the time of the study phase/design, detailed by E. B. Msaddek, Z. Bouaziz, M. Baili, and G. Dessein [2]. Very high spindle speeds are needed to achieve cutting speeds, that can been predicted using dedicated software, G. Patrascu and G. Carutasu in [3]. High advance speeds can be achieved only with the appropriate essential transmissions and stable structure of the machine tool with good vibration damping, shortcuts are necessary for implementing high cutting speed range, expressed by K. Jauhari, A. Widodo, and I. Haryanto in [4]. Although the variety of machines rotors (as types and sizes) is great even within the same sub-class machines, however, they have a common element: the rotor, concluded by V. Gagnol, B. C. Bouzgarrou, P. Ray, and C. Barra in [5].

The study case is made for a milling and drilling CNC machine. In this case, the rotor is equated with the machine tool spindle and gears, elements running around propyl rotation axes are treated as discs that are assembled on the spindle (Fig. 1).

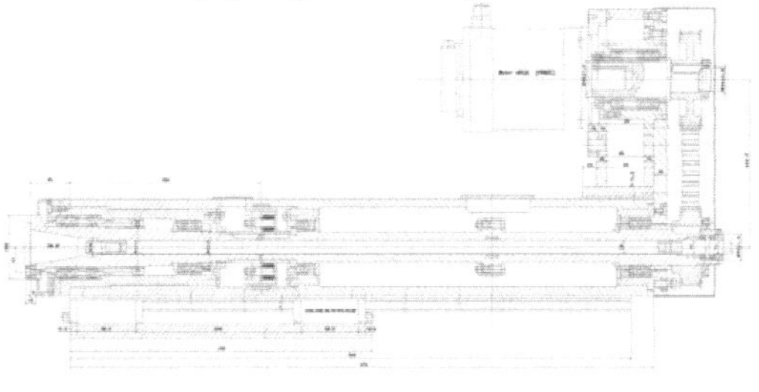

Fig. 1. The main kinematics chain of horizontal milling and drilling CNC machine. Numerical simulation of dynamic response of spindle assembly at the rotation speed of 10 000 RPM

Numerical simulation of dynamic response of spindle system (first section) - bearings, rotation speed of 10 000 rpm, is based on all use DYNROT program [6]. Similar studies driven by K. Jauhari, A. Widodo, and I. Haryanto [7], C. E. H. Ventura and A. Hassui [8] and H. Cao, T. Holkup, and Y. Altintas [9] were made combining Finite Element Method (FEM) method using ANSYS, in case of static behavior and ANSYS Parametric Design Language (APDL) for dynamic behavior. Also, for the presented horizontal milling and drilling machine spindle, presented by N. L. Carutasu [10] the static behavior analyses using FEM method and ANSYS software.

We have achieved, in a first step, the spindle meshing with beam elements four degrees of freedom for each node, of those eight degrees of freedom for each element to obtain the same number of elements. Fig. 2 presents

* Corresponding author: nicoletacarutasu@yahoo.com

sketch highlighting the main spindle nodes have been placed elastic elements. In this case, the placement of them has been taken into consideration, and the manner of mounting of the bearings: the "O" or "X".

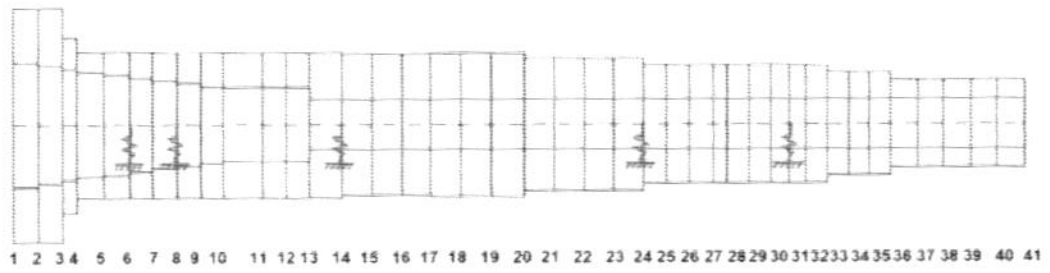

Fig. 2. Sketch of the mine spindle

The graphical representations contain both the deformed shape of the mine shaft and ellipses precession motion of the shaft center of each section. Along with graphical representations are offered information on shaft speed expressed in rpm and natural frequency value expressed in Hz.

Due to the relatively high rigidity of bearings, natural frequencies and critical rotation speeds that are relatively high (the lowest value is approx. 16207 rpm, presented in Table 1) resulting from this that the mine shaft will not achieve a critical rotation speed when idle. The graphical space representations of the first eight own modes precession is presented in Fig. 5.

Table 1. Values of first eight natural frequency for 10 000 rpm

Module	Quantity Natural frequency (Hz) for 10000 rpm	Critical rotation speed of the spindle (rpm) for 10000 rpm
1	270,12	16.207
2	290,59	17.436
3	332,49	19.949
4	446,86	26.811
5	519,65	31.179
6	554,32	33.259
7	951,96	57.117
8	997,32	59.839

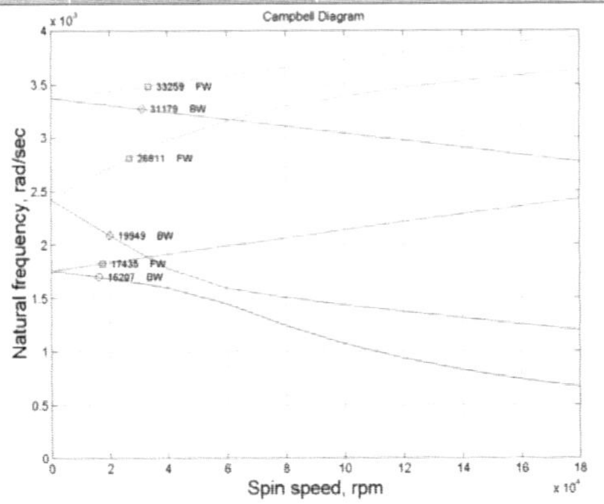

Fig. 3. Campbell diagram, for 10 000 rpm

Backward whirl (BW) represents deformed shaft rotates around the axis in the opposite bearings than the sense that rotates around its axis shaft and Foreword whirl (FW) it is deformed shaft rotates around the axle bearings in the same sense that also rotates on its own axis.

2 Numerical simulation of dynamic response of spindle assembly at the rotation speed of 50 000 RPM

Using the computer program DYNROT, it performed a numerical simulation of the dynamic response of 50000 rpm to determine critical rotation speeds of the system by drawing Campbell diagram (Fig. 4). The graphical space representations of the first four own modes precession is presented in Fig. 6.

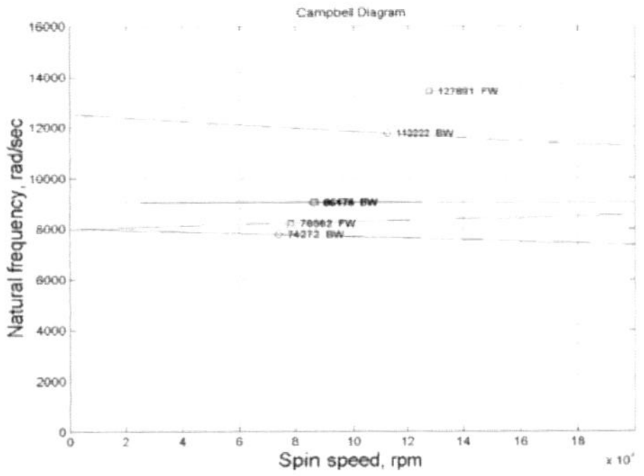

Fig. 4. Campbell diagram, for 50 000 rpm

Table 2. Values first six natural frequency for 50 000 rpm

Module	Quantity Natural frequency (Hz) for 50000 rpm	Critical rotation speed of the spindle (rpm) for 50000 rpm
1	1237,40	74272
2	1308,90	78532
3	1436,30	86175
4	1441,30	86477
5	1870,50	112222
6	2131,50	127891

* Corresponding author: nicoletacarutasu@yahoo.com

DOI: 10.1051/matecconf/201712603004

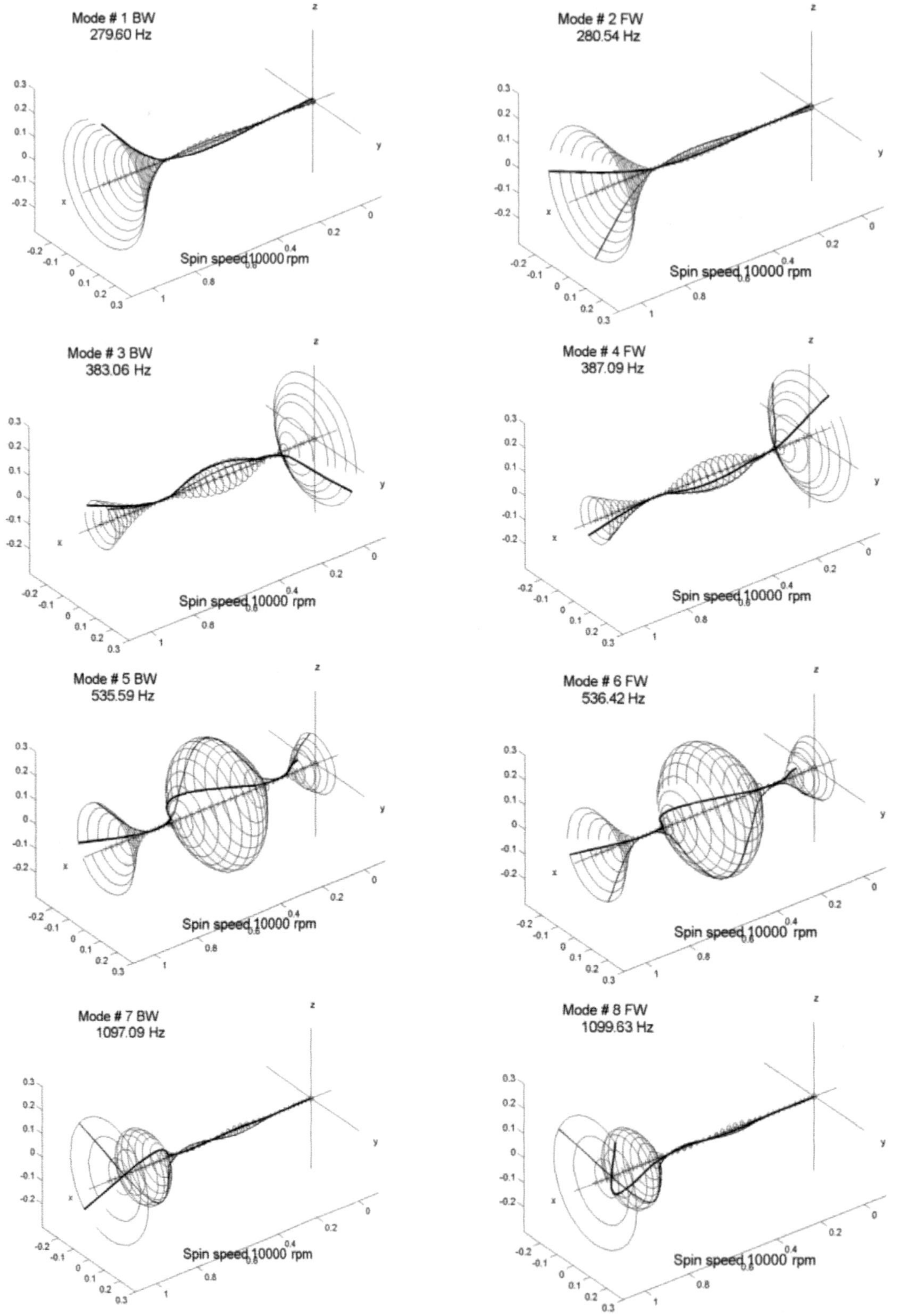

Fig. 5 Graphical space representations of deflection shape

* Corresponding author: nicoletacarutasu@yahoo.com

DOI: 10.1051/matecconf/201712603004

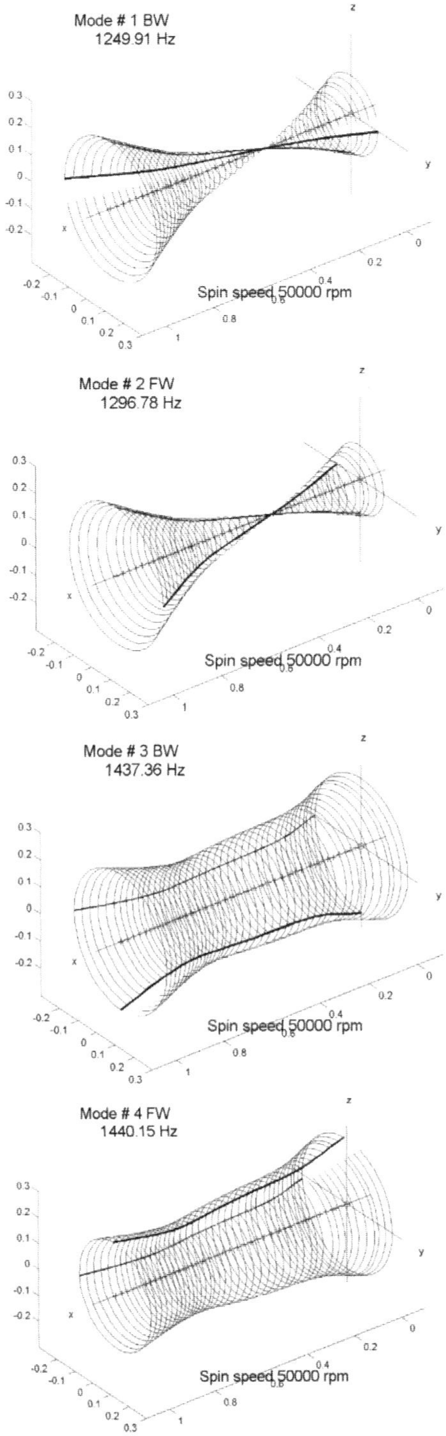

Fig. 6 Graphical space representations of deflection shape corresponding to own the precession modes for 50 000 rpm.

3 Conclusions

Comparing numerical simulations of the dynamic response of spindle assembly at 10 000 rpm and 50 000 rpm rotation speeds, can be seen that the natural frequency decrease with backward whirl (BW) with increasing spindle speed and increase with foreword whirl (FW). Also, precession own modes are pairs (FW and BW) which is observed in the form of precession own modes and differ as form. Natural frequencies and critical rotation speeds that are high in case with 50 000 rpm rotation speed (the lowest value is approx. 74 242 rpm), self-excited vibrations may occur but when certain conditions are met related to the cutting process, but they should not be confused with critical rotation speeds of the mine spindle. Campbell diagrams are different; the variation curves traced its pulsations spindle - bearings system on the main shaft rotation speed (Fig. 3 and 4). The occurrence of resonance and hence a critical rotation speeds occurs when the own pulsation (in rad/sec, or natural frequency expressed in Hz), is equal to the corresponding shaft rotation speed (Campbell diagrams appear that marked these intersections and values critical rotation speed). In conclusion, it can say that in terms of reuse system, it can be used in machine tools with an extended working a speed of the mine spindle structure is stable in terms of dynamic response.

References

[1] A. Dugas, J.-J. Lee, and J.-Y. Hascoët, "High Speed Milling," in *Integrated Design and Manufacturing in Mechanical Engineering*, Dordrecht: Springer Netherlands, 2002, pp. 287–294.

[2] E. B. Msaddek, Z. Bouaziz, M. Baili, and G. Dessein, "Modeling and simulation of high-speed milling centers dynamics," *Int. J. Adv. Manuf. Technol.*, vol. 53, no. 9–12, pp. 877–888, Apr. 2011.

[3] G. Patrascu and G. Carutasu, "Using virtual manufacturing simulation in 3D cutting forces prediction," *Ann. ORADEA Univ.*, vol. 5, pp. 1423–1426, 2007.

[4] K. Jauhari, A. Widodo, and I. Haryanto, "Evaluation of Dynamic Behavior a Machine Tool Spindle System through Modal and Unbalance Response Analysis," *World Acad. Sci. Eng. Technol. Int. J. Mech. Aerospace, Ind. Mechatron. Manuf. Eng.*, vol. 9, no. 2, pp. 400–406, 2015.

[5] V. Gagnol, B. C. Bouzgarrou, P. Ray, and C. Barra, "Dynamic Analyses and Design Optimization of High-Speed Spindle-Bearing System," in *Advances in Integrated Design and Manufacturing in Mechanical Engineering II*, Dordrecht: Springer Netherlands, 2007, pp. 505–518.

[6] Sobriety, "DYNROT User Manual." 2016.

[7] K. Jauhari, A. Widodo, and I. Haryanto, "Identification of a Machine Tool Spindle Critical Frequency through Modal and Imbalance Response Analysis," *Am. J. Eng. Appl. Sci.*, vol. 9, no. 2, pp. 213–221, 2016.

[8] C. E. H. Ventura and A. Hassui, "Evaluation of static cutting forces and tool wear in HSM process applied to pocket milling," *Int. J. Adv. Manuf. Technol.*, vol. 65, no. 9–12, pp. 1681–1689, Apr. 2013.

[9] H. Cao, T. Holkup, and Y. Altintas, "A comparative study on the dynamics of high speed spindles with respect to different preload mechanisms," *Int. J. Adv. Manuf. Technol.*, vol. 57, no. 9–12, pp. 871–883, Dec. 2011.

[10] N. L. Carutasu, "Virtual simulation for static behavior of the main spindle assembly of a horizontal drilling and milling CNC machining with a high-speed cutting," *Ann. ORADEA Univ. Fascicle Manag. Technol. Eng.*, no. 2, pp. 125–128, 2016.

* Corresponding author: nicoletacarutasu@yahoo.com

Ability of managers for crisis management in small enterprises: study in Bosnia and Herzegovina

Vlado Medaković[1*], *Slaviša* Moljević[2], *Ranka* Gojković[3], *Srđan* Vasković[4]

[1]University of East Sarajevo, vlado.medakovic@gmail.com, Bosnia and Herzegovina
[2]University of East Sarajevo, slavisavgd@gmail.com, Bosnia and Herzegovina
[3]University of East Sarajevo, rankagojkovic@gmail.com, Bosnia and Herzegovina
[4]University of East Sarajevo, srdjan_vaskovic@yahoo.com, Bosnia and Herzegovina

Abstract—Since the enterprise have been existing, crisis of enterprise is well-known. Researches in area of possible appearance crisis in small and medium size enterprises, and sciense enterprise management which is crisis, have large significance when we talk about survival those enterprises, apropos possible prevention their bancrot. We can see that theory is mostly dedicated to enterprises repairing. The early symptom in sight of crisis and prevention latent crisis of enterprise are pointed up. Crisis management and analysis of strategy for turn out from the crisis, as we can see in this is paper, expand views and enable giving certain recomendations for appliance in practice.

1 Introduction

The bankruptcy of small and medium enterprises all over the world, ranging between 50% and 60% in the first year of operation (start-up), Medaković [1], Jojić and Božić [2], David [3].

The causes of bankruptcy are different, not the existence of the mission, vision and strategy to the poor product range, marketing, and poor organizational structure. The main reason for bankruptcy, the company's poor management, ie. management incompetence and his inability to recognize the threats facing the company in the early and transitional stage of its existence.

In theory and practice, we often encounter the dilemma of demarcation functions of entrepreneurs and managers. Of course there are differences, however, this distinction depends on the quantity of the enterprise in various companies, or by way of corporate management. In any case, it is impossible to imagine the company's operations outside of the chain (Ownrship - Market - Entrepreneurship - Management), Medaković [1], Ford [4].

Max Weber advocated the view that bureaucratic organization is an ideal type of organization. He, however, was aware of the possibility of abuse of power in the modern organization. Misuse of power may be internal, when participants are exploited or neglected or are not otherwise involved in the organization of public goods and services. Pathology of the modern business organization is struggling with one another and with the problem. As it seems these problems are based on the abuse of power.

Problems that affect the individual participante include alienation, inequality or ritualism. Alienation can be defined as a subjective feeling of weakness or self-alienation or objectively as a condition under which workers are losing control over the products of their labor or the value they have created.

Since the time of Adam Smith onwards, the researchers examined the consequences of organizational involvement, and in particular, the employment of individual participants - the ways and forms of employment in the organization and management efficiency.

In the Republic of Srpska and Bosnia, Serbia, Croatia segregation in employment is made on the basis of belonging to a political party or a privileged group. At the organizational level segregation of jobs in origin, or membership in a group is not just alienation but ill highly criminal society and its institutions.

All organizations providing benefits to external audiences - consumers, customers, citizens - as a condition for its continued existence. Use of this audience requirements vary according to the nature of the organization, they may include direct payments for goods or services received, indirect support in the form of taxes and normative support in the form of goodwill and legitimacy.

* Corresponding author: vlado.medakovic@gmail.com

The response to the needs of external audiences is a concern for all types of organizations, especially those that are external users and/or people connected as primary users. Since the private sector is expected to respond to economic signals - for example, the decline in business because customers are looking for better quality and lower prices. However, the decentralization of ownership and control, and encouraging managers still do not answer the wishes of customers.

2 The crisis of the life cycle company

Stage of development of small business is the most important period in the life cycle of the company, and this is the period in which the most common crisis companies, even in 60% of cases, Jojić and Božić [2], Senić [5].

At this level of growth, the company may either continue to grow and begin to use the profits to block roads or restricting its growth. Some companies survive only during development. Usually, but not always, the development phase begins in the second year of business and takes about two years.

The following scenario, shown in Fig. 1. helps to understand the life cycle of a competitive firm and a sense of each stage of the cycle.

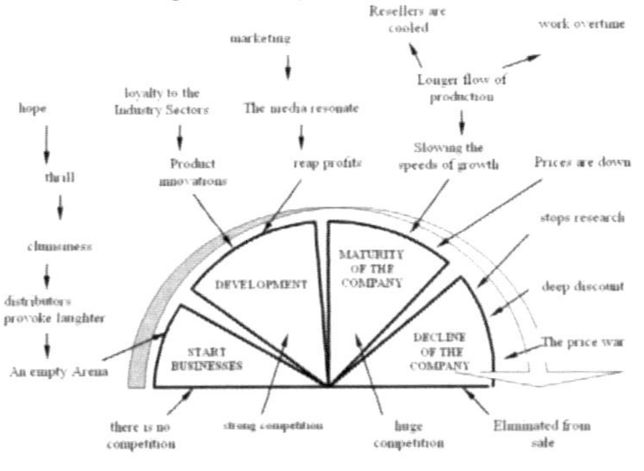

Fig. 1. Crisis scenario life cycle of the company, Medaković [1]

In the embryonic stage, the market is exciting, euphoric naive collision with the truth, that causes laughter, a high failure rate and a lot of negotiation. Price is experimental. The sales volume is low, because the market is very small and the production and marketing costs are high. Dealers are difficult to find, and the sellers are looking for a huge margin. Profit is a risky and speculative. Shrewd entrepreneur, however, can be approximated assess the "core markets". The competition has not yet emerged.

Growth phase was identified as product innovation, strong acceptance of products, beginning loyalty industry, the promotion that "bursting" through the media, the price is indicative. Product innovation continues. Distribution becomes all important. Resellers who were "laughing" during the initial phase now loudly complaining of product distribution. Strong competition, excited scent of money entering the market arena as find the group of target customers superior profits shows signs of growth.

Stage of maturity has been marked as the peak number of customers and generating zero modification. The design is focused on production differentiation rather than product promotion. Competitors are now blinded, they give impulse even when the speed slows shelves. Production is extended, so that firms can exploit the full advantage of capital equipment and management experience. Resellers anticipate rapid collapse, the growing cold products. Investing in advertising is growing compared to the competition. Prices are falling slowly. Any competitor who enters the market, it is now or dumb or over-confident, or both. Once the market becomes hot, it pervades the breath of depression. Decay phase is marked as extreme depression in the market. Competition is becoming desperate. Promotion disappears. Price war continues. Relentless fight for what is left of the core market. Reseller is impossible to find "they disappeared."

The crisis the company largely depends on the vested interests and political interaction between, the influence of organizational and adhokratije anarchy and chaos, and ultimately self-organization.

The politicians are competing with each other in order to obtain a favorable status as an entrepreneur dynamic forces in the private sector, which searches for profitable projects by offering goods and services in a competitive market depends on supply and demand. Today we are seeing that political power has an increasing impact on small businesses and the entrepreneurs. With the support of policy and interest groups are trying to provide the best possible position and as quickly become favorites in their industry, and to provide power.

3 Empirical studies of crisis in the small and medium enterprises

Complete information about the characteristics of a set gives only statistical list. Since the census requires a lot of time to create a large cost, it is replaced by the sample, which is part of the basic set and chosen without bias, ie. objective and whose purpose is to provide a reasonably accurate information about the characteristics of the entire sample set from which it originates.

To be credible conclusions about the characteristics of the basic set, we make based on the sample, the sample should be representative, that should be their composition similar to a basic set.

The study was conducted in the Republic of Srpska, closer location from which the sample is appropriate Podrinje region or territory following municipalities of Bratunac, Srebrenica, Zvornik, Višegrad and Foča. Investigations were carried out in the business at this location, whose random sample I came up. The sample companies are: companies face - singular and partner companies, a capital company: joint stock companies and cooperatives.

* Corresponding author: vlado.medakovic@gmail.com

Research on this topic, not only in the Podrinje region, but also in the Republic of Srpska and Bosnia and Herzegovina are very rare or not implemented at all, so it is difficult from the standpoint of patients eligible and unpopular, mainly due to fear of public presentation of certain data.

The sample is formed by 40 enterprises, which by their nature, organization, number of employees, total annual income, be representative and fully meet the requirements set out in the order of this paper.

4 Results and discussion

The survey covered 34 enterprises whose legal form of organization singular - a partnership firm, then we have 4 companies that are organized as a corporation and two enterprises that are organized as a agricultural cooperatives.

The number of managers is 9 women and 31 men. In order guaranteed discretion of managers, their age will not be shown here, and the age of the company is classified into several categories, as shown in Fig. 2.

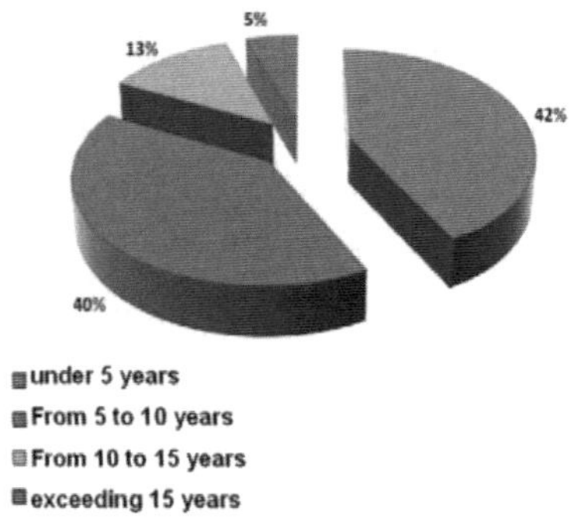

Fig. 2. The age of enterprises, Medaković [1]

It is obvious that small and medium-sized enterprises in the region of Podrinje fairly young, because the representation of companies under the age of 5 years 42%. Therefore subject to all the influences, both external and internal factors of instability.

Activities of companies that are the subject of the research are presented in Fig. 3.

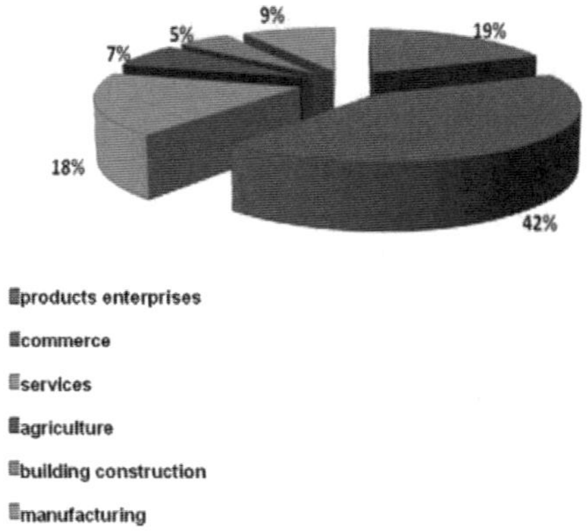

Fig. 3. Activities of the company represented, Medaković [1]

Generally given the third graph, conclusions can be drawn that a large number of companies engaged in commerce (42%) and that there is market saturation and competition is getting stronger, and those who want to survive have to adapt to that situation or reorient to a different activity. In the future business of the company in the field of services, or the provision of services in all areas of social, technical, educational, health, and so on., Tend to increase and the majority of small businesses will be exactly the service of character.

The survey covered enterprises employing different number of workers, as shown in Fig. 4, where one can see four intervals of number of employees and the percentage of workers employed in small and medium-sized enterprises.

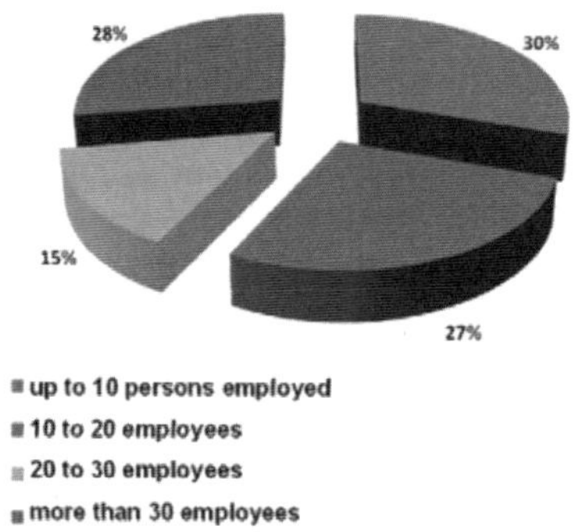

Fig. 4. Number of employees in small and medium-sized enterprises, Medaković [1]

Based on Figure 4 it can be concluded that a substantial number of small companies, 30% employ less than ten workers, indicating that a significant number of micro enterprises participating in the small and medium-sized enterprises.

As far as managerial experience, analysis of the survey can be concluded that included managers from small and managers with extensive experience. In Fig. 5. management experience has shown that is divided into three categories, time intervals Conducting managers.

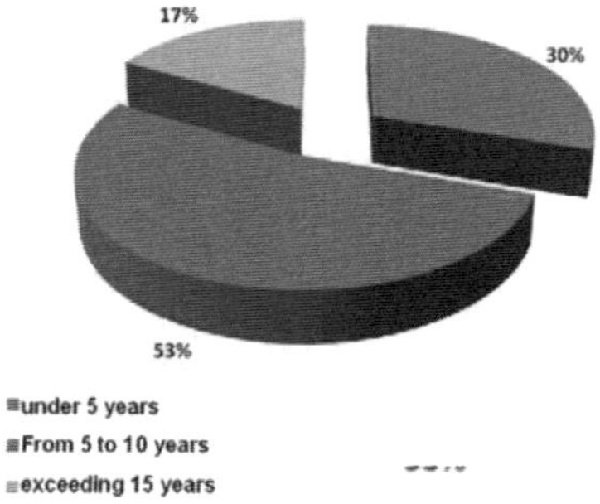

Fig. 5. Years of managerial experience, Medaković [1]

The percentage of 30% of managers with experience

* Corresponding author: vlado.medakovic@gmail.com

of 5 years indicates that just recently there was a rapid development of the private sector and the emergence of small and medium enterprises of different industries.

The third part of the survey effectiveness and creativity has a psychological test that is related to the effectiveness and creativity of managers.

This test demonstrates the extent to which managers have the ability to manage the crisis and which companies are the characteristics that are dominant in their personalities.

The analysis is presented Fig. 6 which displays the points depending on years of managerial experience, where we also had a manager is that the three groups. Manager with experience of 5 years, then a group of managers with experience of 5 to 15 years and a group of managers with over 15 years experience.

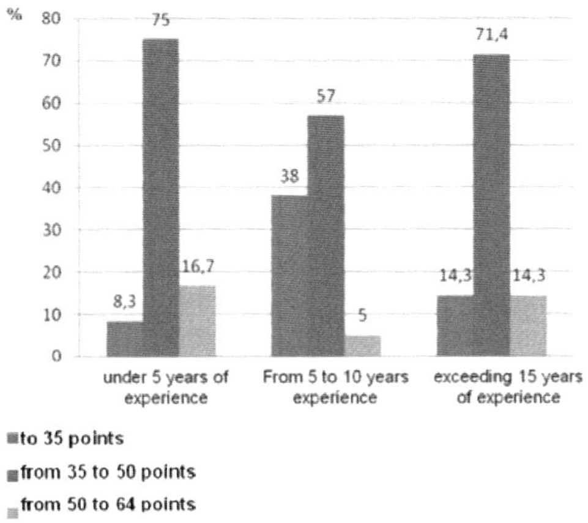

Fig. 6. Procentuala ability to manage a crisis managers in small and medium-sized enterprises, Medaković [1]

With Figure 5 that at first glance conclude that years of managerial experience are crucial when it comes to crisis management in small and medium-sized enterprises.

We see that in all three groups, which were formed on the basis of years of managerial experience, the number of points in the interval from 36 to 50 represented a large percentage, it gives us hope that the managers of small and medium-sized companies willing to venture enterprise management which threatens crisis or is already in crisis. Managers with experience of 5 to 15 years are less involved in monitoring and comprehensive changes that were "put to sleep" in their work, and would for that reason you should pay more attention to innovation in leading companies.

5 Conclusion

We are aware that the environment in which companies operate is becoming more dynamic. Today we live in a time of faster, complex and unpredictable changes, all of which significantly affect the operations and management services. Response to rapid changes in the environment have become more discontinuous character, which asks managers of companies to achieve major shifts in the short term.

Empirical studies have been conducted on the territory of the Republic of Serbian shown that small and medium-sized enterprises in a number are in crisis and that the necessary use of such knowledge and skills of crisis management.

Corporate Responsibility (owners of small and medium enterprises) as well as manager of the Republic of Serbian is at a high level as well as the temptation of finding the right path out of the crisis in which we find ourselves. If we lose way and start to be afraid of new technology, new types of managers, voice of other developed countries and cultures, then inevitably remain in the vicious circle of crisis. Managers who are able to bring to the organization a passion for change and a competitive spirit can count on the future.

References

[1] V. Medakovic, *Development of a model for crisis management in small and medium-sized enterprises* (original *„Razvoj modela za upravljanje krizom u malim i srednjim preduzecima"*), *magistarski rad*, FTN Novi Sad, 2008.

[2] R. Jojić, R. Božić, *Entrepreneurship for new century* (original "Preduzetništvo za novi vijek"), Srpsko Sarajevo - Priština, 1998.

[3] R. F. David, "Strategic management", Fifth Edition, Prentice – Hall International, Inc. Englewood Cliff, New Yersey, 1995.

[4] J. D. Ford, "The Management of Organizational Crisis", Business Horizont, May/June 1981.

[5] R. Senić, *Crisis management* (original "Krizni menadžment"), Beograd, 1996.

* Corresponding author: vlado.medakovic@gmail.com

MATEC Web of Conferences **126**, 04002 (2017) DOI: 10.1051/matecconf/201712604002
Annual Session of Scientific Papers IMT ORADEA 2017

Aspects of primary production of solar thermal and photovoltaic energy in European Union

Marian Zaharia[1], *Aniela* Bălăcescu[2], *Aurelia* Pătraşcu[3]

[1]Petroleum-Gas University of Ploieşti, marianzaharia53@gmail.com, Romania
[2]"Constantin Brâncuşi" University of Târgu Jiu, anielabalacescu@yahoo.com, Romania
[3]Petroleum-Gas University of Ploieşti, patrascuaura@yahoo.com, Romania

Abstract. The green energy production is an imperative of the sustainable development. In this context, the energy production based on solar radiation is an important alternative. Taking into account these aspects, the paper analyses the evolutions of primary productions of solar thermal and solar photovoltaic energy between 2000 and 2015 both in absolute values and in per capita values. The results of the analyses emphasize the exponential development of the productions of these types of energy. They also highlight the existence and even the emphasizing of the Europe Union productions concentration in some states like Spain and Germany that have produced 73.96% of the primary production of solar thermal energy in 2015, respectively Germany and Italy that have produced 62.2% of the primary production of solar photovoltaic energy, in the same year.

1 Introduction

Although in the last decade of the last century the primary renewable energy production has had a general growth trend that, in relative values, have surpassed the primary energy production from classical sources, the real boom of renewable energy production has occurred after 2000. Thus, if in 2000 the primary renewable energy production has represented 11.06% of the total primary energy production, in 2005 it has reached to 14.13% and in 2015 to 28.34%.

The sun has been used as a source of thermal energy since ancient times. However, the thermal energy production was only 149.1 Thousand tonnes of oil equivalent (TOE) at European Union (28 countries) level (EU-28), in 1990, representing less than 0.02% of total primary energy production.

The photovoltaic energy was practically inexistent in 1990, its primary production volume being of only 1.1 TOE. However, it has recorded an explosive growth since 2000. These aspects are the results of the significance given to the renewable energy production at EU level, K. Traube [1], H. Lund [2], J. Andrei, J. Subic, and D. Dusmanescu [3], as well as of the imperatives of sustainable development, A. G. Simionescu, M. C. Dragomir [4], A. L. Dumitrescu [5], J. V. Andrei, R. A. Ion, G. H. Popescu, E. Nica, and M. Zaharia [6].

Starting from this aspect, as well as from the 28 / European Commission Directive 2009/28 [7] and from the European Commission Communication 572/2015 [8] regarding the renewable energy in the EU-28, the paper emphasizes, on the one hand, the evolution that the primary production of solar thermal and solar photovoltaic energy has recorded during 2000 and 2015 and, on the other hand, highlights the place occupied by the EU-28 member states both in the total energy production based on solar radiation and in per capita production of solar thermal and solar photovoltaic energy.

2 Methodology

The analysis of the evolution of the primary productions of solar thermal and solar photovoltaic energy in the EU-28 is based on the statistical data series [9] regarding the two sources of renewable energy that form the two matrices of this type:

$$X = \left\{x_{i,j}\right\}_{i=\overline{1,n},\, j=\overline{1,m}} \quad (1)$$

In relation (1), the variable n=28 that corresponds to EU-28 member states and variable m=4 that corresponds to data series from 2000, 2005, 2010 and 2015.

In the first part of the analysis, the significance of the primary productions means of solar thermal and solar photovoltaic energy that have been calculated at EU-28

* Corresponding author: marianzaharia53@gmail.com

level for those 8 data series has been tested. The tested hypotheses were:

H_0: the mean value is not statistically significant (the mean does not significantly differ by zero).

H_1: the mean value is statistically significant (the mean significantly differs by zero).

In order to test them, the bilateral *t test (Student)* has been used. The statistics of the test (t_c) for the data series corresponding to year *k* is:

$$t_c = \frac{\bar{x}_k}{\frac{s}{\sqrt{n}}}, \quad s = \sqrt{\frac{\sum_{i=1}^{n}\left(x_{i,k} - \bar{x}_k\right)}{n-1}} \tag{2}$$

The condition of accepting the null hypothesis (H_0) is:

$$t_c \in \left[-t_{\frac{\alpha}{2},n-1}, t_{\frac{\alpha}{2},n-1}\right] \tag{3}$$

where $t_{\frac{\alpha}{2},n-1}$ is the critical value of *t test* (2 - tailed) for a significance threshold α. In particular, in the analyses that have been carried out *n* is equal to 28.

To test the statistical hypotheses, the 95% Confidence level (significance threshold α=0.05), has been chosen. The unit of measure used for primary production of solar thermal and solar photovoltaic energy is thousand tonnes of oil equivalent (TOE).

3 Results and discussions

The achieved analyses and the presented results refer both to the primary production of solar thermal and solar photovoltaic energy in absolute values and in per capita primary energy production.

Solar energy rank in the primary renewable energy production

In the early 90, the places occupied by solar thermal energy and solar photovoltaic energy were modest. At EU-28 level, in the total primary renewable energy production, they have represented 0.1877% and, respectively, 0.0015%, being practically negligible. Although during the period from 1990 and 2000, there have been increases in the volume of primary production of both types of energy sources, in 2000, the share of solar thermal energy at EU-28 level has represented 0.4093% of the total primary renewable energy (an increase of 0.2216 percentage points) and the share of solar photovoltaic energy has been of 0.0098% (an increase of only 0.0083 percentage points).

The annual growth rates of primary production from the two sources based on solar energy have overtaken the growth rates of most renewable energy production obtained from other sources since 2000. In this context, their productions volumes begin to be significant. Thus, from a primary production of 426.7 TOE in 2000, the solar thermal energy has reached to 703.0 TOE in 2005, 1788.3 TOE in 2010 and 4252.0 TOE in 2015. In the analysed period, the annual growth rates of the primary production based on solar thermal energy have ranged between a minimum of 7.03% in 2004 and a maximum of 35.23% in 2010.

Regarding the solar photovoltaic energy, this type of energy source has reached from a primary production of 10.2 TOE in 2000 to 125.6 TOE in 2005, 1935.0 TOE in 2010 and 8798.9 TOE in 2015. The annual growth rates of primary energy production from this source have evolved between a minimum of 14.09% in 2014 to a maximum of 101.37% in 2011. The explosive increase of the primary production of solar photovoltaic energy has led to the change in the ratio between the two energy sources. Thus, in 2009 and 2010 the primary production of solar photovoltaic energy has overtaken the primary production of solar thermal energy.

The annual growth rates of primary production of two energy sources have led to an increase of the production share of solar thermal and solar photovoltaic energy in the total primary renewable energy production at the EU-28 level (Fig. 1).

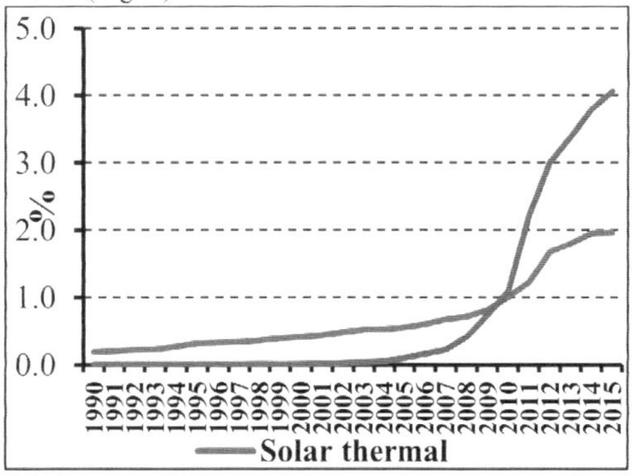

Fig. 1. Evolutions of shares of primary productions of solar thermal and solar photovoltaic energy in the total primary renewable energy production, in EU-28, in 1990-2015 period.

In the period between 2000 and 2010, the share of primary production of solar thermal energy in the total primary renewable energy production, at EU-28 level, has been almost linear with an annual average increase of 0.027 percentage points. In the last five years of the analysed period, we have noticed an exponential growth. However, in 2014 and 2015 a stabilization has occurred around the value of 1.95%.

The share of total production of solar photovoltaic energy in the total primary renewable energy production, at EU-28 level, has had a relatively similar trend but with a much higher intensity. If the increase has been almost linear between 2000 and 2006 with an annual average increase of 0.006 percentage points, after 2007, the increase has become explosive, so that in only 8 years, from a share of 0.2242% in the total primary renewable energy production in 2007, at EU-28 level, it has reached to 4.0548% in 2015. This change of share is the result of the increase of the primary production of solar photovoltaic energy from 324.5 TOE in 2007 to 8798.9 TOE in 2015 (an increase of 27.12 times).

* Corresponding author: marianzaharia53@gmail.com

EU countries rank in the total primary production of solar thermal and solar photovoltaic energy

The statistical significances of the mean values of the two indicators have been determined and tested in order to see if the hierarchy and the EU-28 member states grouping by the total primary production of solar thermal energy and, respectively, solar photovoltaic energy bring relevant information in relation to the primary mean production from these energy sources (Table 1).

Taking into account that the standard deviation values (Std. Dev.) are much higher than the mean values (Mean), the 99% confidence level (α=0.01) has been chosen to test the statistical significance of the mean values. The critical value of *t test* (2-tailed) for the 99% confidence level is $t_{\frac{\alpha}{2},27} = 2.771$.

Excepting the primary mean production of solar thermal energy for 2000 for which the null hypothesis (H_{0_1}) is rejected and the alternative hypothesis (H_{1_1}) is accepted, for all other mean values the null hypothesis is accepted (H_{0_1}) and, consequently, the obtained values are not statistically significant and cannot be used in analyses. This fact emphasizes a greater diversity and requires sorting and grouping of EU-28 member states by the primary productions of solar thermal and solar photovoltaic energy.

Table 1. Testing the statistical significance of primary mean production of solar thermal and solar photovoltaic energy, at eu-28 level

Year	Source	Mean	Std.Dev.	t_c	Acc.H.
2000	ST	15.24	29.13	2.768	H_{1_1}
	SP	0.36	1.03	1.852	H_{0_1}
2005	ST	25.10	53.49	2.483	H_{0_1}
	SP	4.48	20.76	1.142	H_{0_1}
2010	ST	63.86	128.36	2.632	H_{0_1}
	SP	69.10	212.91	1.717	H_{0_1}
2015	ST	151.86	473.85	1.696	H_{0_1}
	SP	314.24	717.47	2.324	H_{0_1}

In order to emphasize the distribution of EU-28 member states by groups depending on the primary productions of solar thermal energy, they have been sorted descending and, after that, six groups have been formed for each of the four years included in the analysis. The first group includes the first three states that contain the highest values of the primary production of solar thermal energy. The other groups contain five states. The primary means productions of energy have been determined for each group.

The graphical representation of the accumulated values corresponding to the primary means productions of solar thermal energy, at group level, highlights not only a high concentration of this type of energy but also an emphasis of it during the period between 2000 and 2015 (Fig. 2).

Some changes regarding the shares of primary production of solar thermal energy by groups of states in the total primary production recorded from this type of energy source at EU-28 level have been produced between 2000 and 2015. However, in the groups structures of states have not been major changes, so that

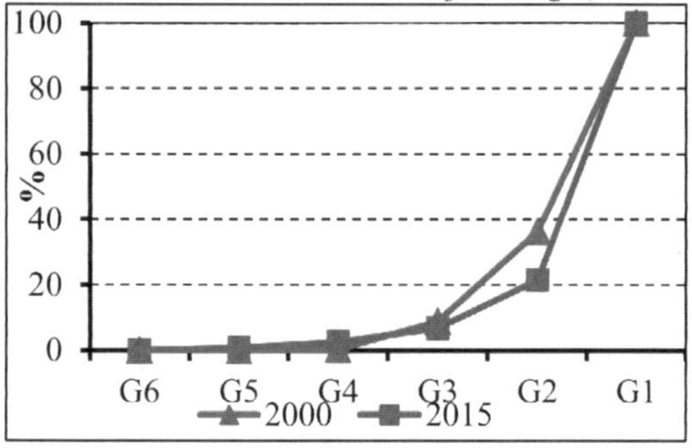

Fig. 2. Concentration of primary productions of solar thermal energy, by groups of states, in 2000 and 2015.

the groups structure of states in 2015 (Table 2) does not fundamentally differ from their structure from 2000.

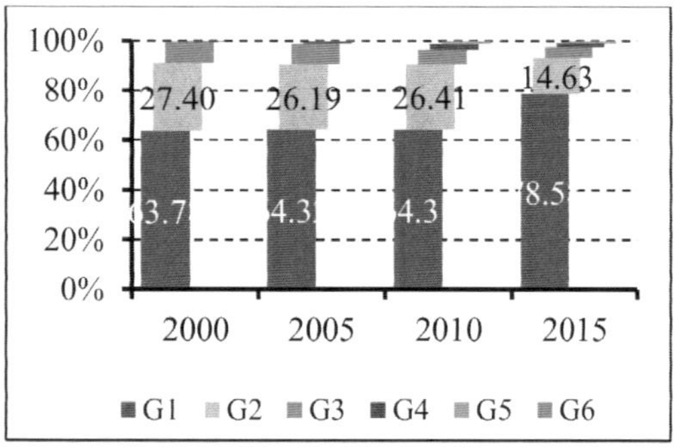

Fig. 3. Evolutions of shares of primary productions of solar thermal energy by groups of states, in 2000-2015 period.

In 2000, the share of primary production of solar thermal energy of the states from the first group (G1) in total primary energy production from this source has

Table 2. States groups structures in terms of the share of primary production of solar thermal energy, in 2000 and 2015

Year	Group	Countries
2000	G1	Germany, Greece, Austria
	G2	Cyprus, Spain, France, Portugal, UK
	G3	Italy, Netherlands, Denmark, Sweden, Croatia
	G4	Belgium, Finland, Ireland, Slovakia, Slovenia
	G5	Romania, Poland, Malta, Hungary, Luxemburg
	G6	Lithuania, Latvia, Estonia, Czech Republic, Bulgaria
2015	G1	Spain, Germany, Greece
	G2	Italy, Austria, France, Portugal, Cyprus
	G3	UK, Poland, Denmark, Netherlands, Belgium
	G4	Bulgaria, Czech Republic, Ireland, Sweden, Slovenia
	G5	Hungary, Croatia, Slovakia, Malta Luxemburg
	G6	Finland, Romania, Lithuania, Latvia, Estonia

* Corresponding author: marianzaharia53@gmail.com

been of 63.78% that corresponded to a primary production of 272.1 TOE, the highest productions being recorded in Germany (110.9 TOE) and in Greece (98.8 TOE).

The second group (G2) has produced 27.4% of the total primary production of solar thermal energy, respectively 116.9 TOE. The highest production has been recorded in Cyprus (35.5 TOE) and lowest in the UK (11.2 TOE). In the same year, the states from the third group (G3) have produced 8.46% of total primary production of solar thermal energy, respectively 36.1 TOE, on the first places from the group being placed Italy (10.9 TOE) and Netherlands (10.8 TOE). Regarding the other 15 states (groups G4-G6), the share of their total primary production in the total primary production of solar thermal energy, at EU-28 level, has been only of 0.35%. In 2000, the primary production of solar thermal energy has been practically concentrated in the 13 states of the groups G1-G3.

In 2015, the share of the primary production of solar thermal energy of the states from the first group (G1) in the total primary production of energy from this source has reached to 78.58% (an increase of 14.8 percentage points). At the same time, the production shares of the states from the group G2 have been reduced from 27.4% to 14.63% (a decrease of 12.77 percentage points) and the production shares of the states from the group G3 have decreased from 8.46% to 4.21%. Also, we have noticed the fact that the share of the states from the groups G4-G6 has recorded significant increases reaching to 2.58%. Excepting Lithuania, Latvia and Estonia, in all other 12 states the primary production of solar thermal energy has been greater than 0.

These changes of shares are due to the significant increases of the primary production of the solar thermal energy. If we consider only the first group (G1), the highest increase of production has been recorded in Spain, from 31.1 TOE to 2473.8 TOE (an increase of 79.54 times). Consequently, in 2015, Spain has produced 58.18% of total thermal solar energy, at EU-28 level. This fact has generated its transition from group G2 to group G1.

Italy has moved from group G3 to the group G2 due to an increase of the production from 10.9 TOE to 190.0 TOE (an increase of 17.43 times). At the same time, UK passes from group G2 to group G3 due to a lower annual increase rate of the production than the other states from group G2.

In the analysed period, due to the national energy policies, significant increases of the primary production of solar thermal energy have been recorded in states of EU-28 where the production from this energy source was practically null, in 2000. Thus, there have been recorded the following productions: 21.8 TOE in Bulgaria, 17.7 TOE in Czech Republic, 10.9 TOE in Slovenia, 10.7 TOE in Hungary, 5.5 TOE in Slovakia and 4.3 TOE in Malta. Romania with a production of only 0.5 TOE is placed in the group G6 with Finland and Baltic States.

The most spectacular increase of the solar energy use in the renewable energy production has been recorded, in the analysed period, by the solar photovoltaic energy, especially after 2005. In 2005, Germany has owned 87.89% of the total primary production of the solar photovoltaic energy at EU-28 level, with a production of 110.3 TOE. Spain, Netherlands, Italy, Austria and Luxembourg have owned, in turn, a percent of 9.96%, with a production ranged between 1.5 TOE and 3.5 TOE. In the other 22 states, the primary productions of solar photovoltaic energy have been practically insignificant.

The results are spectacular in most states for the period between 2005 and 2010, as well as for the period between 2010 and 2015 as a result of EU energy policies. This aspect has generated significant changes in the share of groups of states (Fig. 4). The groups' structures of states depending on these shares, in 2010 and 2015, are emphasized in Table 3. Excepting the first group (G1) that contains the same states both in 2010 and in 2015, in the other groups they have occurred changes.

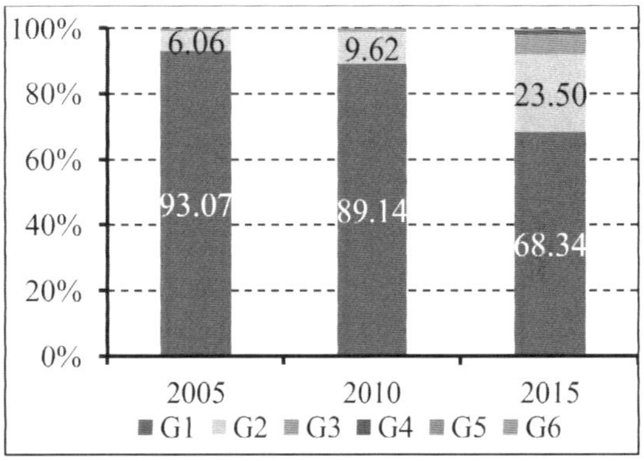

Fig. 4. Evolutions of share of primary productions of solar photovoltaic energy by groups of states, in 2005-2015 period.

Although the primary production of solar photovoltaic energy generated by the stated from the first group (G1) has increased from 1724.8 TOE in 2010 to 6013.4 TOE in 2015 (an increase of 3.48 times), its share in the total primary production, at EU-28 level, has decreased with 20.8 percentage points, reaching to 68.34%. However, it must be emphasized the fact that, in 2015, Germany and Italy have produced 37.8% and, respectively, 22.4% of the EU-28 production at this type of renewable energy.

Excepting Portugal, the other four states that are included in the group G2, in 2010, remain in this group also in 2015, with productions ranging between 194.7 TOE in Czech Republic and 624.2 TOE in France. The highest primary production of solar photovoltaic energy in this group, in 2015, is generated by UK whose production has increased from 3.5 TOE in 2010 to 650.1 TOE in 2015, representing 7.4% of the production of this energy type, at EU-28 level.

The primary production of solar photovoltaic energy for the third group (G3) has increased from 19.2 TOE to

* Corresponding author: marianzaharia53@gmail.com

534.8 TOE (an increase of 27.9 times), in the period between 2010 and 2015. Unlike the first two groups, in this group, there are significant changes. Thus, must be emphasized the contributions of Romania and Bulgaria whose productions of solar photovoltaic energy have increased from very low values to 170.4 TOE and, respectively, 118.9 TOE that have placed them on the first two places in this group. However, in 2015, the states from this group have produced only 6.08% of EU-28 production.

In 2015, in the fourth group, Denmark with a production of 52.0 TOE, Slovenia with 23.6 TOE and Cyprus with 10.9 TOE are maintained. Also, in this group, are added Slovakia with a production of 43.5 TOE that has come from group G3 and Hungary that has reached from a production of 0.1 TOE in 2010 to a production of 10.5 TOE in 2015. In 2015, the primary production of solar photovoltaic energy for the entire group has been of 140.5 TOE that has represented only 1.6% of the total production of this type of renewable energy, at EU-28 level.

Table 3. States groups structures in terms of the share of primary production of solar photovoltaic energy, in 2000 and 2015

Year	*Group*	*Countries*
2000	G1	Germany, Spain, Italy
	G2	France, Czech Republic, Belgium, Portugal, Greece
	G3	Austria, Netherland, UK, Luxemburg, Slovakia
	G4	Bulgaria, Slovenia, Sweden, Cyprus, Denmark
	G5	Finland, Malta, Hungary, Romania, Poland
	G6	Lithuania, Latvia, Croatia, Ireland, Estonia
2015	G1	Germany, Italy, Spain
	G2	UK, France, Greece, Belgium, Czech Republic
	G3	Romania, Bulgaria, Netherlands, Austria, Portugal
	G4	Denmark, Slovakia, Slovenia, Cyprus, Hungary
	G5	Luxembourg, Sweden, Malta, Lithuania, Poland
	G6	Croatia, Finland, Ireland, Latvia, Estonia

Finally, in 2015, the groups G5 and G6 include states where the primary production of solar photovoltaic energy represents less than 0.1% of the primary production of solar photovoltaic energy, at the EU-28 level.

If we consider both primary production of solar thermal energy and primary production of solar photovoltaic energy, the first five producers of renewable energy based on solar radiation, in 2015, are: Germany with 40001.1 TOE, representing 30.66% of the total EU-28 production, Spain with 3184.6 TOE (24.40%), Italy with 2162.7 TOE (16.57%), France with 723.2 TOE (5.54%), and UK with 700.8 TOE (3.37%). Overall, these countries produce 82.54% of total primary energy production based on solar radiation at EU-28 level.

In this ranking, Romania has been placed, in 2015, on the 10th place, with a production of 170.9 TOE that have represented 1.31% of total EU-28 production.

Aspects of per capita primary production of solar thermal and solar photovoltaic energy

In the previous sections, the primary energy productions obtained from the solar radiations, by states and groups of states, in absolute values have been analysed. However, taking into account the fact that the sizes and the economic powers of the EU-28 member states are totally different, we emphasize some aspects of the primary production of solar thermal and solar photovoltaic energy reported to the number of inhabitants in each state. The chosen unit of measure was TOE per one hundred thousand inhabitants (TOE/HTI).

The hierarchy of EU-28 member states where the primary production of energy based on solar radiation is greater than 1 TOE / HTI is presented in Fig. 5.

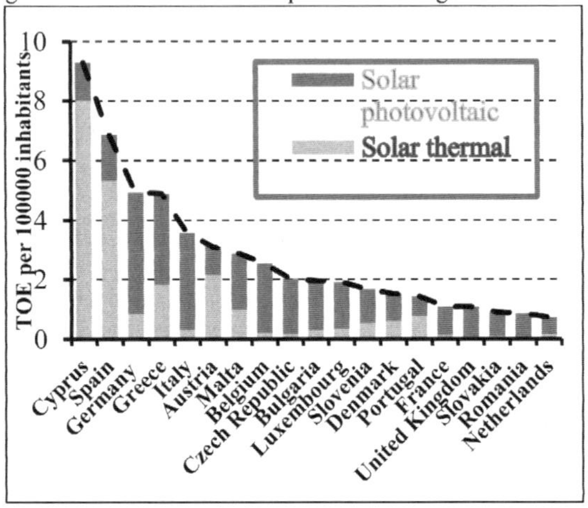

Fig. 5. Primary production of solar thermal and solar photovoltaic energy per 100000 inhabitants, in 2015.

A first observation is the fact that small states such as Cyprus and Malta due to their geographical positions and to their limited traditional resources of energy record significant values of this indicator. Thus, Cyprus is on the first place with a production of 9.3 TOE/HTI and Malta on the 7th place with a production of 2.86 TOE/HTI.

A second observation is that from the 2nd place to 6th place there are states that have been also placed on the first places at the primary production of solar thermal energy or solar photovoltaic energy: Spain with 6.86 TOE/HTI, Germany with 4.94 TOE/HTI, Greece with 4.9 TOE/HTI, Italy with 3.56 TOE/HTI and Austria with 3.1 TOE/HTI.

A third observation is the fact that important states with significant economic powers such as France and UK that have recorded productions of 1.08 TOE/HTI and, respectively, 1.08 TOE/HTI, in terms of primary production of solar thermal and solar photovoltaic energy per one hundred thousand inhabitants, are overtaken by much smaller states, among them three are former communist states: Czech Republic with productions of 2.02 TOE/HTI, Bulgaria with productions

* Corresponding author: marianzaharia53@gmail.com

of 1.95 TOE/HTI and Slovenia with productions of 1.67 TOE/HTI.

We must also emphasize the fact that the shares of primary production of solar thermal and solar photovoltaic energy per one hundred thousand inhabitants in total significantly differ from one state to another. Thus, in states like Cyprus, Spain, Austria and Portugal, the primary production of solar thermal energy prevails, while in the other 12 states represented in Fig. 5 the primary production of solar photovoltaic energy predominates.

Finally, one last observation is about Romania that with a production of energy based on solar radiation of 0.86 TOE / HTI has been on 18th place. Also, we must highlight that 99.71% of this production is obtained from solar photovoltaic energy.

4 Conclusions

In the context of sustainable development, the renewable energy production is a necessity widely recognized by all EU-28 member states, as well as by most countries of the world. Although various renewable energy sources have been used since the last century, in the last 15-20 years the production of green energy has grown exponentially.

Among the renewable energy sources, the use of solar radiation, especially in the production of solar photovoltaic energy, has seen an unprecedented boom, an aspect that is due, to some extent, to the development of technologies and to the increase of the growth rates in this field. Although after 2010, the primary production of solar photovoltaic energy in 26 of the 28 EU member states has been higher than 0.1 TOE, in 2015, 60.2% of the primary production of the solar photovoltaic energy has been concentrated in two states: Germany and Italy that have produced 3329.9 TOE (37.8%) and, respectively, 1972.7 TOE (22.4%). Romania with a production of 170.4 TOE (1.94%) has been on the 9th place, in the EU-28.

Although the primary production of solar thermal energy has recorded significant increases, the growth rates have been lower than in the primary production of solar photovoltaic energy. In the period between 2000 and 2015, the primary production of solar thermal energy has increased from 426.6 TOE to 4252.1 TOE, at EU-28 level. However, the growth rates have significantly differed from one state to another. This fact has led to the increase of concentration. Thus, in 2015, 73.96% of the primary production of solar thermal energy (3145.0 TOE) has been provided by two states: Spain and Germany. Spain, with a production of 2473.8 TOE, has ensured 58.18% of the primary production of solar thermal energy.

In terms of the primary energy production based on solar radiation calculated per one hundred thousand inhabitants, Cyprus has been on the first place in EU-28 with a production of 9.3 TOE/HTI of which 86.17% is solar thermal energy. This fact is due, to some extent, to its geographical position that has led to the massive use of this type of energy. This phenomenon has been manifested, in time, also in Spain, Greece, Italy and Malta which are among the first seven EU-28 states, in this regard. However, we must emphasize the fact that Germany is on the third place with a production of 4.93 TOE/HTI. In this case, we cannot speak about a favorable geographical position, but about an economic power, a characteristic emphasized by the fact that 83.22% (4.10 TOE/HTI) of 4.93 TOE/HTI represents solar photovoltaic energy.

The characteristics of the primary productions evolutions of solar thermal and solar photovoltaic energy emphasize the conclusion that solar radiation is and will be an important source of renewable energy that will continue to develop based on technologies development, from the field.

References

[1] K. Traube, "Renewable Energy and Nature Conservation", *Energy & Environment*, vol. 15, issue 4, pp. 625-631, 2004.
[2] H. Lund, "Renewable energy strategies for sustainable development", *Energy*, vol. 32, issue 6, pp. 912-919, 2007.
[3] J. Andrei, J. Subic, and D. Dusmanescu, "Using dynamic programming for optimizing the investment strategy for an agricultural sheep holding: an investment case simulation", *Актуальні проблеми економіки*, vol. 4, no. 142, pp. 252-261, 2013.
[4] A. G. Simionescu, M. C. Dragomir, "Using Renewable Energy for a Sustainable Development", *Annals of "Dunarea de Jos" University of Galati Fascicle I. Economics and Applied Informatics*, issue 3, pp. 39-44, 2012.
[5] A. L. Dumitrescu, "The Energy Union pillars: competitiveness, security and sustainability", *The Journal of Global Economics*, vol. 8, issue 4, 2016.
[6] J. V. Andrei, R. A. Ion, G. H. Popescu, E. Nica, and M. Zaharia, "Implications of agricultural bioenergy crop production and prices in changing the land use paradigm—the case of Romania", *Land Use Policy*, vol. 50, pp. 399-407, 2016.
[7] European Commission, DIRECTIVE 2009/28/EC OF THE EUROPEAN PARLIAMENT AND OF THE COUNCIL, http://eur-lex.europa.eu/legal-content/EN/TXT/PDF/?uri=CELEX:32009L0028&from=en, accessed on January 2017.
[8] European Commission, State of the Energy Union 2015, https://ec.europa.eu/transparency/regdoc/rep/1/2015/EN/1-2015-572-EN-F1-1.PDF, accessed on January 2017.
[9] Eurostat Database, Primary production - all products - annual data (nrg_109a), http://appsso.eurostat.ec.europa.eu/nui/show.do?dataset=nrg_109a&lang=en, accessed on January 2017.

* Corresponding author: marianzaharia53@gmail.com

Characteristics of the evolution of renewable energy production in European Union

Marian Zaharia[1*], *Rodica Manuela* Gogonea[2], *Ana* Tănăsescu[3]

[1]Petroleum-Gas University of Ploieşti, marianzaharia53@gmail.com, Romania
[2]Academy of Economic Studies from Bucharest, manuela.gogonea@gmail.com, Romania
[3]Petroleum-Gas University of Ploieşti, atanasescuro@yahoo.com, Romania

Abstract. Starting from the evolution of the primary energy production from renewable energy sources, in the EU-28, from 1990 to 2015, the paper emphasizes both the changes in the primary production volumes and the mutations in the share of their production in the total primary renewable energy production recorded, especially, in the second part of the analysed period. Based on them, models are identified and primary renewable energy productions for 2020 are estimated from renewable energy sources like: solid biofuels, hydropower, wind power, biogas, biodiesels and solar photovoltaic. Excepting the production of energy based on hydropower, significant increases are recorded for the other five renewable energy sources.

1 Introduction

The renewable energy production has been an objective for forty years, N. D. Mortimer [1]. The exponential growth of the energy requirement, on the one hand, as well as the sustainable development imperatives J. Andrei, J. Subic, and D. Dusmanescu [2], H. Lund [3], J. V. Andrei, R. A. Ion, G. H. Popescu, E. Nica, and M. Zaharia [4], on the other hand, have made the energy sources problem to become one of the most important concern of this beginning of millennium A. G. Simionescu, and M. C. Dragomir [5], A. L. Dumitrescu [6] for most countries of the world.

At EU level, the production and use of energy from renewable sources constitutes an important target. Thus, since 2009, the Directive 28/EC [7] provided that in 2020 at least 20% of the final energy consumption to come from renewable sources and in the Communication 572/2015 was emphasized the fact that *energy from renewable sources and the energy efficiency require new abilities and investments and create jobs in Europe*, European Commission. State of the Energy Union (website)[8]. The energy security correlated with the sustainable development of the EU Member States economies in 2030 should reduce by 40% the greenhouse gas emissions compared to 1990 levels and ensure at least 27% from energy consumption, from renewable sources, European Commission. 2030 Energy Strategy(website) [9].

Based on these considerations, the paper analyses the evolutions of primary energy productions provided, for the period between 1990 and 2015, from 15 renewable energy sources: hydropower (HP), wind power (WP), solar thermal (ST), solar photovoltaic (SP), tide, wave and ocean (TWO), solid biofuels (SB), biogas (BG), municipal waste renewable (MRW), municipal waste non-renewable (MNW), biogasoline (BGL), biodiesels (BD), other liquid biofuels (OLB), bio jet kerosene (BJK), geothermal energy (GE) and industrial waste (IW).

In the paper first part, both the evolutions of the energy production from the 15 sources that are taken into account and the change of their share in the total energy production from nonconventional sources are analysed.

In the second part of the paper, the evolutions models of the renewable energy sources with significant development of production in the second part of the analysed period are identified and statistically tested. The energy production volumes from these sources, in 2020, are estimated, based on them.

2 Methodology

For the analysis of the evolution of primary renewable energy production in the EU-28, we have used the initial data series, Primary production - all products - annual data(website) [10] corresponding to those 15 primary renewable energy sources included in the achieved analysis. These describe the evolutions of renewable energy productions for a period of 26 years

* Corresponding author: marianzaharia53@gmail.com

DOI: 10.1051/matecconf/201712604003

(1990-2015), thus the variable n representing the number of years is equal to 26.

We have considered the data series $Y = \{y_i\}_{i=n}$. The polynomial model (1) used to determine the evolution of analysed variables is:

$$y = \hat{y} + \varepsilon, \quad \hat{y} = a_0 + \sum_{j=1}^{k} a_j \cdot t^j \tag{1}$$

The validation of model (1) was carried out using ANOVA methodology and *F test*. The *F statistics* is:

$$F_c = \frac{\sum_{i=1}^{n}(\hat{y}_i - \bar{y})}{k} \bigg/ \frac{\sum_{i=1}^{n}(y_i - \hat{y}_i)}{n-k-1} \tag{2}$$

Considering that α=0.05 and according to the values of $F_{0.05,\,k,\,n-k-1}$, the test hypotheses are:

H_{0_1}: the polynomial model (1) is not statistically significant ($Fc < F_{0.05,\,k,\,n-k-1}$).

H_{1_1}: the polynomial model (1) is statistically significant ($Fc > F_{0.05,\,k,\,n-k-1}$).

The estimation of the analysed variables values for year 2020 has been carried out based on the valid models that are specific to each indicator. Taking into account the values of bilateral *t test (Student)*, the limits of the confidence intervals of estimated values, for significance threshold α, are given by the relation:

$$y_{2020} \in \left[\hat{y}_{2020} \mp t_{\frac{\alpha}{2},n-k-1} \cdot S_{\hat{y}_{2020}}\right] \tag{3}$$

where:

$$S_{\hat{y}_{2020}} = \sqrt{\frac{\sum_{i=1}^{n}(y_i - \hat{y}_i)^2}{n-k-1}\left[1 + \frac{1}{n} + \frac{(x_{2020} - \bar{x})^2}{\sum_{i=1}^{n}(x_i - \bar{x})^2}\right]} \tag{4}$$

and $t_{\frac{\alpha}{2},n-k-1}$ represents the critical values for *Student distribution* for significance threshold α and k independent variables. In particular, in the achieved analysed n is equal to 26.

The tested hypotheses are:

H_{0_2}: the estimated value is not statistically significant (the confidence interval for the variable values includes the 0 value).

H_{1_2}: the estimated value is statistically significant (the limits of the confidence interval have the same sign).

To test the statistical hypotheses, 95% Confidence level (significance threshold α=0.05) has been chosen. The unit of measure used for primary renewable energy production is thousand tonnes of oil equivalent (TOE).

The SPSS, E. Jaba, A. Grama [11] and Excel (the Data Analysis module) have been used for data processing and analysis.

3 Results and discussions

In the period between 1990 and 2015, the renewable energy production had an ascending evolution that has led us to the conclusion that the established objectives at EU level for 2020 and 2030 can be fulfilled.

3.1 Characteristics of the evolution of primary renewable energy productions

The total primary renewable energy production at EU - 28 level between 1990 and 2015 has recorded significant increases from 75584.7 TOE (TOE - thousand tonnes of oil equivalent) in 1990 to 216997.7 TOE in 2015 (an increase of 2.87 times). However, the increase was not linear. If until 2002 the annual growth rates have evolved between 5.54% in 1993 (4504.3 TOE) and 0.36% (360.9 TOE) in 1999, in the period between 2002 and 2015 the annual growth rates have evolved between a maximum value of 9.89% in 2010 and a minimum value of 1.90% in 2014 that correspond to some absolute increases of 16132.3 TOE and, respectively, 3901.9 TOE. In consequence, if in the first half of the analysed period the total renewable energy production has increased with 41.55%, in the second half of the analysed period an increased with 150.45% has been recorded.

The recorded increases significantly differ in the analysed period, by renewable energy sources (figure 1). Thus, on the one hand, in absolute values, the highest increase has been recorded at the primary production of solid biofuels (49749.7 TOE), followed by de wind power (25889.2 TOE), biogas (14946.4 TOE) and biodiesels (11070.5 TOE). On the other hand, insignificant increases have been recorded at sources like: bio jet kerosene, other liquid biofuels and tide, wave and ocean.

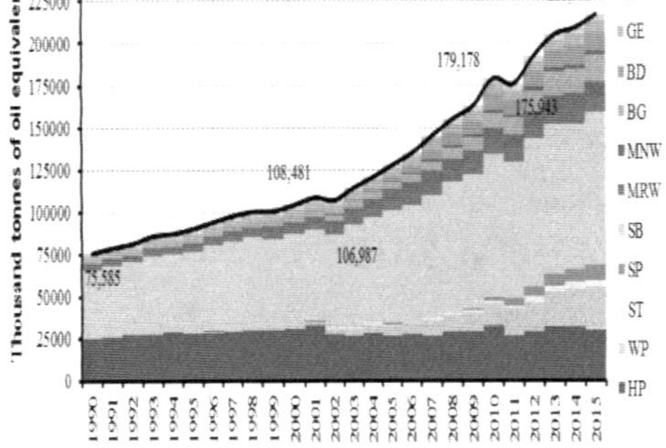

Fig. 1. Evolutions of primary renewable energy productions, in 1990-2015 period.

* Corresponding author: marianzaharia53@gmail.com

Source: elaborated by authors based on the data from Primary production - all products - annual data(website) [10]

In relative values, the differences are even higher. Thus, at the end of the first half of the analysed period, while in the case of 9 of the 15 renewable energy sources have been recorded increases between 0.7% (tide, wave and ocean) and 73.6% (municipal non-renewable waste), the primary energy production from solar thermal source was with 153% higher than in 1990 and at energy sources such as solar photovoltaic and wind power the increases were with 509.1% and, respectively, with 1348.9% higher.

Table 1. The hierarchy of renewable energy sources depending on production volume (toe)

Place	1990		1995		2000	
	Source	Prod.	Source	Prod.	Source	Prod.
1	SB	40627	SB	47646	SB	53835
2	HP	24972	HP	28547	HP	30687
3	GE	3185	GE	3439	GE	4587
4	MRW	2094	IW	3020	MRW	3801
5	MNW	2023	MRW	2661	MNW	3663
6	IW	1759	MNW	2638	IW	2395
7	BG	665	BG	1136	BG	2186
8	ST	142	WP	350	WP	1911
9	WP	67	ST	284	BD	634
10	TWO	43	BD	188	ST	427
11	BD	6	TWO	44	BGL	59
12	SP	1	BGL	24	TWO	44
13	BGL	0	OLB	10	OLB	16
14	OLB	0	SP	4	SP	10
15	BJK	0	BJK	0	BJK	0

Place	2005		2010		2015	
	Source	Prod.	Source	Prod.	Source	Prod.
1	SB	67303	SB	85467	SB	90421
2	HP	26940	HP	32408	HP	29327
3	MNW	6205	WP	12842	WP	25956
4	WP	6058	BD	8931	BG	15612
5	MRW	6025	BG	8530	BD	11077
6	GE	5309	MRW	7864	MRW	9485
7	BG	4000	MNW	7594	MNW	9189
8	BD	2499	GE	5517	SP	8799
9	IW	1633	IW	3466	GE	6466
10	ST	703	BGL	1972	ST	4252
11	BGL	480	SP	1935	IW	3780
12	OLB	394	ST	1788	BGL	2177
13	SP	126	OLB	823	OLB	414
14	TWO	41	TWO	41	TWO	42
15	BJK	0	BJK	0	BJK	1

These evolution trends are emphasized in the second part of the analysed period so that in 2015 compared to 2002 the primary energy production from renewable energy sources was of 8.31 times higher at wind power, of 8.34 times higher at solar thermal, of 11.1 times higher at biodiesels and of 13.75 times higher at biogasoline. Regarding the solar photovoltaic primary energy production, the increase has been explosive, so that in 2015 this increase was of 363.57 times higher than in 2002. The different evolutions that have been recorded by the renewable energy production in the analysed period have led to significant changes of the share of energy sources production in the total renewable energy production (figure 2).

Until the end of the first half of the analysed period significant changes are not recorded, the shares of renewable energy production from solid biofuels and hydropower representing 51.95% and, respectively, 25.64% of total.

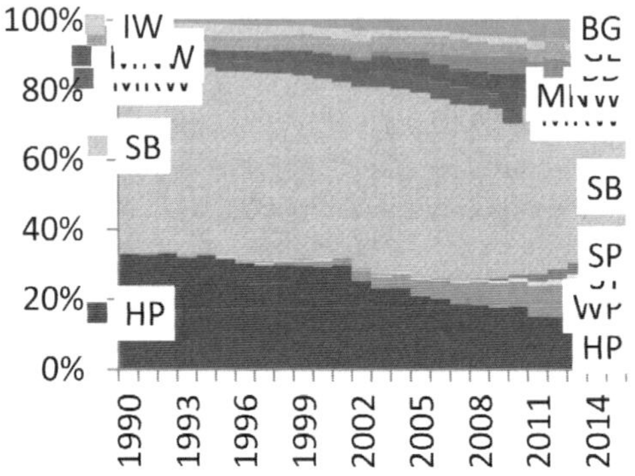

Fig. 2. Evolutions of the shares of primary renewable energy productions, by energy sources, in 1990-2015 period.

However, the changes are significant in the second part of the analysed period. Thus, in 2015, the shares of renewable energy production from solid biofuels and hydropower decrease to 41.67% and, respectively, to 13.51% of total. Due to the explosive increase, the renewable energy production based on wind power reaches to 11.96% of total. This is followed by biogas (7.19%), biodiesels (5.10%), municipal renewable waste (4.37%), municipal non-renewable waste (4.23%), solar photovoltaic (4.05%), geothermal energy (2.98%), solar thermal (1.96%) and industrial waste (1.74%).

The evolutions of the renewable energy productions by main energy sources, presented in table I, emphasize the changes that occur regarding the place occupied by the different renewable energy sources, in 1990-2015 period.

A first characteristic is represented by the fact that the energy produced based on solid biofuels and hydropower remains on the first place, for the entire analysed period.

In 1990, the main renewable energy source was municipal renewable waste (53.75% of total), followed by hydropower (33.04% from total) and geothermal energy (4.21% from total), the other 12 sources generating only 9% from the total renewable energy.

A second characteristic of the renewable energy production evolution is that the most significant advancements in the hierarchy have been recorded by the following energy sources: wind power and biodiesels with an advance of 6 places, solar photovoltaic with an

* Corresponding author: marianzaharia53@gmail.com

advance of 4 places and biogas with an advance of 3 places.

A third characteristic is that, although, the municipal renewable waste and municipal non-renewable constitute important renewable energy sources, in the production volume hierarchy they have passed from the 4th place and 5th place that were maintained until 2000 to the 6th place and 7th place in 2015, being overtaken by wind power, biogas and biodiesels. Significant regresses regarding the occupied place have been also recorded on geothermal energy and industrial waste. Although the energy production for geothermal energy has increased from 3185 TOE, in 1990, to 6466 TOE in 2015, it has passed from 3rd place to 9th place. In terms of industrial waste, it has passed from 6th place, in 1990, to 11th place in 2015.

A forth characteristic is the fact that if in 1990 the biogasoline production is practically null, in 2015 it has reached to 2177 TOE.

On the last two places, with renewable energy productions that are relatively insignificant, are placed tide, wave and ocean (approximate 43 TOE), as well as bio jet kerosene. Tide, wave and ocean energy source has passed from 10th place to 14th place, the production being relatively constant for the entire period.

3.2 Considerations regarding the primary renewable energy production for 2020

Taking into account the renewable energy productions evolutions, the growth rates, as well as the changes of the renewable energy sources rankings for 1990-2015 period, six energy sources have been chosen in order to identify evolution models and to carry out a forecast of renewable energy production.

Table 2. The parameters' values, quality and test results for quantitative model of primary renewable energy production, in 1990 - 2015 period

Variable	*k*	*Coefficients*					*Quality*	*Test results*	
		a_0	a_1	a_2	a_3	a_4	(R^2)	F_c	$F_{0.05,k,n-k-1}$
SB	3	42827	-172.56	149.96	-2.7219	-	0.981	375.131	3.05
HP	4	22165	2391.5	-262.48	10.889	-0.1496	0.446	4.222	2.84
WP	2	1665.7	-658.54	59.066	-	-	0.995	2469.518	3.42
BG	4	85.145	417.59	-56.866	3.6553	-0.0445	0.994	885.492	2.84
BD	3	1241.6	-586.96	56.941	-0.6911	-	0.973	260.717	3.05
SP	2	1795.7	-577.15	31.271	-	-	0.896	99.309	3.42

These six sources are represented by: solid biofuels (SB), hydropower (HP), wind power (WP), biogas (BG), biodiesels (BD) and solar photovoltaic (SP).

Polynomial models of the form described by the relation (1) have been tested using ANOVA methodology, based on the data series corresponding to the annual renewable energy production. Thus, second order models for variables WP and SP, third order models for variables SB and BD and, also, forth order models for variables HP and BG have been obtained.

5 of the 6 models have a value of the coefficient of determination (R squared) higher than 0.89. These values signify the fact that their models ensure a very good approximation of the real evolution of the primary renewable energy production based on solid biofuels, wind power, biogas, biodiesels and solar photovoltaic.

F statistics values corresponding to them (relation 2) are much higher than the critical values ($F_{0.05,\ k,\ n-k-1}$) that leads us to reject the null hypothesis (H_{0_1}) and to accept the alternative hypothesis (H_{1_1}). Therefore, the models are statistically significant and can be used to estimate the values of renewable energy production based on those sources.

A model with a coefficient of determination better than 0.464 cannot be obtained from the data series corresponding to variable HP. The evolutions of the primary renewable energy production based on hydropower are fluctuating from one year to another, this fact being mainly caused by the climate influences on the water flows and, implicitly, on the water level of reservoirs. Taking into account the fact that *F statistics* value (Fc=4.222) is higher than the critical value ($F_{0.05,4,21}$=2.84), the null hypothesis is also rejected (H_{0_1}) and the alternative hypothesis is accepted (H_{1_1}): the forth order polynomial model corresponding to the evolution of renewable energy production based on hydropower is statistically significant.

The evolutions of primary energy productions based on solid biofuels, hydropower, wind power, biogas, biodiesels and solar photovoltaic have been estimated starting from the polynomial models that are statistically validated. Their evolutions and the empirical data series corresponding to their productions between 1990 and 2015 period are graphically represented in figure 3.

A first characteristic that results from the evolutions of the six indicators for 2020 is the fact that the primary renewable energy production based on hydropower will be overtaken by the primary renewable energy production based on wind power.

The maintenance of the ascending trend of the primary energy production volume for the next period (2015-2020) for the other five analysed sources is the second characteristic. The estimated values as well as the results of the testing of their statistical significances are presented in table 3.

* Corresponding author: marianzaharia53@gmail.com

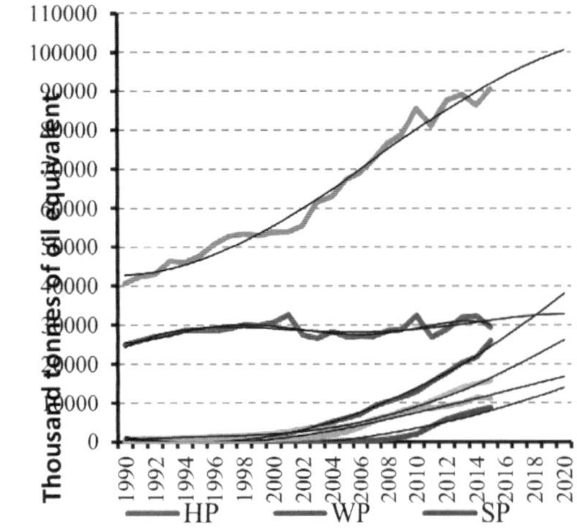

Fig. 3. Evolutions of primary renewable energy productions based on solid biofuels (SB), hydropower (HP), wind power (WP), biogas (BG), biodiesels (BD) and solar photovoltaic (SP), in the 1990-2015 period and the estimations of their values by 2020. Source: elaborated by authors

Taking into account that the minimum and maximum limits of the 95% confidence intervals have the same sign (the zero value is not included) for all the 6 estimated values, the null hypothesis is rejected (H_{0_2}) and the alternative hypothesis is accepted (H_{1_2}). Consequently, the estimated values are statistically significant.

Table 3. The estimated values of renewable energy production, in 2020, from the six sources (toe)

Variable	Estimated production	95% Confidence level		Accepted hypothesis
		Lower	Upper	
SB	100501	94867	106134	H_{1_2}
HP	32787	28958	36615	H_{1_2}
WP	38013	36675	39350	H_{1_2}
BG	26181	25254	27108	H_{1_2}
BD	16745	15935	19354	H_{1_2}
SP	13904	11685	16122	H_{1_2}

Taking into account the estimated values, it results that the renewable energy production based on biofuels will be placed, with a 95% probability, between 94867 TOE and 106134 TOE that corresponds to an increase between 4.9% and 17.3%, the most probable value of production being of 100501 TOE.

In 2020, the highest absolute increases of renewable energy compared to 2015 will be recorded by energy production based on wind power. These increases will range between 10719 TOE and 13394 TOE. At 2020 level, we estimate that the energy production based on wind power will be between 36675 TOE and 39350 TOE (relative increases between 41.3% and 51.6%).

Regarding the relative values compared to 2015, it is expected that the highest increase that ranges between 61.7% and 73.7% to be recorded by the renewable energy production based on biogas (an absolute increase between 9642 TOE and 11496 TOE), followed by biodiesels with a relative increase between 43.8% and 74.7% (an absolute increase between 4058 TOE and 8277 TOE).

Significant increases will be also recorded to the renewable energy production based on solar photovoltaic with absolute increases that belong to an interval between 2886 TOE and 7323 TOE, so that this type of renewable energy production will range between 11684 TOE and 16122 TOE that corresponds to a relative increase between 32.8% and 83.22%.

Regarding the renewable energy production based on hydropower, the increase with a maximum 7288 TOE (24.8%) of the energy production in 2020 compared to 2015 must be reservedly regarded, taking into account the limits of the used model.

4 Conclusions

From the analysis of the evolution of primary renewable energy production from the period between 1990 and 2015, it has resulted that the productions volume from those 15 analysed energy sources have increased. The increases have not been linear and as it results from the models presented, the increases have been emphasized in the second part of the analysed period. However, on the one hand, the energy produced based on solid biofuels and the one generated by hydropower have been maintained on the first place for the entire analysed period, representing in 2015 41.67% and 13.51% from the total renewable energy production at EU-28 level.

On the other hand, the increases that have been recorded significantly differ by energy source type, the highest increase being recorded on the primary production of solid biofuels (49749.7 TOE), followed by de wind power (25889.2 TOE), biogas (14946.4 TOE) and biodiesels (11070.5 TOE). The increases have been insignificant in terms of renewable energy sources like: bio jet kerosene, other liquid biofuels, as well as tide, wave and ocean.

These evolutions have determined the changing of the hierarchy of renewable energy production by sources. Thus, the most significant advancements in the hierarchy have been recorded by energy sources like wind power and biodiesels with an advance of 6 places, solar photovoltaic with an advance of 4 places and biogas with an advance of 3 places. In 2015, the productions from these sources represented 11.96 % (WP), 5.1% (BD), 4.05% (SP) and, respectively, 7.19% (BG) from the total primary renewable energy production at EU-28 level.

Although the municipal renewable waste and the municipal non-renewable waste have passed from the 4th and 5th places, in the hierarchy of the primary production volume, places that were maintained until 2000, to the 6th place and 7th place in 2015, they still represent important renewable energy sources. Thus, they ensure

* Corresponding author: marianzaharia53@gmail.com

4.27% and, respectively, 4.23% from the production recorded in 2015, at EU-28 level.

For the next period, the ascending trends of the primary energy production volume are maintained, with a 95% confidence level, for the other 5 analysed sources. Also, another important conclusion it that the primary renewable energy production based on wind power will overtake the energy production based on hydropower.

References

[1] N. D. Mortimer, "Energy analysis of renewable energy sources", *Energy Policy*, vol. 19, issue 4, pp. 374-385, May 1991.

[2] J. Andrei, J. Subic, and D. Dusmanescu, "Using dynamic programming for optimizing the investment strategy for an agricultural sheep holding: an investment case simulation", *Актуальні проблеми економіки*, vol. 4, no. 142, pp. 252-261, 2013.

[3] H. Lund, "Renewable energy strategies for sustainable development", *Energy*, vol. 32, issue 6, pp. 912-919, 2007.

[4] J. V. Andrei, R. A. Ion, G. H. Popescu, E. Nica, and M. Zaharia, "Implications of agricultural bioenergy crop production and prices in changing the land use paradigm—the case of Romania", *Land Use Policy*, vol. 50, pp. 399-407, 2016.

[5] A. G. Simionescu, M. C. Dragomir, "Using Renewable Energy for a Sustainable Development", *Annals of "Dunarea de Jos" University of Galati Fascicle I. Economics and Applied Informatics*, issue 3, pp. 39-44, 2012.

[6] A. L. Dumitrescu, "The Energy Union pillars: competitiveness, security and sustainability", *The Journal of Global Economics*, vol. 8, issue 4, 2016.

[7] European Commission, DIRECTIVE 2009/28/EC OF THE EUROPEAN PARLIAMENT AND OF THE COUNCIL, http://eur-lex.europa.eu/legal-content/EN/TXT/PDF/?uri=CELEX:32009L0028&from=en, accessed on January 2017.

[8] European Commission. State of the Energy Union, COM (2015) 572 final, https://ec.europa.eu/transparency/regdoc/rep/1/2015/EN/1-2015-572-EN-F1-1.PDF, accessed on January 2017.

[9] European Commission. 2030 Energy Strategy https://ec.europa.eu/energy/en/topics/energy-strategy, accessed on January 2017.

[10] http://appsso.eurostat.ec.europa.eu/nui/show.do?dataset=nrg_109a&lang=en Primary production - all products - annual data (nrg_109a)

[11] E. Jaba, A. Grama, *Analiza statistică cu SPSS sub Windows*, Ed. Polirom, Iaşi, 2004.

* Corresponding author: marianzaharia53@gmail.com

MATEC Web of Conferences **126**, 04004 (2017) DOI: 10.1051/matecconf/201712604004
Annual Session of Scientific Papers IMT ORADEA 2017

The effect of marketing expenses on car sales – an empirical analysis

Mihaela Brîndușa Tudose[1*], *Lidia* Alexa[2]

[1]"Gheorghe Asachi" Technical University, Iasi, brindusa.tudose@tuiasi.ro, Romania
[2]"Gheorghe Asachi" Technical University, Iasi, lidia.alexa@tuiasi.ro, Romania

Abstract. The paper assesses empirically the relationship between marketing expenditures and sales in a highly competitive industry, namely automotive, by analyzing the marketing expending of Automobile Dacia S.A. The first part of the paper presents the state-of-the-art and discusses the studies previously conducted which focus on the structure, dynamic and the impact of marketing expenses, while the second part consists in an empirical analysis conducted on Automobile Dacia S.A. marketing spending. The results of the study show that the company managed to increase its' market share by adopting differentiated marketing for each geographical area. Although the research revealed that the allocation percentage from sales for marketing spending is relatively low (5-6%), the analysis conducted on the cost per unit sold reveals a share of 3% on marketing spending.

1 Introduction

In the context of globalization and increased competitive pressure, the client becomes the most valuable asset for the company and so it needs to valorize the competitive advantage in order to ensure not only maximizing client satisfaction but also profit growth. Consequently, the consumer centered approach needs to be conceived and implemented to guarantee increased company performance and profitability.

Rethinking and implementing the marketing strategy in accordance with specific client profiling requires continuous investments and while the marketing costs have a high degree of certainty, the extensive studies conducted on the impact of the marketing efforts on performance metrics such as revenue, sales, profits or firm value reveal a high degree on uncertainty. Most relevant are S. Srinivasan, K. Pauwels, D. M. Hanssens and M. G. Dekimpe's [1] paper discussing marketing efforts impact over revenue, N. Zhou, D. Zhou and M. Ouyang's [2] article analyzing the correlation between marketing expenses and sales, O. Notta and K. Oustapassidis's [3] research regarding the relationship between advertising and profits or M. Singh, S. Faircloth and A. Nejadmalayeri [4] paper discussing the link between marketing expenses and the firms' market-imposed weighted average cost of capital.

The marketing costs volume, dynamic and structure are directly linked to the activities aimed at increasing costumer satisfaction, loyalty and retention. The main benefits of marketing efforts can be evaluated on two levels: 1) direct financial benefits, generated by increased revenue and consequently higher ROI (Return on investment); 2) indirect benefits resulting from costumer portfolio that can be exploited in the future.

The marketing costs versus benefits management has particularities according to the main objective of the company: increasing the customer portfolio, and preserving (loyalty and retention) of existing customers.

According to S. Pete and I. R. Cardos [5], the first objective entails higher investments, as the cost for acquiring new costumers is significantly higher than the one for retaining existing ones, thus, the second objective is often considered more competitive, financial wise.

The fact that marketing is an important activity for enterprises has caused an increase in marketing related expenditure. L. Kosan [6] considers that a higher level of investment in marketing activities in terms of budgeted

* Corresponding author: brindusa.tudose@tuiasi.ro

amounts will increase the enterprise performance. In terms of technological and internet development, many new opportunities have been created, necessitating the management of the relationship between enterprises and clients. However, D. Krajicek [7] highlights that the ambiguity of the calculation of return on investment has left questions regarding strategic marketing decisions without suitable answers.

A gradually relevant element in conceiving and implementing the marketing strategies in the last decades refers to the fact that the quality of attention/perception to marketing stimuli is in a constant decrease, as costumers lost interest in watching and listening to information coming from advertising. As a consequence, the cost of "buying" attention in the marketplace is constantly rising, namely, nine times in the last two decades, according to T. S. Teixeira [8].

The combination of higher advertising costs and lower attention forces companies and advertisers rethink how they secure their marketing budget and allocate it across different in order to reach their costumers.

The main objective of the paper was to identify the dynamic, structure and impact of marketing efforts over Romanian companies' financial performance by using a hypothetical deductive methodology and combining qualitative and quantitative analysis. In order to reach this objective, the paper addresses the following issues: a brief literature review on marketing spending and an analysis on S.C. Automobile Dacia S.A marketing expenses and their impact. As a consequence, the paper is organized as follows: the second part treats aspects regarding marketing expenses research elements, discussing marketing budgets cots and revenue sources, the third part covers S.C. Automobile Dacia S.A.'s marketing strategies, sales evolution, cost structure and dynamics of its marketing budget. The last section presents the conclusions, limitations and further research directions.

2 Marketing expenses research elements

A marketing budget typically covers costs for advertising, promotion and public relations. Each amount varies according to business size, annual sales and competitors marketing activities.

Depending on the specific industry patterns, marketing budgets can range from as low as 1% of sales to over 30%. New companies can spend as much as 50% of sales for marketing programs in the first year, depending on the product/services life cycle stage; in the introductory stages the marketing budget being larger.

2.1 Marketing budget – costs

A *cost* represents all the expenses used for acquisition, allocation and consumption of production factors, in order to achieve the productive process and the sale of the goods (commodities and services). M. B. Tudose [9] appreciates that, including the expenses for manufacturing and selling, the cost implies a comparable consumption of factors of production.

The cost (production, marketing, management) occupies a central role in producers' decision making process, as the company seeks to adjust factor inputs to either maximize output at a given cost or minimize cost for a determined level of production. The central concern of the company is to associate the sale price of the manufactured item with an offer at a cost that will allow it to obtain the highest profit. Marketing costs include all the costs related to delivering the goods or services to customers. According to the Business Dictionary [10], the most relevant marketing expenses refer to: the costs of transferring the title of goods to the client, storing the goods until delivery, advertising costs or distribution to the point of sale. In other words, marketing costs include expenses related to the development, sale and distribution of goods and / or services.

In terms of marketing costs overall value, research by J. A. Weber [11], reveals the following results: marketing costs have registered a rapid increase from only 20% (after 1950s) to over 50% in the early 2000s. This significant upsurge in marketing costs combined with the increased pressure from stakeholders, forces managers to better validate each sum spent on marketing activities and to find ways to show how marketing expenditure adds to shareholder value. As a result, marketing managers have to implement strategies to enhance the efficiency of marketing efforts, respectively, to increase marketing productivity. The first category of strategies managers can use focuses on increasing efficiency by reducing costs. The second category emphases the methods to estimate the potential Return on Investment for different marketing scenarios / alternatives combined with adjusting the marketing budget in order to contribute to increasing the overall value of the company.

In terms of spending, the marketing budget can include an array of activities, depending on the profile of the company in case. The overall marketing budget can incorporate costs for printing and broadcasting advertising materials, designing and printing for all types of materials, such as newsletters, brochures and press releases, direct mail costs, website development and maintenance, public relations activities, organization of trade shows or any other special events needed etc.

Another classification of marketing related activities is offered by S. Hardesty and P. Leff [12] who studied the direct marketing approach and developed three main categories of marketing activities: packing and storage, transportation, and selling and administration.

The first step in evaluating the marketing costs consists in identifying the relevant marketing activities included in the company's marketing strategy and plans. Once the list is created, the next stage refers to group the activities on categories and determine the resources needed for implementation: human, material and financial. The resources consumption value will

* Corresponding author: brindusa.tudose@tuiasi.ro

represent the basis for determining specific costs of marketing activities.

2.2 Marketing budget – revenue sources

Another important step in establishing the marketing budget consists in determining the sources of funding. The marketing literature identifies three main methods that companies use to allocate funds for marketing activities:

1) *Percentage-of-Sales* is considered to be one of the most commonly used method for founding marketing budgets. Depending on the company size, the average marketing allocations can range between 2% (for small companies) and 9-12% (for medium and large companies). For startups or companies launching a new product/service the marketing budgets can be significantly higher in terms of percentage of sales. The main advantage of this specific method refers to the fact that the marketing budget will increase, or decrease, simultaneously with the sales revenue of the company.

2) *The Competitive-Parity Method*, presented by J. H. Murphy, L. S. DeLewis and I. C. Cunningham [13], correlates the marketing budget with the product/service's market share being also based on analyzing the marketing budgets of competitors and trying to match or outspend their budget.

3) *The Objective-and-Task Method* is often considered the most effective budgeting method. In this specific case, the marketing budget is based on the company's marketing objectives included in the marketing plan. Compared to the first two methods, this one has the advantage that there is a direct correlation between the budgetary allocation and a specific objective, which allows a better evaluation of ROI, according to J. H. Murphy, L. S. DeLewis and I. C. Cunningham [13].

Regardless of the method used, the final marketing budget needs to cover in detail the company's marketing activities and expenses and the manner to cover those expenses.

3 Marketing costs analysis for s.c. Automobile dacia s.a.

In 1999, Renault acquired 51% of the capital of the Automobile Plant from Mioveni; today the company owns 99,43% of the business. Automobile Dacia S.A. is one of the most important companies in Romania with a significant contribution to the gross domestic product. In 2014, Automobile Dacia had the largest turnover in Romania and in the past years, more than 93% of the company's output is being exported to 34 countries on four continents. Initially, the company's products were categorized as „low-cost" (especially due to Logan and Logan break models); later the products managed to revolutionize the market, especially through Sandero model, being ranked in the medium class (semi-premium).

The general marketing strategy of the company is a differentiated one, adjusted according to geographical areas with three specific approaches: on Romanian local market where the brand is leader, the core of the strategy focuses on promoting pride and confidence; in developing countries such as Algeria, Morocco or Turkey the strategy is focused on a more traditional approach, while in Western European saturated markets, Dacia's strategy aims at o more revolutionary approach focused on affordability, under the motto "cross the line, dare".

The overall number of cars sold and the evolution of the market share (on the new cars market) in Romania is presented in Table 1.

Table 1. Automobile dacia s.a. Market Share and Number of Cars Sold

	Market share	Cars sold		
		Total	in Romania	Abroad
2016	31%	584.219	38.861	545.258
2015	30%	550.920	36.946	513.974
2014	30%	511.465	29.625	481.840

Source: own processing after the Annual Financial Statements of S.C. Automobile Dacia S.A.

Based on the information included in the Balance sheet we have identified the main categories of marketing expenses of the company (Table 2).

Table 2. The Structure of the Marketing Expenses at Automobile Dacia s. a.

	2014	2015	2016
Total marketing expenses, out of which:	970,8	1129,7	1307,9
- collaborators expenses – research studies	16,2	18,8	190,0
- market studies regarding competition	0,3	0,4	0,4
- image research studies – financial institutions	1,4	1,5	1,6
- advertising MCX	100,4	129,2	125,6
- trades and fairs	0,4	0,8	0,7
- protocol, invitations & collaborators	0,4	0,5	0,5
- public relations, invitations, receptions	26,6	30,9	28,7
- other promotional channels	0,2	0,3	0,3
- transportation services for buyers	547,5	667,1	673,1
- sales shipments	211,3	202,5	206,3
- collective shipments	36,9	46,6	51,0
- travel expenses sales representatives	0,6	0,7	0,6
- travel expenses delegate partners	28,6	30,4	31,1

Source: Own processing after the Balance sheet, December 2016 – S.C. Automobile Dacia S.A.

The information included in table 2 reveal that:

1) most part of the marketing expenses is related to distribution (circa 80% of the total marketing budget);

2) advertising expenses represent, an average of 10% of the marketing budget;

3) other expenses (research studies, collaborators, fairs and trades, public relations, delegations) represent

* Corresponding author: brindusa.tudose@tuiasi.ro

about 10% of the total marketing budget. The dynamic analysis of the correlation between the marketing budget and the company's turnover is presented in Table 3.

Table 3. Marketing budget (share in turnover) and marketing cost per unit

Indicators	2014	2015	2016
1. Turnover (mil. RON)	18833	19165	22044
2. Marketing costs (mil. RON)	970,8	1129,7	1307,9
3. Marketing costs as percentage of sales	5,2%	5,9%	5,9%
4. No. of cars sold	511.465	550.920	584.219
5. marketing costs per unit of product sold (RON/car)	1898	2050	2239

Automobile Dacia S.A. allocates an average of 5-6% of sales for marketing activities. Taking into consideration the company's size, one would be tempted to appreciate that this value is insignificant, but interpreting it in terms of unit value and number of sold products, the overview changes considerably. For each sold car, the company spent for marketing activities an average of 2000 RON. At an average value per sold car of 67.500 RON (respectively 15.000 Euro, estimated in accordance with Romanian sales), the marketing expenses represent almost 3%.

The most significant part of this budget is allocated for distribution (shipment) activities.

Overall, the impact of marketing activities is a positive one, as the company has registered constant increase in sales, and consequently market share.

4 Conclusions

Globalization and increased competitive pressure forces producers and sellers alike to carefully manage not only their marketing strategies and activities but also the costs entailed by them. This is an increasingly important element, as the costs are specific and have a high degree of certainty, while the benefits can have a higher degree of uncertainty, even under the conditions of a rigorous customer relationship management.

Determining the volume and structure of the marketing budget needs to take into account two types of constraints: the first one refers to the customers and shareholders needs and expectations and the second one to the fact that once the marketing budget is being increased, investors expect proportionally elevated profits.

The differentiated marketing strategy adopted by Automobile Dacia S.A. focusing on different geographical areas proved to be successful as it led to an increased market share for the company.

In terms of marketing costs, the highest amount goes to expenses related to distribution (approximately 80% of the total marketing budget).

The research revealed that the company allocates an average of 5-6% of sales for marketing activities; the analysis based on cost per unit sold disclosed that approximately 3% represent marketing costs.

Taking into consideration the dynamic of the industry and the specificities of the sold goods (cars) – high value and long term use – the strategy to attract new customers involves high marketing budgets.

Research limitations and further directions. The research has a significant limitation due to the fact that the analysis and interpretation of the activity cost structure was done for a single company, but apart from this, the research team considers that the study results are of substantial value and can represent a starting point for future research. We are also considering further studied for identifying the determinant factors of strategies for substantiating marketing budgets of the most important operators in the automotive industry, as well as determining the impact of marketing cost dynamics on the performances of these companies.

References

[1] S. Srinivasan, K. Pauwels, D.M. Hanssens, M.G. Dekimpe, "Do promotions benefit retailers, manufacturers, or both", in *Management Science*, Issue 50, 2004, pp. 617–629.
[2] N. Zhou, D. Zhou, M. Ouyang, "Long-term effects of television advertising on sales of consumer durables and nondurables", in *Journal of Advertising*, issue 32, 2003, pp. 45–54.
[3] O. Notta, K. Oustapassidis, "Profitability and media advertising in Greek food manufacturing industries", Review of Industrial Organization, 18, 2001, pp. 115–126.
[4] M. Singh, S. Faircloth, A. Nejadmalayeri, "Capital market impact of product marketing strategy: Evidence from the relationship between advertising expenses and cost of capital", in *Journal of the Academy of Marketing Science* 33, 2005, pp. 432–444.
[5] S. Pete, I. R. Cardos, "A managerial and cost accounting approach of customer profitability analysis", in *Annals of the University of Oradea*, Economic Science Series, 19(1), 2010, pp. 570-576.
[6] L. Kosan, "Accounting for Marketing: Marketing Performance Through Financial Results", in *International Review of Management and Marketing*, Vol. 4, No. 4, 2014, pp. 276-283.
[7] D. Krajicek, "The ROI of everything, defining a new philosophy of marketing value", in *Marketing Insights*, Summer/2013, pp. 8-9.
[8] T. S. Teixeira, "The Rising Cost of Consumer Attention: Why You Should Care, and What You Can Do about It", Working Paper 14-055, Harvard Business School, 2014, available at http://www.hbs.edu/faculty/ Publication %20Files/14-055_2ef21e7e-7529-4864-b0f0-c64e4169e17f.pdf
[9] M. B. Tudose, *Bazele economiei. Microeconomie (suport de curs)*, 2016, Universitatea Tehnică Gh. Asachi, Iaşi.
[10] http://www.businessdictionary.com/definition/marketing-cost.html
[11] J. A. Weber, "Managing the marketing budget in a cost-constrained environment", in *Industrial Marketing Management*, 31, 2002, pp. 705 – 717.
[12] S. Hardesty, P. Leff, "Determining Marketing Costs and Returns in Alternative Marketing Channels", *Renewable Agriculture and Food Systems*, volume 25, Issue 1, 2010, pp. 24-34.
[13] J. H. Murphy, L. S. DeLewis, I. C. Cunningham, *Determining the Advertising Appropriation and Budgeting* in Integrated Brand Promotion Management, Kendall Hunt Publishing Company, 2011, pp. 123-165.

* Corresponding author: brindusa.tudose@tuiasi.ro

Multiple stakeholders's co-creation process in new product development: an exploratory analysis

Lidia Alexa[1*], *Silvia* Avasilcăi[2], *Adriana* Bujor[3]

[1]"Gheorghe Asachi" Technical University, Iasi, lidia.alexa@tuiasi.ro, Romania
[2]"Gheorghe Asachi" Technical University, Iasi, silvia.avasilcai@tuiasi.ro, Romania
[3]"Gheorghe Asachi" Technical University, Iasi, adbujor@gmail.com, Romania

Abstract. In the this highly competitive market, a company's capacity to generate and market creative and original ideas is a key for success. But most companies have limited resources and so, knowledge creation can not be generated solely from within the firm. In order to expand their knowledge base, organizations begun to implicate stakeholders in all phases of the new product development process, from idea generation, selection, development and eventually, even to marketing the new products or services. In this context, the Internet and the new technologies represent a valuable instrument for companies, due to the fact that they can enhance the firms' ability to actively engage all their stakeholders in collaborative innovation. Our paper presents and evaluates the development and implementation of an online co-creation platform – E-PICUS addressed to multiple stakeholders of a new electronic product - Video Intercom providing insights into the specific capabilities a firm needs in order to manage co-creation and into partial results obtained through costumers' involvement in the innovation process.

1 Introduction

The fact of the matter is that the only constant truth these days is that everything is in a constant and rapid change, starting with technology and ending with the costumers needs and expectations. So, if a company wants to survive and succeed it needs to change and adjust as well just to keep the pace. In many industries, the ability to develop new products quickly, effectively, and efficiently has become the single most important factor driving a firm's success as presented by M. Schilling [1] and in order to do that, companies need to constantly create knowledge and innovate. But at the same time, most companies have limited resources and so knowledge creation can not be generated only from within the firm. In order to expand their knowledge base, organizations begun to implicate stakeholders in all the phases of the new product development process, from idea generation, selection, development and eventually, even to marketing the new products or services. In terms of the type of actors involved in the co-creation process, most often companies relay on primary stakeholders, such as customer, analyzed by N. E. Coviello and R. M. Joseph [2], competitors, discussed by W. Amaldoss and A. Rapaport [3] or suppliers, examined by M. Song and J. Thieme [4], but research and practice have shown an important shift towards collaborating with multiple stakeholders simultaneously during the innovation process. Previous research shows that the involving different types of stakeholders throughout the innovation process represents an important factor for successful product and service development, as it aids in obtaining more detailed information about a firm's external environment, as emphasized by P. H. Driessen and B. Hillebrand [5].

For example, G. Cuccureddu [6] discuses DHL case which has implemented a multiple stakeholders' co-creation process by "working together with academics, politicians, public authorities and citizens in order to co-create new offerings which address the challenge of decreasing urban traffic and a need for a greener economy".

2 The E-picus experiment

2.1 Project Development

The E-PICUS co-creation platform is being developed through the project „*E-solutions for innovation through customer pro-active involvement in value creation to*

* Corresponding author: lidia.alexa@tuiasi.ro

DOI: 10.1051/matecconf/201712604005

increase organizational competitiveness (E-PICUS)" and the project main scope is to develop an experimental model for e-solutions of innovation through customer pro-active involvement in product innovation, in order to improve organizational competitiveness on the international market. The platform was designed and tested using a video-intercom product developed by a highly innovative Romanian technology company located in Iasi, Electra. In this specific phase, the goal was to design a user friendly platform focused mainly on enhancing the back-stages of the new product development process (product design and testing) involving three types of stakeholders, namely, partners and distributors which are selling and installing the devices produced by the company, costumers (current users of intercoms or video intercom systems and potential users), and students from technical universities.

The platform development process had two separate stages: the first one consisted in an extensive literature review in order to determine the state-of-the-art and to gain a better understanding of the co-creation area, the existing open innovation and co-creation platforms and instruments, followed by a benchmarking analysis, which included an extensive number of online co-creation platforms and instruments developed, among others by Dell, analyzed by L. Alexa, M. Alexa and S. Avasilcăi [7], Heineken, presented in detail by S. Avasilcăi and G. Rusu [8], BMW, studied by S. Avasilcăi and E. Gălățeanu (Avram) [9], Lego, reviewed by D. Zwick, S.J. Bonsu and A. Darmody [10], Barilla, examined by A. Bujor and S. Avasilcăi [11], IBM assessed by V. Blazevic and A. Lievens, [12], etc.

The goal of the benchmarking analysis was to identify the most frequent common elements included in all platforms, the best practices and the overall process of involving and engaging the stakeholders in the co-creation process in order to generate consistent and useful feedback. The analysis took into account the fact that the platform was designed for a multiple stakeholders' approach, involving costumers (current users of video intercom systems and potential users), partners and distributors which were selling and installing the devices produced by the company and students, mainly from technical universities.

The second stage of the development process focused mainly on the internal analysis of the company and materialized in several focus-groups with members of the research & development, marketing & sales and engineering departments. The qualitative research results assisted the implementation team in the process of identifying useful features for the online co-creation instrument, designing the main structure of the platform and deciding on the focal topics to be included in the co-creation community section, such as various aspects regarding the aesthetics and the functionality of the product. Another element discussed during the focus-groups focused on the challenges imposed by a multiple stakeholders' approach, because, as V.M. Waligo, J. Clarke and R. Hawkins [13] emphasize, bringing a diverse group of stakeholders together leads to potential divergent goals and interests, communication difficulties, distrust among stakeholders, or conflict over value appropriation. Taking into account this element, the multiple stakeholders issue, in P. H. Driessen and B. Hillebrand opinion [5], the company needs to have a complex bundle of knowledge, skills and mechanisms in place to enable it to incorporate the voice of the stakeholders in its decision making processes, because in practice, stakeholders interests can often be conflicting due to divergent needs and expectations.

2.2 Project Implementation

The co-creation platform structure is simple and intuitive, with five sections in the main menu: Home, About us (a description of the project consortium), How it works (users manual), Our proposals (a description of the product in question – the Video Intercom and a list of functionality and design elements proposed to be enclosed in the final product, to be voted and evaluated/modified/improved by users) and Propose your idea (the online community feature that offers users the possibility to propose their own ideas for debate and to vote and comment on the ideas posted by other users).

In order to motivate the target group to access the platform and engage in the co-creation process they are to receive tangible benefits: the costumers have the opportunity to win (free of charge) a video intercom system, the partners received discounts and the students could earn an internship in the research and development department of the company.

In the end, the co-creation platform has two separate components: the first component provides users access into the community where they have the options to vote and comment the proposed functionalities and to suggest new ideas for product development and improvements. The second component focuses on a quantitative research and has a questionnaire designed for each of the three stakeholders' groups regarding the product features and options, asking for specific feedback from each target group, but with a set of common questions.

2.3 Project Intermediary Results

The co-creation platform has been online for users starting with October 2016. After six months, the platform has registered 993 sessions with an average duration of 5:44 minutes and 5,482 page views. At this point, the platform has 225 registered users and 221 subscribers.

There are also 33 new proposals and 49 comments coming from registered users, mostly referring to security functions, from adding new sensors to establishing connections to smartphones or to security interventions firms. Apart from commenting the

* Corresponding author: lidia.alexa@tuiasi.ro

proposals posted in the community, registered users can vote them with ratings from 1 to 5 and at this point there are 51 votes; the popularity of each proposal being another element taken into account when evaluating whether a feature/proposal should be integrated in the end-product. Most of the proposals regarding technical aspects are received from the partners and distributors stakeholder group, as they are the ones who have a direct contact with the end-users and they have to respond to potential malfunctions and/or customization requests. They have also added proposals and suggestions regarding after-sale services.

The other two stakeholder groups, customers and students, made suggestions concerning mainly aspects referring to aesthetics and customization/personalization of the video intercom.

The proposals receive feedback both from the other users on the platform and from members of the research development team of the company specifically assigned to interact and communicate with the users that bring ideas and suggestions for improvements.

Each idea will be further evaluated by the research development team in order to decide if the proposed feature or modification will be implemented in the final product.

In order to evaluate and decide on the features of the final product the company is developing a multiple criteria analysis of each proposal: an economic evaluation in terms of investment needed and increased cost of the end-product, an utility evaluation, in terms of specific needs for a higher number of consumers, a differentiation analysis: if the proposed feature ensures a significant differentiation from other products developed by competitors, an evaluation of the added value perception, if the proposal/feature is perceived as valuable by customers.

The platform will be online for this specific project until the end of June 2017, when all the feedback, the users' proposals and comments will be analyzed, evaluated and integrated (if the case) in the final product.

In terms of the quantitative research, at this point there are 25 questionnaires completed by partners/ distributors, 49 completed by customers, out of which 70,2% have an intercom, 29,8% don't own one and only 4,3% own a video intercom and 124 completed by students from technical universities.

In an effort to evaluate if there are any divergent perspectives between the three types of stakeholders, we conducted a brief comparative analysis of the answers provided at the common questions regarding the functionality features of the video intercom.

The leading part of the questionnaire focused mainly of functionality features and so the first question referred to users' interest toward additional warning options, with four alternatives provided by the company: fire sensor, flood sensor, window breaking in sensor and panic button. The answers used a 5 points rating scale, ranging from uninterested (1) to very interested (5) and our analysis focused on the 4 and 5 range. At the same time, users had the possibility to add new warning options after evaluating the four alternatives initially provided. For the first option, the fire sensor, 75% of partners/distributors, 89% of clients and 74% of students declared that they are interested and very interested. For the flooding sensor, 55% of partners/distributors, 57% of clients and 57% of students declared that they are interested and very interested. For the window breaking in sensor, 55% of partners/distributors, 78% of clients and 66% of students declared that they are interested and very interested. For the panic button, 60% of partners/distributors, 57% of clients and 67% of students the declared that they are interested and very interested. There are no significant differences between the three type of stakeholders regarding the additional warning options. However, the choice to integrate the additional sensors will be made by the company after the project completion and after taking into account all the answers to the questionnaires and all the votes registered on the platform for each alternative.

The next question referred to sensor-terminal connection with two options: cable and Wi-Fi on a 5 points rating scale ranging from strongly disagree (1) and strongly agree (5). Again, the analysis focused on the 4 and 5 range. For the cable connection option, 50% of partners/distributors, 28% of clients and 44% of students declared that they agree and strongly agree with this possibility. The Wi-Fi option was preferred by 65% of partners/distributors, 85% of clients and 81% of students. For this question as well there are no significant differences between the three type of stakeholders, most stakeholders leaning toward the Wi-Fi option.

The next question referred to warning communication options for various events with five options: acoustic alarm, light alarm, message on the outdoor display, SMS/mobile alert, message to a security company. The answers used a 5 points rating scale, ranging from uninterested (1) to very interested (5) and the analysis focused on the 4 and 5 range. 65% of partners/distributors, 78% of clients and 63% of students declared that they are interested and very interested about the acoustic alarm. 50% of partners/distributors, 59% of clients and 44% of students opted for the light alarm, while the message on the outdoor display was rated as interesting and very interesting by 40% of partners/distributors, 44% of clients and 48% of students. The highest values were registered for SMS/mobile alert: 80% of partners/distributors, 94% of clients and 76% of students, while the message to a security company was rated as interesting and very interesting by 70% of partners/distributors, 73% of clients and 82% of students. The answers regarding the warning communication options for various events were relatively similar between the three stakeholders, with no significant differences.

The next question discussed customization

* Corresponding author: lidia.alexa@tuiasi.ro

alternatives with seven options: keys sound, keys sound volume control, keys sound length control, ringtone selection, ringtone volume control, ringtone length control, acoustic alarm volume control, each one rated on a 5 points rating scale, ranging from uninterested (1) to very interested (5).

The aspect regarding keys sound was rated as interesting and very interesting by 20% of partners/distributors, 29% of clients and 23% of students. The keys sound volume control was rated as interesting and very interesting by 40% of partners/distributors 38% of clients and 30% of students.

The keys sound length control was rated with 4 and 5 points by 5% of partners/distributors, 25% of clients and 28% of students. The ringtone selection was rated with 4 and 5 points by 50% of partners/distributors, 68% of clients and 43% of students. The ringtone volume control was rated with 4 and 5 points by 70% of partners/distributors, 68% of clients and 46% of students.

The ringtone length control was rated with 4 and 5 points by 70% of partners/distributors, 68% of clients and 43% of students. The acoustic alarm volume control was rated with 4 and 5 points by 60% of partners/distributors, 74% of clients and 58% of students.

The question regarding customization alternatives registered a wider range of values, with differences such as 25% (ringtone selection – costumers vs. students) to 27% (ringtone length – partners vs. students), the differences can be explained both by the fact that the question treats specific technical aspects and that it refers to customization and personalization. However, in order to evaluate the relevance for the end product, we need more data from a wider sample.

3 Conclusion

As useful and valuable co-creation can be for a company's performance, addressing the interests of a wide set of stakeholders can be a daunting task in terms of knowledge management and information integration in the new product development process due to possible divergences between the different stakeholders' needs and expectations.

In terms of managing the information, the company has appointed personnel from the research and development departments to actively engage in the platform and to interact with users regarding their ideas and proposal and at the end of the project an interdisciplinary team will further evaluate the proposals using a multiple criteria analysis to decide which functionality and design aspects will be integrated in the final product.

In terms of the quantitative analysis, our research so far has not detected significantly conflicting perspective from the three stakeholders involved in the co-creation process, but the results can register changes once the sample becomes larger.

This research was undertaken within the framework of the National Research Program PN II, financed by MEN – UEFISCDI, project PN-II-PT-PCCA-2013-4-1811.

References

[1] M. Schilling, *Strategic Management of Technological Innovation*, 4th ed., 2013, McGraw Hill Education.

[2] N.E. Coviello, R.M. Joseph, "Creating major innovations with customers: Insights from small and young technology firms". *Journal of Marketing*, 76(6), 2012, 87–104.

[3] W. Amaldoss, A. Rapoport, "Collaborative product and market development: Theoretical implications and experimental evidence", *Marketing Science*, 24(3), 2005, 396–414.

[4] M. Song, J. Thieme, "The role of suppliers in market intelligence gathering for radical and incremental innovation", *Journal of Product Innovation Management*, 26(1), 2009, 43–57.

[5] P. H. Driessen, B. Hillebrand, "Integrating Multiple Stakeholder Issues in New Product Development: An Exploration", *Journal of Product Innovation Management*, 30 (2), 2013, 364-379.

[6] G. Cuccureddu, "DHL's open innovation contest and the quest for radical decentralization", accessed April, 12, 2017, from:http://www.innovationmanagement.se/2011/10/07/dhl-open-innovation-contest-and-the-quest-for-radical-decentralization/, 2011.

[7] L. Alexa, M. Alexa, S. Avasilcăi, "An Empirical Research On Open Innovation and Co-Creation: The Ideastorm Project By Dell", *Review of Management and Economic Engineering*, Volume 13, No. 4 (54), 2014, 779-788.

[8] S. Avasilcăi, G. Rusu, "Co-Creation Value Through Customers' Proactive engagement: A Case Study on Heineken", *Annals of The University Of Oradea, Fascicle of Management and Technological Engineering*, Issue 2, 2015, 100-105.

[9] S. Avasilcăi, E. Gălățeanu (Avram), "Innovation through developing consumers communities. Part II: Digitalizing the innovation processes", *IOP Conf. Series: Materials Science and Engineering*, 95, 2015.

[10] D. Zwick, S.J. Bonsu, A. Darmody, "Putting consumers to work: 'Co-creation' and new marketing govern-mentality", *Journal of Consumer Culture*, 8 (2), 2008, pp. 163–196.

[11] A. Bujor, S. Avasilcăi, "Co-creation innovation in consumer goods industry: The case of Barilla Group (B)", *Annals of the Oradea University. Fascicle of Management and Technological Engineering*, XXIV (XIV), 2015, 1-6.

[12] V. Blazevic, A. Lievens, "Managing innovation through customer cocreated knowledge in electronic services: an exploratory study", *Journal of the Academy of Marketing Science*, 6 (1), 2008, 138–151.

[13] V.M. Waligo, J. Clarke, R. Hawkins, "The 'leadership–stakeholder involvement capacity' nexus in stakeholder management", *Journal of Business Research*, 67(7), 2014, 1342–1352.

* Corresponding author: lidia.alexa@tuiasi.ro

MATEC Web of Conferences **126**, 04006 (2017) DOI: 10.1051/matecconf/201712604006
Annual Session of Scientific Papers IMT ORADEA 2017

A fuzzy quality function deployment approach to improve a component of a supervisory control and data acquisition system

Ciprian Cristea[1*], *Ciprian* Saşa[2], *Maria* Cristea[3]

[1]Technical University of Cluj-Napoca, Faculty of Electrical Engineering, ciprian.cristea@emd.utcluj.ro, Romania
[2]Technical University of Cluj-Napoca, Faculty of Electrical Engineering, sasa_ciprian@yahoo.com, Romania
[3]Technical University of Cluj-Napoca, Faculty of Electrical Engineering, fagarasan_maria@yahoo.com, Romania

Abstract—Monitoring and control of electric transformer stations, frequently spread out over small or large geographical areas, are achieved with supervisory control and data acquisition (SCADA). Quality function deployment (QFD) is a valuable analyzing tool in product design and development. To solve the uncertainty or inherent imprecision in QFD, many researchers have applied the fuzzy set theory to QFD and have developed various fuzzy QFD approaches. The literature regarding applying fuzzy QFD for analyzing subsystems of SCADA, to the best of our knowledge, remains inexistent. In this paper, a fuzzy QFD approach is used to effectively determine the design requirements of a SCADA component.

1 Introduction

The SCADA (supervisory control and data acquisition) systems play a vital role in modern power generation systems. In the SCADA networks, data acquisition systems, data transmission systems and Human Machine Interface (HMI) software are integrated for providing the centralized monitoring and control system for processing outputs and inputs A. Rezai, P. Keshavarzi, Z. Moravej [1]. SCADA system monitors the status of different equipments in substation and accordingly sends control signals to the remote control equipments. Historical data of the substation are collected and alarms in the event of electrical accidents or faults are generated. Thus, substations rely on SCADA for remote supervision and control, improving the reliability of the network and minimizing the downtime, their proper functioning is vital to modern society.

The rapidly increasing globalization of economic environment has decreased the life cycles of products. Companies have to develop new products that meet customer requirements in a shorter time to improve their competitive advantage. Companies realize the importance of effectively translating customer requirements into engineering characteristics and quality factors that should be considered in product design and development H.-T. Liu [2], C.C. Otel [3], I.A. Iancu [4], C.E Stoenoiu [5].

There are various product design and development approaches that have been developed and applied in several areas. QFD (quality function deployment) is a useful method for quality planning, continuous product improvement and decision making which translates the customer requirements into design or engineering characteristics that are taken into account in product design and then into specific plans and production requirements, associated to its manufacturing processes C.K.M. Lee, C.T.Y. Ru, C.L. Yeung, K.L. Choy, W.H. Ip [6].

Traditional QFD is based on communication with customers and market survey to acquire customer requirements and effectively decrease product development time. In order to set different parameters, linguistic variables have to be used by product developers. Mostly, the result of market survey and linguistic variables used are imprecise or uncertain, usually resulting in biased analysis results. In order to cope with this problem, a number of scholars have applied the fuzzy set theory to QFD and developed various fuzzy QFD approaches H.-T. Liu [2]. The approaches contain conventional QFD computation using fuzzy variables E. Bottani, A. Rizzi [7], fuzzy tendency analysis X.X. Shen, X. Min, K.C. Tan [8], fuzzy MCDM (multi-criteria decision making) Y.S. Sohn, I.S. Choi [9], fuzzy integral C.Y. Tsai [10], fuzzy analytical network process C. Kahraman, T. Ertay, G. Buyukozkan [11], fuzzy expected value Y. Chen, R.Y.K. Fung, J. Tang [12], fuzzy goal programming L.S. Chen, M.C. Weng [13], fuzzy expert systems C.K. Kwong, Y. Chen, H. Bai, D.S.K. Chan [14], etc.

QFD is composed of four successive matrices each

* Corresponding author: ciprian.cristea@emd.utcluj.ro

corresponding to a stage of the product development cycle. These are product planning, part deployment, process planning, and production planning matrices, respectively. Customer requirements are translated into design characteristics by product planning matrix; important design characteristics are translated into product/part characteristics by the part deployment matrix; important product/part characteristics are translated into manufacturing operations by the process planning matrix; important manufacturing operations are translated into day-to-day operations and controls by the production planning matrix M. Dursun, E. E. Karsak [15]. Here, the current paper concentrates on the first matrix (customer planning matrix), that is also called the "House of Quality (HOQ)". HOQ show the relationship between customer requirements (what to do) and engineering characteristics (how to do it). It represents the engine that drives the entire QFD process, most QFD researches focusing only on this stage. The main aim of this paper is to propose a fuzzy QFD approach to support the decision making process in improving a component of a SCADA system.

The remainder of the paper is organized as follows. In the next paragraph, the fuzzy QFD approach methodology is described. In the third section, a case study is discussed with the results and, finally, the last section summarizes the conclusions.

2 Methodology

The major steps D.H. Akbas, B. Bilgen [16], F. R. Lima-Junior, L. C. R. Carpinetti [17] of conducting fuzzy QFD approach to analyze the component of a SCADA system requirement are described below.

1) *Identify customer requirements* – represent the initial input for the HOQ and point out those product specifications that should be took into account.

2) *Determine the importance of customer requirements* – usually, customer requirements are of different degrees of importance. A fuzzy set represents a class of objects with a continuum of grades of membership ranging between zero and one L.A. Zadeh [18]. If the value assigned is one, then the element belongs completely to the set and if the assigned value is zero, the element does not belong to the set G. Buyukozkan, A.G. Ciftci [19]. Finally, the value between 0 and 1 belongs to the fuzzy set only partially. A triangular fuzzy number (TFN) is represented with three points as follows. $\widetilde{M} = (l, m, u)$, where the parameters l, m, u, respectively, point out the smallest possible value, the most promising value, and the largest possible value that describe a fuzzy event A.R. Ghazikalayeh, M. Amirafshari, H.M. Mkrchyan, M. Taji [20]. In this paper, the linguistic variables are represented by TFN. The membership function of a TFN is given by (1) DH. Akbas, B. Bilgen [16].

$$\mu_{\widetilde{M}}(x) = \begin{cases} \dfrac{x-l}{m-l}, & l \le x \le m \\ \dfrac{u-x}{u-m}, & m \le x \le u \\ 0, & \text{otherwise} \end{cases} \qquad (1)$$

Table 1. Linguistic terms and corresponding fuzzy numbers on satisfaction value D.H. Akbas, B. Bilgen [16]

Linguistic term	Fuzzy number
Very low (VL)	(1, 1, 2)
Low (L)	(1, 2, 3)
Medium (M)	(2, 3, 4)
High (H)	(3, 4, 5)
Very high (VH)	(4, 5, 5)

The linguistic variables of importance ratings are listed in Table 1.

In this study, fuzzy numbers are applied to model the linguistic judgments of the decision makers. The degree of importance of a customer requirement can be evaluated using the linguistic terms very low, low, medium, high and very high. The aggregated judgments of the t decision makers (d = 1, 2, . . ., t), concerning the ith customer requirement (i = 1,2, . . ., n), are represented by $\widetilde{x}_i$, given by (2) F.R. Lima-Junior, L.C.R. Carpinetti [17].

$$\widetilde{x}_i = \frac{\sum_{d=1}^{t} \widetilde{x}_i^d}{t} \qquad (2)$$

where:

$\widetilde{x}_i^d$ - the fuzzy number corresponding to the linguistic judgment oft the ith requirement, made by the dth decision maker;

After aggregation of the decision makers' judgments, the absolute weight x_i is calculated by defuzzification, according to (3) F.R. Lima-Junior, L.C.R. Carpinetti [17].

$$x_i = \frac{l_{\widetilde{x}_i} + 2 \cdot m_{\widetilde{x}_i} + u_{\widetilde{x}_i}}{4} \qquad (3)$$

The value of the absolute weight x_i is then converted to the relative weight wr_i according to (4) F.R. Lima-Junior, L.C.R. Carpinetti [17].

$$wr_i = \frac{x_i}{\sum_{i=1}^{n} x_i} \qquad (4)$$

3) *Identify competitors and perform a competitive analysis* – in order to improve its competitiveness in the market, the team has to assess the current performance of the company's product as well as its competitors' for each customer requirements.

4) *Identify engineering characteristics* – for capturing the customer requirements in technical terms.

5) *Determine the relationships between engineering characteristics and customer requirements* – the

* Corresponding author: ciprian.cristea@emd.utcluj.ro

relationship matrix shows how engineering characteristics affects each customer requirement. The linguistic variables are used to indicate these relationships, as indicated in table 2.

Table 2. Linguistic terms indicating the relationship between engineering characteristics and customer requirements a.r. ghazikalayeh, m. Amirafshari, h.m. mkrchyan, m. Taji [20]

Linguistic term	Fuzzy number
No relationship (NR)	(0, 0, 0)
Weak (W)	(1, 1, 3)
Average (A)	(1, 3, 5)
Strong (S)	(5, 9, 9)

The aggregated judgments of the t decision makers ($d = 1, 2, \ldots, t$), concerning the relationship between the ith requirement ($i = 1, 2, \ldots, n$) and the jth characteristic ($j = 1, 2, \ldots, m$), represented by $\tilde{u}_{ij}$, is given by (5) F.R. Lima-Junior, L.C.R. Carpinetti [17].

$$\tilde{u}_{ij} = \frac{\sum_{d=1}^{t} \tilde{u}_{ij}^{d}}{t} \tag{5}$$

where:

$\tilde{u}_{ij}^{d}$ - the fuzzy number corresponding to the linguistic judgment of the relationship between the ith requirement and j^{th} characteristic, made by the dth decision maker;

The absolute weight of the jth criterion, $\tilde{w}_j$, is computed as in (6) F.R. Lima-Junior, L.C.R. Carpinetti [17].

$$\tilde{w}_j = \sum_{i=1}^{n} \tilde{u}_{ij} \times wr_i \tag{6}$$

where:

wr_i - the value of relative weight of the ith customer requirement;

The absolute weight of each characteristic is defuzzified as in (7) and converted to the relative weight wc_j according to (8) F.R. Lima-Junior, L.C.R. Carpinetti [17].

$$w_j = \frac{l_{\tilde{w}_i} + 2 \cdot m_{\tilde{w}_i} + u_{\tilde{\tilde{x}}_i}}{4} \tag{7}$$

$$wc_j = \frac{w_j}{\sum_{j=1}^{m} w_j} \tag{8}$$

6) *Determine the ratings of engineering characteristics* – the engineering characteristics with higher ratings are more important for the company's product to be successful in the market.

7) *Perform a technical competitive analysis* – the team has to assess the current performance of the company's product and its competitors' for each engineering characteristics.

3 Case study

In order to illustrate the implementation of the fuzzy QFD to support the decision making process in improving a subsystem of a SCADA system, a case study conducted in collaboration with the management of Romanian transmission and system operator (referred to as A company) is presented. The electrical substations are the key element for transmission and distribution of electrical energy. Designing the SCADA system for an electrical substation can be a difficult task, but has become an indispensable tool for power dispatching. Due to the fact that QFD can effectively collect customer requirements, support in product development, and enhance product quality, thus this study apply the fuzzy QFD approach in the process of designing a subsystem (central substation management unit) of a SCADA system.

The assessment was performed by five SCADA experts. In order to identify the customer requirements, the decision makers were interviewed. The customer requirements are the following: continuous availability (CR_1), data concentrator (CR_2), protocol converter (CR_3), communication server (CR_4), synchronization with all equipment's time (CR_5), communication security and access control (CR_6), hot standby redundant configuration (CR_7), real-time data processing (CR_8), no moving parts (CR_9), redundant power supply (CR_{10}) and real-time database (CR_{11}). These specialists (EX_1,... EX_5) were responsible for providing the linguistic judgments required for assessing the degree of importance of the customer requirements. The results in the weights of customer requirements are shown in Table III.

Table 3. Weights of customer requirements

Customer requirements	EX_1	EX_2	EX_3	EX_4	EX_5	Average fuzzy number	Relative weight
CR_1	(4,5,5)	(4,5,5)	(4,5,5)	(4,5,5)	(4,5,5)	(4,5,5)	0.11
CR_2	(3,4,5)	(3,4,5)	(2,3,4)	(3,4,5)	(2,3,4)	(2.6,3.6,4.6)	0.08
CR_3	(2,3,4)	(2,3,4)	(3,4,5)	(3,4,5)	(3,4,5)	(2.6,3.6,4.6)	0.08
CR_4	(3,4,5)	(3,4,5)	(3,4,5)	(3,4,5)	(2,3,4)	(2.8,3.8,4.8)	0.08
CR_5	(2,3,4)	(3,4,5)	(3,4,5)	(3,4,5)	(3,4,5)	(2.8,3.8,4.8)	0.08
CR_6	(4,5,5)	(4,5,5)	(3,4,5)	(4,5,5)	(4,5,5)	(3.8,4.8,5)	0.1
CR_7	(4,5,5)	(4,5,5)	(4,5,5)	(4,5,5)	(4,5,5)	(4,5,5)	0.11
CR_8	(2,3,4)	(3,4,5)	(2,3,4)	(3,4,5)	(3,4,5)	(2.6,3.6,4.6)	0.08
CR_9	(4,5,5)	(3,4,5)	(4,5,5)	(4,5,5)	(4,5,5)	(3.8,4.8,5)	0.1
CR_{10}	(4,5,5)	(4,5,5)	(4,5,5)	(4,5,5)	(4,5,5)	(4,5,5)	0.11
CR_{11}	(2,3,4)	(3,4,5)	(2,3,4)	(3,4,5)	(2,3,4)	(2.4,3.4,4.4)	0.07

In the next stage, a competitive analysis was performed. Company A's ability to meet customer requirements on a scale of 1 to 5 (1 worst – 5 best) was ranked. This case study deals with four competitors, denoted B, C, D and E company. The competitive analysis is shown in fig. 1. It can be noticed that A company has to improve data parameter.

* Corresponding author: ciprian.cristea@emd.utcluj.ro

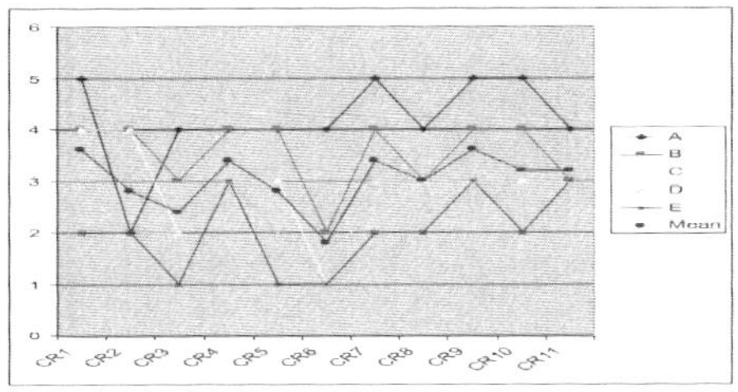

Fig. 1. Competitive analysis for customer requirements

In the next step, the decision makers agreed the following list of engineering characteristics: warm standby power supply (EC_1), data acquisition from the substation control systems, protection, automation service equipments (EC_2), communication system (EC_3), independent and redundant communication ports (EC_4), GPS time servers (EC_5), secure database connection (EC_6), hot standby system (EC_7), time stamping application (EC_8), modular construction (EC_9), hot-swap enabled power supplies (EC_{10}) and Random Access Memory (EC_{11}).

Table 4. Fuzzy number of the aggregated degrees of relationship and values of the relative weights of the engineering characteristics

	EC_1	EC_2	EC_3	EC_4	EC_5
CR_1	(5,9,9)	(0,0,0)	(0,0,0)	(0,0,0)	(0,0,0)
CR_2	(0,0,0)	(3.4,6.6,7.4)	(1.2,6,4.6)	(1,3,5)	(0,0,0)
CR_3	(0,0,0)	(0,0,0)	(3.4,6.6,7.4)	(0.8,0.8,2.4)	(0,0,0)
CR_4	(0,0,0)	(1,2.2, 2)	(0,0,0)	(4.2,7.8,8.2)	(0,0,0)
CR_5	(0,0,0)	(1,1,3)	(0,0,0)	(0,0,0)	(4.2,7.8,8.2)
CR_6	(0,0,0)	(0,0,0)	(0,0,0)	(0,0,0)	(0,0,0)
CR_7	(5,9,9)	(0,0,0)	(0,0,0)	(0,0,0)	(0,0,0)
CR_8	(0,0,0)	(1.2,6,4.6)	(1,1,3)	(0,0,0)	(4.2,7.8,8.2)
CR_9	(1, 1.8,3.8)	(0,0,0)	(0,0,0)	(0,0,0)	(0,0,0)
CR_{10}	(5,9,9)	(0,0,0)	(0,0,0)	(0,0,0)	(0,0,0)
CR_{11}	(0,0,0)	(3.4,6.6,7.4)	(0,0,0)	(0,0,0)	(1,2.6,4.6)
Relative weight	0.1619	0.1074	0.0592	0.0788	0.0676

	EC_6	EC_7	EC_8	EC_9	EC_{10}	EC_{11}
CR_1	(0,0,0)	(4.2,4.6,8.2)	(0,0,0)	(1.2,6,4.6)	(5,9,9)	(0,0,0)
CR_2	(0.8,0.8,2.4)	(0,0,0)	(1,3,5)	(0,0,0)	(0,0,0)	(1,3,5)
CR_3	(0,0,0)	(0,0,0)	(0,0,0)	(0,0,0)	(0,0,0)	(0,0,0)
CR_4	(0,0,0)	(0,0,0)	(1.2,6,4.6)	(0,0,0)	(0,0,0)	(1,1,3)
CR_5	(0,0,0)	(0,0,0)	(0,0,0)	(0,0,0)	(0,0,0)	(0,0,0)
CR_6	(4.2,4.6,8.2)	(0,0,0)	(0,0,0)	(0,0,0)	(1,3,5)	(0,0,0)
CR_7	(1,2.6,4.6)	(4.2,4.6,8.2)	(0,0,0)	(1.2,6,4.6)	(4.2,4.6,8.2)	(0,0,0)
CR_8	(0.8,0.8,2.4)	(0,0,0)	(5,9,9)	(0,0,0)	(0,0,0)	(1,2,2,4.2)
CR_9	(0,0,0)	(0,0,0)	(0.8,0.8,2.4)	(4.2,4.6,8.2)	(1,2,2,4.2)	(0,0,0)
CR_{10}	(0,0,0)	(1.2,6,4.6)	(0,0,0)	(1,3,5)	(4.2,4.6,8.2)	(0,0,0)
CR_{11}	(0.8,0.8,2.4)	(0,0,0)	(1,3,5)	(0,0,0)	(0,0,0)	(5,9,9)
Relative weight	0.0657	0.0727	0.0695	0.0981	0.1493	0.0697

Table IV presents these results regarding the degrees of relationship between the customer requirements and engineering characteristics, based on the linguistic terms and the relative weight.

In the final stage, a competitive analysis was performed. Company A's ability to meet engineering characteristics on a scale of 1 to 5 (1 worst – 5 best) was ranked and then was compared to competitors. The competitive analysis is illustrated in fig. 2.

It can be noticed that A company has to improve the independent and redundant communication ports and the time stamping application.

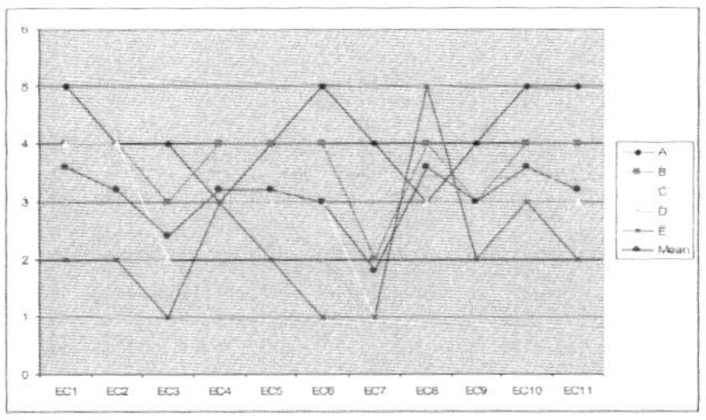

Fig. 2. Competitive analysis for engineering characteristics

I. CONCLUSIONS

SCADA systems have many advantages, such as handling a large amount of data required to monitor the electrical state of all power lines, equipments and can help in a short period of time diagnose the failure state of the system. This paper presented a fuzzy QFD approach to support the decision making process in improving a subsystem of a SCADA system. By integrating fuzzy set theory, this approach is also capable to capture the vagueness and subjectivity in expert's assessment and to streamline the analysis of QFD information. The results reveal that the fuzzy QFD approach may be a very useful tool to support decision makers to perform HOQ analysis without difficulties.

REFERENCES

[1] A. Rezai, P. Keshavarzi, Z. Moravej, "Key management issue in SCADA networks: A review", *JESTECH*, 20, pp. 354–363, 2017.
[2] H.-T. Liu, "Product design and selection using fuzzy QFD and fuzzy MCDM approaches", *Appl. Math. Model.*, 35, pp. 482–496, 2011.
[3] C.C. Otel, "Conceptul de calitate", Revista de Management şi Inginerie Economică, 5,(18), pp.199-200, 2006.
[4] I.A. Iancu, "Marketing Mix in Financial Investment Services Companies", SEA-Practical Application on Science, IV(10), pp. 59-64, 2016.
[5] C.E Stoenoiu, "Economic and financial analysis of a company–support for users of information", J. Int. Sci. Publ. : Econ. Bus., 6(3), pp. 333-347, 2012.
[6] C.K.M. Lee, C.T.Y. Ru, C.L. Yeung, K.L. Choy, W.H. Ip, "Analyze the healthcare service requirement using fuzzy QFD", *Comput. Ind.*, 74, pp. 1–15, 2015.
[7] E. Bottani, A. Rizzi, "Strategic management of logistics service: a fuzzy QFD approach", *Int. J. Prod. Econ.*, 103, pp. 585–599, 2006.
[8] X.X. Shen, X. Min, K.C. Tan, "Listening to the future voice of the customer using fuzzy trend analysis in quality function deployment", *Qual. Eng.*, 13, pp. 419–425, 2001.
[9] Y.S. Sohn, I.S. Choi, "Fuzzy QFD for supply chain management with reliability", *Reliab. Eng. Syst. Safe.*, 72, pp. 327–334, 2001.
[10] C.Y. Tsai, "Using fuzzy QFD to enhance manufacturing strategic planning", *J. Chin. Inst. Ind. Eng.*, 18, pp. 33–41, 2003.
[11] C. Kahraman, T. Ertay, G. Buyukozkan, "A fuzzy optimization model for QFD planning process using analytic network approach", *Eur. J. Oper. Res.*, 171, pp. 390–411, 2006.

* Corresponding author: ciprian.cristea@emd.utcluj.ro

[12] Y. Chen, R.Y.K. Fung, J. Tang, "Rating technical attributes in fuzzy QFD by integrating fuzzy weighted average method and fuzzy expected value operator", *Eur. J. Oper. Res.*, 174, pp. 1553–1566, 2006.
[13] L.S. Chen, M.C. Weng, "An evaluation approach to engineering design in QFD processes using fuzzy goal programming models", *Eur. J. Oper. Res.*, 172, pp. 230–248, 2006.
[14] C.K. Kwong, Y. Chen, H. Bai, D.S.K. Chan, "A methodology of determining aggregated importance of engineering characteristics in QFD", Comput. Ind. Eng., 53, pp. 667–679, 2007.
[15] M. Dursun, E. E. Karsak, "A QFD-based fuzzy MCDM approach for supplier selection", *Appl. Math. Model.*, 37, pp. 5864–5875, 2013.
[16] D.H. Akbas, B. Bilgen, "An integrated fuzzy QFD and TOPSIS methodology for choosing the ideal gas fuel at WWTPs", *Energy*, 125, pp. 484-497, 2017.
[17] F.R. Lima-Junior, L.C.R. Carpinetti, "A multicriteria approach based on fuzzy QFD for choosing criteria for supplier selection", *Comput. Ind. Eng.*, 101, pp. 269–285, 2016.
[18] L.A. Zadeh, "Fuzzy sets", *Inf. Control*, 8, pp. 338–353, 1965.
[19] G. Buyukozkan, A.G. Ciftci, "Combined fuzzy AHP and fuzzy TOPSIS based strategic analysis of electronic service quality in healthcare industry", *Expert. Syst. Appl.*, 39(3), pp. 2341–2354, 2012.
[20] A.R. Ghazikalayeh, M. Amirafshari, H.M. Mkrchyan, M. Taji, "Application of fuzzy hybrid analytic network process in equipment selection of open-pit metal mines, *Int. J. Res. Ind. Eng.*, 2(3), pp. 35–46, 2013.

* Corresponding author: ciprian.cristea@emd.utcluj.ro

Statistical descriptions of delivered quantity of water by sources in the federation of Bosnia & Herzegovina

Amna Aščić[1*], *Mirsad* Imamović[2]

[1] Institute for Statistics of Bosnia and Herzegovina, amnatravnik@gmail.com, Bosnia and Herzegovina
[2] International University Travnik, mimo.mirsad@hotmail.com, Bosnia and Herzegovina

Abstract—Bosnia and Herzegovina is a country rich in unpolluted water resources which could in the future become the driving force of its economic development. In accordance with EU legislation, adopted in 2006, the Federal Law on Water, which among other things regulates the amount of water delivered in order for their sustainable use. The purpose of this study is to determine the trend and statistical descriptions of the amount of water delivered to the sources in the Federation of Bosnia & Herzegovina (FB&H), for the period 2001-2015. The minimum value of the total amount of water delivered in FB&H for the period 2001-2015 (in thousands m^3) was 216620×10^3 (m^3) of water in 2014 and the maximum $237\ 480 \times 10^3$ (m^3) of water in 2005.

1 Introduction

BOSNIA and Herzegovina is a country in Southeastern Europe, located in the west part of the Balkan Peninsula. Border states of Bosnia and Herzegovina are the Republic of Serbia at north-east, Republic of Croatia at the north, west and south and Republic of Montenegro at south-east.

It is administratively divided in to entities and one district: Federation of Bosnia & Herzegovina (FB&H) and Republic of Srpska (RS) and Brčko District.
According to the census from 2013, the total number of people living in FB&H is 3531159.

Total surface of FB&H is 51209,2 km², of which the land surface is 51197 km² and the surface of coastal sea is 12,2 km². Territory of FB&H covers two river basins: basin of the river Sava that includes 75,7% and the basin of Adriatic sea that includes 24,3% of the total surface of the country. Bosnia and Herzegovina is rich in salt and fresh water resources. There are listed 262 rivers on its territory. Surface waters of FB&H are, according to the global standards, the waters of high quality. Bosnia and Herzegovina is rich in underground waters. Thermal and mineral waters are one of its most important natural resources. Coast of B&H is south from the delta of Neretva river, its total length is 22 km. Bosnia and Herzegovina has the access to the sea which ahs the surface of 8 km².

Waters of Bosnia and Herzegovina are unpoluted and in the future they could becoe the initiator of its economic development. Insufficient spatial and temporal distribution of water flow requires the construction of the plant for managing the waters of significat size and complexity, in order to provide rational exploitation of waters, protection of quality and quantity of waters and protection against harmful effects of the water.

Federal law on waters that is under jurisdiction of the Federal Ministry of Agriculture, Waterpower Engineering and Forestry and Federal Ministry of Environment and Tourism has appropriately related competences by this Law, regulates the manner of water management within the territory of Federation of Bosnia & Herzegovina (water protection, water usage, protection against harmful effect of waters and regulation of waterflow and other waters), water resources, public water resources, water objects, legal entities and other institutions competent for particular issues of water management and other issues related to the waters of FB&H. The purpose of this law is to reduce the water polution, achieve good state of waters and prevent waters degradation; achievement of sustainable water usage; ensuring a just access to waters; achievement of social and economic development; ecosystem protection; reduction of risk against floods and other negative water impacts; ensuring the participation of the public in making decisions that refer to waters; prevention and solving of the conflicts related to the protection and water usage; meeting the

* Corresponding author: amnatravnik@gmail.com

obligations from international contracts that are obligatory for Bosnia and Herzegovina.

The most important characteristic of water is its quality. In the world there is a defined set of indicators of water quality, which are incorporated in the so-called Water Quality Index (WQI). In table 1 is given Water Quality Index (WQI) and status of water quality by C. Chaterjee and M. Razuddin [1].

Table 1. Water quality index (wqi) and status of water quality by c. Chaterjee and m. Razuddin [1]

Water Quality Index (WQI)	Water Quality Status or Category
0-25	Excellent Water Quality
26-50	Good Water Quality
51-75	Poor Water Quality
76-100	Very Poor Water Quality
>100	Unfit for drinking

Analysis of WQI index as an indicator for evaluation and classification of different water types and in different world territories is presented in the following papers: for Lagos (Nigeria) by T. A. Adesalu and D. I. Nwankwo [2], for Douro River by A. A. Bordalo, R. Teixeira and W. J. Wiebe [3], for Warri River (Nigeria) by A. B. M. Egborge and J. Benka-Coker [4], for Tuticorin coastal city (south India) by S. Selvam, G. Manimaran, P. Sivasubramanian, N. Balasubramanian and T. Seshunarayana [5], for five river basins in Europe by C. P. Von der Ohe, A. Prüß, R. B. Schäfer, M. Liess, E. De Deckere and W. Brack [6].

Water quality index (WQI) as management tool is given by N. C. Ferreira, C. Bonetti and W. Q. Seiffert [7] and as classification tool is given by H. Boyacioglu [8] and by P. R. Kannel, S. Lee, Y.-S. Lee, S. R. Kanel and S. P. Khan [9].

WQI for coastal water is given by A. K. Gupta, S. K. Gupta and R. S. Patil [10] and for evaluating surface water quality by F. W. Kaurish and T. Younos [11].

Prediction of WQI by regression analysis (RA) and artificial neural networks (ANN) is given by E. R. Rene and M. B. Saidutta [12].

2 Data sources and methods

Data on values of delivered amounts of water according to the springs in FB&H (in thousands m^3), are taken from Statistic Yearbooks of the Federation of Bosnia & Herzegovina (FB&H) Bureau of Statistics, for the period 2001-2015, Statistical yearbook of Federation of Bosnia & Herzegovina for 2006 [13], Statistical yearbook of Federation of Bosnia & Herzegovina for 2009 [14], Statistical yearbook of Federation of Bosnia & Herzegovina for 2012 [15], Statistical yearbook of Federation of Bosnia & Herzegovina for 2016 [16], with a certain calculations from the part of the authors. u

For the trend analysis, we used the following parameters: annual growth rate (AGR) and cumulative growth index (CGI), described in the papers P. Dašić [17] and R. Tošović, P. Dašić and I. Ristović [18].

For the calculation of statistical descriptions parameter we used software system MS-Excel.

For the graphical presentation of data we used standard statistical analysis methods and software system MS-Excel which is described in the book G. Briand [19], G. Harvey [20], J. Schmuller [21] and W. Winston [22].

3 Results and Discussion

Values of the supplied amounts of waters according to the springs in FB&H (in thousands m^3), according to the data taken frojm Statistical Yearbooks of the Federation of Bosnia & Herzegovina (FB&H) Bureau of Statistics, for the period 2001-2015, Statistical yearbook of Federation of Bosnia & Herzegovina for 2006 [13], Statistical yearbook of Federation of Bosnia & Herzegovina for 2009 [14], Statistical yearbook of Federation of Bosnia & Herzegovina for 2012 [15], Statistical yearbook of Federation of Bosnia & Herzegovina for 2016 [16],, are given in Table 2.

Table 2. Supplied amounts of water according to the springs in FB&H, for period from 2001-2015 (in thousands m^3)

Year	TVWPWSS	VWTWSS	Total
2001	219255	4074	223329
2002	218292	5888	224180
2003	221554	7843	229397
2004	229168	7936	237104
2005	229573	7907	237480
2006	220860	7271	228131
2007	217123	6437	223560
2008	223156	6789	229945
2009	218021	7016	225037
2010	219313	6570	225883
2011	220814	6783	227597
2012	219926	6438	226364
2013	219401	6971	226372
2014	209668	6952	216620
2015	216481	7486	223967

Note:
TVWPWSS - Total volume of water from the public water supply system,
VWTWSS - Volume of water taken from other water supply systems.

Fig.s 1-3 show a graphical presentation of the trend of supplied amounts of water in FB&H according to the springs, for the period 2001-2015 (in thousands m^3) as well as their annual growth rate (AGR) in (%) for:

1) *TVWPWSS (total volume of water from the public water supply system) (Fig. 1);*
2) *VWTWSS (volume of water taken from other water supply systems) (Fig. 2);*
3) *Total (Fig. 3).*

Value of supplied amounts of water from TVWPWSS (total volume of water from the public water supply system) in FB&H for period from 2001-2015 (in thousands m^3) is reduced by $2774 \cdot 10^3$ (m^3) water (from $219255 \cdot 10^3$ (m^3) water in 2001 to $216481 \cdot 10^3$ (m^3) water in 2015), with cumulative growth index (CGI) of 98,73%

* Corresponding author: amnatravnik@gmail.com

in relation to the year 2001., and it also had a continuous trend of supplied amounts of water from TVWPWSS in FB&H (Fig. 1). Mean value of delivered amounts of water from TVWPWSS in FB&H for period from 2001-2015 (in thousands m^3) is $220174 \cdot 10^3$ (m^3) of water.

The highest annual growth of supplied amounts of water from TVWPWSS in FB&H was in 2004 by $7614 \cdot 10^3$ (m^3) water or by 3,44%, and then in 2015 for $6813 \cdot 10^3$ (m^3) water or by 3,25% etc. (Fig. 1).

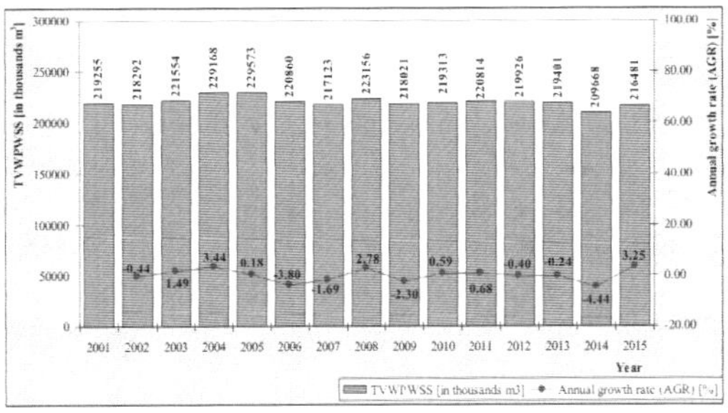

Fig. 1. Graphical presentation of supplied amounts of water from TVWPWSS in FB&H and their annual growth rate (AGR) in (%).

Value of the supplied amounts of water from VWTWSS (volume of water taken from other water supply systems) in FB&H for period from 2001-2015 (in thousands m^3) was increased by $3412 \cdot 10^3$ (m^3) water (from $4074 \cdot 10^3$ (m^3) water in 2001 to $7486 \cdot 10^3$ (m^3) water in 2015), with cumulative growth index (CGI) by 183,75% in relation to 2001., and it mostly had the trend of growth wavering of the supplied amounts of water from VWTWSS in FB&H (Fig. 2).

The highest annual growth of supplied water amount from VWTWSS in FB&H was in 2002 by $1814 \cdot 10^3$ (m^3) water or by 44,53%, and then in 2003 by $1955 \cdot 10^3$ (m^3) water or by 33,20% etc. (Fig. 2).

The highest annual reduction of supplied water amounts from VWTWSS in FB&H was in 2007 by $636 \cdot 10^3$ (m^3) water or by 8,04%, and then in 2006 by $834 \cdot 10^3$ (m^3) water or by 11,47% etc. (Fig. 2).

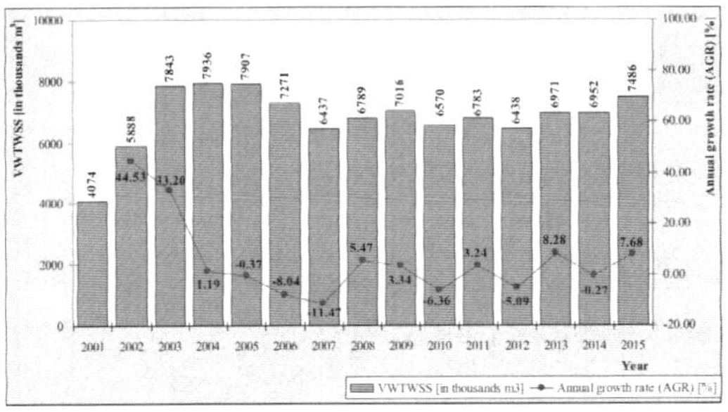

Fig. 2. Grpahical presentation of supplied amounts of water from VWTWSS in FB&H and their annual growth rate (AGR) in (%)

The highest annual reduction of delivered amounts of water from TVWPWSS in FB&H was in 2014 by $9733 \cdot 10^3$ (m^3) water or by 4,44%, and then in 2006 by $8713 \cdot 10^3$ (m^3) water or by 3,80% etc. (Fig. 1).

Value of the total supplied amount of water in FB&H for period from 2001-2015 (in thousands m^3) was increased by $638 \cdot 10^3$ (m^3) of water (from $223329 \cdot 10^3$ (m^3) water in 2001 to $223967 \cdot 10^3$ (m^3) water in 2015), with cumulative growth index (CGI) of 100,29% in relation to 2001, and it had a continuous trend of total supplied waters in FB&H (Fig. 3). Mean value of total supplied water amount in FB&H for the period 2001-2015 (in thousands m^3) is $226998 \cdot 10^3$ (m^3) water.

The highest annual growth of total supplied water amounts in FB&H was in 2015 by $7347 \cdot 10^3$ (m^3) water or by 3,39%, and then in 2004 by $7707 \cdot 10^3$ (m^3) water or by 3,36% etc. (Fig. 3).

The highest annual reduction of total supplied water amount in FB&H was in 2014 by $9752 \cdot 10^3$ (m^3) water or by 4,31%, and then in 2006 by $9349 \cdot 10^3$ (m^3) water or by 3,94% etc. (Fig. 3).

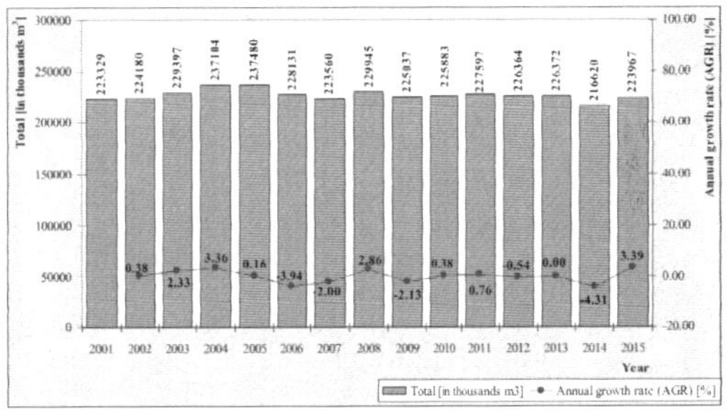

Fig. 3. Graphical presentation of total supplied water amounts in FB&H and their annual growth rate (AGR) in (%)

Fig. 4 presents a graphical presentation of the structure and share in percents of the springs of supplied water amounts in FB&H by 2015 (in thousands m^3).

From the Fig. 9, we can observe that the highest share in percents of the spring of supplied water in FB&H for 2015 (in thousands m^3) have the underground waters (46,72 %), and then springs (39,29 %) etc. Other water sources of the supplied water amount in FB&H for 2015 (in thousands m^3) have only 13,99 % water, and underground waters and springs have 86,01 %.

* Corresponding author: annatravnik@gmail.com

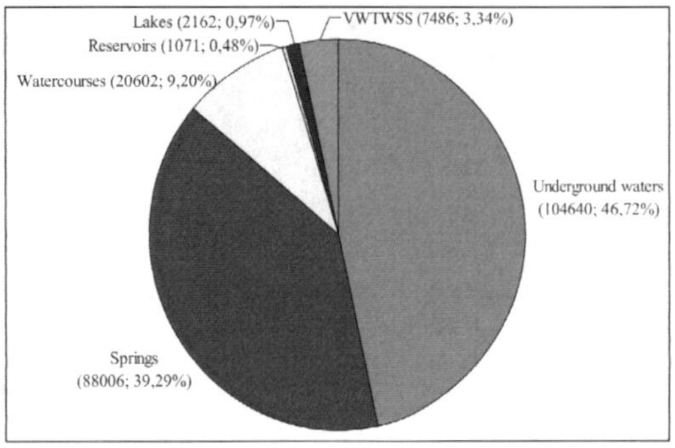

Fig. 4. Graphical presentation of the structure and share in percents of the sources of supplied water amount in FB&H for 2015 (in thousands m^3)

Statistical descriptions parameter of delivered quantity of water by sources in the FB&H is given in table 3.

Table 3. Statistical descriptions parameter of delivered QUANTITY OF WATER BY SOURCES IN THE FB&H

Measures	Sign	TVWPWSS	VWTWSS	Total
Minimum	Min	0.21 mil	4074	216620
Maximum	Max	0.22 mil	7936	237480
Range	Rx	0.02 mil	3862	20860
Total	Sum	3.3 mil	102361	3404966
Arithmentic mean	Aver	0.22 mil	6824.067	226997.733
Geometric mean	GM	0.22 mil	6748.025	226941.704
Harmonic mean	HM	0.22 mil	6655.340	226886.032
Median	Med	0.22 mil	6952	226364
Std. deviation	SD	0.004 mil	962.344	5237.782
Variance	Var	23.18 mil	926106.210	27434357.924
Coef. of variation	CV	2.187	14.102	2.307
Skewness	Sk	0.244	-1.633	0.549
Kurtosis	Ku	1.732	4.204	1.297

Conclusion

Continuous trend of supplied water amounts in FB&H for the period 2001-2015 had the water from TVWPWSS (total volume of water from the public water supplysystem) (Fig. 1) with cumulative growth index (CGI) by 98,73% in relation to 2001. and mean value of $220174 \cdot 10^3$ (m^3) water and total supplied water amount (Fig. 3) with the cumulative growth index (CGI) by 100,29% in relation to 2001 and mean value of $226998 \cdot 10^3$ (m^3) water.

Trend of a great growth wavering of the value of delivered amounts of water in FB&H for the period 2001-2015 had the waters from VWTWSS (volume of water taken from other water supply systems) (Fig. 2)

* Corresponding author: amnatravnik@gmail.com

Fig. 5 graphically presents arithmentic (Aver), geometric (GM) and harmonic mean (HM) and median (Med) for delivered quantity of water by sources in the FB&H.

Minimum value of delivered amounts of water from TVWPWSS in FB&H for period from 2001-2015 was 209668 (in thousands m^3) in 2014, and maximum 229573 (in thousands m^3) in 2005.

Minimum value of supplied water amounts from VWTWSS in FB&H for period from 2001-2015 was 4074 (in thousands m^3) in 2001, and maximum 7936 (in thousands m^3) in 2004.

Minimum value of the total supplied water amounts in FB&H for period from 2001-2015 was 216620 (in thousands m^3) in 2014, and maximum 237480 (in thousands m^3) in 2005.

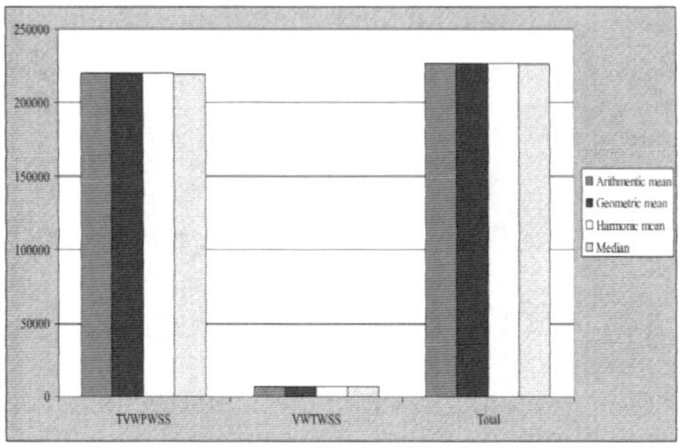

Fig. 5. Graphical representation arithmentic (Aver), geometric (GM) and harmonic mean (HM) and median (Med)

with cumulative growth index (CGI) by 183,75% in relation to 2001.

Based on the structure and share in percents of the sources of supplied water amounts in FB&H for 2015 (in thousands m^3) (Fig. 4) have the waters from underground waters (46,72 %), and then the waters from springs (39,29 %). Waters from underground waters (46,72 %) and waters from springs have a percentage share of 86,01 % in supplied water amounts in FB&H for 2015 (in thousands m^3) while the other sources have a percentage share of only 13,99 %.

The arithmetic mean value of the delivered amount of water in FB&H for the period 2001-2015 (in thousands of m^3) is 226998×10^3 (m^3) of water, geometric mean is 226942×10^3 (m^3) and harmonic mean is 226886×10^3 (m^3). Sum of total delivered amount of water in FB&H for period 2001-2015 (in thousands of m^3) was 3404966×10^3 (m^3) of water. The value of the total delivered amount of water in FB&H for the period 2001-2015 (in thousands of m^3) had a constant trend of the total delivered amount of water in FB&H, and has increased by 638×10^3 (m^3) of water (from 223329×10^3 (m^3) of water in 2001 to 223967×10^3 (m^3) of water in 2015), with a cumulative growth index (CGI) of 100.29% compared to 2001. Largest annual growth of total delivered amount of water in FB&H was in 2015 for 7347×10^3 (m^3) of water or for 3,39% etc. Highest annual decrease of total delivered amount of water in FB&H was in 2014 for 9752×10^3 (m^3) of water or for 4,31% etc.

References

[1] C. Chaterjee, and M. Razuddin, "Determination of Water Quality Index (W.Q.I.) of a degraded river in Asanil Industrial area, Ranigunj, Burdwan, West Bengal Nature," *Environment and Pollution Technology*, vol. 1, no. 2, pp. 181-189, 2002.

[2] Adesalu, T.A. and Nwankwo, D.I.: "Effect of water quality indices on phytoplankton of a sluggish tidal creek in Lagos, Nigeria," *Pakistan Journal of Biological Sciences*, vol. 11, no. 6, pp. 836-844, 2008. doi: 10.3923/pjbs.2008.836.844.

[3] A. A. Bordalo, R. Teixeira, and W. J. Wiebe, "A water quality index applied to an international shared river basin: The case of the Douro River," *Environmental Management*, vol. 38, no. 6, pp. 910-920, 2006. doi: 10.1007/s00267-004-0037-6.

[4] A. B. M. Egborge, and J. Benka-Coker, "Water quality index: Application in the Warri River, Nigeria," *Environmental Pollution. Series B, Chemical and Physical*, vol. 12, no. 1, pp. 27-40, 1986. doi: 10.1016/0143-148X(86)90004-2.

[5] S. Selvam, G. Manimaran, P. Sivasubramanian, N. Balasubramanian, and T. Seshunarayana, "GIS-based evaluation of Water Quality Index of groundwater resources around Tuticorin coastal city, south India," *Environmental Earth Sciences*, vol. 71, no. 6, pp. 2847-2867, 2014. doi: 10.1007/s12665-013-2662-y.

[6] C. P. Von der Ohe, A. Prüß, R. B. Schäfer, M. Liess, E. De Deckere, and W. Brack, "Water quality indices across Europe - A comparison of the good ecological status of five river basins," *Journal of Environmental Monitoring*, vol. 9, no. 9, pp. 970-978, 2007. doi: 10.1039/b704699p.

[7] N. C. Ferreira, C. Bonetti, and W. Q. Seiffert, "Hydrological and Water Quality Indices as management tools in marine shrimp culture," *Aquaculture*, vol. 318, no. 3-4, pp. 425-433, 2011. doi: 10.1016/j.aquaculture.2011.05.045.

[8] H. Boyacioglu, "Utilization of the water quality index method as a classification tool," *Environmental Monitoring and Assessment*, vol. 167, no. 1-4, pp. 115-124, 2010. doi: 10.1007/s10661-009-1035-1.

[9] P. R. Kannel, S. Lee, Y.-S. Lee, S. R. Kanel, and S. P. Khan, "Application of water quality indices and dissolved oxygen as indicators for river water classification and urban impact. assessment," *Environmental Monitoring and Assessment*, vol. 132, no. 1-3, pp. 93-110, 2007. doi: 10.1007/s10661-006-9505-1.

[10] A. K. Gupta, S. K. Gupta, and R. S. Patil, "A comparison of water quality indices for coastal water," *Journal of Environmental Science and Health - Part A Toxic/Hazardous Substances and Environmental Engineering*, vol. 38, no. 11, pp. 2711-2725, 2003. doi: 10.1081/ESE-120024458.

[11] F. W. Kaurish, and T. Younos, "Developing a standardized water quality index for evaluating surface water quality," *Journal of the American Water Resources Association*, vol. 43, no 2, pp. 533-545, 2007. doi: 10.1111/j.1752-1688.2007.00042.x.

[12] E. R. Rene, and M. B. Saidutta, "Prediction of water quality indices by regression analysis and artificial neural networks," *International Journal of Environmental Research*, vol. 2, no. 2, pp. 183-188, 2008.

[13] *Statistical yearbook of Federation of Bosnia & Herzegovina for 2006*. Sarajevo, Bosnia & Herzegovina: Institute for Statistics of the FB&H, 2006, pp. 465.

[14] *Statistical yearbook of Federation of Bosnia & Herzegovina for 2009*. Sarajevo, Bosnia & Herzegovina: Institute for Statistics of the FB&H, 2009, pp. 513.

[15] *Statistical yearbook of Federation of Bosnia & Herzegovina for 2012*. Sarajevo, Bosnia & Herzegovina: Institute for Statistics of the FB&H, 2012, pp. 532.

[16] *Statistical yearbook of Federation of Bosnia & Herzegovina for 2016*. Sarajevo, Bosnia & Herzegovina: Institute for Statistics of the FB&H, 2016, pp. 506.

[17] P. Dašić, "Application of polynomial regression models for approximation of time series," *Journal of Economic and Management Based on New Technologies*, vol. 1, no. 2, pp. 81-160, 2012.

[18] R. Tošović, P. Dašić, and I. Ristović, "Sustainable use of metallic mineral resources of Serbia from an environmental perspective," *Environmental Engineering and Management Journal*, vol. 15, no. 9, pp. 2075-2084, 2016.

[19] G. Briand, *Using Excel for principles of econometrics*. (4th Edition), Hoboken, New Jersey: John Wiley & Sons Inc., 2011, pp. 484.

[20] G. Harvey, *Excel 2016 for dummies*. Hoboken, New Jersey: John Wiley & Sons Inc., 2016, 432 pp.

[21] J. Schmuller, *Statistical analysis with Excel for dummies*. (4th Revised Edition). Hoboken, New Jersey: John Wiley & Sons Inc., 2016, 552 pp.

[22] W. Winston, *Microsoft Excel data analysis and business modeling*. (5th Edition). Redmond, Washington: Microsoft Press, 2016, pp. 864.

* Corresponding author: amnatravnik@gmail.com

DOI: 10.1051/matecconf/201712604008

Case study using analysis of variance to determine groups' variations

Flavius A. Ardelean[1]

[1]CONTINENTAL Automotive, flavius.a.ardelean@continental-corporation.com

Abstract - This paper aims to present the analysis of a part manufactured in three shifts, which has a specific characteristic dimension, using DFSS (Design for Six Sigma) ANOVA (Analysis of Variance) method. In every shift, the significant characteristic, "SC", dimension should be produced within the given tolerance. The question that arises is: "Does the shift have any influence on the "SC" dimension realization?" By using the one way ANOVA method, one can observe the variation between the means of each of the three shifts. Afterwards, specific action can be undertaken to adjust, if necessary, the differences between the shifts.

1 About anova

Anova, which is the abbreviation of "analysis of variance", tests the hypothesis that the means of three or more populations are equal. ANOVA assess the importance of one or more factors by comparing the response variable means at the different factor levels. The null hypothesis states that all population means (factor level means) are equal, while the alternative hypothesis states that at least one is different, http://support.minitab.com [1].

We are using the one-way ANOVA method because the sample data are separated into groups according to one characteristic, which is the "SC" dimension. Instead of referring to the main objective of testing for equal means, the term analysis of variance refers to the method we use, which is based on an analysis of sample variances, M. F. Triola [3].

What are we doing is comparing the variance between samples with variance within sample.

$$F = \frac{variance\ between\ sample}{variance\ within\ sample} \quad (1)$$

A correlation between the p-value and test statistic for one way ANOVA, F, states that for larger values of F, we get smaller p-values and for that the ANOVA test is right-tailed. Also smaller values of F result in larger values of p-values and the graph will be left-tailed.

The P-value is the probability of obtaining a sample statistic with a value as extreme as, or more extreme than the one determined by the sample data.

Fig. 1, below, shows the relationship between F test statistic and p-value.

2 Data under anova analysis

The part that has been observed is an assembly component on which, from the design, a specific characteristic dimension is given.

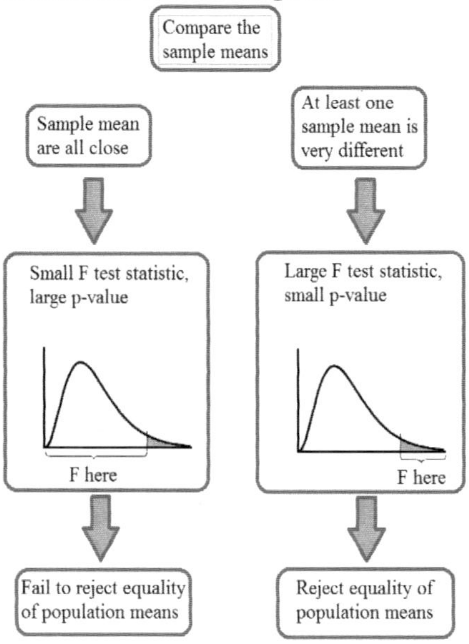

Fig. 1. Relation between F test statistic and p-value

That has a major impact over the functionality of the part and, for that, systematic measurements are taken during every shift.

Fig. 2 presents a detail from the drawing of the part and with the specific characteristic dimension marked on it. That is Φ4.15±0.025 and it represents the diameter of the hole. Geometrical tolerance, circularity, presented also in this figure, is not considered for this observation even if it had the SC specification on it.

Also the coaxiality tolerance is not a part of the actual observation. First thing that influences the quality of the part is the significant dimension, respectively the

* Corresponding author: flavius.a.ardelean@continental-corporation.com

DOI: 10.1051/matecconf/201712604008

diameter of the hole. All other information are to be taken in the next phases of observations and control.

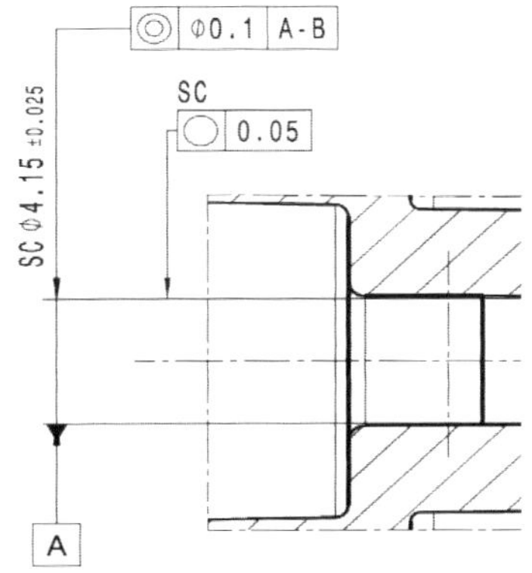

Fig. 2. Drawing of the part

Those measurements are used to determine, by the ANOVA method, the differences of the mean of every shift, regarding this specific dimension. For that, 15th measurements are taken in every single shift.

A measurement report is given and it includes the 15th measurements of the specific characteristic dimension on every shift. In the table below these measured values can be seen.

Table 1. Values from measurement report

	SHIFT 1	SHIFT 2	SHIFT 3
	4.159	4.169	4.162
	4.143	4.136	4.151
	4.145	4.135	4.172
	4.126	4.166	4.167
	4.151	4.140	4.146
	4.148	4.174	4.137
	4.150	4.136	4.167
	4.173	4.140	4.139
	4.138	4.137	4.148
	4.154	4.147	4.140
	4.137	4.165	4.141
	4.134	4.136	4.148
	4.136	4.139	4.134
	4.150	4.151	4.155
	4.168	4.151	4.165
MEAN	**4.147**	**4.148**	**4.151**

From this table we can see that the mean of every single shift is given in the last raw.

First of all, we can observe from this measurements table a small variation of the means of the part during the three shift. Thus we can say that every shift produces good parts regarding the upper and lower tolerances.

To have an overall opinion over the part variation we can use the "one-way ANOVA method".

3 Using one way anova to compare the means of the three shifts, DfSS trainings materials [4]

One way ANOVA is used to compare the mean of at least three conditions in a certain experiment considering every shift as a group.

Data for this experiment is given in table 1. We can observe that we have three groups (representing the three shifts) and 15 measurements of a specific dimension for every group.

To begin with the ANOVA method, the first thing that we have to do is to define the statements of *no* and *alternative hypothesis*.

4 Hypothesis of one way ANOVA

Statistical tests prove, or attempt to disapprove, if assumptions, statements or hypothesis about unknown populations are valid or not. The goal is to be able to decide if a factor or more have a significant influence on a certain response. Sometimes, the differences are significant, other times they are not and they have to be observed.

The hypothesis tests will help us decide with a certain confidence if a statistical difference between samples exists or not. Always assume that the *null hypothesis* (H_0) is true, unless we find a strong evidence otherwise. The alternative, called *alternative hypothesis* (H_a), is when a strong evidence is found and then we have to reject the null hypothesis.

In our case, for *NO hypothesis* (or null hypothesis) we will say that there is no difference between the means of every shift. If we fail to reject H_o hypothesis, that means that we can accept the H_o hypothesis and also the fact that the factor shift has no influence on the functional results.

Alternative hypothesis or H_a will state that there is at least one difference among the means or the factor has an influence on the functional results.

The two statements are written as bellow:

$H_0: \mu_1 = \mu_2 = \mu_3$

$H_a: at\ least\ one\ difference\ among\ the\ means$

We will use α_{level} =0.05, significance level. By definition, the alpha level is the probability of rejecting the null hypothesis when the null hypothesis is true, http://support.minitab.com [1].

Using the standard $\alpha_{level} = 0.05$ cutoff, the null hypothesis is rejected when $p < 0.05$ and not rejected when $p > 0.05$. The p-value does not, in itself, support reasoning about the probabilities of hypotheses but is only a tool for deciding whether to reject the null hypothesis, R. L. Wasserstein, N. A. Lazar [5].

P-value is better represented in the fig. 3 which shows where and how it influences the decision to reject or fail to reject the null hypothesis.

* Corresponding author: flavius.a.ardelean@continental-corporation.com

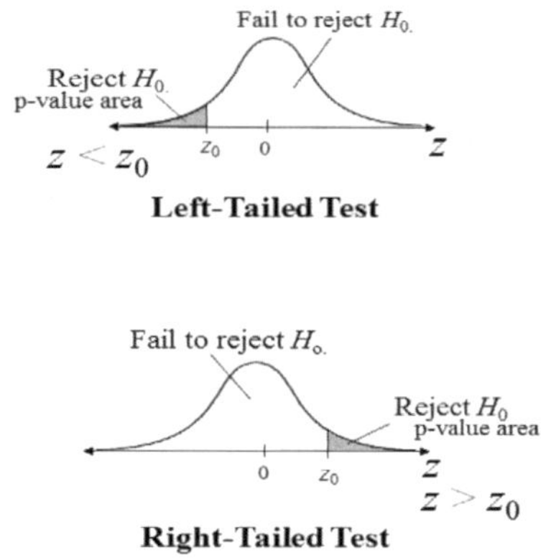

Fig. 3. P-value, on the left and right tailed graphic, with null hypothesis

5 Analyzing the degree of freedom to determine the critical value

Using the degree of freedom (d_f) the statistic test will be compared. There are two ways to calculate the degree of freedom: between the groups and within the groups.

For calculating the d_f between the groups:

$$\mathbf{d_{f_{between}} = k - 1} \tag{2}$$

where k represents the number of conditions (we have three groups then there are three conditions).
Results that $d_{f_{between}}$ will be then 2.

For $$\mathbf{d_{f_{within}} = N - k} \tag{3}$$

where N represents the number of values in groups.

Then,

$$\boldsymbol{d_{f_{within}} = 42} \tag{4}$$

Total degrees of freedom will be :

$$\mathbf{d_{f_{within}} = 44} \tag{5}$$

6 F-critical value

Using table (or FINV function in excel, e.g. =FINV(0.05,2.42), fig. 2), we get a $F_{crit} = 3.22$.

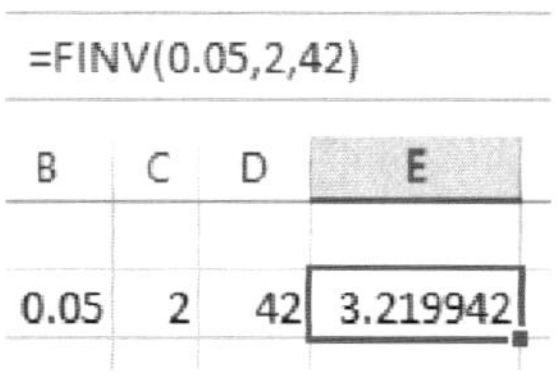

Fig. 4. Using F_{crit} function in excel

7 Analysis of the sum of the squares

The mean for each group is given below:
Group 1 (Shift 1): $\bar{x}_1 = 4.147$
Group 2 (Shift 2): $\bar{x}_2 = 4.148$
Group 3 (Shift 3): $\bar{x}_3 = 4.151$
The grand mean, $\bar{\bar{X}}$, will be:

$$\bar{\bar{\mathbf{x}}} = \frac{\mathbf{G}}{\mathbf{N}} = \frac{\mathbf{186.706}}{\mathbf{45}} = \mathbf{4.149}$$

where G is the sum of total values between groups and N is the total conditions, representing the mean of all groups.

7.1 Sum of squares total

Will be calculated as per following equation:

$$\mathbf{SS_{TOTAL}} = \sum(\mathbf{x} - \bar{\bar{\mathbf{x}}})^2 = \mathbf{0.007267} \tag{7}$$

7.2 Sum of squares within groups

$$\mathbf{SS_{within}} = \sum[(\mathbf{x_1} - \bar{\mathbf{x}}_1)^2 + (\mathbf{x_2} - \bar{\mathbf{x}}_2)^2 + (\mathbf{x_3} - \bar{\mathbf{x}}_3)^2] = \mathbf{0.007129} \tag{8}$$

7.3 Sum of squares between the groups

From the equation bellow, we find that $SS_{between}$ is 0.000138

$$\mathbf{SS_{TOTAL}} = \mathbf{SS_{within}} + \mathbf{SS_{between}} \tag{9}$$

8 Calculation of the variance between and the variance within

First, we calculate the mean square between, which is:

$$\mathbf{MS_{between}} = \frac{\mathbf{SS_{between}}}{\mathbf{d_{f_{between}}}} = \mathbf{0.0000688} \tag{10}$$

Second, the mean square within:

$$\mathbf{MS_{within}} = \frac{\mathbf{SS_{within}}}{\mathbf{d_{f_{within}}}} = \mathbf{0.000169} \tag{11}$$

9 Calculate the F-value for specific set

This is to compare with F_{crit} in order to reject or not the H_0 hypothesis.

F-value is calculated as a ratio between the $MS_{between}$ and MS_{within}. If the result is less than F_{crit}, then we are fail to reject the null hypothesis and that means that the mean of each group is almost the same and there is no significant difference between the three groups.

$$\mathbf{F} = \frac{\mathbf{MS_{between}}}{\mathbf{MS_{within}}} = \mathbf{0.4058} \tag{12}$$

F-value of 0.4058 is smaller than F_{crit} which is 3.22

* Corresponding author: flavius.a.ardelean@continental-corporation.com

and gives us the possibility to reject the null hypothesis.

We can say, as we can observe from the measurement table, that there is no big difference between shifts, even if the 3rd shift has the mean bigger than the other two shifts. The difference is not so big and no further action is needed to be taken.

10 Using excel add-in, "Data analysis"

Excel has an add-in function that allows easy calculations of various statistic elements. Through those functions, one way ANOVA is presented and it give us all the values as we calculated before.

For the three groups that we have evaluated, the following results are shown in excel data analysis add-in.

In table 2 it can be observed the main information regarding the group structure: count of observations, sum and average and the variance as well.

Table 2. Main information regarding groups under analyze summary

Groups	*Count*	*Sum*	*Average*	*Variance* $x10^{-4}$
G1	15	62.212	4.147466667	1.6241
G2	15	62.222	4.148133333	1.9141
G3	15	62.272	4.151466667	1.5541

The ANOVA functions, which we've already calculated in this paper, are presented in table 3. Here we can find the sum of squares (within, between and total), the degrees of freedom, the mean square, F-value, p-value and also F-critical.

Table 3. Main information of anova

Source of Variation	*SS*	*df*	*MS*	*F*	*P-value*	*F crit*
Between Groups	0.0001	2	6.889E-05	0.406	0.669	3.22
Within Groups	0.0071	42	0.0001697			
Total	0.0073	44				

With a p-value of 0.66 calculated, bigger than α_{level} of 0.05 that we had at the begging of the process (which means that we have 95% of confidence that the analysis is correct, using one tailed test), we can ascertain again that we fail to reject the null hypothesis and to accept that there are no big differences between the mean of the part during the three shifts. In other words, even if there is a slight difference of the third shift in respect to the other two, the difference is too small to influence the quality of the part. The significant characteristic dimension is respected, the variation not being too influent.

11 Conclusion

We saw that by using the one way ANOVA method, we were able to determine if there is a statistically significant difference among the groups that are not related to sampling error. If we find that there is a difference, then we'll need to examine where the groups' differences lay and undertake proper measures. For the analysis presented here, we observed that there is no significant difference between the groups (shifts), null hypothesis failed to be rejected, so no further action should be taken.

References

http://support.minitab.com
http://www.statisticssolutions.com
M. F. Triola, "Elementary Statistics" (11th Edition), Publisher: Addison Wesley, 2009
DfSS trainings materials (internal trainings materials)
R. L. Wasserstein, N. A. Lazar, "The ASA's Statement on p-Values: Context, Process, and Purpose", Publisher: Taylor & Francis, 2016
Y. Kai, E-H. Basem, "Design for Six Sigma: A Roadmap for Product Development", (2nd Edition), Publisher: McGraw Hill, 2008
K. Hogreve, "Design for Six Sigma (The Six Sigma Series)", Publisher: Createspace Independent Publishing Platform, 2015
A.Asefeso, "Design for Six Sigma", Publisher: Createspace Independent Publishing Platform, 2014

* Corresponding author: flavius.a.ardelean@continental-corporation.com

MATEC Web of Conferences **126**, 04009 (2017) DOI: 10.1051/matecconf/201712604009
Annual Session of Scientific Papers IMT ORADEA 2017

Determinants of corporate dividend policy: evidence from romanian listed companies

Ciprian Cristea[1*], *Maria* Cristea[2]

[1]Technical University of Cluj-Napoca, Faculty of Electrical Engineering, ciprian.cristea@emd.utcluj.ro, Romania
[2]Technical University of Cluj-Napoca, Faculty of Electrical Engineering, fagarasan_maria@yahoo.com, Romania

Abstract—Although there is a vast literature that has investigated the dividend policies of firms from developed countries, relatively little research has been published exploring the dividend policies of firms from emerging countries. The literature regarding establishing the relationship between dividend policy and the attributes of non-financial companies listed on Romanian stock market, to the best of our knowledge, remains inexistent. The aim of this study is to identify the main factors influencing dividend policy for the non-financial companies listed on the Bucharest Stock Exchange for a period of ten years from 2007 to 2016. In order to achieve this aim, panel data were collected from the listed companies' reports and financial statements. The study reveals that dividend policy is positively related to corporate profitability and liquidity and negatively associated with leverage, size, growth, and the state of the economy.

1 Introduction

The dividend policy is one of the most researched topics in corporate finance over the past decades. Dividend policy represents the set of guidelines a firm uses to dispose how much of its financial resources will payout to its shareholders, when it is not required by law, as mentioned by K. Kato, U. Loewenstein, W. Tsai [1]. M. Miller and F. Modigliani [2], pioneers in this field, demonstrate that dividend payments have no effect on company value and the payout ratios should not matter under perfect capital market assumptions. Yet, in the real world where markets that are far from being perfect, the irrelevance theory proposed by M. Miller, F. Modigliani [2] is no more an acceptable answer.

Dividend policy continues to retain the interest of academics, creditors, management, and shareholders. The importance attached to this topic arises from its interconnection with other corporate decisions, such as financing and investments, and its effect on shareholders' wealth and on the whole economy I. Jabbouri [3]. Dividend income represents a part of the national income, hence, it helps in understanding the overall performance of the economy D.L. Papadopoulos, P.D. Charalambidis [4]. Choosing the dividend policy is a strategic decision, generally made by top managers, which requires the final approval of the board of directors. Dividends account for roughly thirty percent of the corporate profits of publicly-traded firms around the world A. Fatemi, R. Bildik [5]. The dividend policy literature is vast and contains many hypotheses, and explanations for dividends, financial academics proposing many competing theories about why firms pay, or do not pay, dividends and, despite extensive debate and ample empirical research, no universally accepted explanation is achieved on the actual motivation for paying dividends to be published H.K. Bakera, E. Kilincarslanb, A.H. Arsalc [6].

The continuous growth of empirical studies dealing with the firm's payout policy identifies mixed results. E.F. Fama, K.R. French [7] show a decrease in the propensity to pay dividends by US companies during 1978–1999. Similar findings are recorded for six developed economies during 1994–2002 D.J. Denis, I. Osobov [8], in the UK L. Renneboog, G. Trojanawski [9], for firms in the EU for 1989–2005 H. Von Eije, W.L. Megginson [10], for companies in India for 1991–2001 Y.S. Reddy, S. Rath [11], for a couple of companies from twenty-three countries S.P. Ferris, N. Jayaraman, S. Sabherwal [12], for a large sample of firms in 33 countries A. Fatemi, R. Bildik [5]. H. DeAngelo, L. DeAngelo, D.J. Skinner [13] contradict these findings, showing that dividends paid by US industrial firms actually increased between 1978 and 2000. B. Julio, D. Ikenberry [14] support H. DeAngelo, L. DeAngelo, D.J. Skinner [13] conclusions with regard to the US companies. R. Bildik, A. Fatemi, I. Fooladi [15] compare the dividend payout behavior of US firms with

* Corresponding author: ciprian.cristea@emd.utcluj.ro

those of firms in 32 other countries for the period between 1985–2011 and found that the proportion of firms that pay dividends in the US is smaller than in the rest of the world.

G. Bekaert, C.R. Harvey [16] mention that corporate finance models are developed taking into account that are consistent with developed countries, which may cause that these models fail when tested in emerging ones. T. Lagoarde-Segot [17] specifies that managerial models are developed in Western countries, and when are applied in a different institutional context become poor guides to business decisions. Dividend policy is a topic of ongoing debate in both developed H.K. Baker, G.E. Farrelly, E.T. Veit [18] and developing countries A. Hafeez, Y.J. Attiya [19].

In this paper, we investigate the relationship between dividend policy and the attributes of non-financial companies listed on the Bucharest Stock Exchange Market for a period of ten years from 2007 to 2016. In this study, panel data analysis is applied to investigate the determinants of dividend policies of the Romanian companies mentioned above. This research has important implications for both theory and practice. No study, to the best of our knowledge, has examined the determinants of dividend policy on the Romanian market. Our findings have implications for corporate finance and governance theories, academics, investors, regulators, and policymakers in emerging markets.

The rest of the paper is organized as follows: in the next paragraph the methodology is described, furthermore, the empirical results are presented in the third section and, finally, the last section summarizes the conclusions.

2 Methodology

The objective of this paper is to explore dividend policy in Romania and identify its main determinants. In order to test the impact on dividend policy of the most important factors detected in literature, this study uses panel data analysis. These factors include: size of the firm, financial leverage, growth, current profitability, liquidity, and the state of the economy. These factors were chosen due to their influence on dividend behavior in developed and emerging markets. The financial data were collected manually from the annual reports and financial statements of Romanian non-financial firms listed on the Bucharest Stock Exchange Market over the period 2007-2016, thus having 701 complete company-years observations.

In order to measure the amount of dividend payment, we used the annual cash dividend per share over the book value of assets per share (*Div*) of a company, following the case presented by K. Li, X. Zhao [20], Y. Grinstein, R. Michaely [21]. The dependent variable is cash dividend over book value of assets.

Most of the independent variables were intensively used in similar previous reported empirical work: size of the firm, financial leverage, growth, current profitability, liquidity, and the state of the economy. Firm size (*Size*) is measured as natural logarithm of total assets, total book value of debt divided by total assets (*Leverage*) will proxy for financial leverage. For the growth opportunities, annual growth in sales is used as a proxy (*Growth*). In order to quantify the company current profitability, return on equity is used as a proxy (*Profitability*). Return on equity is a firm's net income divided by its shareholder's equity. Quick or acid test ratio shows the ratio of cash and other liquid resources of a company in comparison to its current liabilities, being employed as a measure of liquidity (*Liquidity*). Finally, gross domestic product growth rate (*GDP*) will be used to control for the state of the economy.

In order to examine the impacts of these indicators (size of the firm, financial leverage, growth, current profitability, liquidity, and the state of the economy) on dividend policy, the study uses a panel analysis. For estimating the regression equation, the ordinary least square (OLS) method was used. The basic regression takes the following form:

$$\mathbf{Div}_{it} = \alpha_i + \beta_1 \cdot \mathbf{Size}_{it} + \beta_2 \cdot \mathbf{Leverage}_{it} + \beta_3 \cdot \mathbf{Growth}_{it} + \beta_4 \cdot \mathbf{Profitability}_{it} + \beta_5 \cdot \mathbf{Liquidity}_{it} + \beta_6 \cdot \mathbf{GDP} + \mu_{it} \quad (1)$$

In this equation, the subscript t represents the time-series dimension and i denotes the cross-sectional dimension.

3 Results

Table 1 presents the descriptive statistics of the dependent and independent variables used in the empirical analyses. The annual cash dividend per share over the book value of assets per share of a company is on average 0.055 which is higher that of Argentinian (0.034) and Brazilian (0.027) companies J. Benavides, L. Berggrun, H. Perafan [22]. Average leverage is lower than the average corporate indebtedness for the Argentinan (0.449) and Brazilian (0.539) companies J. Benavides, L. Berggrun, H. Perafan [22].

Table 1. Descriptive statistics of variables

	Mean	Median	Standard deviation
Div	0.055	0.032	0.079
Size	17.802	17.556	1.983
Leverage	0.217	0.153	0.187
Growth	0.137	0.034	0.715
Profitability	6.968	5.087	7.473
Liquidity	5.577	2.08	13.933
GDP	4.822	10.05	32.598

The dividend policy trend is shown in fig. 1. As revealed in fig. 1, an upward trend is evident during the global financial crisis years.

* Corresponding author: ciprian.cristea@emd.utcluj.ro

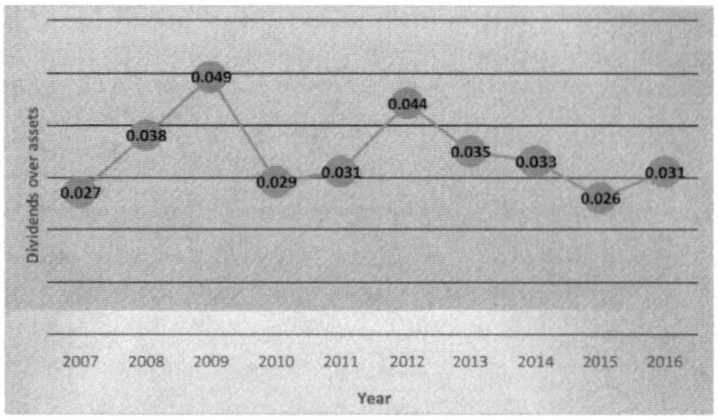

Fig. 1. Dividend policy trend during 2007–2016

It can be noticed that the values for annual cash dividend per share over the book value of assets per share were fairly stable over the study period, the lowest median is 0.026 in 2015 and the highest is 0.049 in 2009.

In Table 2, we present the Pearson correlation coefficients for the variables used in this paper.

Table 2. Pearson correlation coefficients for the variables

	Div	Size	Leverage	Growth	Liquidity	Profitability	GDP
Div Sig. (2-tailed)	1 -						
Size Sig. (2-tailed)	- 0.1324 (0.00)	1 -					
Leverage Sig. (2-tailed)	- 0.1318 (0.00)	0.1134 (0.002)	1 -				
Growth Sig.(2-tailed)	- 0.0141 (0.70)	- 0.0219 (0.561)	0.1 (0.008)	1 -			
Liquidity Sig. (2-tailed)	0.0903 (0.01)	- 0.0856 (0.023)	-0.3038 (0.000)	0.1326 (0.000)	1 -		
Profitability Sig. (2-tailed)	0.5258 (0.00)	- 0.1083 (0.004)	0.1698 (0.0000)	0.0905 (0.0165)	-0.0674 (0.0742)	1 -	
GDP Sig. (2-tailed)	0.0144 (0.701)	0.0629 (0.095)	0.0253 (0.502)	0.1264 (0.000)	-0.0512 (0.174)	0.1123 (0.0029)	1 -

According to our assumption and to the results obtained in other researches we found a statistically positive correlation coefficient between dividend policy and company profitability, implying that if the return on equity decreases it will have a negative impact on the annual cash dividend per share over the book value of assets per share. We found a statistically negative correlation between leverage and dividend policy, which means that more leveraged companies are likely to pay lower dividends. There is a statistically negative correlation between liquidity and leverage, which indicates that the more liquid assets firms have, the less they are leveraged.

Table III shows the results of estimating regression model by investigating the relationship between dividend policy and the attributes of non-financial companies listed on the Bucharest Stock Exchange market.

Table 3. Estimated results of panel data analysis

Div	Coefficient	Standard Error	Probability
Constant	0.0472	0.0049	0.0000
Size	-0.0012	0.0000	0.0000
Leverage	-0.0630	0.0029	0.0000
Growth	-0.0038	0.0015	0.0138
Liquidity	0.0005	0.0001	0.0007
Profitability	0.0038	0.0000	0.0000
GDP	-0.0006	0.0001	0.000
R^2	0.7947		
Adj. R^2	0.7930		

The R-Squared represents a measure of the overall fitness of the model and specifies that the model is capable of explaining about 80% of the systematic variation in the dependent variable.

The empirical findings indicate that the firms' profitability have a positive impact on the dividend policy decisions of listed companies, which means that the firms with high profits show an increase in the propensity to pay dividends more than less profitable companies. This is in line with I. Jabbouri [3], C. Adao˘glu [23].

The analysis documents a negative relationship between size and dividend policy, which means that the response of small companies' stock prices to dividend announcements is higher than the reaction of larger companies. This is in line with Z. Jin [24], but this result does not agree with the findings of I. Jabbouri [3], H. DeAngelo, L. DeAngelo, D.J. Skinner [13] where they mentioned the fact that firm size is positively associated with dividend payout.

Consistent with previous findings, the study reports a negative relationship between financial leverage and dividend policy I. Jabbouri [3], D.L. Papadopoulos, P.D. Charalambidis [4]. Thus, more financially indebted firms may decrease dividend payments.

Furthermore, empirical findings from the regression analysis on the relationship between growth and the dividend payout of listed firms indicate that there is an inverse relationship, which can be explained by the fact that investment opportunities would deplete cash resources available for dividend payments. This is in line with the findings of I. Jabbouri [3].

As expected, the study reveals a positive relationship between company's liquidity and dividend policy. The result is similar with prior findings, companies facing liquidity risk are unlikely to issue dividends H. DeAngelo, L. DeAngelo, D.J. Skinner [13], I. Jabbouri [3].

Finally, in addition to the aforementioned findings, table III also shows the result on the relationship between state of the economy and the dividend payouts decisions of listed firms. Regression analysis result shows that there is a negative relationship between the state of the economy (proxied by GDP growth rate) and the dividend policy decisions of listed firms in Romania. The international economic crisis had a significant impact over Romanian capital market C.E Stoenoiu, A. Nedelcut

* Corresponding author: ciprian.cristea@emd.utcluj.ro

[25], I.A. Iancu [26]. The result specify that management tends to increase dividend payments in periods of economic downturns and decrease them in good economic times, which is in line with I. Jabbouri [3].

For detecting the multi-collinearity among predictors in the multiple regression model, the Variance Inflation Factors (VIF) for explanatory variables were determined and presented in Table IV.

Table 4. Variance inflation factors

Variable	VIF
Size	1.04
Leverage	1.40
Growth	1.06
Liquidity	1.35
Profitability	1.06
GDP	1.06

All the VIF are relatively small and none of them is greater than 1.4. Thus, there is no problem of multi-collinearity, which means there is not necessary to reduce the collinearity by eliminating variables from the analysis.

4 Conclusions

This paper examines the main determinants of dividend policy using a sample of Romanian non-financial companies listed on the Bucharest Stock Exchange market between 2007 and 2016. The study noticed that there was a positive association between the profitability of firms and dividend payout of companies. The paper, also, validates the positive relationship between firm's liquidity and dividend policy. Thus, firms with a lack of liquidity are unlikely to distribute dividends. The paper revealed that there is a negative relationship between firms' financial leverage and the dividend payouts decisions of listed firms. Thus, riskier and more financially indebted companies are likely to pay lower dividends. Likewise, growth, firm size, and the state of the economy are negatively related to dividend policy. The results of this paper are useful for academics, analysts, investors, and regulators in emerging markets.

References

[1] I. K. Kato, U. Loewenstein, W. Tsay, „Voluntary dividend announcements in Japan", *PAC-BASIN FINANC J.*, 5, pp. 167–193, 1997.

[2] M. Miller and F. Modigliani, "Dividend policy, growth, and the valuation of shares", *J BUS*, 34, pp. 411–433, 1961.

[3] I. Jabbouri, "Determinants of corporate dividend policy in emerging markets: Evidence from MENA stock markets", *RES INT BUS FINANC*, 37, pp. 283–298, 2016.

[4] D.L. Papadopoulos, P.D. Charalambidis, "Focus on present status and determinants of dividend payout policy: Athens stock exchange in perspective", *J FINANC MANAG ANAL*, 20 (2), pp. 24–37, 2007.

[5] A. Fatemi, R. Bildik, "Yes: dividends are disappearing: worldwide evidence", *J BANK FINANC*, 36, pp. 662–677, 2012.

[6] H.K. Bakera, E. Kilincarslanb, A.H. Arsalc, "Dividend policy in Turkey: Survey evidence from Borsa Istanbul", *GLOB FINANC J*, to be published.

[7] E.F. Fama, K.R. French, "Disappearing dividends: Changing firm characteristics or lower propensity to pay?", *J FINANC ECON*, 60, pp. 3–43, 2001.

[8] D.J. Denis, I. Osobov, "Why do firms pay dividends? International evidence on the determinants of dividend policy, *J FINANC ECON*, 89, pp. 62–82, 2008.

[9] L. Renneboog, G. Trojanawski, "Patterns in payout policy and payout channel choice of UK firms in the 1990s, *ECGI Working Paper Series in Finance*, 34, pp. 411–433, 2005.

[10] H. Von Eije, W.L. Megginson, „Dividends and share repurchases in the European Union", *J FINANC ECON*, 89, pp. 347–374, 2008.

[11] Y.S. Reddy, S. Rath, "Disappearing dividends in emerging markets: Evidence from India", *EMERG MARK FINANC TR*, 41, pp. 58–82, 2005.

[12] S.P. Ferris, N. Jayaraman, S. Sabherwal, "Catering effects in corporate dividend policy: International evidence", *J BANK FINANC*, 33, pp. 1730–1738, 2009.

[13] H. DeAngelo, L. DeAngelo, D.J. Skinner, "Are dividends disappearing? Dividend concentration and the consolidation of earnings", *J FINANC ECON*, 72, pp. 425–456, 2004.

[14] B. Julio, D. Ikenberry, „Reappearing dividends", *J APPL CORP FINAN*, 16(4), pp. 89–100, 2004.

[15] R. Bildik, A. Fatemi, I. Fooladi, "Global dividend payout patterns: The US and the rest of the world and the effect of financial crisis", *GLOBAL FINANCE J*, 28, pp. 38–67, 2015.

[16] G. Bekaert, C.R. Harvey, "Foreign speculators and emerging equity markets", *J FINANC*, 55, pp. 565–614, 2000.

[17] T. Lagoarde-Segot, "Firms and markets behaviours in emerging markets", *RES INT BUS FINANC*, 27, pp. 145–146, 2013.

[18] H.K. Baker, G.E. Farrelly, E.T. Veit, "Revisiting managerial perspectives on dividend policy", *J ECON FINANC*, 26, pp. 267-283, 2002.

[19] A. Hafeez, Y.J. Attiya, "The determinants of dividend policy in Pakistan", *INT RES J FINANC ECON*, 25, pp. 148–171, 2009.

[20] K. Li, X. Zhao, "Asymmetric information and dividend policy", *FINANC MANAGE*, 34, pp. 673–694, 2008.

[21] Y. Grinstein, R. Michaely, „Institutional holdings and payout policy", *J FINANC*, 60, pp. 1389–1426, 2005.

[22] J. Benavides, L. Berggrun, H. Perafan, "Dividend payout policies: Evidence from Latin America", FINANC RES LETT, 17, pp. 197–210, 2016.

[23] C. Adao˘glu, "Instability in the dividend policy of the Istanbul stock exchange (ISE) corporations: evidence from an emerging market", *EMERG MARK REV*, 1(3), pp. 252–270, 2000.

[24] Z. Jin, "On the differential market reaction to dividend initiations", *Q REV ECON FINANC*, 12, pp. 263–277, 2000.

[25] C.E Stoenoiu, A. Nedelcut, "The economic crisis in the context of globalization", *J. Int. Sci. Publ. : Econ. Bus.*, 7(1), pp. 195-207, 2013.

[26] I.A. Iancu, "Investing Strategies of Romanian Retail Investors Before and During the Crisis (2006-2009)", *SEA-Practical Application on Science*, III (9), 23-28, 2015.

* Corresponding author: ciprian.cristea@emd.utcluj.ro

MATEC Web of Conferences **126**, 04010 (2017)
Annual Session of Scientific Papers IMT ORADEA 2017
DOI: 10.1051/matecconf/201712604010

The nature of the creative workforce

Adriana Bujor[1*], *Silvia* Avasilcai[2], *Lidia* Alexa[3]

[1]"Gheorghe Asachi" Technical University of Iasi, adbujor@gmail.com, Romania
[2]"Gheorghe Asachi" Technical University of Iasi, silvia.avasilcai@gmail.com, Romania
[3]"Gheorghe Asachi" Technical University of Iasi, lidia.alexa@tuiasi.ro, Romania

Abstract. Considering the fact that creative, creativity, co-creation are so very used terms in the last years, that creative industries and entrepreneurship in creative industries are the subject to many conferences, symposiums, courses, curricula, etc., discussions on creative economy is a subject of current interest, as well. To better understand creative economy, one must understand the nature of the creative workforce. The aim of this paper is to identify the nature of creative workforce. The foreseen result is to highlight the differences between creative industries and creative jobs, starting from the identified nature of the creative industries

1 Introduction

If in general terms, almost all industries use / contain at least an element of creativity, creative industries differ in that the value they offer to their customers / consumers is determined / provided by the creativity only, according to UNCTAD, and UNDP [1]. Basically entries are of a cultural / creative dimension, even if the results have a functional size.

Having as standard the definition of the creative industries offered by DCMS (Department for Culture, Media and Sport), T. Flew [2], the creative / cultural dimension inputs occur only due to the individual talent and skills, and the outputs are innovative products and services, that needs to be protected by copyright (intellectual property).

If we consider, as an example, a furniture design project, the creative dimension is given by the level of which that designer uses his / her creativity, individual talent and skills in order to span all the needed resources to create that piece of furniture that usually has a functional size. But what makes them to qualify as industries, namely creative industries, it is their potential to generate / make profit, to provide a way of living and the possibility to create and develop a business, capable of generating (new) workforce, (new) jobs.

The project's functional size is determined by the clients' feedback, the last step of the design process, which analyzes the degree of their requirements fulfillment.

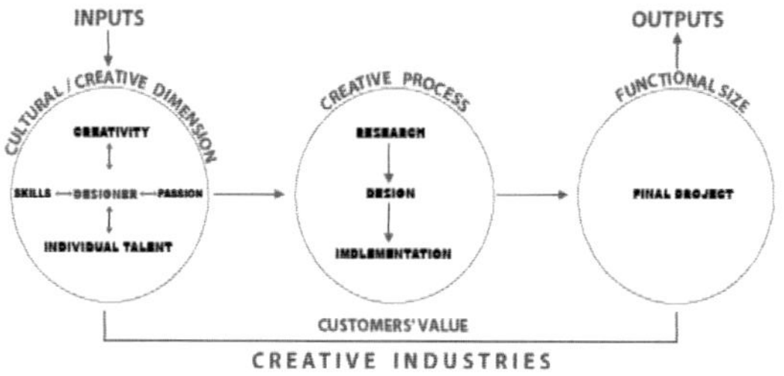

Fig. 1. Inputs and outputs in creative industries.

Even though most businesses that are part of the creative industries are often micro, small or medium sized enterprises that have started mainly on local markets, most of them can develop into strong economic clusters (creative clusters) capable of inducing economic growth.

2 Creative industries and the work foundation model

During the researches done so far on creative industries in Romania many suspicions and questions have arisen. There are still doubts that culture's outputs can develop into profit, and, even more, into businesses, no matter the size.

For this reason, for those working in cultural domains or connected with cultural activities, the Concentric Circles Model proposed by the Work Foundation suit best.

Unlike the model proposed by NESTA (National Endowment for Science, Technology and the Arts) [3], the Work Foundation [4] has made a distinction between creative contents and industries that produce and distribute them, according to the *expressive value* of the

* Corresponding author: adbujor@gmail.com

DOI: 10.1051/matecconf/201712604010

creative products and services.

The expressive value term is defined as "any dimension (in ideas), which, in its broadest sense, extends the cultural meaning and understanding", according to the Work Foundation [4]. The term incorporates elements such as:

1) *aesthetic value;*
2) *spiritual value;*
3) *historical value;*
4) *symbolic value;*
5) *authentic value.*

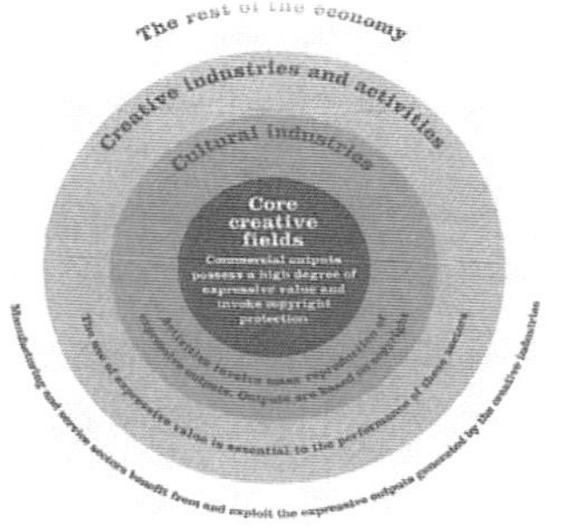

Fig. 2. The Concentric Circles Model proposed by the Work Foundation [4].

Expressive value is used to differentiate creation and performing arts of commercial media, precisely because of the aesthetic value and the meaning that the first two have, and to justify the investment that the public make in them.

2.1 The nature of creative industries

Once with the appearance of the creative industries, the creative economy term has appeared and aroused much interest. In order to better understand the term of creative economy, one must understand which the nature of the creative workforce is.

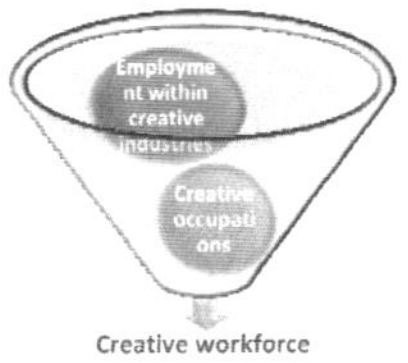

Fig. 3. The nature of the creative workforce.

As shown in fig. 3, creative workforce does not strictly refer to the workforce within creative industries. It actually represents the combination of creative occupations and employment within creative industries.

Another question that arose during the research on creative industries and their classification, especially in Romania, referred to the level of understanding the difference between creative industries and creative workforce / creative jobs.

Starting from a question like: "Why the automotive industry is not a creative industry?" a better differentiation can be offered, giving in the same time a clear explanation on a creative industries' sector, with related jobs, and a creative job that can be found in any type of industry.

For this, Queensland University of Technology Center of Excellence for Creative Industries and Innovation created the Creative Trident, representing a useful tool / methodology to show the different values of the creative jobs and the creative sectors / segments. According to this trident described by Creative Industries Innovation Centre [5], there are:

6) *specialist creatives;*
7) *support workers;*
8) *embedded workers.*

The specialist creative is the one that actually works within creative industries, being creatively occupied (doing creative jobs), in contrast to the support worker, that even though he or she works as well within creative industries, does not do creative jobs. The last type of worker, the embedded one, is creatively occupied, as the first type, but does not work within creative industries.

Table 1. The Creative Trident

		Industries		
		Employed in creative industries	Employed in non-creative industries	
Occupations	Employed in creative occupations	**Specialist creatives**	**Embedded creatives**	Total employment in creative occupations
Occupations	Employed in non-creative occupations	**Support workers**	Non-creative occupation in non-creative industries	
		Total employment in creative industries		Total creative workforce

According to the creative trident, the best answer / explanation to the previous question is that within an automotive industry embedded workers are found. This type of industry has not been classified as a creative industry, but within it there are many creative jobs, among non-creative others, such as the (product) designer within an automotive industry, or a graphic designer in different non-creative industries, so on.

What can be added to this trident, is another category of workforce that lately has arisen. This category is formed of so called prosumers that can be considered a creative workforce, with certain limitations.

Defined as one "who blurs the distinction between a consumer and a producer", as stated by W. Gerhardt [6],

* Corresponding author: adbujor@gmail.com

a prosumer can be considered a type of workforce as a prosumer can participate to the co-creation of goods, or the development of different services for a company.

The main difference among all these types of workforce is that a consumer involved in a company's co-creation process (another way to define a prosumer) becomes a form of free workforce, raising many controversies among labor specialists, and it can be found in any occupations and in any industries from the trident.

The "job markets" for a prosumer, as emphasized by A. Bujor, and S. Avasilcai [7], are represented by:

1) traditional consumer channels, such as *advertising and mail;*

2) nontraditional channels, such as: e-mail, online sites (Google);

3) business-to-business channels, such as: industry site advertising, and trade publications.

Table 2. The Creative Trident and Prosumer's place within it

		Industries		
		Employed in creative industries	Employed in non-creative industries	
Occupations	Employed in creative occupations	**Specialist creatives**	**Embedded creatives**	Total employment in creative occupations
		Prosumers		
	Employed in non-creative occupations	**Support workers**	Non-creative occupation in non-creative industries	
		Total employment in creative industries		Total creative workforce

3 The creative workforce in Europe-28 (EU-28): a comparative analysis

The economic value of creative industries has been increasingly recognized by now, all over the world, despite the fact that 80% of the businesses in the creative industries fields consist of SMEs (with many sole traders or with only no more than three employees) or micro-enterprises with just few employees, as well.

3.1 Creative workforce in Europe

If in 2008, according to Terraconsult, the creative employment in UK and Germany was of 2.7 million, in France of 1.7 million, in Italy of 1.4 million and in Spain of 1.2 million, the percentage of jobs in creative industries was as it follows: 9.2% in UK, 6.2% in France, 6.9% in Germany, 6.1% in Italy, and 5.9% in Spain.

From all sectors of creative industries, the statistical analysis has shown that in Fashion can be found the most workers employed with 31.41% of total employees, followed by Design with 20.12%, Architecture with 10.74%, and Book&Press with 9.89% of total employees, as presented by Hogeschool vor de Kunsten Utrecht, [8].

Many creative entrepreneurs are also employed in other sectors of the economy, contributing this way to the development of the creative capacity of non-creative industries. They represent the embedded creatives from the trident.

According to NESTA, the 2011-2013 average of all creative industries EU-28's employment was of 11,218,000, accounting for 5,21% of the EU workforce, as emphasized by M. Nathan, A. Pratt, and A. Rincon-Aznar [9].

3.2 Creative Trident for Europe-28: a comparative Analysis

The data found for this comparative analysis did not allow comparing all 28 European countries, between 2011-2013, due to the absence of the 4 digit occupational resolution, in the following countries: Bulgaria, Cyprus, Denmark, Greece, Italy, Portugal, Latvia and Spain, also Belgium and Germany but only for 2011. Thus, due to the above and wishing to obtain accurate information and data, the comparative analysis has been limited to only 18 European countries, even though general data on workforce in countries like Denmark, Germany, Portugal and Spain are relevant at European level and not only.

Table 3. Creative Tridents for Europe-28 (2011-2013)

	Creative industries	Non-creative industries	Creative industries
Creative occupations	2,921,000	3,273,000	6,194,000
Non-creative occupations	6,094,000	150,046,000	156,140,000
All occupations	11,387,000	206,178,000	217,565,000

Of the 18th EU member states for which we consider the creative economy, U.K., registering so far the larger cultural and creative industries in Europe, is definitely the leader in creative specialists (816,000 working in both creative occupations and creative industries), followed by France, at a considerable distance (264,000), and Netherlands (190,000). Romania ranks 11th place out of 18 (35,000), Luxembourg being the last ranked (1,000).

As for embedded creatives (working in both creative occupations and non-creative industries), U.K. has the largest employment (570,000), followed again by France (449,000) and Poland this time (278,000). Romania ranks 6th place out of 18 (122,000), Luxembourg being once again the last ranked (1,000).

The top three of support workers/non-specialists creative (employed in both non-creative occupations and creative industries) is as it follows: U.K. (1,405,000), France (1,169,000), and Poland (381,000). This time

* Corresponding author: adbujor@gmail.com

Romania ranks 10th (109,000), and Malta ends the top (5000).

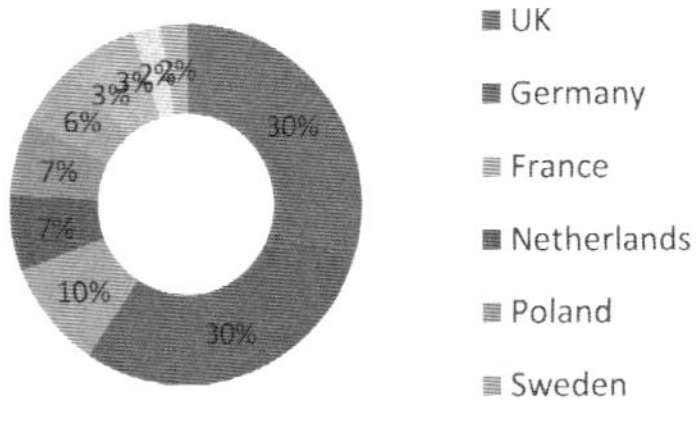

Fig.4. Top 10 creative specialists working in both creative occupations and creative industries

Poland once again finds itself in top three, even though to a considerable distance (8,923,000), while Malta closes once again the list (158,000). For this category, Romania manages this time to rank 4th out of 18, employing considerable less than top three.

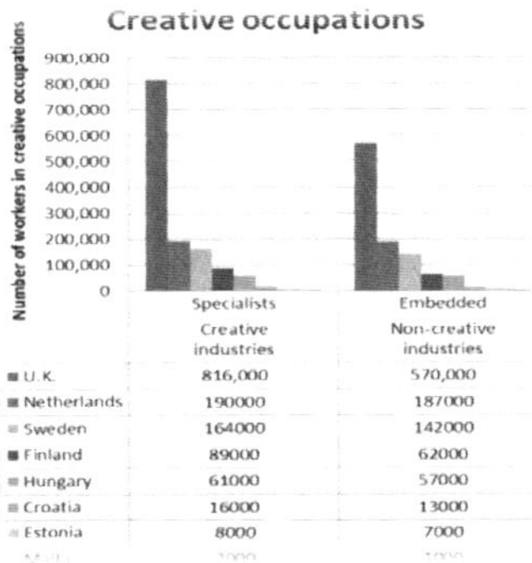

Fig.5. Creative workers from creative industries vs. creative workers from non-creative industries

What can be concluded from this analysis is that all EU countries experienced, during the years, great growth in each creative economy workforce, especially in specialist creatives and embedded creatives, as the importance of creatives' presence proved to be of great help in both creative and non-creative industries.

Another conclusion that emerges from this analysis is that there are countries that managed to employ more creative workers inside their creative industries than outside: the U.K. (816,000 vs. 570,000), Netherlands (190,000 vs. 187,000), Sweden (164,000 vs. 142,000), Finland (89,000 vs. 62,000), Hungary (61,000 vs. 57,000), Croatia (16,000 vs. 13,000), Estonia (8000 vs. 7000), Malta (2000 vs. 1000). In Luxembourg the number of creative workers employed in creative industries is similar to those employed in non-creative industries (1000).

4 Conclusion

Creative industries are made up of different sectors whose outputs are also different, of functional size, even though their institutional organizations and employment patterns have many things in common. What is sure is that the inputs are of cultural / creative dimension, based on individual talent, passion, skills and craftsmanship.

Creative workforce does not refer only to the workforce within creative industries, but to the workforce whose core is creativity. According to the Creative Trident there are: specialist creatives (employed in creative occupations within creative industries), support creatives (employed in non-creative occupations within creative industries), and support creatives (employed in creative occupations within non-creative industries). To this trident, prosumers can also be added as a creative workforce, if we take into consideration the way they are engaged in a company's co-creation process.

Taking into account all the data, European creative economies manage to exceed the best they can, in their ways. At European level, U.K. is the leader, registering so far the larger cultural and creative industries.

This research was undertaken within the framework of the National Research Program PN II, financed by MEN – UEFISCDI, project PN-II-PT-PCCA-2013-4-1811.

References

[1] UNCTAD, UNDP, *Creative Economy: A Feasible Development Option*, 2010 Report.
[2] T. Flew, *The Creative Industries. Culture and Policy*, SAGE Publications Ltd, 2012.
[3] NESTA, *Creating Growth: How the UK Can Develop World Class Creative Business*, London, 2006.
[4] The Work Foundation, *Staying ahead: the economic performance of the UK's creative industries*, Department for Culture, Media and Sport, 2007.
[5] Creative Industries Innovation Centre, *Valuing Australia's Creative Industries. Final report*, University of Technology, Sydney, December 2013.
[6] W. Gerhardt, *Prosumers: A New Growth Opportunity*, Cisco Internet Business Solutions Group (IBSG), March 2008, Retrieved from CISCO Web Site: http://www.cisco.com/c/dam/en_us/about/ac79/docs/wp/Prosumer_VS2_POV_0404_FINAL.pdf.
[7] A. Bujor, and S. Avasilcai, "Co-creation in Romanian consumer goods industry", *Annals of the Oradea University, Fascicle of Management and Technological Engineering*, Issue #2, August 2016.
[8] HKU, *The Enrepreneurial Dimension of the Cultural and Creative Industries*, Hogeschool vor de Kunsten Utrecht, 2010.
1. M. Nathan, A. Pratt, and A. Rincon-Aznar, *Creative Economy Eomployment in the EU and the UK. A comparative Analysis*, NESTA, London, December 2015.

* Corresponding author: adbujor@gmail.com

Benchmarking in Romanian industrial environment

Gina-Maria Moraru[1*]

[1]"Lucian Blaga" University of Sibiu, gina.moraru@ulbsibiu.ro, Romania

Abstract. Benchmarking is a managerial tool that can assist the organizational change and the innovation. The paper aims to discover the degree in which Romanian managers in various industrial fields use this modern tool in the improvement of business strategy or organizational processes. In this context, we presented some results of a selective research made in Romanian industrial environment. The respondents were experts in creativity management and benchmarking, acting in big, medium or small enterprises. They offered many solutions for increase the rate of use of benchmarking and creativity couple in the management of Romanian organizations.

1 Introduction

Benchmarking is a process through which participants can identify what they need to improve in organization, learn how to share information with other participants, and discover how to make the best improvements, by APO [1]. Benchmarking can assist the organizational change, by D. Gillen [2], and the innovation, by APO [1]. Experts in various fields can implement creatively in their organizations solutions generated by benchmarking participants, by G.M. Moraru [3].

In the first stage, a correct benchmarking process will help the management to discover where performance blockages are most serious, APO [1]. Benchmarking can then focus on the areas with problems.

In the elaboration of the business strategy stage, benchmarking can help management to select the optimal improvements by assisting with breakthrough initiatives, proposing new ideas or process innovation, APO [1]. Therefore, managers all around the world use benchmarking as a modern tool to create a complete organizational database for the future innovations. Moreover, it is a management tool for improving the organizational performance, by R. Scott [4].

2 Selective Research in Romanian Industry

2.1 Premises of the Research

During the last years, we have developed many studies regarding the possibilities of using the benchmarking - creativity couple in organizations, in order to increase their performances, G.M. Moraru [3], and G.M. Moraru [5]. Comparing the Romanian managers' opinions regarding the real use of this couple in organizations, by G.M. Moraru [3], with those of other experts in creativity management and benchmarking, acting in big, medium or small enterprises, by G.M. Moraru [5], we notify that experts are more reserved than managers regarding the use of creativity in Romanian management, but more optimist regarding the use of benchmarking (Fig. 1).

Using a scale from 0 to 5 (0 points for "I don't know" and 5 points for the use of the specified element to a very large extent) the averages of experts' responses were 1.917 for creativity and 1.833 for benchmarking. The averages of managers' responses were 2.134 for creativity and 1.354 for benchmarking. These values are under the mean of the scale (2.5) and show a poor use of creativity and benchmarking in Romanian management in the opinions of both categories of respondents.

We have to mention that this paper presents a few results from the phase of a larger research developed with experts in creativity management and benchmarking, acting in big, medium or small enterprises, G.M. Moraru [5].

The first limitation of our study consisted in the difficulty to discover in the Romanian industry these experts. Even academics in Romanian universities and top managers of many firms suggested us a list with the name of experts, based on their professional achievements, many of these people were very modest and did not accept the status of experts. Being in full professional development, they have declared that they do not have enough experience and knowledge to be named "experts".

* Corresponding author: gina.moraru@ulbsibiu.ro

The second limitation of this exploratory study partially derived from the first one. If it was difficult for us to convince the experts to participate to the research, it was even more difficult to find experts in creativity management and benchmarking who do not work in research and development but in production, services,

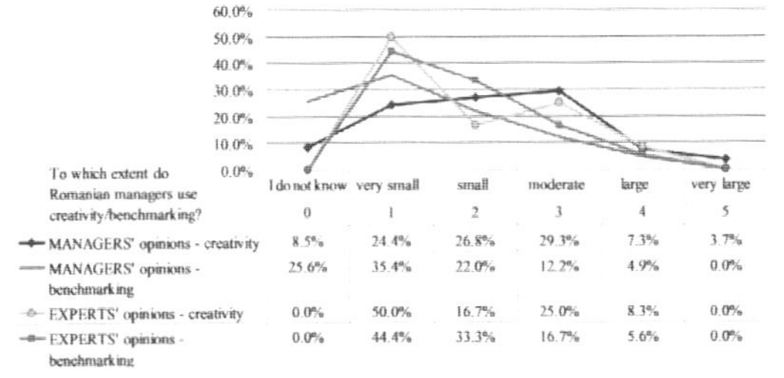

Fig. 1. Comparative opinions of experts and managers regarding the use of benchmarking and creativity in Romanian organizations

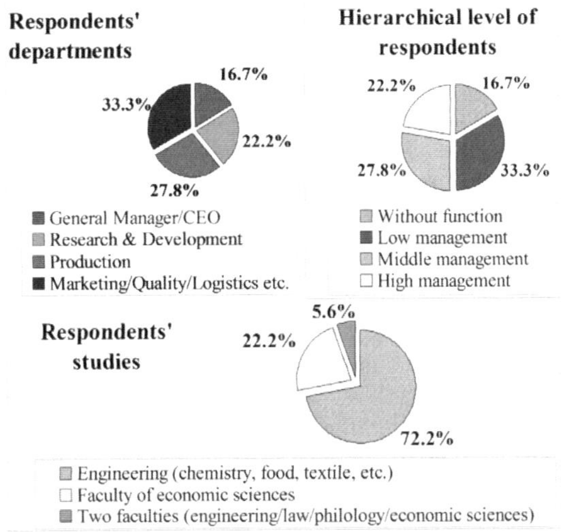

Fig. 2. Respondents' characteristics

So, the sample is not representative for the experts' population. The study is an investigation, not a survey.

2.2 The main results

One of the questions asked respondents to formulate solutions for expanding the use of benchmarking and creativity in the management of Romanian organizations. They provided many strategic, tactical and/or operational solutions (Fig. 3). We accorded:
3 points – to the questionnaires with strategic solutions;
2 points – to those with tactical solutions;
1 point – to those with operational solutions;
0 point – to those without solutions.

Using this scale, we obtained an average of 2.056, a standard deviation of 0.893 and a homogeneity coefficient of 0.434. Even the responses are partial not homogeneous (and the coefficient is between 0.4 and

human resources, marketing or finance.

The third limitation of the study is the lack of information regarding the personal characteristics of the whole population of experts in creativity management and benchmarking in Romania. Fig. 2 presents a few of the respondents' characteristics. 0.45), the average obtained show more concerning of the respondents with the strategic measures than with the operational ones. It is a positive aspect that reflects their orientation on long terms.

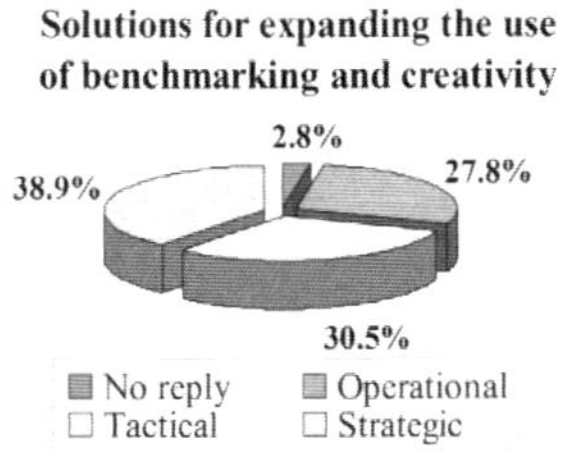

Fig. 3. Experts' suggestions for expanding the use of benchmarking and creativity

We mention the most important strategic solutions provided by respondents:
1) Motivating creativity at all organizational levels;
2) Including creativity in the strategic plans;
3) Making an organizational guide for assessing employees' ideas;
4) Developing the technology transfer chains;
5) Founding scientific concerns in various fields;
6) Assuming the risks of pioneering managerial actions;
7) Ensuring a legislation that stimulates creativity.

From the tactical respondents' suggestions we selected the most relevant ones and we grouped them in several categories:
1) Supporting the research and development of the new products in the organization's own centers;
2) Increasing budgets for research;
3) Developing new projects with universities and research institutes;
4) Lifelong learning, emphasizing the development of human creativity in Romanian organizations;

5) Making national advertising to the firms that used benchmarking.

Regarding the last proposal, we remember that in the specialty literature there are opinions that support the necessity to establish national specific institutions which are concerned with benchmarking, for the benefit of the national economy, by G.M. Moraru [5].

We enumerate several operational solutions provided by the respondents:

* Corresponding author: gina.moraru@ulbsibiu.ro

1) Training all employees for creativity;
2) Combining various managerial methods for stimulating human resources' creativity;
3) Educating the young managers by the oldest ones in the spirit of customer respect;
4) Creating benchmarking procedures in the company;
5) Rewarding any process, activity or product improvement made by an employee.

Only 2.8% of the experts did not answer to this question (Fig. 3).

Another question for the experts in creativity management and/or benchmarking was: "In how many benchmarking trials was your organization involved in the last five years?" We centralized their responses in Fig. 4. We can observe that 66.7% of respondents declared that their organization was not involved in any benchmarking process in the last five years.

The average of the answers was low, 1.833 on a scale from 1 to 5. Even if the standard deviation is high – 1.404 – and the sample answers are not homogeneous – with a homogeneity coefficient of 0.766, the graphics demonstrates a poor use of benchmarking in Romanian industrial management (Fig. 4).

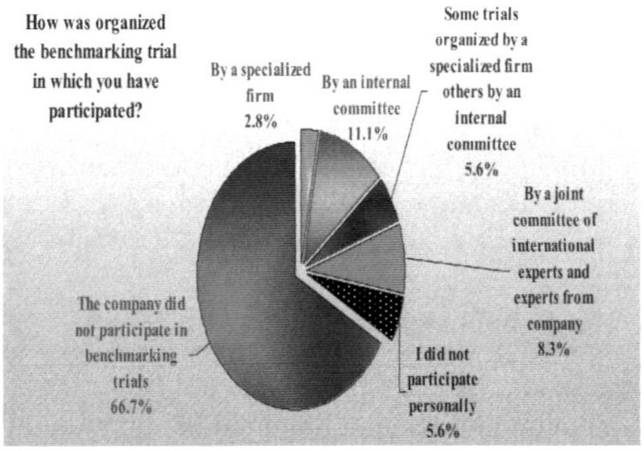

Fig. 4. The organization of benchmarking trials in Romanian industry.

On the second place are the trials organized by a joint committee made from international experts and experts who work in company (8.3%). So, in Romanian industry, internal benchmarking is preferred to the external one.

Moreover, only 2.8% of respondents declared that their company was involved in benchmarking trials

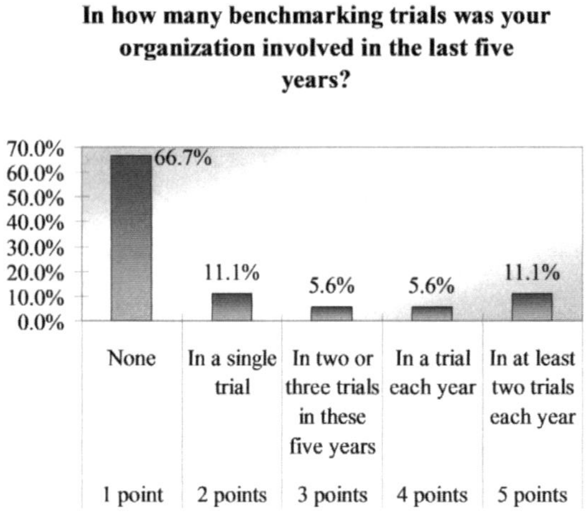

Fig. 5. The number of benchmarking trials in which respondents' organizations were involved.

Then respondents were asked to specify how was organized the benchmarking trial (trials) in which they have participated. Centralizing their answers, we obtain the graphic in Fig. 5. We can see that the most trials were organized by an internal committee (11.1%). developed by a specialized firm. A possible explanation could be the Romanian managers' reluctance to use benchmarking and share information with other organizations.

We wanted to find out if the specialty literature helps managers and experts to achieve new and important knowledge in the field of creativity management and benchmarking. So, another question was: "Do you think that Romanian literature does provide enough information about:

a) Scientific research in your field?
b) Creativity management?
c) Benchmarking?"

The experts signaled the gap in the Romanian specialty literature with information at all previous points (Fig. 6). For evaluation, we used the scale: 0 points for the answer "no", 1 point for the answer "only on certain aspects" and 2 points for "yes". The averages were very low: 0.361 for information offered in the experts' research fields, 0.278 for those in creativity management, and 0.111 for information about benchmarking.

* Corresponding author: gina.moraru@ulbsibiu.ro

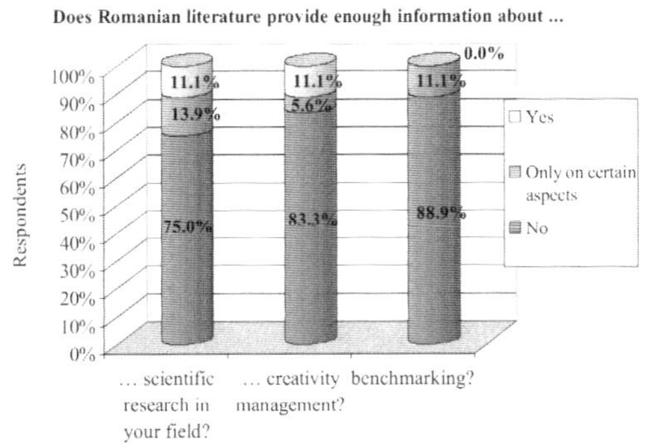

Fig. 6. Experts' opinions regarding the information offered by the Romanian specialty literature.

3 Conclusions

Highlighting both organizational problems and their improvement potential, benchmarking is a tool that can support managers in various fields. Modern benchmarking can be developed between partners from various industries (G.M. Moraru [5]), with different functions or locations (S. Rohlfer [6]). Benchmarking can help managers to build learning organizations, by C.J. McNair, K.H.J. Leibfried [7].

We presented some results of a selective research made in Romanian industrial environment, with the aim of discovering the degree in which Romanian managers in various industrial fields use this modern tool in the improvement of business strategy or organizational processes.

Our respondents were experts in creativity management and/or benchmarking, acting in big, medium or small enterprises. They understand one of the most important roles of the modern benchmarking, that of triggering creative ideas through inspiring from similar organizations. They also signaled a gap in the Romanian specialty literature in this field.

The experts in creativity management and/or benchmarking offered many solutions for increase the rate of use of benchmarking - creativity couple in the management of Romanian organizations, in order to improve their performances. We remember only the necessity of developing the technology transfer chains and those of ensuring a legislation framework that stimulates creativity.

Acknowledgment

This work was supported by the grant LBUS-IRG-2016-02, co-financed by the "Lucian Blaga" University of Sibiu (Romania).

References

[1] Asian Productivity Organization (APO), *Benchmarking Training Manual*, Tokyo, Japan: APO Best Practice Network, 2005, pp. 1-15, http://www.apo-tokyo.org/publications/wp-content/uploads/sites/5/ind-13-bmtm.pdf, accessed on March 2017.

[2] D. Gillen, "Benchmarking and Performance Measurement: The Role in Quality Management", School of Business & Economics Wilfrid Laurier University Waterloo, Canada, 2000, https://legacy.wlu.ca/documents/4293/Benchmarking.pdf, accessed on May 2017.

[3] G.M. Moraru, "Creativity and Benchmarking in Romanian Management", *EDULEARN15 Poceedings*, Barcelona, Spain: IATED Digital Library, 2015, pp. 3996-4002.

[4] R. Scott, "Benchmarking: A Literature Review", Edith Cowan University, 2011, https://intranet.ecu.edu.au/__data/assets/pdf_file/0010/357193/Benchmarking-Literature-Review.pdf, accessed on May 2017.

[5] G.M. Moraru, "Creativity Management and Benchmarking Promoting Performance and Competitiveness in Modern Organizations" ("Managementul creativităţii şi benchmarkingul în promovarea performanţei şi competitivităţii în organizaţiile moderne"), PhD Thesis, "Lucian Blaga" University of Sibiu, Romania, sustained April 2011, unpublished to a publishing house

[6] S. Rohlfer, "Benchmarking Concepts in the UK and Germany: Between Standardisation and Local Variation?", *Warwick Papers In Industrial Relations*, No. 69, University of Warwick, UK: Industrial Relations Research Unit, 2005, pp. 1-36, https://www2.warwick.ac.uk/fac/soc/wbs/research/irru/wpir/wpir_sylvia_rohlfer.pdf, accessed on May 2017.

[7] C.J. McNair, K.H.J. Leibfried, *Benchmarking: A Tool for Continuous Improvement*. New York: Wiley, 1993, pp. 320-321.

* Corresponding author: gina.moraru@ulbsibiu.ro

Stochastic optimization model for random demand stocks, with storage expenses accounting

Gheorghe Ciolan[1], *Ion* Preda[1,*], and *Mircea* Nastasoiu[1]

[1]Transilvania University of Brasov, Brasov, Romania

Abstract. The paper presents a possible stock level optimization method, based on a stochastic model. The consume demand for the stored product is considered a discrete random quantity. It was adopted the hypothesis that the repartition law of the demand probability is known for the time interval of stock existence (operation). The main aim of the optimization procedure is to minimize the total expenses (costs) involved by the existence or lack of the reserve stock. For a better understanding of the proposed algorithm, a calculation example is presented.

1 Introduction

The management of the stocks needed for the different economical activities represents today an important source for the company's profits. This is the reason for which the problem of cost optimizations was and still is intensively studied.

The works of D. Constantinescu [1], G. Hadley, T. M. Whitin [2], C. Bălan [3], [4], N. Florea [5], S. Chopra, P. Meindl [6], J. Gattorna [7], and M. Udrescu, S. Cuturela [8] are only few examples of systematic approaches in this respect.

The present article was written with the intention to present a possible way of mono-product stock optimization, useful and easy to implement mainly for small and medium production or servicing companies.

2 Presentation of the stochastic model for stock-optimization

To establish the mathematical model for stocks optimization, the following hypotheses were considered:
- the consumer demand V for the product has a random magnitude;
- the probability distribution law $p(V)$ of the demand V in the time interval T of stock existence is known;
- the aim of the model use is to minimize the total storage costs.

In these conditions, two different situations may be possible for the consumption of stock products (Fig. 1):

a) when consumer's product demand V in the time interval T is smaller as the stock Q;

b) when consumer's product demand V in the time interval T is bigger as the stock Q.

Supposing the stock variation is linear, it results:
- for the first case, in which the stock Q is bigger as- or equal with the demand V in the time interval T (Fig. 1.a), the mean stock Q' is established with the equation:

$$Q'=[Q+(Q-V)]/2=Q-V/2 \quad (1)$$

- for the second case, in which the stock Q is smaller as the demand V in the considered time interval T (Fig. 1.b), the mean stock Q'' is established with the equation:

$$Q''=[(Q+0)/2]\cdot(T_1/T)=(Q/2)\cdot(T_1/T) \quad (2)$$

where $T1$ is the depletion time of the stock.

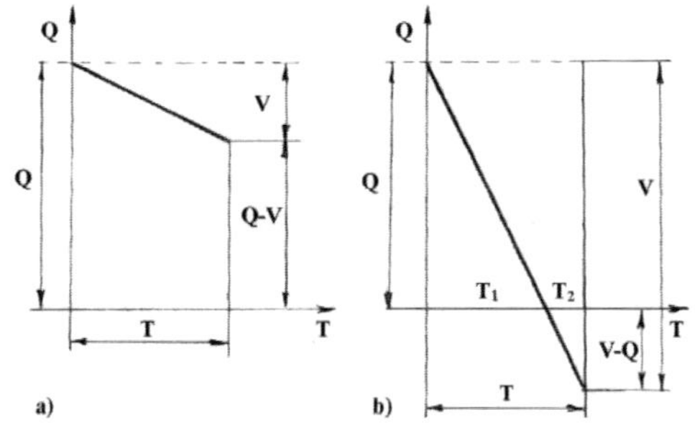

Fig. 1. Possible situations for the stock consumption during the time T: a) the stock is bigger as- or equal with the demand ($Q \geq V$); b) the stock is smaller as the demand ($Q < V$).

From the Figure 1.b it can be also observed that

$$T_1/T=Q/V \quad (3)$$

and replacing in (2) it results:

$$Q''=(Q/2)\cdot(T_1/T)=Q^2/(2V). \quad (4)$$

Reasoning in a similar way, the mean lack of stock Q''' in the considered time interval T may be established with the equation:

$$Q'''=[(V-Q)/2]\cdot(T_2/T)=(V-Q)^2/(2V), \quad (5)$$

because the maximum lack of stock is

* Corresponding author: pion@unitbv.ro

$$V-Q=V\cdot(T_2/T) \quad (6)$$

as can be observed again from the Figure 1.b.

For the calculation of the total storage cost, two constant values will be considered:

- c_1, that represents the storing cost per product unit during the time T;
- c_2, that represents the cost (loss) for the lack of stock per product unit during the time T.

Using the previously determined mean values Q', Q'' of the stocks and Q''' of the lack of stock, the three partial contributions to the storage cost can be calculated with the equations:

$$z_1(Q)=c_1\cdot Q'=c_1 \sum_{V=0}^{Q}\left(Q-\frac{V}{2}\right)p(V) \quad (7)$$

$$z_2(Q)=c_1\cdot Q''=c_1 \sum_{V=Q+1}^{\infty}\frac{Q^2}{2V}p(V) \quad (8)$$

$$z_3(Q)=c_2\cdot Q'''=c_2 \sum_{V=Q+1}^{\infty}\frac{(V-Q)^2}{2V}p(V) \quad (9)$$

and then the total storage cost z results summing these three partial costs z_1, z_2 and z_3:

$$z(Q)=c_1\cdot Q'+c_1\cdot Q''+c_2\cdot Q'''=z_1(Q)+z_2(Q)+z_3(Q). \quad (10)$$

Using the equation (10) of the mean value $z(Q)$ of the total storage costs, one calculates a series of values z for different stock values Q and one retains the value Q_{opt} for which the possible total costs depending on Q present the minimum value $z_{min}=z(Q_{opt})$.

3 Analytic solution

An analytic solution to obtain the optimal stock level Q_{opt} and the minimal storing cost z_{min}, demonstrated by G. Ciolan, F. Kirstein, I. Preda, P. Petre in [9], but not presented here, exists and may also be used. That solution states that the optimal value Q_{opt} of the stock verifies the condition:

$$L(Q_{opt}-1) < \rho < L(Q_{opt}), \quad (11)$$

where L is a monotonically increasing function and the ratio

$$\rho = c_2/(c_1+c_2) \quad (12)$$

is obtained from c_1, the unitary storing cost during the time unit T, and c_2, the unitary cost (loss) for the lack of stock during the same time period.

The function

$$L(Q) = L_1(Q) + L_3(Q) \quad (13)$$

may be calculated with the help of the next three intermediate functions:

$$L_1(Q)=P(V\leq Q)=\sum_{V=0}^{Q}P(V) \quad (14)$$

which is the probability that the product demand V to be smaller as- or equal with the existing stock Q, and

$$L_2(Q)=\sum_{V=Q+1}^{\infty}\frac{P(V)}{V}; \quad (15)$$

$$L_3(Q)=(Q+0.5)\cdot L_2(Q). \quad (16)$$

If one compare the ratio ρ with the series of calculated values $L(Q)$, the optimal stock level Q_{opt} will be obtained.

The minimum total cost for the products storage will be determined by replacing the founded value Q_{opt} in the equation (10) of the total mean cost: $z_{min} = z(Q_{opt})$.

4 Application example

The problem. An auto service ensures, between others activities, the replacement of the oil filter for a car type. During a week (the time period T), the demand for oil filter change has a random discrete size and is statistically characterized by a known discrete probability distribution $p(V)$ (also called probability mass function). The values of this function are given in the Table I and obey to the equation

$$\sum_{V=0}^{\infty}p(V)=1. \quad (17)$$

The workshop it is supplied once per week with the ordered number of spare parts.

The cost c_1 needed to store a product unit (an oil filter) for the period of time T (one week) will be considered constant and equal with 1 r.c. (reference unitary cost): c_1 = 1 r.c.

If the demand of oil filter replacements exceeds the existent stock, the workshop can order a supplementary oil filter which will be delivered in short time, but with a penalty of transport cost and customer delay. That unitary loss involved by the unsatisfied product demand is bigger as c_1. In this example: $c_2 = 5\cdot c_1 = 5$ r.c.

In these conditions, one intends to determine the optimal stock level Q_{opt} to be ensured at any beginning of the working week and the mean cost z_{min} involved by the storage and lack of oil filters in that time.

The solution. The probability distribution function $p(V)$ describes a random process and may give useful information about this. In the present example, such function may be obtained by observations noted in a long period of time (for example, one year in this case).

The meaning of the probability distribution law $p(V)$ indicated in the Table I (and presented graphically in the Fig. 2 – the histogram) is that from 100 working weeks considered, in 10 weeks it is no command to replace oil filters, in 10 weeks it is needed to replace only 1, in 30 weeks it is needed to replace 2, and so on.

The cumulative frequency distribution

$$R(V)=\sum_{j=0}^{V}P(j) \quad (18)$$

can be obtained by summation from the probability distribution $p(V)$ and indicates the probability that in one week to be replaced up to V oil filters. For example, according with the data in the Table I (and presented in

Fig. 2), the probability to replace maximum 3 filters is 0.8 (or 80%).

Table 1. Density of probability for the parts demand.

V	0	1	2	3	4	5	≥6
$p(V)$	0.1	0.1	0.3	0.3	0.15	0.05	0
$R(V)$	0.1	0.2	0.5	0.8	0.95	1	1

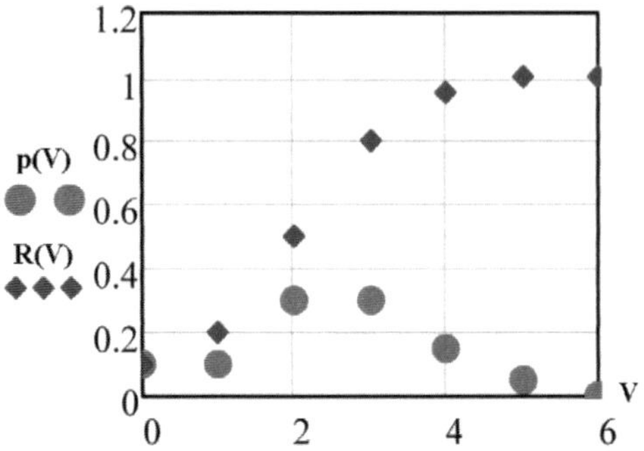

Fig. 2. Discrete probability functions used in the algorithm application example (Table I): density of probability (red circles); cumulated probability (blue diamonds).

The probability distribution $p(V)$ can be used also to calculate the mean number of oil filter interventions per week:

$$N_m=\sum_{V=0}^{\infty}[V\cdot p(V)] \tag{19}$$

In this example, $N_m=\sum_{V=0}^{5}[V\cdot p(V)]=2.45$.

The solving of the problem starts with the calculation of the ratio $p(V)/V$, used to obtain the values $L(Q)$.The corresponding values of this ratio for different demand amounts V are indicated in the Table II.

Table 2. Calculated values for the ratio $p(V)/V$.

V	0	1	2	3	4	5	≥6
$p(V)/V$	-	0.1	0.15	0.1	0.038	0.01	0

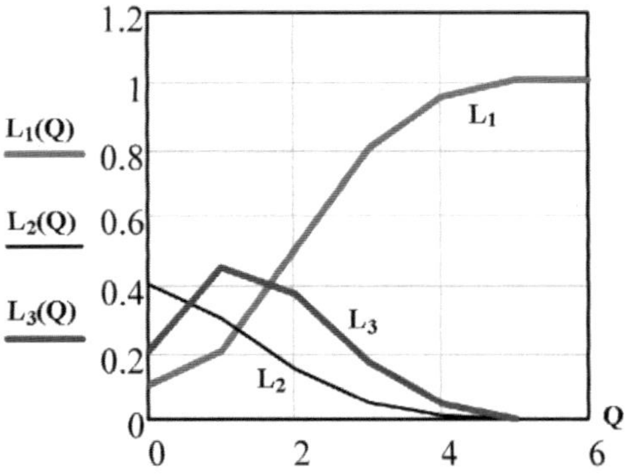

Fig. 3. Graphic representations of the expressions L_1, L_2 and L_3 (equations (14), (15) and (16)) for the considered example.

The values $L(Q)$ are obtained with the equations (14), (15), (16) and (13). These calculated values are presented in the Table III and represented graphically in the Figures 3 and 4.

Table 3. Results of calculation example ($L=L_1+L_3$).

Q	$L_1(Q)$	$L_2(Q)$	$L_3(Q)$	$L(Q)$
0	0.1	0.397	0.199	0.299
1	0.2	0.297	0.446	0.646
2	0.5	0.147	0.369	0.869
3	0.8	0.048	0.166	0.966
4	0.95	0.01	0.045	0.995
5	1	0	0	1.000

The value of the ratio from equation (12) results as:

$$\rho = c_2 / (c_1 + c_2) = 5\cdot c_1 / (c_1 + 5\cdot c_1) = 1/6 = 0.8333.$$

Comparing the value $\rho = 0.8333$ with the series of the calculated values $L(Q)$ in Table III, it retains 0.869 (the first value bigger as ρ), for which corresponds the optimum stock level $Q = 2$. A graphical representation of that searching process it is given in Fig. 4. It can be observed the monotonic increase of the function $L(Q)$ and the finding of the optimal stock level Q_{opt} when the function $L(Q)$ exceeds the level ρ.

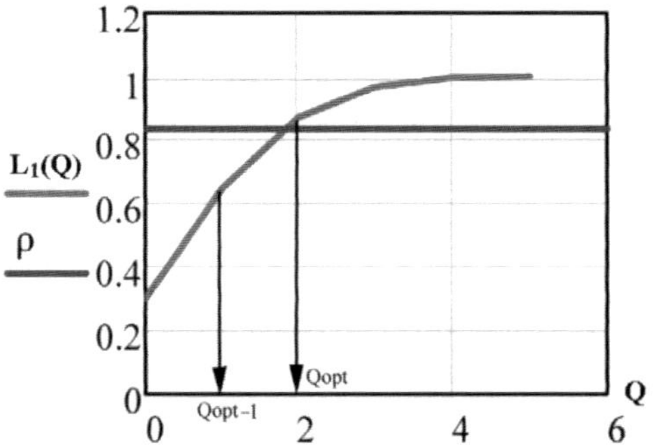

Fig. 4. Graphic representations of the stock-problem analytic solution: $L(Q_{opt}-1) < \rho < L(Q_{opt})$.

For this optimal number of spare parts (Q=2), one can calculate now the mean value $z(Q_{opt})$ of the storage costs:

$$z_1(Q_{opt}) = z_1(2) = 1\cdot\sum_{V=0}^{2}\left(2-\frac{V}{2}\right)p(V) = 0.65$$

$$z_2(Q_{opt}) = z_2(2) = \frac{1}{2}\cdot\sum_{V=3}^{6}2^2\frac{p(V)}{V} = 0.295$$

$$z_3(Q_{opt}) = z_3(2) = \frac{5}{2}\cdot\sum_{V=3}^{6}(V-2)^2\frac{p(V)}{V} = 0.85$$

$$z(Q_{opt}) = z(2) = z_1(2) + z_2(2) + z_3(2) = = 0.65 + 0.295 + 0.85 = 1.795\ r.c.$$

Table 4. Total mean storage costs $z(Q)$ vs. stock level Q.

Q	0	1	2	3	4	5
$z(Q)$	6.125	2.917	1.795	2.007	2.805	3.775

In the Figure 5 there are presented the partial costs z_1, z_2, z_3 as are calculated with the equations (7), (8) and (9) for different stock levels Q. In the same figure it is moreover presented the total cost z, also calculated in the Table IV.

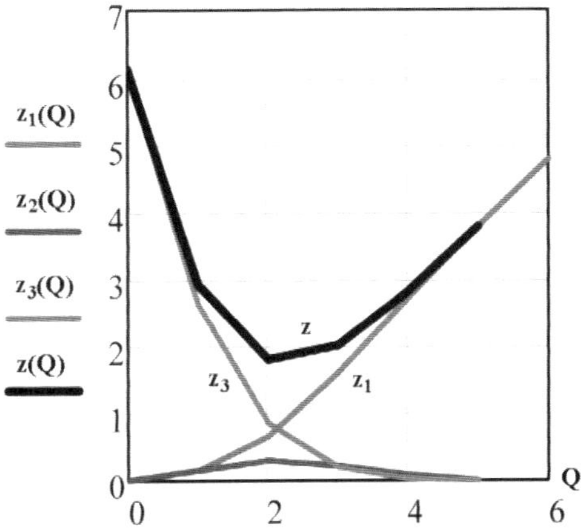

Fig. 5. Contributions of the terms z_1, z_2, z_3 (equations (7), (8) and (9)) in the total cost z of the stock management.

For comparison, the cost z_m involved by a stock level equal with the maximal number of oil filter interventions per week $V_{max} = 5$ is:

$$z_m = c_1 \cdot V_{max} = 1 \cdot 5 = 5 \ r.c.,$$

which shows the economy realized with an optimized stock level ($1.795 < 5$).

The optimal stock magnitude Q_{opt} is influenced not only by the probability distribution function $p(V)$ of demands (interventions) per week (which determines also the mean number N_m of demands), but also by the ratio c_2/c_1 of the unitary costs involved by the existence (c_1) and lack (c_2) of stock.

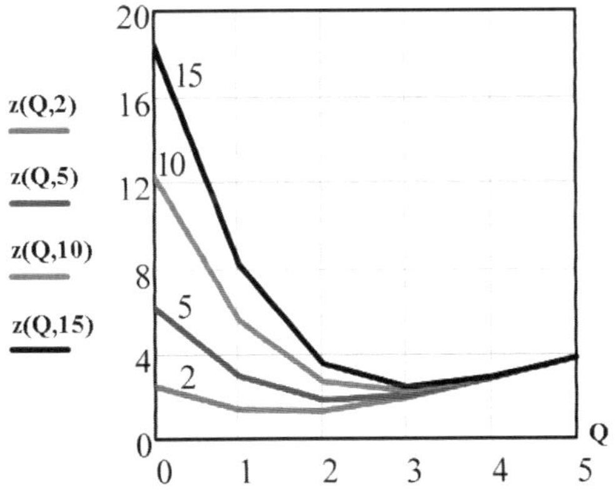

Fig. 6. Influence of the stock magnitude and ratio c_2/c_1 over the cost of the stock management.

The Figure 6 shows comparatively the total storage costs for different stock levels Q and component costs ratios c_2/c_1 (the values 2, 5, 10, 15). It can be observed that if c_2 is much bigger as c_1, then the optimal stock level Q_{opt} and the minimal total cost z_{min} increase also.

5 Conclusions

The paper presented an algorithm allowing to determine the optimum size of the reserve stock so that the expenses to be minimal.

It was considered the case of a company with a random demand for products or activities which implies the existence of a reserve stock. The probability density function of the demand in a considered working time it is considered known.

A model, easy to be implemented in a computer program, was presented.

The model may be modified for different particular cases, as for the situations of variable unitary cost, dependent of the demand level or stock product packaging.

References

1. D. Constantinescu, *Conducerea operativă a producției* (Ed. Mondo-ec, Craiova, 1994)
2. G. Hadley, T. M. Whitin, *Etude et practique des modeles des stocks* (Dunod, Paris, 1966)
3. C. Bălan, *Logistica* (Ed. Uranus, Bucureşti, 2004)
4. C. Bălan, *Logistica funcție integratoare şi factor de competitivitate* (Ed. Uranus, Bucureşti, 2004)
5. N. Florea, *Supply chain management. Curse notes*, (Ed. Univ. Al. I. Cuza, Iaşi, 2004)
6. S. Chopra, P. Meindl, *Supply Chain Management Strategy, Planning and Operation*, Third Edition, (Pearson Prentice Hall, 2006)
7. J. Gattorna, *Managementul logisticii şi distribuției*, (Ed. Teora, Bucureşti, 2006)
8. M. Udrescu, S. Cuturela, *Unele considerații despre managementul resurselor materiale şi logistică*, Revista Română de Statistică Trim I/2013-Supliment, pp. 137-147 (2013)
9. G. Ciolan, F. Kirstein, I. Preda, P. Petre, *The stocks optimization for a random discrete consumption, with several stochastic models* (The Xth International Automotive Congress CAR 2011, paper 1166, Piteşti)

DOI: 10.1051/matecconf/201712605002

Analysis of the cars lane changes accidents

Nicolae Ispas[1*], *Mircea* Năstăsoiu[2]

[1]Transilvania University of Braşov, inicu@unitbv.ro, Romania
[2]Transilvania University of Braşov, m.nastasoiu@unitbv.ro, Romania

Abstract. Experimental cars crashes test are valuable tools for improve overall automotive safety. Lane change crashes (or more properly, the lane change family of crashes) are defined in this paper, in according with generally accepted sense when a car collides with a vehicle running on a neighboring band when the first leaves its lane. Such collision results from various vehicle maneuvers including typical lane change or others. For present paper, the main aim is to quantify the post lane changes collisions parameters for endorsed influences over possible more dangerous traffic accidents occurring. Other goal of the paper was the study of speeds differences over changes in cars initials trajectories.

1 Introduction

Lane change collisions occur when driving on motorways or on urban and/or interurban roads with two or more lanes on the same direction. Accidents of this type can have the more serious consequences as speed differences (relative speeds) between cars involved and impact angles are greater. Often collisions in the lane change occur when lane change the car traveling on the neighboring lane is in blind spot mirrors.

The paper's experimental results were obtained by support of DSD, Dr. Steffan Datentechnik GmbH - Linz, Austria in "Easter 2016 PC-Crash Seminar", using the same instrumentation as that described in: U.S. Department of Transportation, National Highway Traffic Safety Administration [1], N. Ispas and M. Năstăsoiu [2] and N. Ispas and M. Năstăsoiu [3] papers.

Four crash experiments were made for determination of velocities, accelerations and rotation of the cars involved in lane changes collisions using crashes design showed in the fig 1 to fig. 4.

The main technical data of the cars used in the crashes experiments together with the cars shapes are presented in the same fig. 1 to fig.4.

Knowing that the cars weight and cars dimensions influences over post collision consequences we are uses motor vehicle with mass and dimensions "compatible" to avoidance. is inversely proportional to car mass or mass difference: in respect of Jan van der Sluis [4] "the heavier the car the lower the fatality or injury risk (and the higher the aggressiveness). Some authors also described the fact that in collisions between cars of equal mass, the outcome was better for heavier than for lighter cars".

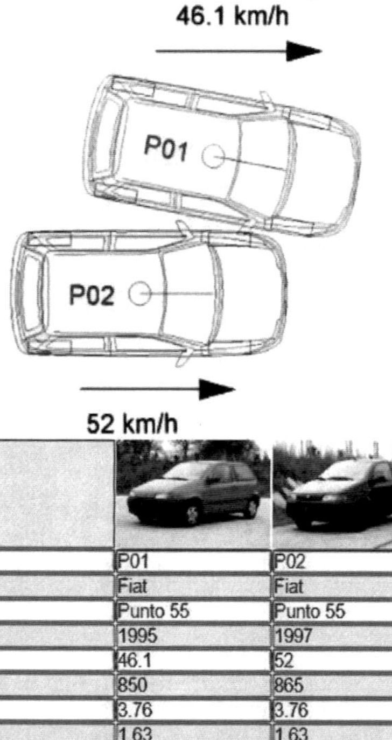

	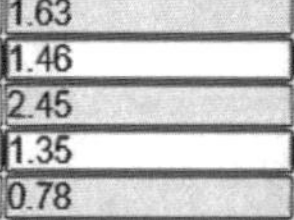	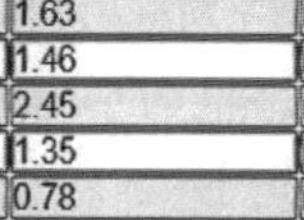	
Label	P01	P02	
Make	Fiat	Fiat	
Model	Punto 55	Punto 55	
Year	1995	1997	
Velocity	46.1	52	km/h
Weight	850	865	kg
Length	3.76	3.76	m
Width	1.63	1.63	m
Height	1.46	1.46	m
Wheelbase	2.45	2.45	m
Trackwidth	1.35	1.35	m
Front overhang	0.78	0.78	m
Axle load front	530	535	kg
Axle load rear	320	330	kg
Dist. COG to front axle	0.92	0.93	m

Fig. 1. First collision and cars involved characteristics in according with occurring tests

* Corresponding author: inicu@unitbv.ro

DOI: 10.1051/matecconf/201712605002

Despite low difference in cars speed, in all collision cases the collision angle in near in blind spot mirrors.

In all four experimental tests, human cars drivers were uses.

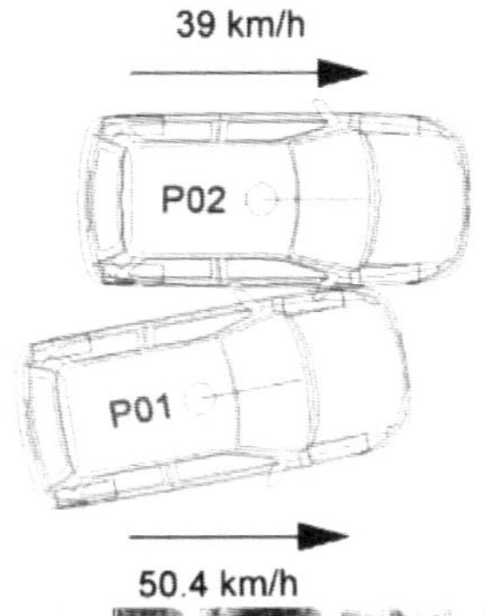

Label	P01	P02	
Make	Fiat	Fiat	
Model	Punto 55	Punto 55	
Year	1995	1997	
Velocity	50.4	39	km/h
Weight	850	865	kg
Length	3.76	3.76	m
Width	1.63	1.63	m
Height	1.46	1.46	m
Wheelbase	2.45	2.45	m
Trackwidth	1.35	1.35	m
Front overhang	0.78	0.78	m
Axle load front	530	535	kg
Axle load rear	320	330	kg

Fig.2. Second collision test and cars involved specifications.

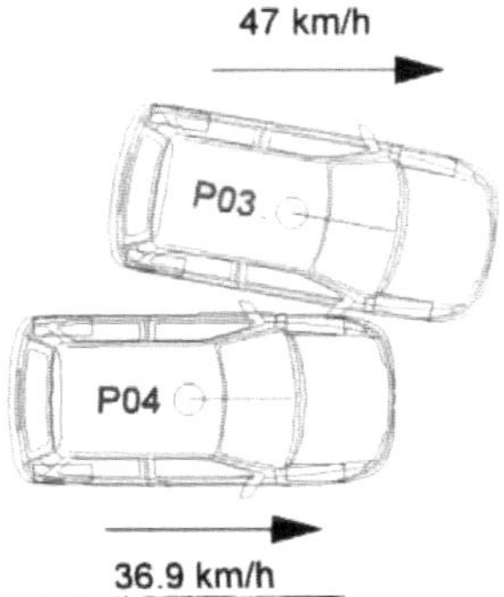

Label	P03	P04	
Make	Fiat	Fiat	
Model	Punto 55	Punto 55	
Year	1998	1997	
Velocity	47	36.9	km/h
Weight	900	885	kg
Length	3.76	3.76	m
Width	1.63	1.63	m
Height	1.46	1.46	m
Wheelbase	2.45	2.45	m
Trackwidth	1.35	1.35	m
Front overhang	0.78	0.78	m
Axle load front	555	545	kg
Axle load rear	345	340	kg
Dist. COG to front axle	0.94	0.94	m

Fig.3. The third collision test and cars involved parameters.

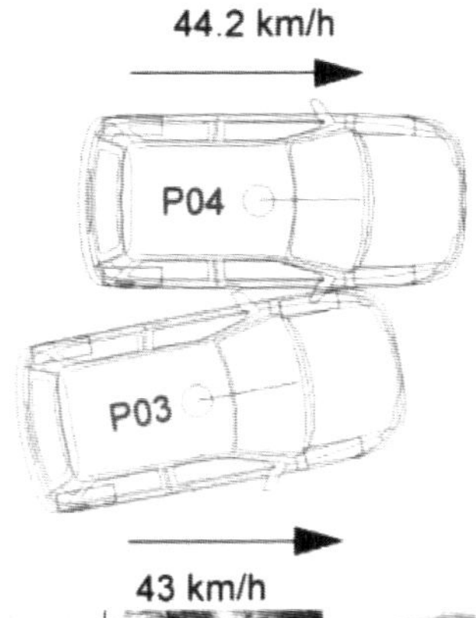

Label	P03	P04	
Make	Fiat	Fiat	
Model	Punto 55	Punto 55	
Year	1998	1997	
Velocity	43	44.2	km/h
Weight	900	885	kg
Length	3.76	3.76	m
Width	1.63	1.63	m
Height	1.46	1.46	m
Wheelbase	2.45	2.45	m
Trackwidth	1.35	1.35	m
Front overhang	0.78	0.78	m
Axle load front	555	545	kg
Axle load rear	345	340	kg
Dist. COG to front axle	0.94	0.94	m

Fig.4. The fourth collision test and cars involved characteristics.

2 Experimental results and discutions

Four crash tests were performed according with EN1317 and EN12767. In each of them were use human's car drivers in both in crash cars. Complex accelerometers were mounted in the Center of Gravity (CG) of each cars

Velocities, speeds (by GPS), accelerations and rotations of the cars were also measured.

For quantify the influences over the cars after lane change collision, we used valuable data obtained from real world experimental crashes.

All attempts have been made so that the speeds of the vehicles involved can be considered relative, and the experimental research scenarios, in all four cases, can be assimilated to accidents on the highway when changing the lane.

Assimilating the collisions of the four cases with those produced on the highway when changing the lane, it can be considered that the speeds of the cars involved are ordered in increasing order, starting from the cars that run on the first right lane.

This kind of test data enable the possibilities to analyze influences of collisions caused by lane changes on subsequent, often more dramatic accidents.

* Corresponding author: inicu@unitbv.ro

DOI: 10.1051/matecconf/201712605002

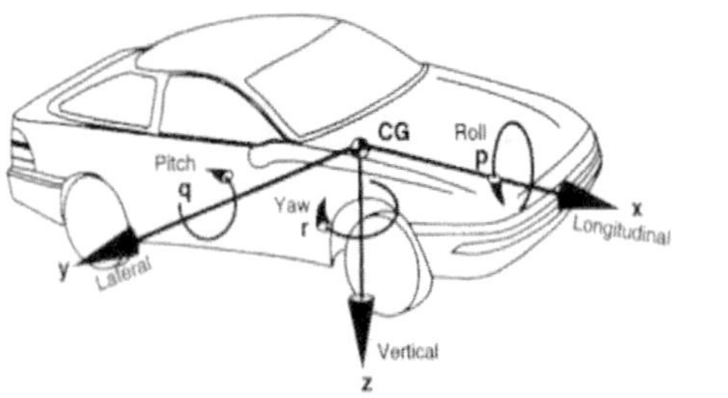

Fig.5. The automotive coordinate system used for experimental tests.

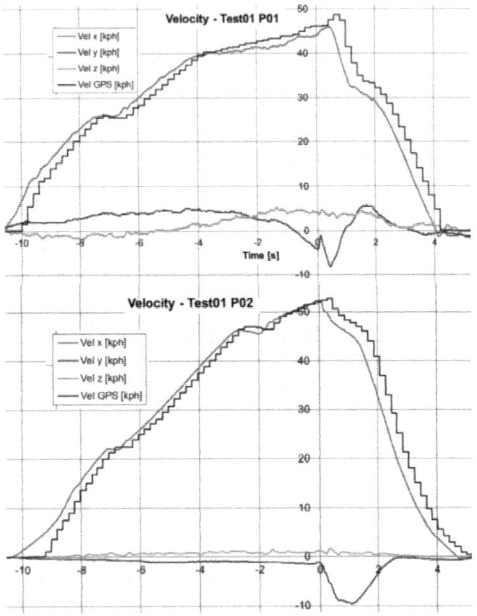

Fig.6. Velocities and GPS speeds of the cars involved in collision test

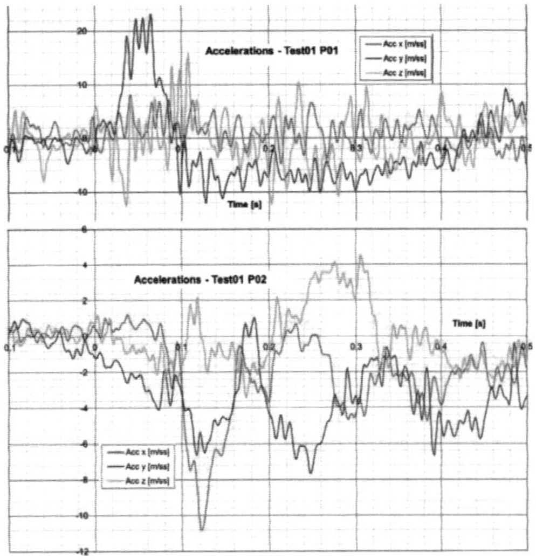

Fig.7. Accelerations of the cars involved in first collision test

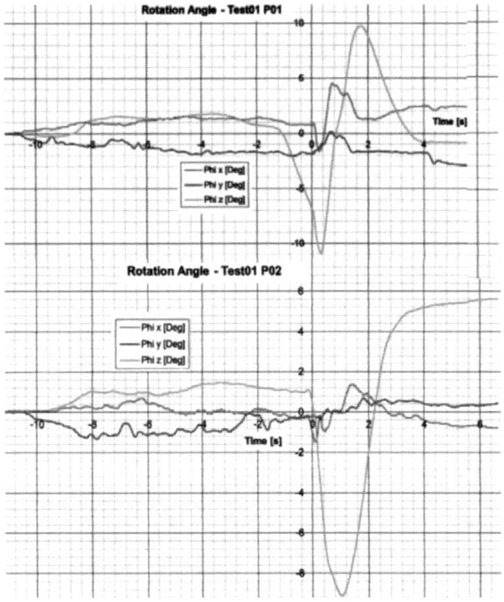

Fig.8. Rotation angles of the cars involved in first collision test.

In the fig. 5 shows the coordinate system of the vehicle in relation to which the velocities, accelerations and angles of rotation have been determined in all four test cases.

Fig. 6 to 17 show the variations in the velocities, speeds, accelerations and rotation angles of the cars involved in the four cases of lane-change collisions described in the previous chapter.

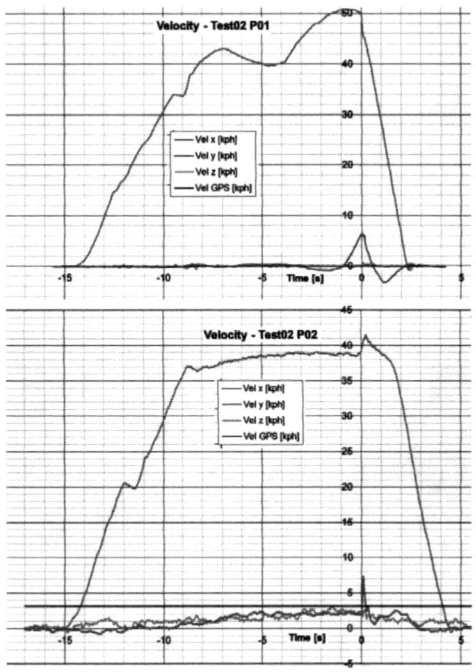

Fig.9. Velocities and GPS speeds of the cars involved in the second collision test

* Corresponding author: inicu@unitbv.ro

DOI: 10.1051/matecconf/201712605002

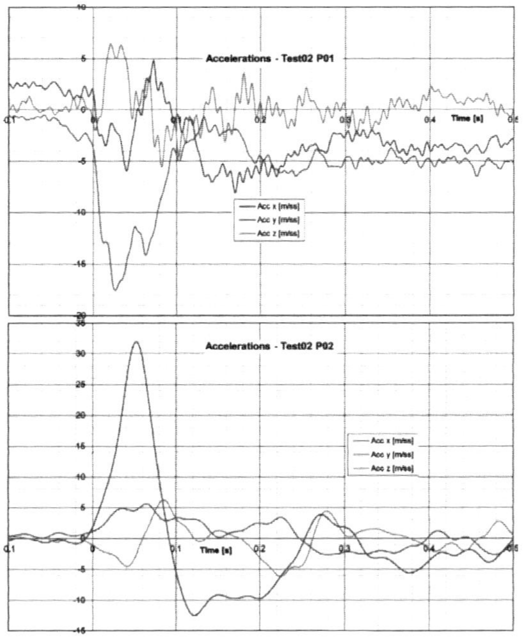

Fig.10. Accelerations of the cars involved in the second collision test

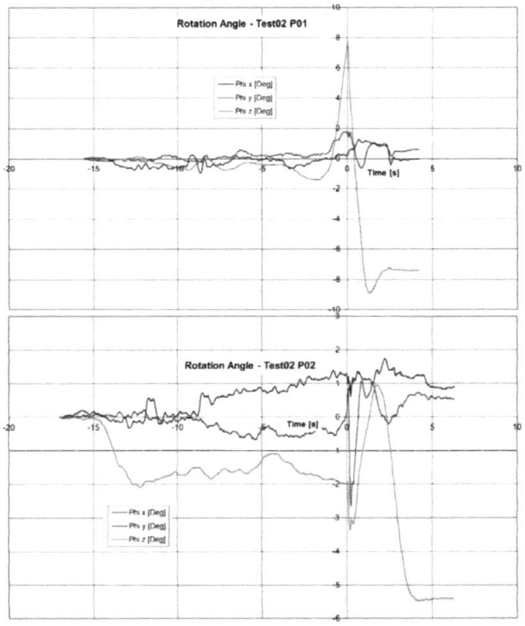

Fig.11. Rotation angles of the cars involved in the second collision test.

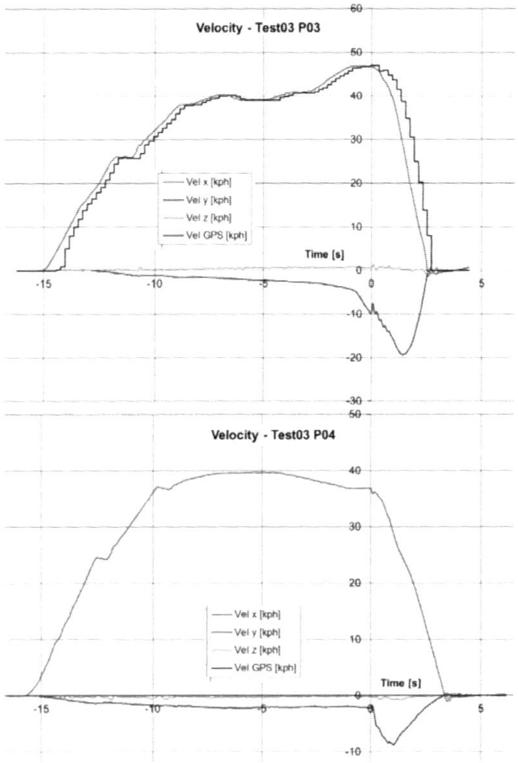

Fig.12. Velocities and GPS speeds of the cars involved in the third collision test.

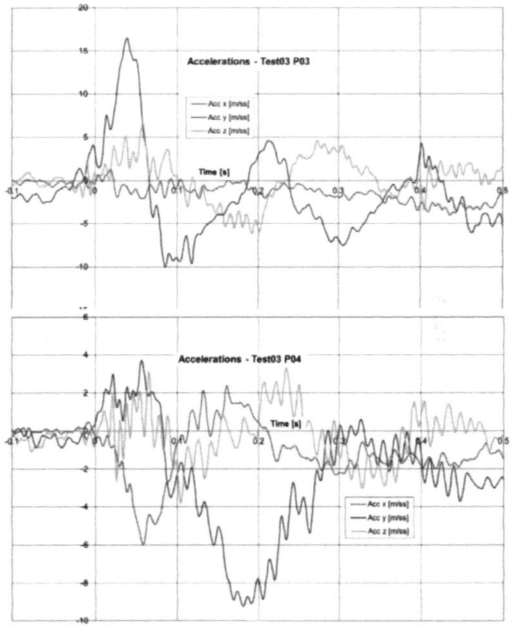

Fig.13. Accelerations of the cars involved in the third collision test.

* Corresponding author: inicu@unitbv.ro

DOI: 10.1051/matecconf/201712605002

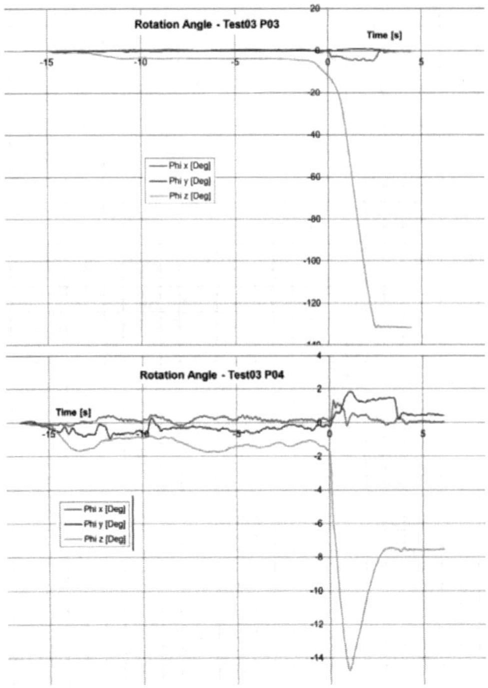

Fig.14. Rotation angles of the cars involved in the third collision test.

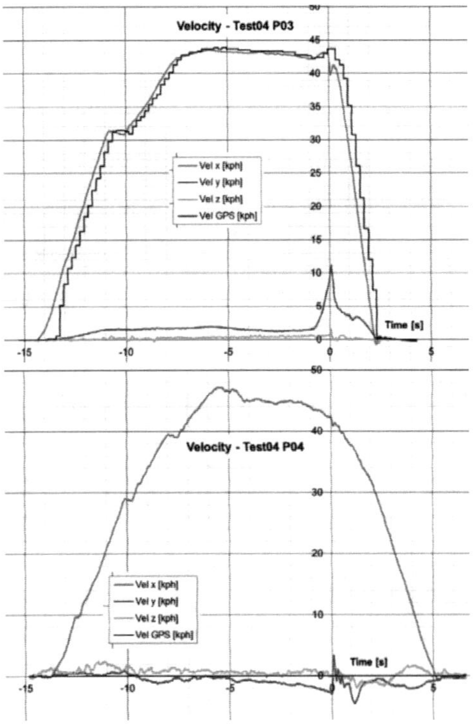

Fig.15. Velocities and GPS speeds of the cars involved in the fourth collision test.

* Corresponding author: inicu@unitbv.ro

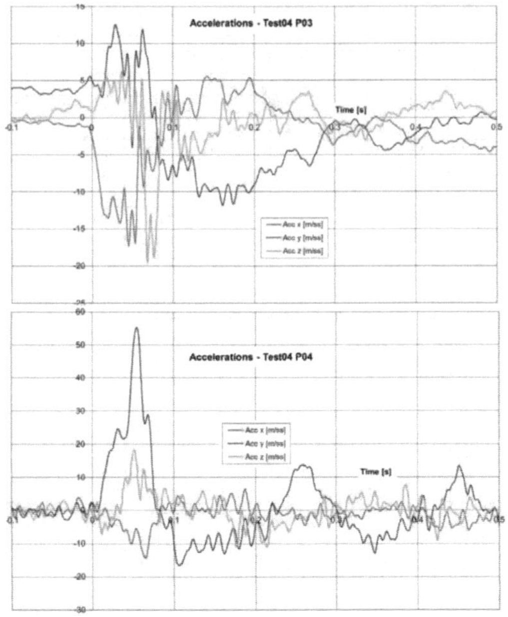

Fig.16. Accelerations of the cars involved in the fourth collision test.

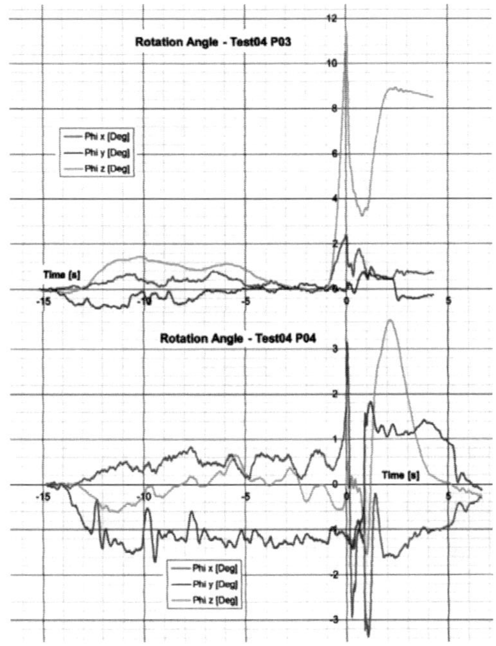

Fig.17. Rotation angles of the cars involved in the fourth collision test.

3 Conclusions

The novelty of the paper are the comparisons of data set from two cars involved in each of four experimental crashes. Another novelty consists in possibilities to analyze the influences of the crashes parameter over both cars involved damages.

The data obtained are highly reliable given by the quality of the equipment used (N. Ispas, M. Nastasoiu [5]).

Using for each lane change collision case the experimental obtained data, we can write the followers main conclusions:

3.1 First crash test:

1. Cars crash was at low collision relative speed (5.9 km/h);

2. In the hypothesis of the relative speed between the two cars and the similarity with highway traffic, the collision was caused by the car running on the higher speed lane:

3. For the P01 (the impactor car), a maximum acceleration of 23 m/s² is recorded in the Y (transverse) direction, and for the other car the maximum acceleration value is -12 m/s² recorded along the X axis (longitudinal);

4. The maximum rotation angle for the P01 was -11 degrees around the Z axis and for the P02 the maximum angle was -8 degrees around the same Z axis.

3.2 Second crash test:

1. *Cars crash was at collision relative speed (11.4 km/h);*

2. In the hypothesis of the relative speed between the two cars and the similarity with highway traffic, the collision was caused by the car running on the lower speed lane:

3. For the P01 (the impactor car), a maximum acceleration of -17,5 m/s² is recorded in the X axis (longitudinal) and for the other car the maximum acceleration value is -32 m/s² recorded along the Z axis;

4. The maximum rotation angle for the P01 was -9 degrees around the Z axis and for the P02 the maximum angle was -5.5 degrees around the same Z axis.

3.3 Third crash test:

1. *Cars crash was at collision relative speed of 10.1 km/h;*

2. In the hypothesis of the relative speed between the two cars and the similarity with highway traffic, the colision was caused by the car running on the higher speed lane;

3. For the P03 (the impactor car), a maximum acceleration of 16.5 m/s² is recorded in the Y (transverse) direction, and for the other car the maximum acceleration value is -8 m/s² recorded along the Y axis;

4. The maximum rotation angle for the P03 was -130 degrees around the Z axis and for the P02 the maximum angle was -15 degrees around the same Z axis.

3.4 Fourth crash test:

1. *Cars crash was at low collision relative speed (1.2 km/h);*

2. In the hypothesis of the relative speed between the two cars and the similarity with highway traffic, the collision was caused by the car running on the lower speed lane:

3. For the P03 (the impactor car), a maximum acceleration of -19 m/s² is recorded in the Z direction, and for the other car the maximum acceleration value is 55 m/s² recorded along the Y axis;

4. The maximum rotation angle for the P03 was -11.5 degrees around the Z axis and for the P04the maximum angle was 4 degrees around the same Z axis.

References

[1] U.S. Department of Transportation, National Highway Traffic Safety Administration "Analysis of Lane Change Crashes", Report, 52 p.DOT-VNTSC-NHTSA-02-03, 2003.

[2] N. Ispas and M. Năstăsoiu "Crash Tests and the Loads over Driver Head in Different Side Impact Cases", Current Solutions in Mechanical Engineering pp 181-186, 2016

[3] N. Ispas and M. Năstăsoiu "A Study Concerning the Loads Over Drivers Heads in the Cases of Cars Crashes with Involved Cars of the Same or Different Generation Proceedings of the European Automotive Congress EAEC-ESFA", 2015 Springer pp 325-336.

[4] Jan van der Sluis, "Vehicle compatibility in car-to-car collisions," Literature review in the framework of the European research project "Improvement of crash compatibility between cars", Workpackage, SWOV Institute for Road Safety Research, The Netherlands. Report, 2000.

[5] N. Ispas, M. Nastasoiu "Cars Crashes with Cars of Same or Different Generation – Occupant's Loads, Timings and Acceleration's Effects", 12th International Congress of Automotive and Transport Engineering (CONAT) Location: Brasov, 2001

* Corresponding author: inicu@unitbv.ro

AUTHOR INDEX

EDP Sciences – Web of Conferences
17, Avenue du Hoggar
Parc d'Activité de Courtabouf
BP 112
F-91944 Les Ulis Cedex A
France

ISBN 978-1-5108-4969-3

9 781510 849693

CURRAN ASSOCIATES INC.
proceedings
.com